THE FUTURE OF REMEDIES IN EUROPE

The Future of Remedies in Europe

Edited by
CLAIRE KILPATRICK, TONIA NOVITZ
and PAUL SKIDMORE

• HART •
PUBLISHING
OXFORD – PORTLAND OREGON
2000

Hart Publishing
Oxford and Portland, Oregon

Published in North America (US and Canada) by
Hart Publishing c/o
International Specialized Book Services
5804 NE Hassalo Street
Portland, Oregon
97213-3644
USA

Distributed in the Netherlands, Belgium and Luxembourg by
Intersentia, Churchillaan 108
B2900 Schoten
Antwerpen
Belgium

Hart Publishing Ltd is a specialist legal publisher based in Oxford, England.
To order further copies of this book or to request a list of other
publications please write to:

Hart Publishing Ltd, Salter's Boatyard,
Folly Bridge, Abingdon Road, Oxford OX1 4LB
Telephone: +44 (0)1865 245533 or Fax: +44 (0)1865 794882
e-mail: mail@hartpub.co.uk
WEBSITE: http//www.hartpub.co.uk

British Library Cataloguing in Publication Data
Data Available
ISBN 1 84113–082–6 (cloth)

Typeset by Hope Services (Abingdon) Ltd.
Printed and bound in Great Britain on acid-free paper by
Biddles Ltd, www.biddles.co.uk

Foreword

The contributions to this book have evolved from papers presented at the Fifth EU/International Law Forum held by the Law Department of the University of Bristol in May 1999. This series of fora, initiated by Malcolm Evans and Stratos Konstadinidis, allows a variety of participants the opportunity to explore issues concerning and connecting EU and international law. This volume is intended to complement the collection of essays, *Remedies in International Law: The Institutional Dilemma*, edited by Malcolm Evans, published by Hart Publishing in 1998.

As organisers of the Forum in 1999, we would like to thank the University of Bristol Law Department and the Faculty of Law Trust for their financial and other support of this event. As always, the careful administrative planning provided by Shirley Knights ensured its success. We also wish to thank all those who attended the Forum and those whose comments and advice shaped this volume. In particular, we are grateful to Giorgios Anagnostaras, Kenneth Armstrong, Benjamin Capps, Michael Dougan, Malcolm Evans, Chris Harding, Jonathan Hill and Phil Syrpis.

As editors, we owe a considerable debt of gratitude to Pat Hammond for her invaluable assistance with the preparation of the manuscript. Many thanks go to Richard Hart for his encouragement and continued commitment to this series.

During the time we have spent together as colleagues at the University of Bristol, we have enjoyed the opportunity to collaborate on this joint enterprise. It has been an exciting task, in which we were able to draw upon our different areas of expertise. However, the realisation of this project depended on the contributors. We hope that their thought-provoking chapters will inform future debates in this field. It is to them that we owe our final thanks.

Claire Kilpatrick
Tonia Novitz
Paul Skidmore

Abbreviated contents

Contents

IV ACCESS TO COURTS AND OTHER FORMS OF REMEDIAL CONTROL

Biographies of Contributors

Paul Beaumont is Professor of European Union and Private International Law, University of Aberdeen.

Leo Flynn is a Legal Secretary at the European Court of Justice. He is writing in his own personal capacity and not as a representative of the Court.

Carol Harlow is Professor of Public Law, London School of Economics and Political Science.

Claire Kilpatrick is a Lecturer in Law at Queen Mary and Westfield College, University of London, and a Jean Monnet Fellow at the European University Institute (2000).

Miguel Poiares Maduro is Professor of European and International Law at the New University of Lisbon, Portugal.

Tonia Novitz is a Lecturer in Law at the University of Bristol.

Richard Rawlings is a Reader in Law at the London School of Economics and Political Science.

Bernard Ryan is a Lecturer in Law at the University of Canterbury, Kent.

Henry G. Schermers is a Professor of Law at the University of Leiden.

Paul Skidmore is a Lecturer in Law at the University of Bristol.

Phil Syrpis is a Lecturer in Law at the University of Bristol.

Takis Tridimas is a Professor of Law at the University of Southampton.

Angela Ward is a Reader in Law at the University of Essex.

Stephen Weatherill is Jacques Delors Professor of EC Law, Somerville College, Oxford University.

Robin C.A. White is a Professor of Law at the University of Leicester

Table of Cases

EUROPEAN

European Court of Justice

Court of First Instance

European Commission and Court of Human Rights

NATIONAL

France

Ireland

Italy

Netherlands

UK

US

Table of Conventions and Treaties

EUROPEAN

INTERNATIONAL

Table of Legislation

EUROPEAN

Regulations

Directives

NATIONAL

Germany

Ireland

Italy

Netherlands

UK

Statutory Instruments

Abbreviations

ACAS	–	Advisory Conciliation and Arbitration Service
ArbGG	–	*Arbeitsgerichtgesetz*
BGB	–	*Bürgerliches Gesetzbuch*
BYBIL	–	*British Yearbook of International Law*
CCP	–	Collective Complaints Protocol
CDE	–	*Cahiers de droit Européen.*
CEEP	–	Centre Européen de l'Enterprise Publique
CFI	–	Court of First Instance
CFSP	–	Common Foreign and Security Policy
CIE	–	Committee of Independent Experts
CMLR	–	Common Market Law Reports
CMLRev	–	*Common Market Law Review*
EAT	–	Employment Appeal Tribunal
EC	–	European Community
ECHR	–	European Convention on Human Rights
ECJ	–	European Court of Justice
ECR	–	European Court Record
ECSC	–	European Coal and Steel Community
EEA	–	European Economic Area
EEC	–	European Economic Community
EELR	–	*European Environmental Law Review*
EFTA	–	European Free Trade Association
EHRR	–	European Human Rights Reports
EHRLR	–	*European Human Rights Law Review*
EIRR	–	*European Industrial Relations Review*
ELJ	–	*European Law Journal*
ELRev	–	*European Law Review*
ERPL	–	*European Review of Public Law*
EPL	–	*European Public Law*
ESA	–	European Space Agency
ETUC	–	European Trade Union Confederation
ETUI	–	European Trade Union Institute
EU	–	European Union
GATS	–	General Agreement on Trade and Services
ICCPR	–	International Covenant on Civil and Political Rights
ICESCR	–	International Covenant on Economic, Social and Cultural Rights
ICJ	–	International Court of Justice

ICLQ – *International Comparative Law Quarterly*
ICR – Industrial Cases Reports
IGC – Inter-Governmental Conference
IJCLLIR – *International Journal of Comparative Labour Law and Industrial Relations*
ILJ – *Industrial Law Journal*
ILO – International Labour Organisation
ILRM – *Irish Law Reports Monthly*
IRLR – Industrial Relations Law Reports
JCMS – *Journal of Common Market Studies*
JCP – *Journal of Consumer Policy*
JEPP – *Journal of European Public Policy*
JHA – Justice and Home Affairs
JLS – *Journal of Legislative Studies*
LGDJ – *Librairie générale de droit et de jurisprudence*
LIEI – *Legal Issues of European Integration*
LSE – London School of Economics
MJ – *Maastricht Journal of European and Comparative Law*
MLR – *Modern Law Review*
NGO – Non-Governmental Organisation
OJ – Official Journal [of the European Community]
OJLS – *Oxford Journal for Legal Studies*
PJCC – Police and Judicial Co-operation in Criminal Matters
PL – *Public Law*
RTDE – *Revue trimistrielle de droit européen*
TEU – Treaty on European Union
UDHR – Universal Declaration of Human Rights
UEAPME – Union Europèene de l'Artisanat et des Petites et Moyennes Entreprises
UNICE – Union des Confédérations de l'Industrie et des Employeurs d'Europe
WTO – World Trade Organisation
YEL – *Yearbook of European Law*

The Future of Remedies in Europe

CLAIRE KILPATRICK

1. THE FUTURE OF REMEDIES IN EUROPE

HOW DO EC lawyers think about remedies in Europe? Most accounts focus on how one specific institution, the Court of Justice, has considered remedies for EC law in the national legal orders. Almost all accounts within this perspective aim at rational reconstruction of the Court's case-law on remedies. We argue that while this type of analysis is essential to examine remedies in EC law, no amount of crystal-ball gazing into solely this kind of account will allow us to predict – or try to change the direction of – the future of remedies in Europe.

This chapter starts by briefly highlighting three important underlying themes which can be found in the most thoughtful accounts focusing on the development of remedial jurisprudence by the Court of Justice. These three themes are closely linked. The first is the invention by the Luxembourg Court of a private enforcement model of EC law in the Member States. The second is the development of remedies in the private enforcement model. The third is the contrast between the Court's development of remedies against Member States in the private enforcement model and its development of remedies against the Community institutions.

The analysis proceeds by indicating perspectives which are obscured, denied or insisted upon in the classic "rational reconstruction" account of remedies in EC law. By developing one way of reading the contributions to this book, the chapter outlines new ways of thinking about remedies in Europe and sketches an agenda for the future. Many of these perspectives involve placing remedies in EC law in their geographical home – Europe. We argue that much is to be learnt by placing the legal visions of remedies in Europe within the EC (and EU) systems alongside other legal visions such as those of national legal systems and other European systems such as private international law and the Council of Europe regimes. We also contend that remedial visions are central in constituting institutional narratives of legal orders, particularly those constructed by courts. This is explored by examining various meanings ascribed to the development of "economic" and "constitutional" discourses within European legal orders. Finally we consider the impact courts, especially European level courts, have had on how remedies are talked about in Europe.

2. THE LUXEMBOURG COURT AND REMEDIES

The invention of the private enforcement model

The focus on remedies for EC law in the national legal orders cannot be analysed without seeing it as one of the by-products of the "great leap" taken by the Court of Justice in the twin doctrines of direct effect and supremacy to ensure that private individuals, through litigation before national courts, and the use of the preliminary reference mechanism in Article 234 EC (ex Article 177) would provide both more and better compliance by Member States with EC law obligations they had assumed. The increased potential penetration into the national legal orders effected by the system of "private Attorney-Generals" thereby created becomes clear when we compare it with the mechanisms explicitly written into the Treaty of Rome for ensuring compliance.[1] Its only mechanisms for ensuring compliance by the Member States with EC law were infringement proceedings by the Commission under Article 226 EC (ex Article 169)[2] or, under Article 227 EC (ex Article 170), by one Member State against another. Both suffered from similar problems. First, lack of resources, both financial and informational, would lead to sporadic and scarce enforcement as well as failure to probe depth of compliance, although individuals were to provide the Commission with valuable information on Member States' compliance failures.[3] Second, politicisation could lead to highly selective pursuit of Member States and negotiated agreements concerning (non) compliance. Finally, these public enforcement models risked non-compliance by Member States found to be in breach of Community law. The Community had no law enforcement personnel and, at that time, no sanctions whatsoever at its disposal.[4] The private Attorney-General model solved all of these problems. The success of the private enforcement model of EC law rights, combined with the Luxembourg Court's institutional mission to sustain and promote the Community legal order, has had a number of crucial consequences for the development of remedies in EC law.

[1] See P. Craig, "Once Upon A Time in the West: Direct Effect and the Federalization of EEC Law" (1992) 12 *OJLS* 453. See also R. Craufurd Smith, "Remedies for Breaches of EC law in National Courts: Legal Variation and Selection" in P. Craig and G. de Búrca *The Evolution of EU Law* (Oxford: Oxford University Press, 1999), 287at 287–92.

[2] See further Weatherill, this volume.

[3] See Rawlings, this volume.

[4] See, now, introduced by the Maastricht Treaty, Article 228 EC, allowing fines to be imposed on Member States which fail to comply with a judgment of the European Court of Justice. See below Rawlings at 289.

Remedies in the private enforcement model – national procedural autonomy, effectiveness and effective judicial protection

The Court of Justice set out a division of remedial competencies which recognised the inevitable reliance of the Community legal order and the Court of Justice on national courts and remedies in the private enforcement model. Rights or substantive issues concerning EC law were for the *Court of Justice* while remedies and procedural issues concerning the enforcement of EC law rights were for the *national legal orders and the national courts*.

This division of competence clearly emerged in the 1976 *Rewe (Saarland)* case. Here, apple importers were prevented from recovering inspection charges levied contrary to EC law because of a thirty-day time limit for making such claims in German law. The Court held that in the absence of harmonisation measures, "it is for the domestic legal system of each Member State to designate the courts having jurisdiction and to determine the procedural conditions governing actions at law intended to ensure the protection of the rights which citizens have from the direct effect of Community law".[5] The Community right to recover the inspection charges had to be exercised in accordance with the thirty-day national time-limit. Similar restraint is evident in the 1981 *Rewe (Kiel)* case where the ECJ declared that the Treaty, "was not intended to create new remedies in the national courts to ensure the observance of Community law other than those already laid down by national law".[6]

This initial pact, or base-line, is usually called *national procedural autonomy*, in recognition of the fact that national courts and laws were entrusted with the task of affording adequate mechanisms to take care of the procedural and remedial aspects of EC law claims. However, the Court of Justice's trust that the national legal orders could adequately safeguard EC law rights only went so far. The base-line of national procedural autonomy came accompanied by two provisos, widely viewed (at least until recently) as minimal safeguards for the protection of EC law rights, rather than as substantial threats to national procedural autonomy.

The first proviso is called variously the "practical impossibility", "excessively difficult" or "effectiveness" proviso. This indicates, broadly speaking, that it should not be impossible for an individual either to assert EC law rights before a national court or to obtain redress for violation of such rights.[7] An example of

[5] Case 33/76 *Rewe* v. *Landwirtschaftskammer für das Saarland* [1976] ECR 1989, especially para. 5; see also Case 45/76 *Comet* v. *Productschap voor Siergewassen* [1976] ECR 2043, paras. 12–16; Case 68/79 *Hans Just* v. *Danish Ministry of Foreign Affairs* [1980] ECR 501, para. 25 (a national rule permitting the State not to pay back levies imposed contrary to EC law where such costs had been defrayed by passing them on to consumers was compatible with EC law).

[6] Case 158/80 *Rewe* v. *Hauptzollamt Kiel* [1981] ECR 1805, para. 44.

[7] See now the qualitative development of this proviso in Cases C–430 and 431/93 *Van Schijndel & Van Veen* v. *Stichting Pensioenfonds voor Fysiotherapeuten* [1995] ECR I–4705 and Case C–312/93 *Peterbroeck, Van Campenhout & Cie* v. *Belgian State* [1995] ECR I–4599. Contrast

a national rule which the Court found made it "excessively difficult" to exercise EC law rights is *San Giorgio*.[8] This case once again concerned traders seeking the refund of inspection charges they had had to pay which had been levied contrary to EC law. Italian law had a rule similar to that the Court had accepted in *Just*[9] which allowed Member States not to pay back unlawfully levied charges where they had been "passed on" by the traders to third parties. However, in addition, the Italian law had a rule providing that the charges would be presumed to have been passed on unless the trader produced documentary evidence to the contrary. The latter condition failed the first "practical impossibility" proviso of the national procedural autonomy base-line.

The second proviso is usually known either as the "equivalence" or "comparability" proviso. This indicates that EC law rights should not be subject to worse treatment in the national procedural and remedial environment than equivalent or comparable domestic law rights. Until very recently, this received extremely limited examination by the Court of Justice. This was mirrored by lack of academic comment.[10]

Why is it that accounts of remedies in EC law call this national *procedural* rather than *remedial* autonomy? This illustrates another characteristic of the Luxembourg Court's approach to remedies. As Harlow's chapter indicates it has adopted a very broad definition of what counts as a "remedy" encompassing development of access to EC law rights, their temporary protection through interim measures as well as redress for infringement of those rights. Commentators have followed this and have placed under the shorthand of "remedies" or, indeed, "procedure" all of these aspects concerning the judicial enforcement of EC law rights. Remedies and procedure have not been clearly distinguished *inter se* as being distinctive parts of a legal claim. Rather, they are

T. Tridimas and C. Harlow below at 36–8 and 71–2. For extended comment on the implications of these twin cases contrast G. de Búrca, "National Remedies for Breach of EC law: the Changing Approach of the ECJ" with F.G. Jacobs, "Enforcing Community Rights and Obligations in National Courts: Striking the Balance" both in J. Lonbay and A. Biondi (eds.), *Remedies for Breach of EC Law* (Chichester: Wiley, 1997) at 37–46, 25–36.

[8] Case 199/82 *Amministrazione delle Finanze dello Stato* v. *San Giorgio* [1983] ECR 3595. See, now, the stricter scrutiny applied to national "passing on" rules in Joined Cases C–192 to C–218/95 *Société Comateb and Others* v. *Directeur Général des Douanes et Droits Indirects* [1997] ECR I–165, discussed by T. Tridimas, *The General Principles of EC Law* (Oxford: Oxford University Press, 1999) 289*ff*.

[9] See note 5, above.

[10] Hence, it is not discussed in P. Craig and G. de Búrca, *EU Law: Text, Cases and Materials* (Oxford: Oxford University Press, 1998), chapter 5. Nor is it given more than one brief footnote (note 31) in Craufurd Smith's recent survey of remedies in EC law (above note 1,). See the discussion by Tridimas, this volume. More discussion is emerging as a result of the Court having to confront the issue in a series of references from Italian courts on time–limits imposed on restitution of charges levied contrary to EC law: see, in particular, Case C–231/96 *Edilizia Industriale Siderugica Srl (Edis)* v. *Ministero delle Finanze* [1998] ECR I–4951 and Case C–228/96 *Aprile Srl* v. *Amministrazione delle Finanze dello Stato* [1998] I–7141, and a UK reference on the meaning of both provisos to national procedural autonomy: Case C–326/96 *Levez* v. *T.H. Jennings (Harlow Pool) Ltd* [1998] ECR I–7835. See also A. Biondi, "The European Court of Justice and Certain National Procedural Limitations: Not Such a Tough Relationship" (1999) 36 *CMLRev* 1271.

identified through contradistinction to issues of substance concerning the content of EC law rights.[11]

Why such an overwhelming focus on Court of Justice case-law? Two reasons can be identified. First, the exponential expansion of supranational rights was not accompanied by EC legislation on remedies and procedures for EC law claims. Academic attention has been firmly fixed on the Court of Justice's activities in the field of remedies because there was not much other EC-level action. Hence the Public Procurement Directives, which contain provisions on damages, interim measures and appeal are an exception.[12] The construction of procedural and remedial protection in the gender equality in employment area has relied on inventive use by the Court of Justice of a provision which, on its face, promises rather less.[13] More generally, the Court's activism in the area of remedies has been heavily dependent on the sketchy foundations of Article 10 EC (ex Article 5). Neither Member State governments nor the Commission have been dedicated proponents of EC-led programmes to partially harmonise procedural and remedial law in the national legal systems. Some academics, and certain judges and Advocates General, have been the main source of proposals to harmonise aspects of procedural and remedial law in the Member States.[14] This is well illustrated by the genesis of the group which produced the Storme Report.[15] This report is the most sustained attempt to date to produce proposals – in this case, a substantial draft directive – to harmonise significant aspects of procedural law in the Member States. The group, made up of twelve academics, was formed on its own initiative, rather than as a result of national or supranational institutional prompting, in 1987. It received only limited and belated funding three years later after presenting a Memorandum to the Commission on its work.[16]

[11] See Harlow, below at 73, discussing the difficulty of maintaining clear distinctions between procedure, substance and remedies.

[12] Directives 89/665 and 92/13 EC. See further Weatherill, below at 92.

[13] Comparison with the Court's interpretation of the similarly-worded Article 6 of Directive 79/7 which deals with equal treatment in social security illustrates just how non-inevitable the interpretation of Article 6 of the Equal Treatment Directive 76/207 is. For the former, see Ryan, this volume. For the latter, see Flynn, this volume.

[14] Most noteworthy is the work of Walter Van Gerven, a former Advocate General. See, for example, "Bridging the Gap between Community and National Laws: Towards a Principle of Homogeneity in the Field of Legal Remedies?" (1995) 32 *CMLRev* 679; "Non-Contractual Liability of Member States, Community Institutions and Individuals for Breaches of Community law with a View to a Common Law for Europe" (1994) 1 *MJ* 7. See also C.N. Kakouris, "Do the Member States Possess Judicial Procedure 'Autonomy'?" (1997) *CMLRev* 1389.

[15] M. Storme (ed.), *Approximation of Judiciary Law in the European Union* (Dordrecht/London: Martinus Nijhoff, 1994). For comments on the proposals therein see Harlow, this volume at 75–6. *Cf.* C.M.G. Himsworth, "Things Fall Apart: The Harmonisation of Community Judicial Procedural Protection Revisited" (1997) 22 *ELRev* 291 at 304, "The group's ringing endorsement, coming as it does from procedural experts . . . provides powerful support for the idea of harmonisation and a basis on which it may be implemented in practice".

[16] See P.H. Lindblom, "Harmony of the Legal Spheres: A Swedish view on the construction of a unified European procedural law" (1997) *European Review of Private Law* 11 at 15.

Second, the widening and deepening of supranational rights has meant that the Court of Justice has subsequently had a complex relationship with the national procedural autonomy base-line and its two provisos. The Court has sometimes struggled to manage the off-spring of its own, on occasion bold, initiatives in the area of remedies for EC law rights. The Court of Justice, like other courts, does not "own" its case-law; once created, it is available for use by other courts and litigants who will argue for adapted meanings. The private enforcement model operates through judicial dialogue, part of which becomes visible at supranational level through Article 234 EC references from national courts.[17] The functioning of the private enforcement model made a continual process of adjustment to the initial remedial and procedural pact inevitable.

Most comment has characterised this process of adjustment as a series of moves by the Court from respect and deference for national procedural autonomy to promoting the *effectiveness* of EC law and *effective judicial protection*. This shift to effectiveness has involved substituting national procedural autonomy for Community Court-controlled remedial and procedural competence in a number of ways. Preliminary references revealed that use of national procedures and remedies left "gaps" in the procedural and remedial protection of individual litigants' EC law rights across the Community. Five of the most important "gaps" are named here. First, a litigant could fail to get into court in the first place to plead an EC law infringement because of national procedures permitting certain actions to be immunised from legal challenge. Second, lack of protection of EC law rights occurred when Member States failed to transpose, or had transposed incorrectly, a directive and a national time-limit prevented a litigant who eventually discovered the EC law right she had been deprived of from availing herself of its benefits. Third, there was a "gap" when a national legal order was not equipped with the remedy needed in a particular situation to protect EC law rights. Fourth, a "gap" was created when no-one could challenge non-compliance with a particular obligation in an EC law instrument because it lacked direct effect and was, therefore, incapable of application by national courts. Fifth, a "gap" could be perceived when derisory remedies resulted from a finding that an EC law right had been infringed. This could occur because of national limits on the types of loss which could be recovered, financial limits on compensation, arrears' limits on recovery of past losses or unjust enrichment rules.

The Court of Justice responded to each of these challenges in ways which emphatically suggested interference in national procedural and remedial environments. In *Johnston*,[18] the ouster clause contained in national law which prevented the litigant challenging her exclusion from the Royal Ulster Constabulary was found, by drawing on the European Convention of Human

[17] See generally S. Sciarra (ed.), *Labour Law in the courts: national judges and the European Court of Justice* (Oxford: Hart Publishing, 2000).

[18] Case 222/84 *Johnston* v. *Chief Constable of the RUC* [1986] ECR 1651. See also Case 222/86 *Heylens* v. *UNECTEF* [1987] ECR 4097.

Rights, to contravene EC law by excluding judicial tutelage of EC law rights.[19] It responded to the second situation by deciding in *Emmott*[20] that time would not begin to run against individuals in the national legal orders until Member States had properly implemented their obligations in Community Directives. It plugged the third "gap" in *Factortame I*[21] by stating that the House of Lords should issue interim injunctions against the Crown, even where such power did not exist in national law, in order to protect EC law rights. It responded to the fourth in *Francovich*[22] by creating a new remedy in all the national legal orders of state liability in damages for failure to properly apply EC law. Moreover, such liability was subsequently revealed not to be confined to situations where no alternative means of enforcing EC law was available. In *Marshall II*,[23] it stated that a national ceiling on compensation, the final situation, contravened EC law as it did not afford an effective remedy to a victim of gender discrimination.

The cumulative effect of these five key cases, decided between 1986 and 1993, was to leave the promise of national procedural autonomy looking decidedly threadbare. Emblematic of much assessment of this set of cases by EC lawyers is Caranta.

> For a long time, judicial protection against Member States has been the object of momentous work in progress . . . It is suggested that the subject now shows a remarkable coherence, which allows the observer to trace the development of a set of rules that should be common to all the Member States, and thus replace pre-existing domestic rules. This is to say that a new *jus commune* is slowly taking place, and that great emphasis is now laid on remedies.[24]

Practising lawyers and litigants had an interest in exploiting and clarifying these new judicial developments before national courts. This, in turn, produced a fresh wave of references related to the new Euro-remedy of state liability and national remedial rules to the Court of Justice. But, no sooner had doctrinal comment decided that the journey to a brave new coherent world – in which effectiveness and effective judicial protection had replaced national procedural autonomy as the prevailing paradigm – had been safely undertaken than the Court, in the new wave of remedy-related references, began to retreat in various, not always readily explicable ways, from the implications of whole-hearted application of this case-law. This was accompanied by and not entirely divorced

[19] See further below, note 60.

[20] Case C–208/90 *Emmott* v. *Minister for Social Welfare and Attorney-General* [1991] ECR I–4629.

[21] Case C–213/89 *R* v. *Secretary of State for Transport, ex parte Factortame Ltd and Others* [1990] ECR I–2433.

[22] Cases C–6 and 9/90 *Francovich and Bonifaci* v. *Italy* [1991] ECR I–5357.

[23] Case C–271/91 *Marshall* v. *Southampton & South West Area Health Authority* [1993] ECR I–4367.

[24] R. Caranta, "Judicial Protection Against Member States: A New *Jus Commune* Takes Shape" (1995) 32 *CMLRev* 703; J. Steiner, "From direct effects to *Francovich*: shifting means of enforcement of Community law" (1993) 18 *ELRev* 3.

from, on the one hand, a fleshing out of the conditions of state liability[25] and, on the other, moves by the Court, at times as a result of insistent pressure from national courts, to develop the meaning of the two provisos which accompany national procedural autonomy.

This shifting recomposition of the judicial landscape is explored by Tridimas and Flynn in this book. Tridimas places particular emphasis on the developing meaning of the two provisos to national procedural autonomy and examines the Court's recent case-law on "effectiveness" and "equivalence". Flynn provides an extremely useful scalpel-like examination of the demise of the highly ambitious *Emmott* decision. Taken together, they provide us with a rich sense of the recent paths taken in the Luxembourg Court's jurisprudence *vis-à-vis* national remedial environments.

Remedies against the Community institutions – playing to a different tune?

Remedial developments within the private enforcement model created pressures exerted by comparisons made with mechanisms designed to ensure that the Community institutions themselves acted in accordance with Community law. The Luxembourg Court's desire for effectiveness of EC law at national level which had driven the private enforcement model had been twinned, in justificatory terms, with the principle of effective judicial protection. The latter drew on notions of a necessary role for courts in democracies in the protection of individuals against the (Member) State, the principle of *ubi ius, ibi remedium* as a value inherent in the Community tradition and effective judicial protection of individuals in the EU as a central component of citizenship in that developing polity. In the private judicial enforcement model, the Community institutional desire for effectiveness in the national legal orders dovetailed with justifications linked to effective judicial protection of the individual.

Different institutional priorities prevailed for the Court of Justice when considering compliance with Community law by the Community institutions, including the Community legislature. Here, effectiveness of the Community order and effective judicial protection did not seem to point in the same direction. Adequate protection of individuals (effective judicial protection) involved challenging the activities of the still fragile and young EC institutions (which would not bolster the effectiveness of the new legal order). The Court has been notoriously reluctant to permit private individuals to challenge the legality of Community measures[26] or the exercise of discretion to take infringement proceedings by the Commission[27] or to develop a generous system of Community

[25] See below, note 30.

[26] Under Article 230 EC. See Case 25/62 *Plaumann & Co.* v. *Commission* [1963] ECR 95. See Syrpis, this volume.

[27] Case 247/87 *Star Fruit Co.* v. *Commission* [1989] ECR 291; see also Rawlings, this volume at 276, and Weatherill, this volume at 93.

liability in damages.[28] The contrast between its willingness to protect individuals when anyone but the Community was at fault, and its reluctance to give the EC the same dose of effective judicial protection could only become more and more apparent. Unsurprisingly, many argued that what was sauce for the (Member State) goose should be sauce for the (Community) gander.[29] The most acute manifestation of this so far has been the contrast between the bold pronouncements in *Francovich* which beckoned wide-reaching Member State liability for breaches of Community law and the restrictive conditions under which the Community institutions could be non-contractually liable under Article 288(2) EC. This undoubtedly had a significant impact on how the Court of Justice shaped its post-*Francovich* jurisprudence.[30]

3. RE-EXAMINING THE LUXEMBOURG COURT ACCOUNT OF REMEDIES IN EUROPE

The central EC law remedies analysis traces the Court's activities *vis-à-vis* national remedies for breach of EC law rights. These activities are evaluated by examining the internal coherence of the Court's jurisprudence and its success in offering effective remedies for Community rights in national courts. Tridimas concludes, concurring with most commentators,[31] that the Court's current

[28] See the legacy and application of the *Schöppenstedt* formula: Case 5/71 *Aktien-Zuckerfabrik Schöppenstedt* v. *Council* [1971] ECR 975. The Court's desire to maintain control of the integrity of Community law is also evident in its assertion of a judicial monopoly over the validity of Community acts (Case 314/85 *Foto-Frost (Firma)* v. *Hauptzollamt Lübeck-Ost* [1987] ECR 4199 and its careful detailed control of the circumstances in which national courts can grant interim measures when the validity of Community law is at issue (Cases C–143/88 and C–92/89 *Zuckerfabrik Süderdithmarschen AG* v. *Hauptzollamt Itzehoe* [1991] ECR I–415; Case C–465/93 *Atlanta* [1995] ECR I–3761).

[29] See, for example, Caranta (1995), note 24, above, who states at 724–5: "The Court of Justice seems to use a double standard, depending on whether remedies are sought against Member States or against Community institutions. [. . .] Effective judicial protection seems still to have to come of age, to be no more than an implication of full effects of Community law, as such to be used more to exact obedience from Member States than to protect citizens".

[30] In particular in Cases 46/93 and 48/93 *Brasserie du Pêcheur SA* v. *Germany*, *R.* v. *Secretary of State for Transport, ex parte Factortame Ltd and Others* [1996] ECR I–1029. See also further clarifications of state liability in Case C–392/93 *R.* v. *HM Treasury, ex parte British Telecommunications plc* [1996] ECR I–1631; Cases C–283, 291 and 292/94 *Denkavit International* v. *Bundesamt für Finanzen* [1996] ECR I–5063; Cases C–178–9/94, 188–190/94 *Dillenkofer and Others* v. *Federal Republic of Germany* [1996] ECR I–4845; Case C–5/94 *R.* v. *Ministry of Agriculture, Fisheries and Food, ex parte Hedley Lomas* [1996] ECR I–2553; Case C–319/96 *Brinkmann Tabakfabriken GmbH* v. *Skatteministeriet* [1998] ECR I–5255. See T. Heukels and A. McDonnell (eds.), *The Action for Damages in Community Law* (The Hague/Boston: Kluwer, 1997) and J. Beatson and T. Tridimas (eds.), *New Directions in European Public Law* (Oxford: Hart Publishing, 1998). On the interaction of *Francovich* liability with other methods of private enforcement in the labour law context see Ryan, this volume.

[31] See M. Hoskins, "Tilting the Balance: Supremacy and National Procedural Rules" (1996) 21 *ELRev* 365; see also Craufurd Smith (1999), note 1, above, at 317 who views the Court's activities in this area as "a confident foray, an explicit redrawing of territorial lines". Craufurd Smith identifies a similar three-fold classification of the treatment in academic comment of the Court of Justice's remedies' jurisprudence.

remedial jurisprudence, viewed as the outcome of a process to find the appropriate equilibrium between effectiveness of Community law and national procedural autonomy, "has drawn that balance successfully". A second group are less content with the Court's record desiring more coherence in the case law and, in particular, more evidence of explicitly reasoned distinctions. There are arguments in favour of moves towards, sometimes, more effective judicial protection[32] and, sometimes, more national procedural autonomy.[33] At the other extreme, Judge Kakouris has argued that there have been no significant changes in the Court's approach to remedies; national procedural autonomy was always a misnomer for Court of Justice harnessing of national procedures as ancillary to the effective realisation of Community rights in the national legal orders.[34] In his view, the story has always been one of effectiveness and effective judicial protection and the Court's case law can be best explained by viewing it as such.

We find this type of account necessary but insufficient for understanding remedies in EC law. A number of interrelated shortcomings can be identified, all of which can be attributed to the tendency to adopt an internal perspective *vis-à-vis* the Court of Justice's activities and aspirations. It has very little predictive power. Its methodology is little more than a *post hoc* reconstruction and reaction to whatever the Luxembourg Court happens to have done. So, while it is a valuable descriptive technique, it can only trace shifts to and from national procedural autonomy and effectiveness rather than tell us what the Court may do next and why it will do so, let alone turn to alternative, non-Luxembourg Court-oriented solutions.

The normative assumptions underpinning this account also deserve closer inspection. By saying that an internal perspective is adopted *vis-à-vis* the Luxembourg Court, we mean that it is a *judicial* perspective which defines *success* in terms of the degree to which what are perceived to be the *supranational* objectives pursued by the Luxembourg Court are realised. Measurement of their realisation is largely solely read off from the Court's jurisprudence. We shall call this the "judicial supranational" perspective and those who view remedies from this vantage point "judicial supranationalists".

The affliction of supranationalitis

The judicial supranational perspective of the national and sub-national legal orders fails to take seriously enough the multi-level nature of the EC. It assumes that judicial interaction through the preliminary reference mechanism is

[32] For this kind of argument developed in a specific policy area, see Ryan, this volume.

[33] See, for example, Biondi (1999), note 10, above.

[34] See Kakouris (1997), note 14, above. He achieves this only by dint of categorising (at 1399) Case C–338/91 *Steenhorst-Neerings* [1993] ECR I–5475 and Case C–410/92 *Johnson No.2* [1994] ECR I–5483 together with *Emmott*, note 20, above, as though placing them side-by-side removes any need to explain their utter incompatibility. See further on these cases, Flynn, this volume.

capable, given time, of effecting or provoking procedural and remedial convergence at national level. Harlow's chapter powerfully takes issue with these assumptions by reversing the supranational emphasis to examine these judicial remedial developments within national procedural and remedial environments. She points out the dramatic lack of procedural and remedial uniformity in national judicial systems. However, this does not only, or even importantly, reflect a transnational jumble, in need of a supranational sorting out. Through the example of the balance struck between state liability (in non EC-law cases) and other (in particular, mandatory) remedies in French and English administrative law, she illustrates how such outcomes reflect rather choices about allocation of state resources[35]and the balance between the judicial and other branches of government. The arrival of cases such as *Factortame* and *Francovich*[36] is disruptive of such historically-developed, though non-static, choices at national level.

The judicial supranationalist might respond that this is a lamentable, but unavoidable and worthwhile, price to be paid on the road to judicially-driven EC-wide procedural convergence. In particular, imbalances created between remedies for EC and domestic rights by Luxembourg Court jurisprudence provide the necessary spur towards "levelling-up" towards the EC standard for domestic rights, hence hastening the journey towards convergence.

Harlow is thoroughly unconvinced. She contends that adopting a national perspective dispels the belief that the judicial communication installed by Article 234 EC has, or could ever have, the capacity to bring about wide-scale procedural harmonisation. Rather, the piecemeal supranational judicial incursions carried out in the name of effectiveness and uniformity seem apt to perturb each national legal system differently, leading to new divergences, as well as decreased integrity in the national system.[37]

Moreover, Harlow largely focuses on instances where such procedural and remedial perturbance has occurred. We can add to this picture of non-uniformity instances of widespread judicial resistance to upsetting the status quo reflected in existing remedial landscapes. A good example of this is remedies between private parties in the field of competition law, in particular, the awarding of "competition damages". Caruso has identified judicial resistance in France, Germany and the UK to awarding these which is so effective that few actions are brought before domestic courts by potential plaintiffs who prefer to use instead the EC's public enforcement machinery by filing complaints with the Commission.[38] She draws the following conclusions.

[35] See also by the same author, "*Francovich* and the problem of the disobedient state" (1996) 2 *ELJ* 199.

[36] Notes 21 and 22, above.

[37] G. Teubner, "Legal Irritants: Good Faith in British Law or How Unifying Law Ends Up in New Divergences" (1998) 61 *MLR* 11.

[38] D. Caruso, "The Missing View of the Cathedral: The Private Law Paradigm of European Legal Integration" (1997) 3 *ELJ* 3 at 17*ff*.

> [T]here is, in each of these nations, a strong reluctance to have the system of civil liability changed . . . by European intervention . . . Embedded in national legal cultures is the reluctance of state courts to let European regulation add to their armoury of private remedies.[39]

The judicial supranationalist suffers from supranationalitis. Given that the EC legal order, particularly in the area of remedies, has been and looks set to continue to be heavily dependent on interaction with national remedial and procedural environments via the interlocutor of the national judiciaries, thinking about the future of remedies means taking the national much more thoroughly into consideration.

Economic, constitutional and political enforcement assumptions

The judicial supranationalist frequently assumes, often tacitly, that economic, constitutional and political developments necessitate harmonisation of procedural and remedial issues.[40]

We disagree with the assertion that economic, constitutional or political developments require harmonisation of remedies and procedures. First, as discussed in the previous section, it is impossible for the EC private enforcement model to produce procedural convergence. Second, by looking at other legal orders in Europe which organise forms of economic interaction and rights-based "constitutional" developments, we can question the need to harmonise procedure and remedies as a result of the strengthening of economic and constitutional ties between the states of Europe. This will be done by looking at private international law as an example of a legal order regulating economic interactions[41] and the European Convention on Human Rights as an example of a legal order which attempts to entrench certain "constitutional" rights across its Contracting States.[42]

However, at the same time, the assertion that economic, constitutional and political developments require harmonisation of remedies and procedures is important and interesting. We can see it as a mission statement of the EC insti-

[39] Ibid. at 21–2.

[40] Some examples of explicit comments can be found in E. Szyszczak, "Making Europe More Relevant to its Citizens: Effective Judicial Process" (1996) 21 *ELRev* 351 at 352: "The imperatives for consistent Community principles of effective judicial process are two-fold: economic and constitutional. Economic in that market integration presumes the uniform application of Community law across the internal market. Constitutional in that Citizens are entitled to expect that Community rights are fully respected within national systems". See also Jolowicz at xiii of the Preface to the Storme Report, note 15, above: "The idea of a single "internal market" requires for its complete realisation a single system for the judicial resolution of disputes"; and Himsworth (1997), note 15, above, at 311: "Harmonisation is a seamless process. Political and economic harmony demand legal harmony in all its aspects".

[41] Below at 16

[42] Below at 21

tutions which has guided and justified their activities over time. We can also test the coherence or completeness of this mission statement by examining how the categories of "economic", "constitutional" and "political" have been invoked and combined in the context of providing remedies within EC law.

Before doing so, we need to say what we mean by "economic", "constitutional" and "political". We are not arguing that these three terms have got fixed meanings nor that they are mutually exclusive. Indeed one of the distinctive characteristics of the EC legal order has been to link "economic" with "constitutional" to justify building an "economic constitution" with its own "fundamental freedoms". "Economic rights" within the EC legal order would include these four freedoms as well as associated disciplines dealing with competition law, intellectual property and the creation of the single market.

We can likewise identify a sufficiently stable meaning of "constitutional" and "political" rights in the EC legal order which are presented as counterbalancing respectively the expansion of economic rights and the growth of the EU.

First, the substantive EC agenda has been widened to include "non"-economic rights, though frequently these are concerned with protecting groups or public goods from certain market effects. Primary examples would be the protection of workers, consumers and the environment. These will be called "constitutional" rights in what follows.

Second, as the EU has expanded and increased its power it comes under increasing pressure to endow the process and outcomes of EC law-making and administration with more democratic credentials. The increased powers of the European Parliament and the social partners' law-making role in Articles 138–9 EC may be viewed, at least in part, as responses to such pressures. We can also think of pressures to give atypical institutional actors more possibilities to complain about how the EC institutions operate and the legality of their actions. Key in this regard are the creation of new actors such as the European Ombudsman to deal with complaints by EU "citizens".[43] These will be called "demos" rights.

It must be stressed that there are no watertight divisions between these categories. Indeed, part of the dynamic development of the EU comes from actors arguing that linkages exist between the languages in which these various rights' categories are couched. Hence, the economic actor can demand to be treated as an economic "citizen"[44] while the environmental activist can argue that protecting the environment is as "fundamental" as free movement. However, we do argue that the meanings given to these categories and the linkages between them have become sufficiently stable as to characterise what is distinctive about the EU. What remains to be done is to think about how remedies have interacted with these categories of rights.

First, given the actual development of the EU, remedies for "economic" and "constitutional" rights are likely to be predominantly associated with the

[43] See Rawlings, this volume.
[44] See Poiares Maduro, this volume.

private, rather than the public, enforcement model. It is within the private enforcement model, as we have seen, that the Luxembourg Court has deployed the notions of effectiveness and effective judicial protection to provide "constitutional" encasing for the Luxembourg Court's determination to move enforcement of EC law from an international model to a new *sui generis* EC law model. One issue which arises is whether the Luxembourg Court has used "economic" and "constitutional" rights in the same way in constructing effectiveness and effective judicial protection.

We also need to ask whether the remedial and enforcement options available in the combined operation of the public and private enforcement models permit equal opportunities to enforce the "economic" and "constitutional" parts of the package. More broadly, what can we learn from various methods of sectorally analysing procedure and remedies for enforcement of EC law rights?[45]

Finally, EC "demos" rights are exercisable not against the national legal orders but against EC law and the conduct of EC institutions. Remedy for their breach, if sought judicially, will be through the use of the judicial review and non-contractual liability provisions of the Treaties. The interactions between legal orders, categories of rights and remedies are developed in the sections which follow.

Sectoral approaches to EC remedies

The judicial supranational account aims to reconstruct the Luxembourg Court's jurisprudence, in so far as this is possible, as a seamless canvas. Though it is accepted that this is frequently not possible, the judicial supranationalists' view is that remedies across the many areas covered by Community law should be uniform and are best analysed by seeing to what extent they conform to this aspiration. What if we tried instead to understand the Court's jurisprudence as being driven by different sectoral demands? For instance, *are* procedures and remedies for gender equality in employment currently treated differently by the Court of Justice from those concerning restitution to traders of unlawfully levied inspection charges? Whether that is true or not, *should* they be treated differently and should these different treatments be explicitly articulated by the Court of Justice in its judgments? Might it even be thought that considerations of a sectoral nature have influenced the Luxembourg Court's decisions but that pressures for uniformity and an inadequately developed "sectoral sense" are leading cases decided in one policy area to be applied inappropriately in another? At the very least, this kind of thinking might provide a new and challenging research agenda for re-assessing the past and considering the future of remedies in the Luxembourg Court's jurisprudence.

[45] Below, next section.

We can also use sectoral analyses to move beyond analysis of the internal coherence of Luxembourg Court jurisprudence within the private enforcement model. In particular, we can see more clearly how identifiable actors in specific policy areas interact with the public and private enforcement models available in the EC system. This brings to the fore the question whether the "economic" and "constitutional" parts of the package are given equal enforcement opportunities in the EC. Weatherill's chapter poses this question and answers it in the negative. He substantiates with rigorous and wide-ranging analysis the claim that the EC's two-pronged public and private enforcement regimes, together called the "dual vigilance" model, create a particularly acute gap between those wishing to enforce "economic" EC law rights and those wishing to assert "constitutional" EC law rights. For example, diffuse interests are, by their very nature, more likely to be dependent on accessing public enforcement machinery to perceive and pursue violations of EC rules. Because of this, lack of EC level financial resources, legal powers and administrative structures (such as inspectorates and agencies) has a disproportionate negative impact on the "constitutional" than on the "economic" part of the package. Moreover, the defects of the dual vigilance model are exacerbated by other developments. The increasing tendency in, for example, social law measures to resort to less precise EC rule formulation, with use being made instead of Framework Directives, opt-outs, derogations and delegations, makes finding an EC law right to enforce and obtain remedies for more problematic. It is only in the "economic" area that moves towards "smart" pre-emption of litigation-oriented enforcement are being made through the use of tools such as notification procedures to bring to light non-compliance.[46] Finally, though there is a more pressing need to move beyond the dual vigilance model with regard to "constitutional" rather than "economic" issues, it is also politically more fraught as the former are regarded as areas where EC competence is more contested and Member States' claims are stronger.

By focusing on reverse discrimination, Poiares Maduro is able to provide a different, though by no means incompatible, perspective on the tensions between the national and supranational levels of governance, on the one hand, and between the "economic" and "constitutional" elements in the EC's developing identity on the other. It is well-known that the Luxembourg Court has found that EC "economic" rights, and their corresponding remedial protection, are only available to persons, goods and services which have "moved" across a Member State border. This means that nationals of a particular Member State have, unlike all other EC nationals, no remedies against that State for discriminatory treatment with regard to economic rights. This can be contrasted with EC "constitutional" rights, such as the right to parental leave, equal pay or to continued employment when an undertaking is transferred. These are universal rights, available to all worker-citizens, without their having to move from one

[46] See also Rawlings at 287.

Member State to another. As he states, "The EU is no longer directed to economic agents but to EU citizens. Reverse discrimination will be re-proposed as a problem of discrimination among citizens of the Union". Having argued that reverse discrimination is not a national problem but an EC problem with significant national dimensions, he examines and rejects the Court of Justice's assumption that either the market or national political processes will provide adequate remedial solutions in such cases, proposing instead that reverse discrimination is best remedied through judicial control. But this is not a plea for supranational judicial control. National courts, acting as Community courts, need to be given the appropriate remedial operating space to handle such cases of reverse discrimination; this could be done by the Luxembourg Court relinquishing to national courts the power to decide which reverse discrimination situations should fall within or without the scope of EC law. He concludes by suggesting that the broader lesson from this sectoral examination could be that, where the effects of EC law are internal to a particular State, which is true not only of reverse discrimination but of many cases concerning the horizontal direct effect of directives, national courts should be given more leeway to decide on how EC rights should be enforced in the national environment.

This connects neatly to the final sectoral examination – of EC labour law rights – by Ryan. These have provided the illustration *par excellence* of arbitrary access to remedies arising because of directives lacking horizontal direct effect. He postulates a number of different "economic" and "constitutional" justifications for EU labour law and uses these to examine the different remedial prescriptions which would emerge from a thorough-going application of each to the current mix of enforcement opportunities provided by the combination of direct effect, indirect effect and *Francovich* liability.

4. OTHER EUROPEAN LEGAL ORDERS: CO-EXISTENCE AND INTERACTION WITH EC/EU INSTITUTIONS

Co-existence and interplay of economic legal orders – private international law and EC law

To analyse in parallel the development in Western Europe of private international law and EC law as systems for recognising the existence of increasing interaction between, in particular, economic actors is like spinning around in a hall of mirrors. It provides us with a wealth of contrasting images and oblique reflections which allow us to see the EC legal order more clearly, the better to test hypotheses about the causal factors spurring the nature and extent of its development. This is not the place to develop a detailed analysis of the relationships between private international law and EC law. If, however, for the purposes of developing our analysis of remedies, we take the starting point that both provide ways in Europe of legally dealing with the challenges thrown up by economic activity across the borders of different nation states, we can provide a schematic roadmap of the different conceptions underpinning private international law and, in particular, see where courts, procedures and remedies are situated within that model.

Private international law resolves the difficulties created by economic transactions in which the litigants and the disputed assets are scattered across territories with different legal systems through three key devices; jurisdiction rules, choice of law rules and rules concerning recognition and enforcement of judgments. The first two of these devices are designed to ensure that the most suitable national court – in terms of links to the location of litigants, obligations or assets – will have jurisdiction over the case (application of jurisdiction or forum rules) and will apply the law which appears appropriate, given the parties and the subject matter in dispute, to decide the case (choice of law rules).

It is this combination of the two devices of jurisdiction and choice of law to resolve transnational legal disputes which creates situations whereby an English court which has jurisdiction over, let us say, a contractual dispute may apply French contract law (the choice of law) to resolve that dispute. For our purposes, what is crucial to note is that choice of law rules concern which legal systems' *substantive* law is to govern the dispute. By contrast, the *procedural and remedial* law governing the case is always the law of the forum (*lex fori*).[47] So, in our example, the English court will apply substantive French contract law but English law concerning procedures and remedies will govern the case. Sticking with this example, we now need to turn to the third important element, recognition and enforcement of judgments. If the assets are not all in England but are partly, for example, in Ireland, the English court's judgment may need to be enforced there too. Rules concerning the recognition and enforcement of judgment allow foreign judgments, such as that of the English court, to be recognised and enforced, here before an Irish court.

We can see from this simplest of road maps what a different conception private international law has from EC law of the relationship between nation states with regard to transnational economic activity.

Unlike EC law, private international law accepts the fifteen plus (the UK is made up of two private law systems, Scottish and English) legal systems in the EU as its principal units and engages in a process of co-ordination of the courts

[47] Unsurprisingly, the decision as to whether a matter is one of substance or procedure has proved just as difficult in private international law as in EC law. For EC law see Harlow, this volume, at 73. It is important to note that many matters considered as procedural or remedial under EC law are widely considered as substantive by national systems' conflict of laws rules. Thus, for example, limitation periods are generally classified as substantive by national conflict of laws rules. The English courts' insistence on classifying limitation periods as procedural for conflict of law purposes was so out of line with other countries' conflict rules that the legislature intervened in the Foreign Limitation Periods Act 1984 which provides that all limitation periods shall be regarded as substantive. See J.G. Collier, *Conflict of Laws*, 2nd edn. (Cambridge: Cambridge University Press, 1994). For detailed discussion of the difficulties the Court of Justice has had in dealing with time-limits under EC law, see Flynn, this volume.

and laws in those States in order to resolve disputes where that co-ordination is required. It makes no attempt to evaluate or change the substantive or procedural and remedial laws in those constituent states. It does, however, ask courts to apply substantive laws which are not their own (as a result of the application of choice of law rules). It also asks courts, when recognising and enforcing a judgment, to find ways of achieving within their own remedial system outcomes required by the remedial law of another State (as a result of rules concerning recognition and enforcement of judgments). This can be seen as minimal incursion into the ideal of the autonomy of national legal systems. It is the welcoming of a stranger (foreign law, a foreign judgment) into the national community, not the demand (made by EC law) to change the rules and values of that national community. What can be hailed as the benefits of private international law[48] can, of course, be equally presented as its problems. A balanced assessment is provided by Joerges who depicts the problematic side as follows:[49]

> The dilemma of private international law continues to be its helplessness when applied to the relationship between European and national substantive law. The identification of minimum standards that would promote integration policy, the consideration of European concepts in the application of national law, the consideration of integration policy concerns in domestic law and its coordination with supranational regulatory claims, are all matters that cannot be dealt with by choice-of-law rules, given that they remain committed to the traditional ideal of harmony among decisions.

What can we say about procedural and remedial law on the basis of looking at private international law? We have seen that the procedural and remedial law to be applied will be that of the forum, in turn determined by the application of rules on jurisdiction. So, as with the EC legal order, procedural law travels less and is seen as more territorially grounded than substantive law. As Lindblom puts it, "a choice of procedural law may be made possible only by choosing a certain country as a procedural environment".[50] Joerges points out the access to

[48] Hence, private international law has been invoked frequently in recent years by private lawyers opposed to interference in doctrinal private law cultures and traditions at national level through EC-led harmonisation (which has been most evident in the field of consumer protection). These arguments point out that economic interactions do not require EC legislative initiatives to harmonise private law and that private international law provides a preferable regime for co-ordinating transnational economic interactions, as it does this successfully as well as respecting the integrity of national private law systems. The focus in these discussions tends, however, to be on substantive law rather than on procedural and remedial law. See E. De Boer, "The Relation between Uniform Substantive Law and Private International Law" in A.S. Hartkamp *et al.* (eds.), *Towards a European Civil Code* (Nijmegen: Ars Aequilibri Dordrecht/London: Martinus Nijhoff, 1994); H. Collins, "European Private Law and the Cultural Identity of States" (1995) 3 *European Review of Private Law* 353.

[49] C. Joerges, "The Europeanisation of Private Law as a Rationalisation Process and as a Contest of Disciplines: an Analysis of the Directive on Unfair Terms in Consumer Contracts" (1995) 3 *European Review of Private Law* 175 at 187.

[50] Lindblom (1997), note 16, above, at 14.

justice issues this may raise, especially with regard to the protection of weak groups and diffuse interests.[51]

At the same time it is true that private international law concerns itself explicitly with two important procedural and remedial matters: the question of which court has jurisdiction and issues concerning the execution and enforcement of judgments. Moreover, by virtue of linking procedure and remedies to the law of the forum, it could provide incentives to litigants to forum-shop for the most desirable procedural environments.

The parallel lines between private international law in Europe and EC law with regard to procedure and remedies do not stop here. Private international law has also undergone a process of Europeanisation. Prior to the 1968 Brussels Convention, each Member State of the (then) EEC had its own separate rules concerning when it would have jurisdiction over a case and when it would recognise and enforce a foreign judgment. All EU Member States must accede to the 1968 Brussels Convention,[52] characterised as "the most thorough attempt to co-ordinate Member State civil procedure to date".[53] For our purposes, it does two crucial things. First, it lays down uniform jurisdiction rules for cases concerning EU Member States. For instance, it provides that jurisdiction is normally decided on the basis of the domicile of the defendant. Second, it provides, with very limited exceptions, for the automatic recognition and enforcement of judgments between the EU Member States. This means that while foreign judgments are normally welcome under national conflict of law rules but may be subject to some pedigree checks, under the Brussels Convention judgments of other EU Member States must be automatically welcomed and enforced. Moreover, the Luxembourg Court is the authoritative interpreter of this Convention. The Brussels Convention has its own distinctive preliminary reference procedure which allows appellate courts to make references and obliges courts of last instance to do so.[54] We can see that the parallel lives of private international and EC law are lived through the same institutions, in particular the national courts and the Luxembourg Court.

Developments of the utmost importance have recently occurred in the parallel lives and institutional entangling of procedure and remedies in the Brussels Convention and EC law. These key developments are explored by Beaumont

[51] Joerges (1995), note 49, above, at 187. He points to comments made in the Commission's Green Book on the access of consumers to the law and on the settlement of legal disputes of consumers in the internal market, COM 93 (576) final of 16 November 1993 to the effect that the procedural law of the respective *lex fori* opposes the intervention of foreign authorities or consumers' associations drawing attention to "foreign" interests, while it negates the need of legal protection of domestic authorities and consumers defending "foreign" concerns.

[52] See also the 1989 Lugano Convention to which all EU Member States must also accede. It provides similar rules on jurisdiction and recognition of judgments but is an agreement between EU and EFTA States and to which any state in the world can be admitted if the EU and EFTA States agree on that admittance.

[53] Caruso (1997), note 38, above, at 14.

[54] Found in a 1971 Protocol.

through the lens of interim remedies. The two most important are very briefly highlighted here.

First, efforts are afoot to create a new private international law regime which will provide the EC institutions, in particular the Commission, with greater control than they currently possess. This tale of institutional politics reveals that "Europeanisation", in an era of differential integration,[55] can have more than one meaning and needs to be evaluated in different ways. Hence, the European Commission is pushing for the adoption of a Regulation, the legal base of which will be Article 65 of the new Title IV of the Amsterdam Treaty, which would replace the Brussels Convention and move private international law inside the body of the EC Treaty. Beaumont points out the heavy price to be paid for what would appear in some ways to be a greater "Europeanisation" of the private international law rules concerning jurisdiction and recognition and enforcement of judgments. In most respects it is a "de-europeanisation" as the move from Convention to Regulation under Article 65 EC will create greater intra-EU geographical fragmentation,[56] more remedy shopping possibilities for litigants who can afford the legal costs and more confusion for the rest, input from fewer national courts[57] and immense risks of decreased possibilities for international co-operation in the private international law field. All this to allow the Commission to obtain an "EU" external competence in the private international law field.

Second, the Court of Justice has made key pronouncements on both jurisdiction and recognition and enforcement of interim remedies under the Brussels Convention which have mingled the Brussels Convention with its case-law on interim remedies under EC law. Because assets scattered across different jurisdictions may need to be protected in order for any final judgment on a dispute to be useful, both the Brussels and Lugano Conventions allow courts in any State (not just the court with jurisdiction over the dispute) to grant interim remedies. Beaumont explores how in *Van Uden*[58] the Luxembourg Court has drawn on the parallel world of EC law in order to decide in what circumstances courts should award interim remedies under the Brussels and Lugano Conventions, but has not brought together the standards under EC law and the Brussels Convention. He then turns to discussion of recognition and enforcement of interim measures and how this has been dealt with in the recent complex and often unclear *Mietz*[59] judgment by the Luxembourg Court.

[55] See also Ward, this volume.

[56] Fewer states would be involved than in the Brussels Convention as Denmark has a complete opt-out from Title IV measures and the UK and Ireland have freedom to opt in to measures under that Title. Moreover, the desire to make the Brussels Convention a Regulation has also meant that revision of the Lugano Convention has not been carried out at the same time, and hence risks creating divergence between the two systems.

[57] Fewer courts would be able to refer than under the Brussels Convention because Article 68(1) EC which governs Title IV measures restricts that possibility to courts of last resort.

[58] Case C–391/95, [1998] ECR I–7091.

[59] Case C–99/96, Judgment of 27 April 1999.

Placing private international law beside EC law encourages us to think more carefully about what we mean when we talk about "economic integration" and its connection to both substantive and procedural harmonisation. Neither are necessary for economic interactions across borders. By providing us with an alternative vision which is clearly much more respectful of national procedural (and substantive) autonomy, it forces us to justify more explicitly what it is we want to achieve through EC interventions. Moreover, private international law is a separate European legal regime with its own procedural and remedial developments, deserving attention in their own right. At the same time, Beaumont's exploration of recent developments which highlight the sharing of institutions between the EC legal order and the Brussels Convention regime force us to consider first, who will control the future of procedure and remedies in the EU in private international law and second, what EC legal resources will they draw on to do so?

Co-existence and interplay of "constitutional" legal orders – remedies in Strasbourg and Luxembourg

A central ingredient in the Luxembourg Court's development of effective judicial protection has been the inspiration of the European Convention on Human Rights (the Convention). In particular, as Harlow points out, invoking its provisions has allowed the Court of Justice to read remedies backwards to encompass access to courts. This happened most famously in the *Johnston* case.[60] Three different ways in which it is useful to examine the Convention system from the remedial viewpoint can be identified. The first examines how the Strasbourg Court can be compared with the Luxembourg Court in its development of a remedial framework, the second examines the interaction of the two Courts and orders in the context of "mainstream" EC law while the third does so in the context of TEU and Title IV EC measures.

Of particular interest in comparing remedial frameworks in the EC and the Convention system is the roles played in the latter by the Strasbourg European Court of Human Rights, individuals, States and national courts. EC lawyers might well turn to the Convention system with certain ideas and expectations of what they will find there. They will know that the Strasbourg Court has not insisted on direct effect and supremacy of Convention rights in the national legal orders of the Contracting States. They will also be aware that individuals have played a key role in bringing to the Strasbourg Court violations of Convention rights. So there is an important private enforcement element in the Convention system but one which functions unlike that developed by the Luxembourg Court. If asked to name the key remedial provisions in the Convention, the EC lawyer would, on the basis of her knowledge of Luxembourg Court jurisprudence,

[60] Note 18, above. See Harlow below at 74.

plump for Article 6(1) ECHR as requiring effective remedies before national courts.

To examine the Convention a little more closely is to both confirm and modify these expectations. The main point can be stated immediately. If one was handed the text of the Convention and asked to note its principal remedial and procedural provisions concerning individual enforcement, the list would not contain Article 6(1)[61] and would probably be Article 35 (formerly 26),[62] Article 41 (formerly 50)[63] and Article 13.[64] Yet it is also true that, if asked to compile the same list in the light of the history of the Convention and the jurisprudence of the Strasbourg Court, Article 6(1) would come top of the list by a long margin. How did this come to pass?

Individual enforcement and protection has become, in the lifetime of the Convention, a central focus. As with the EC legal order, it was not originally meant to be thus. Harris, O'Boyle and Warbrick express this clearly.

> The original purpose of the Convention was not primarily to offer a remedy for particular individuals who had suffered violations of the Convention but to provide a collective inter-State guarantee that would benefit individuals generally by requiring the national law of the contracting parties to be kept within certain bounds. An Article 25 (now 34) application was intended as a mechanism for bringing to light a breach of an obligation owed by one State to others, not to provide a remedy for an individual victim.[65]

Moreover, the Convention was organised on the assumption that it played a subsidiary role in the guaranteeing of the human rights it protected, the primary role being played by the States.[66]

Combining these two aspects of the Convention we can understand better the functioning of its remedial provisions. Let us consider first the division of national and Strasbourg judicial competence and the role of individuals which is reflected in the combination of Articles 35 and 41 ECHR. Article 41 ECHR gives the Strasbourg Court the competence to compensate applicants whose rights under the Convention have been violated.[67] It will only come into play if

[61] The relevant part is the first sentence of Article 6(1) ECHR: "In the determination of his civil rights and obligations, or of any criminal charge against him, everyone is entitled to a fair and public hearing within a reasonable time by an independent and impartial tribunal established by law".

[62] "The Court may only deal with the matter after all domestic remedies have been exhausted, according to the generally recognised rules of international law and within a period of six months from the date on which the final decision was taken".

[63] "If the Court finds that there has been a violation of the Convention or the protocols thereto, and if the internal law of the High Contracting Party concerned allows only partial reparation to be made, the Court shall, if necessary, afford just satisfaction to the injured party".

[64] "Everyone whose rights and freedoms as set forth in this Convention are violated shall have an effective remedy before a national authority notwithstanding that the violation has been committed by persons acting in an official capacity".

[65] D.J. Harris, M. O'Boyle and C. Warbrick, *Law of the European Convention on Human Rights* (London: Butterworths, 1995), 32.

[66] See further White, this volume.

[67] This competence illustrates an obvious, but fundamental, difference between the institutional mechanisms linking the Strasbourg Court and the Luxembourg Court to individuals and national

local remedies have been exhausted (Article 35 ECHR), a violation of the Convention is established and that violation would not be fully compensated by the national system. The assumption underlying these two Articles of the Convention is that the national level is primarily responsible for remedying human rights violations and is to be given every opportunity to do so. The interpretation of these two Articles reveals that Strasbourg will assume the national level to have done so unless the applicant can show that they gave the national system every possible chance to provide it with a remedy and it has failed to do so. The case-law consistently shows that applicants have to be extremely diligent in order to satisfy the Strasbourg Court that they have exhausted local remedies.[68]

If an application passes through the admissibility hurdles and a violation is found, then Article 41 ECHR recognises that there is a real plaintiff before the Strasbourg Court which must properly process the claim given that it is, particularly in the light of its interpretation of Article 35, in a very tangible sense, the final court. So, with regard to both Articles 35 and 41 ECHR, we see a picture emerging of the Strasbourg system explicitly positioning itself and reinforcing its position as a very final court for victims of human rights violations with hopes and expectations firmly fixed on the Contracting States to put their own houses in order. To this developing picture we must add the lack of content given to what would seem to be a central remedies provision, Article 13 ECHR, which requires that "everyone whose rights and freedoms as set forth in this Convention are violated shall have an effective remedy before a national authority notwithstanding that the violation has been committed by persons acting in an official capacity". White's contribution to this volume investigates the Strasbourg Court's jurisprudence under Article 41 and Article 13 ECHR from the point of view of their assistance for national, in this case, UK courts, in deciding on remedies for Convention violations. He illustrates how those hoping to find here a well-developed set of principles on remedies under either Article will be disappointed. Let us examine in more detail how and why the promise of Article 13 ECHR has not been fulfilled.

There is no reason of principle why Article 13 could not have been interpreted to require that an effective national remedy be available to determine a claim that national legislation violates the Convention, thus having the effect of demanding national legal orders to accept the automatic incorporation (wholly or partially) of the Convention. It could, in other words, have provided a

courts. An individual plaintiff is an actual party to the case before the Strasbourg Court; it takes over after the national courts have terminated their consideration of the case. By contrast, the Luxembourg Court lacks this competence because, in terms of enforcing EC rights in the national legal orders, individuals do not appear before it; the preliminary reference mechanism is a court-to-court discussion which takes place during the dispute before the national court; a dispute which must always finish its life before the national court. But see Schermers' proposal, this volume, concerning relations between the national courts and the Strasbourg Court.

[68] Appl. 712/60 *Retimag* v. *Federal Republic of Germany*, Yearbook IV (1961), 384 at 404–6. See also Appl. 6452/74 *Sacchi* v. *Italy*, D & R 5 (1976), 43 at 51.

textual basis for both requiring the direct enforceability of Convention provisions before national authorities and providing the Strasbourg Court with a mandate to define what would constitute an "effective" remedy at national level for a breach of a Convention right.

The European Court of Human Rights has not used Article 13 to do either of these two things. The history of its interpretation by that Court has led to Article 13 being defined by two of its judges as "one of the most obscure clauses" in the Convention.[69] It is best described in terms of how it does not require these two things. With regard to enforceability, it does not require Contracting States to provide means by which national legislation could be challenged as not being in conformity with the Convention.[70] With regard to checking "effectiveness" of remedies, Article 13 does not require the State to provide any particular form of remedy for Convention violations; States have a margin of discretion in choosing what sort of remedies are appropriate. Nor does the effectiveness of a remedy for Article 13 purposes depend on the certainty of a favourable outcome for the applicant.[71] Finally, the context of the substantive Convention right affected must be thoroughly integrated into consideration under Article 13 ECHR of whether a given remedial set of possibilities at national level are "effective". The latter consideration in particular makes it very difficult to construct any general criteria about what might constitute an "effective" remedy and provides an extremely low threshold to satisfy the requirements of Article 13 ECHR.[72]

However, the main reason that Article 13 ECHR has assumed a marginal role is that it has been eclipsed by other Convention provisions, in particular, Article 6(1) ECHR. Given that Article 6(1) ECHR on its face is concerned with fair trial guarantees, it does not seem an obvious place to start looking for Strasbourg Court remedies jurisprudence. It is therefore important to try to ascertain how and why it has moved into remedial pole position and what this does to the Convention's broader remedial landscape. Let us look first at how Article 6(1) ECHR has achieved pre-eminence and from there try to work out why the Strasbourg Court has promoted it so extensively. The starting-point is the Strasbourg Court's judgment in *Golder*.[73] In this case, which concerned an English prisoner who was prevented by the prison rules from bringing a defama-

[69] *Malone*, Judgment of 2 August 1984, A/82, at 41, partly dissenting opinion of judges Matscher and Pinheiro Farinha.

[70] See the Commission in *Young, James and Webster* A/44 (1981) *Com. Rep.* para.177. This relies on interpretation of the words "notwithstanding that the violation has been committed by persons acting in an official capacity". The Commission stated, "It cannot be deduced from Article 13 that there must be a remedy against legislation as such which is considered not to be in conformity with the Convention. Such a remedy would in effect amount to some sort of judicial review of legislation because any other review – generally sufficient for Article 13 which requires only a "remedy before a national authority" – could hardly be effective concerning legislation.

[71] See *Vilvarajah*, Judgment of 30 October 1991, A/215 at 37–8 and *Soering*, Judgment of 7 July 1989, A/161 at 27–8; for example, English judicial review, despite the fact that it exercises control only on the procedure and not the merits of an impugned decision, constitutes an "effective remedy" for Article 13 purposes.

[72] This is well-illustrated by *Leander*, Judgment of 26 March 1987, A/116 at 29–30.

[73] Judgment of 21 February 1975, A/18 at 18.

tion action against a prison officer, the European Court of Human Rights, through a very teleological interpretation of Article 6(1), created a right of access to a court out of its provisions by using the following arguments:

> In civil matters one can hardly conceive of the rule of law without their being a possibility of access to the courts . . . The principle whereby a civil claim must be capable of being submitted to a judge ranks as one of the universally recognised fundamental principles of law; the same is true of the principle of international law which forbids the denial of justice. Article 6(1) must be read in the light of those principles.

A dual hierarchy was thereby established with regard to Article 13. First, Article 6(1) gives a right of access to a court for the determination of all "civil rights and obligations" whereas Article 13 only requires an effective remedy for "the rights and freedoms" set out in the Convention. This clearly gave Article 6(1) a broader potential scope than Article 13. Second, in its subsequent jurisprudence the Strasbourg Court has operated on the assumptions that the access to court guaranteed by Article 6(1)[74] is, in the absence of exceptional breakdowns of democracy, *ipso facto* an effective remedy and *more* effective than any other kind of (non-judicial) remedy. This has meant that in cases concerning "civil rights and obligations", that is where Article 6(1) ECHR can be applied, Article 13 is considered redundant and is not examined.[75] Both these assumptions are, of course, questionable.[76] Finally, the Strasbourg Court has widened the coverage of Article 6(1) by interpreting both the right to court access and "civil rights and obligations" in an extremely extensive fashion.[77] Harlow illustrates this in her discussion of *Osman*, concluding that the Strasbourg Court "read access forward to include outcome".[78] This contrasts with the reticence we saw exhibited in its interpretation of Articles 35 and 13 ECHR to interfere in the national legal order making its own choices and running its own course.

The use made of Article 6(1) ECHR by both the Luxembourg and Strasbourg Courts is illustrative of similar tendencies. Both have relied on promoting individual access to courts as their preferred method of justifying extensive interactions with the national legal orders and deepening their claims to be European "constitutional" courts. One outcome of reliance on this method by both the

[74] And by other Convention provisions such as Article 5(4) guaranteeing access to court in specified circumstances.

[75] See, for example, *Campbell and Fell*, Judgment of 28 June 1984, A/80 at 51; *Hokkanen* v. *Finland* A/299–A at 21.

[76] See with regard to whether access to court is an effective remedy in Article 13 terms the dissenting Opinion of judge Walsh in *Brannigan and McBride*, Judgment of 26 May 1993, A/258–B at 69.

[77] See further for detailed analysis of the case-law F. Jacobs and R. White, *The European Convention on Human Rights* (Oxford: Clarendon Press, 1996), 128–33. In particular, access to court has been required for decisions of a public law nature such as social security proceedings, the revocation of licences to serve alcohol, the revocation of a taxi-route licence in order to provide a bus service.

[78] Reports, 1998–VIII. See Harlow below at 74.

Luxembourg and the Strasbourg Courts has been, as Harlow notes, that "procedure is being tailored, piecemeal and haphazardly, to suit the convenience of transnational courts".[79]

Of course the Luxembourg and Strasbourg Courts have relied on the symbolic value of the "individual" in distinctive ways. Luxembourg opted for direct enforceability of EC law before national courts. Its boldest judgments on remedies and procedures have been taken either when there were particularly pressing "effectiveness" needs for the EC legal order[80] or, more typically, where effectiveness was given heavy backing by effective judicial protection; this most commonly occurred where the "individual" seeking protection by the Luxembourg Court was a real, vulnerable, human being (Theresa Emmott, Andrea Francovich, Helen Marshall, Marguerite Johnston). Strasbourg has taken a different path, albeit one informed by the potency of the "individual" for courts. The expansion of Article 6(1) ECHR set beside the strict interpretation of exhaustion of domestic remedies (Article 35) and the underdevelopment of Article 13 ECHR indicates that Strasbourg preferred to widen the influence of the Convention through giving the widest possible group of individuals their opportunity to put their grievance before a *national* court. Article 13 ECHR, confined as it is to Convention rights and freedoms, did not facilitate such a development. Article 6(1), which refers to all "civil rights and obligations", did. Once Article 6(1) ECHR had helped them get inside the national judicial system and ensured through the fair trial guarantee in that Article a degree of procedural fairness, the Strasbourg Court then expected them to stay there and try to get a remedy. Nor would it radically interfere with the choice of remedy given, as indicated by its State-friendly interpretation of Article 13 ECHR.

Schermers' contribution deals with the second way identified of examining the Convention system alongside EC law. He examines their developing institutional co-existence, and how problems of co-ordination have been addressed from both "sides", that is when the Luxembourg Court uses Strasbourg case-law and how the Strasbourg Court deals with claims that Community law breaches the Convention. In particular, he addresses problems arising from the fact that the Luxembourg Court considers that all EC law, even that passed at national level to fulfil EC obligations, should conform with the Convention, and will be struck down by it when it does not. When that is combined with the fact that the path to Strasbourg, requiring exhaustion of domestic remedies, is much longer than the path to Luxembourg, there is a risk that Luxembourg will become *de facto* the court of preference for human rights issues for all those cases which can be fitted within the EC law rubric. Considering this to be undesirable and likely to become a more frequent occurrence, he suggests a solution which is to institute a preliminary reference mechanism between national courts and the Strasbourg Court. From the other "side", his account of the Strasbourg

[79] Harlow below at 75.
[80] Case 35/76 *Simmenthal* v. *Italian Minister for Finance* [1976] ECR 1871.

Court's recent case-law on whether Member States can be held liable for Community law breaches of the Convention demonstrates how a potentially uncomfortable institutional situation has so far been resolved. When Member States implement EC obligations they are, for this purpose, acting as "agents" of the Community. To hold them responsible for breaches of the Convention arising from such activities is to hit the wrong target. On the other hand, the EC is not a Contracting Party to the ECHR[81] and therefore cannot be challenged before the Strasbourg Court. The Strasbourg Court has so far dealt with this by assuming that the Convention is adequately protected with regard to Community law by the Luxembourg Court. However, as the *Matthews*[82] case shows, where Member State acts under Community law are not subject to Luxembourg Court judicial control, the Strasbourg Court will opt for making the Member State responsible. This, moreover, provides further illustration of the Strasbourg Court's attachment to remedies through courts.

The European Court of Human Rights' deference to the Luxembourg Court and judicial control takes on a fresh importance in the context of differential integration developments in the post-Amsterdam EC and TEU. Here, the Luxembourg Court's "constitutional" language guaranteeing uniform, effective judicial protection in the Community legal order is placed under strain as formerly intergovernmental measures move inside the EC. EC law is not what it used to be. Pre-Amsterdam, all EC measures were subject to the same public and private enforcement regimes under Articles 226, 227 and 234 EC. The EC Commission could act against any infringement of Community law, all national courts could make preliminary references on any aspect of EC law, the Luxembourg Court always had jurisdiction and its remedies jurisprudence constituted part of the *acquis communautaire*. Ward's essay traces the post-Amsterdam fracturing of this judicial protection scenario, though the damage had of course been done through the invention of the three pillar structure invented at Maastricht whereby EC coherence was achieved only by dint of creating two non-reviewable TEU pillars. Of particular interest is to consider how both the Luxembourg and Strasbourg Courts may react to this fragmented, partial, conferral of judicial protection in EC and TEU measures in the light of their respective attachments to human rights guarantees.[83]

[81] Opinion 2/94 [1996] ECR I–1759 where the Luxembourg Court concluded that accession of the EC to the ECHR would require a Treaty amendment. On the institutional stakes underpinning this decision see J. Weiler and S.C. Fries, "EC and EU Competence in Human Rights" in P. Alston, M. Bustelo and J. Heenan (eds.), *The EU and Human Rights* (Oxford: Oxford University Press, 1999) 147 at 150: "There is indeed, no small measure of *chutzpah* in a Court which has endless creative resources when it comes to interpretations which consolidate the legal order over which it presides, but discovers the virtues of hermeneutic prudence when its own position may be overshadowed, or where the vaunted European order itself may be seen to be subjected to a higher law judicially enforced by others".

[82] Appl. No. 24833/94, Judgment of 18 February 1999.

[83] See Article 6 (ex Article F) TEU.

5. COURTS AND REMEDIES: PLACING COURTS IN CONTEXT

Judicial supranationalists have a tendency to unthinkingly accept the judicial arena as the principal means of obtaining redress for grievances. This in part, reflects, as we have seen, the strong emphasis in both the EC and ECHR system on promoting remedies through courts. Greater effectiveness, in a remedies-through-courts perspective, will tend to be measured in terms of more procedural possibilities for getting into courts and obtaining their protection and "tougher" remedies, frequently involving the defendant paying out more money or being forced to do something. Judicial recourse is therefore not placed, and evaluated against, other ways of achieving satisfactory outcomes, either by providing mechanisms designed to help prevent the wrong arising in the first place, or by providing for other ways of resolving grievances. This does not mean that access to court is unimportant; for those deprived of it, it can be very important indeed. However, at the same time, there can be no doubt that the remedies-through-courts developed by both the Strasbourg and Luxembourg Courts may have created a path-dependency which sees remedies-through-courts as a cure-all for civil and administrative wrongs and grievances, with no bad side-effects. But bad side-effects there may well be.

An angle from which to observe the benefits and problems associated with remedies-through-courts is to consider various situations where potential litigants have not been allowed to go to court, consider why not, whether these are good reasons for this and what else might be done. The essays of Novitz, Syrpis and Rawlings do this in different ways.

These essays also allow us to develop what might be meant by "constitutional" rights and how this links to remedies. We have argued that within the EC private enforcement model *constitutional remedial language* ("effective judicial protection") was most effectively invoked when it linked to what the Court of Justice could see as men and women invoking *substantive constitutional rights*. In the context of EC law, these rights were often social law rights such as rights under the Insolvency Directive or, even better, rights which could be seen as both social and "fundamental", most significantly gender equality in employment and, at least for a while, gender equality in social security as well.[84] In other words, courts and other constitution-builders build up images of "constitutionality" depending on the map of legal sources they have before them. Legal orders devise distinctive bundles of rights and create different hierarchies between them in path-specific historical trajectories.

This can be demonstrated by showing that the "social law rights" – "effective judicial protection remedies" link achieves stability only within the limited confines of the EC private enforcement model. This is perfectly illustrated in different ways in the essays of Novitz and Syrpis in this volume.

[84] See further the chapters by Ryan (for employment) and Flynn (for social security) of this volume.

Novitz looks at social law rights, not within EC law but within the Council of Europe. The European Convention on Human Rights has a neglected younger sister, the European Social Charter of 1961, which deals with social law rights. However here the reading of the map of legal sources has made the ECHR (civil/political) "more constitutional" than the ESC (social) and this has had a radical impact on how remedial protection for social law rights has developed in the ESC, especially when compared with remedial protection under its sister Convention or with remedial developments *vis-à-vis* social law rights before the Luxembourg Court. Her discussion of the new improved ESC remedial machinery, the Collective Complaints Protocol 1995, further underlines the potency of the "individual" in fuelling remedial developments and the sluggishness of European-level remedial machinery which keeps the individual out.

Syrpis' essay explores EC social rights but from a different perspective from that in the private enforcement model. He is concerned with the possibility to judicially review before the Luxembourg Court a new way of making EC social law measures. Introduced in the Maastricht Treaty, now Articles 138 and 139 EC, the "social dialogue" process requires the European Commission to consult the social partners and allows the social partners to preempt EC legislation by agreeing on how to regulate a particular issue themselves. These agreements may then be implemented by Council Directive or via collective routes in the Member States. There can be no doubt that the social dialogue has been presented as adding substance to EU claims to be a maturing democratic polity. All well and good but would the Community have the capacity to produce the remedial-constitutional maturity to match its democratising and more variegated institutional law-making universe? With regard to the Court, its chance to show its colours came when *UEAPME*, an employers' organisation, sought to obtain standing under Article 230 EC to challenge its exclusion from the EC social dialogue process which eventually produced the Parental Leave Directive. It failed.[85] In one sense, this comes as no surprise. With dreary predictability, the Luxembourg Court has stuck to the narrowest of standing rules in almost all situations. Even the exceptions have been narrowly drawn. Nonetheless Syrpis' perspicacious analysis of the *UEAPME* decision reveals a worrying lack of remedial-constitutional maturity in two respects. First, the standing requirements, though tough on all those seeking judicial review, are particularly effective in excluding from court those representing the public interest such as consumer, environmental or human rights' groups. The second concerns the Court's attitude to new "democracy-enhancing" methods of making EC law through the involvement of new institutional actors. Rather than deciding on standing on the basis of adequate consideration of the specific democratic rationales underpinning this new law-making model, the Luxembourg Court latched onto the only traditional "law-making" component in the process in order to make its

[85] Case T–135/96 *UEAPME* v. *Council* [1998] ECR II–2335.

decision. The Court is having problems developing adequate remedies for "demos" rights.

The Court's reluctance to create new paths of entry into Article 230 EC can be explained (though not necessarily justified) by its fears of an escalating case-docket and its reluctance to hold EC law, as opposed to Member States' compliance with EC law, up to scrutiny.[86] We might therefore turn more optimistically to public enforcement under Article 226 EC to see whether there the fresh breezes of citizenship and democracy have ushered in a new era of remedial maturity on the part of the EU institutions. Rawlings' essay addresses these issues. It is also a fitting conclusion to this volume as it links with and complements the themes developed in preceding contributions.

First he reminds us that, in the excitement of analysing the ascendancy of the private enforcement model which, as we saw at the beginning of this chapter,[87] has dominated the EC remedies debate, it is easy to gloss over the limitations of private enforcement and not adequately focus on the role public enforcement can play.

Having established that both public and private enforcement have a part to play, their roles should be determined by ensuring that public enforcement is targeted at the "gaps in the coverage left by the private model". The analysis developed in this introductory chapter and throughout this volume makes the location of those gaps an easy task. In the EC legal order "constitutional" rights, as Weatherill's chapter also shows, currently lose out in both the public and private enforcement models. Syrpis shows that they fare worse when it comes to challenging the legality of EC law as well. Arguments for sectoral analysis of EC law could make past decisions more understandable. It could also mean that in the future remedies could be customised and sectorally-bounded. This would prevent general case-docket worries inhibiting the remedial developments necessary to keep pace with the changing needs of the Community legal order.

Finally, we know the Commission is heavily reliant on individual complainants in identifying situations of non-compliance under Article 226 EC. We have examined the role of the individual in the private enforcement model. The question now is how is the individual treated in the public enforcement model? Rawlings identifies an initial bipolar model – reflecting an international procedure between the Commission and the Member State – in Article 169 (now 226) EC. He then discusses the pressures placed on that model by the deepening and widening of the EC project, in particular to "the rise of citizenship as a political and social as well as a market construct". This would imply moves towards adapting the bipolar model to take the complainant seriously as a citizen – to give him or her "demos" rights. Rawlings sketches the institutional actors on the Article 226 EC stage – the Court, the Commission, the Member States, the European Ombudsman and the complainants – and investigates how they

[86] Above, at 8–9.
[87] Above, at 3–8.

construct a view of each others' respective roles in public enforcement, depending on how they view their own role in that process and the function of the public enforcement mechanism itself. A picture of remedial maturity does not emerge here either. The Commission handles complaints in a manner that ignores the complainant. The Court places administrative duties on the Commission *vis-à-vis* the Member State but not *vis-à-vis* the complainant, giving judicial sustenance to the bipolar model. The European Ombudsman, rather than "reaching those parts that judges cannot reach", has acted like a surrogate court in monitoring Commission treatment of complainants under Article 226 EC.

6. CONCLUSION

This chapter has presented a picture of Europe as a space in which various legal orders – national, sub-national, supra-national, inter-national – develop, through selective re-reading of their components and those of other legal orders, their own specific institutional rationales. We have shown that remedies is a privileged medium through which this on-going process of legal constitution occurs.

Because of the importance of remedial frameworks in helping legal orders to stabilise themselves internally, to develop their own specific identities and to position themselves *vis-à-vis* other legal orders, their actual, as opposed to rhetorical, contribution to providing remedial protection is often of secondary importance to the institutions constructing remedial protection. This phenomenon is particularly marked in non-national judicially-led European legal orders. Considering the future of remedies involves both a critical understanding of the constitutive functions of remedies in legal orders (seeing how an internal perspective is developed) and measuring the remedial outcomes this produces against other, non-internal, criteria.

PART I

Dialogue Between the European Court of Justice and National Courts

1

Enforcing Community Rights in National Courts: Some Recent Developments

TAKIS TRIDIMAS

1. THE COLONISATION OF THE LAW OF REMEDIES: THREE PHASES IN THE COURT'S CASE-LAW

THE COMMUNITY legal order is supported by a decentralised system of justice. Although Luxembourg is undoubtedly the most dramatic witness of judicial power, the primary venue for the assertion of Community rights are the national courts whose rôle remains pivotal even in relation to policies, such as competition law and state aid, which are administered centrally by the Commission.[1] Community measures rarely prescribe the remedies available for the breach of Community rights so that, where such rights fall to be enforced in national courts, in principle, the national rules of procedure apply. Within the last twenty years, however, the law of remedies has undergone a transformation. One could distinguish three phases in the Court's case-law. Initially, the Court took the view that remedies were a matter for the national laws and relied on national rules of procedure and remedies subject to the dual requirement of equivalence (or non-discrimination) and minimum protection. The *locus classicus* of this early stage is the *Rewe*[2] and *Comet*[3] case-law. The Court's approach was encapsulated in *Rewe* v. *Hauptzollamt Kiel* decided in 1981, where it was stated that the EC Treaty "was not intended to create new remedies".[4] As the case-law progressed, the emphasis shifted from the requirements of non-discrimination and minimum protection to the need to provide effective remedies for the breach of Community rights. Indeed, one of the key features of judicial constitution-building at Community level has been the derivation from the

[1] See, for example, Case C–234/89 *Delimitis* [1991] ECR I–935; Case C–39/94 *SFEI and Others* [1996] ECR I–3547. Note also the Commission's White Paper of May 1999 on the Modernisation of the Rules implementing Articles 85 and 86 of the EC Treaty which proposes the decentralisation of the administration of EC competition rules, OJ 1999, C 132, 1.

[2] Case 33/76 *Rewe* v. *Landwirtschaftskammer für das Saarland* [1976] ECR 1989.

[3] Case 45/76 *Comet* v. *Productschap voor Siergewassen* [1976] ECR 2043.

[4] Case 158/80 [1981] ECR 1805, para. 44.

general principles of primacy and direct effect of a specific duty on national courts to provide full and effective protection of Community rights. This, more interventionist, approach of the Court is evinced by cases such as *Johnston*,[5] *Factortame*[6] and *Peterbroeck*,[7] and reached its apex in the establishment of state liability in damages and the cognate right to reparation for private parties.

Currently, the case-law seems to have entered a third period, the chief feature of which is selective deference to the national rules of procedure. This trend is exemplified in particular by the following developments:

- the post-*Emmott* case-law;
- recent developments on state liability in damages, especially, the judgment in *Brinkmann*;[8]
- the tendency of the case-law to leave discretion to national courts in determining whether the national rules of procedure provide a sufficient level of protection for the Community rights in issue.

The above developments should not be taken as evidence of retreat on the part of the Court. Rather, they illustrate the directed use of judicial power as the legal system matures. The underlying rationale seems to be that, since the general principles of the law governing remedies have now been established, the Court can entrust national courts to apply those principles and be more selective with regard to the national rules with which it takes issue. The purpose of a remedy is to stop the breach of a legal norm and undo its detrimental effects or, to put it in a different way, "to make constitutional ideas into living truths".[9] The starting point of the Court's approach remains the universality of remedies. Where there is a right, there must be a remedy (*ubi jus ibi remedium*), so that national courts must in principle provide a remedy for the protection of Community rights, and offer the individual the opportunity to assert rights derived from Community law.[10] This association between rights and remedies,

[5] Case 222/84 *Johnston* v. *Chief Constable of the RUC* [1986] ECR 1651.

[6] Case C–213/89 *Secretary of State for Transport, ex parte Factortame Ltd and Others* [1990] ECR I–2433.

[7] Case C–312/93 *Peterbroeck* v. *Belgian State* [1995] ECR I–4599.

[8] Case C–319/96 *Brinkmann Tabakfabriken GmbH* v. *Skatteministeriet* [1998] ECR I–5255. In that case, the Court held that where a Member State fails to take implementing measures to transpose a directive into national law, the national authorities may present as a valid defence in an action for damages that they themselves attempted to comply with the directive. In such a case, liability arises only if the incorrect transposition of the directive by the national authorities amounts to a serious breach. *Brinkmann* is the first case where the Court denied state liability on grounds of lack of causation.

[9] *Cooper* v. *Aaron* 358 US 1, 20 (1958).

[10] For a recent example in the field of sex equality, see Case C–185/97 *Coote* v. *Granada Hospitality Ltd* [1998] ECR I–5199; see further Case C–167/97 *R* v. *Secretary of State for Employment, ex parte Seymour Smith and Perez* [1999] ECR I–0623 and, on judicial review, Case C–120/97 *Upjohn Ltd* v. *The Licensing Authority established by the Medicines Act 1968 and Others* [1999] ECR I–223.

which is much clearer in German law,[11] is not as foreign to common law as it is sometimes assumed.[12]

The purpose of this paper is not to give an exhaustive account of the case-law.[13] It intends rather to discuss selectively the dual requirements of equivalence and effectiveness, as applied by the Court especially in recent cases. This paper does not cover state liability in damages.[14]

Before entering into a detailed discussion of equivalence and effectiveness, it is helpful to recall at this juncture the Court's classic formula. According to the established case-law,[15] in the absence of Community rules, it is for the domestic legal system of each Member State to designate the courts and tribunals having jurisdiction and to lay down the detailed procedural rules governing actions for safeguarding the rights which individuals derive from Community law, provided that such rules satisfy two conditions:

- they are not less favourable that those governing similar domestic actions (the principle of equivalence or non-discrimination); and
- they do not render virtually impossible or excessively difficult the exercise of rights conferred by Community law (the principle of effectiveness).

The two principles operate cumulatively so that, in order for a national rule to be compatible with Community law, it must comply with both. For example, a rule of evidence[16] or a time-limit[17] which renders the protection of Community rights virtually impossible must be set aside by the national court even if it applies equally to similar claims arising from an infringement of national law.

In *Peterbroeck*[18] the Court held that, in order to ascertain whether the principle of effectiveness is complied with, the following enquiry should be pursued:

> . . . a national procedural provision . . . must be analysed by reference to the role of that provision in the procedure, its progress and its special features, viewed as a whole before the various national instances. In the light of that analysis the basic principles of the domestic judicial system, such as protection of the rights of the defence, the

[11] See M.Ruffert, "Rights and Remedies in European Community Law: A Comparative View" (1997) 34 *CMLRev* 307 at 332–3.

[12] See the dissenting judgment of Oliver LJ in *Bourgoin SA* v. *Ministry of Agriculture* [1986] 3 All ER 585.

[13] For a more extensive treatment and further bibliography, see T. Tridimas, *The General Principles of EC Law* (Oxford: Oxford University Press, 1999), chapter 8.

[14] For a discussion, see Tridimas, *ibid*, chapter 9 and for recent cases, see *Brinkmann*, note 9, above; Case C–302/97 *Konle* v. *Republic of Austria* [1999] ECR I–3099; Case C–140/97 *Rechberger and Greindl* v. *Republic of Austria* [1999] ECR I–3499; Case C–127/95 *Norbrook Laboratories Limited* v. *Ministry of Agriculture* [1998] ECR I–1531.

[15] See, for example, *Rewe*, note 2, above, para. 5; *Comet*, note 3, above, paras. 12 to 16; Case 199/82 *Amministrazione delle Finanze dello Stato* v. *San Giorgio* [1983] ECR 3595, para. 14; Joined Cases C–6 and C–9/90 *Francovich and Others* v. *Italian Republic* [1991] ECR I–5357, para. 43; Case C–312/93 *Peterbroeck*, note 7, above, para. 12; Case C–231/96 *Edis* v. *Ministero delle Finanze* [1998] ECR I–4951, para. 19.

[16] See, for example, *San Giorgio*, *ibid*.

[17] See, for example, *Peterbroeck*, note 7, above.

[18] *Ibid*.

principle of legal certainty and the proper conduct of procedure, must, where appropriate, be taken into consideration.[19]

Similarly, in order to ascertain whether a provision complies with the principle of equivalence, account should be taken of the function of that provision in the procedure as a whole, as well as the operation and any special features of that procedure before the various national courts.[20]

2. THE PRINCIPLE OF EQUIVALENCE

The principle of equivalence requires that claims based on Community law must be subject to rules which are no less favourable than those governing similar claims based on national law. The requirement of equivalence applies "where the purpose and cause of actions are similar".[21] An obvious question which arises here is the determination of the similarity of claims. What is a similar claim under national law? In principle, it is for the national court to ascertain whether the national rules of procedure comply with the principle of equivalence, since it is the national court alone which has direct knowledge of those rules.[22] Thus, it is primarily for the national court to ascertain what claims under national law may be considered to be comparable with the claim based on Community law in issue in the proceedings. The Court of Justice however may provide guidelines. The determination of comparable claims is by no means a mechanical exercise. In some cases, it may not be necessary to carry out a detailed search for a comparable claim under national law. An example of this is provided by *BP Supergas* v. *Greek State*,[23] a case concerning overpaid VAT contrary to the Sixth Directive. The Advocate General opined that, where a taxable person is entitled to a refund of tax in respect of a particular tax year on grounds recognised by national law, that possibility must extend to grounds based on Community law without need to find a comparable claim under national law. In particular, where national law provides for revision of a tax assessment on the ground that the taxpayer made an excusable error, it must be open to the taxpayer to claim revision on the ground that the national law in accordance with which he calculated the tax applicable to him is incompatible with Community law. This is because in dealing with the tax authorities, an individual is entitled to assume that the State has correctly implemented all Community Directives and complied with Community obligations.[24] In such a

[19] See, for example, *Peterbroeck*, note 7, above, para. 14; see also Joined Cases C–430 and C–431/93 *Van Schijndel and Van Veen* v. *SPF* [1995] ECR I–4705, para. 19.

[20] Case C–326/96 *Levez* v. *T.H. Jennings (Harlow Pools) Ltd* [1998] ECR I–7835, para. 44.

[21] *Levez, ibid*, para. 41; *Edis*, note 15, above, para. 15.

[22] *Levez, op. cit.*, paras. 39–43. Case C–261/95 *Palmisani* v. *Istituto Nazionale della Previdenza Sociale (INPS)* [1997] ECR I–4025, para. 33.

[23] Case C–62/93 [1995] ECR I–1883.

[24] *Ibid*, 1904 *per* Jacobs AG.

case, "[i]t is not . . . necessary to engage in the difficult and somewhat artificial exercise of seeking a comparable claim under national law".[25] The claims however must not be wholly unrelated. Thus the fact that, under domestic law, a national court may exceptionally take into account certain pleas of its own motion even if they have not been raised by the parties, such as the issue that the dispute is *res judicata* or that the action is time-barred, does not mean that the national court may also raise of its own motion any plea based on Community law.[26]

In order to determine whether the principle of equivalence has been complied with, the national court must consider "the purpose and essential characteristics" of allegedly similar domestic actions.[27] In *Palmisani*[28] it was held that an action to recover the loss suffered as a result of the belated implementation of a directive is comparable with a claim for the non-contractual liability of the State brought under ordinary national law and therefore the two claims may be subject to the same limitation period. By contrast, in that case, the Court decided that an action to recover the loss suffered as a result of the failure to implement Directive 80/987[29] is not comparable with an action to claim the benefits guaranteed to employees by that Directive, so that the time-limits applicable to the two actions need not be compared. In *Shinghara and Radiom*[30] it was held that the right of nationals from other Member States to enter the host Member State cannot be equated with the right of the host State's own nationals to enter the national territory and therefore the remedies for breach of the two need not be the same.

It should be accepted that the requirement of equivalence prohibits not only direct but also indirect discrimination against claims based on Community law. Where a procedural rule applies to certain categories of claims most of which are claims based on Community law, and a more favourable rule applies to other categories of claims most of which are claims based on national law, the first rule may run counter to the requirement of equivalence unless it is objectively justified.

The principle of equivalence does not require Member States to extend their most favourable rules to all actions based on Community law. The Court has had the opportunity to elaborate on this issue in a series of recent cases arising as a result of the imposition by the Italian authorities of corporate registration charges incompatible with Directive 69/335 concerning indirect charges on the

[25] *Op.cit.*, para 58. of the Advocate General's Opinion.

[26] See *Peterbroeck*, note 7, above, paras. 23–7 of the Advocate General's Opinion.

[27] *Levez*, note 20, above, para. 43; *Palmisani*, note 22, above, paras. 34–8.

[28] *Palmisani*, note 22, above.

[29] Directive 80/987 relating to the protection of employees in the event of the insolvency of their employer, OJ 1980 L 283, 23.

[30] Joined Cases C–65 and C–111/95 *The Queen* v. *Secretary of State for the Home Department, ex parte Mann Singh Shingara and Abbas Radiom* [1997] ECR I–3343.

raising of capital.[31] In *Edis* v. *Ministero delle Finanze*,[32] an Italian company sought recovery of unduly paid corporate registration charges but, under the case-law of Italian courts, the registration charge fell within the scope of Article 13(2) of Decree No 641/72 according to which the taxpayer may request repayment of charges wrongly paid within a period of three years from the date of payment. The referring court questioned the compatibility of that time-limit with Community law pointing out that, under the ordinary rules provided for in the Italian Civil Code, an action for the recovery of sums paid but not due is subject to a ten year limitation period. The Court held that Community law does not preclude the legislation of a Member State from laying down, alongside a limitation period applicable under the ordinary law to actions between individuals for the recovery of sums paid but not due, special detailed rules, which are less favourable, governing claims and legal proceedings to challenge the imposition of charges and other levies. The position would be different only if those detailed rules applied solely to actions based on Community law for the recovery of such charges. In the case in issue, the three year time-limit applied not only in relation to repayment of the contested registration charge but also to that of all government charges of the same kind. A similar time-limit applied to actions for repayment of certain indirect taxes, and also to actions for repayment of charges or dues levied under domestic laws declared incompatible with the Italian Constitution.[33]

On the basis of similar reasoning, the Court held in *Ansaldo Energia SpA* v. *Amministrazione delle Finanze dello Stato*[34] that Member States may calculate the interest payable in respect of the recovery of fiscal charges paid to the national authorities contrary to Community law in accordance with methods of calculation which are less favourable than those applicable to actions between individuals for the recovery of sums paid but not due, provided that the method in question applies without distinction to actions against national authorities based on Community law and those based on national law.[35]

The reasoning in the above cases seems persuasive. In general, a claim against the national authorities to recover a sum levied contrary to Community law can better be equated to a claim to recover a sum levied contrary to a superior rule of national law, such as the national constitution, rather than to claims of recovery against other individuals. The public–private law distinction reasserts itself and assists the search for comparability. More subtle distinctions however may

[31] OJ, English Special Ed. 1969 (II), 412.

[32] Case C–231/96 [1998] ECR I–4951; see also Case C–260/96 *Ministero delle Finanze* v. *SPAC* [1998] ECR I–4997; Case C–228/96 *Aprile* v. *Amministrazione delle Finanze dello Stato* [1998] ECR I–7141; Joined Cases C–10 to C–22/97 *Ministero delle Finanze* v. *IN.CO.GE '90 Srl* [1998] ECR I–6307.

[33] *Edis*, note 15, above, paras. 37–8; *SPAC*, *ibid*, paras. 21–2.

[34] Joined Cases C–279 to C–281/96 [1998] ECR I–5025.

[35] *Ibid*, para. 30. The Court left open the question whether it makes any difference that the method of calculating the interest is fixed by the authority responsible for the breach of Community law which gave rise to the claim for repayment. See paras. 31–5.

need to be made if other factors are entered into the equation, for example the restitutionary or otherwise nature of the claim.[36] Further enquiry may also need to be pursued if national law provides for a variety of procedures for the recovery of levies charged in breach of national law, depending for example if the levy was simply miscalculated, or *ultra vires*, or even contrary to a fundamental constitutional norm. In general, however, the Court is unwilling to interfere with the way legal relations between the individual and the national authorities are classified under national law.[37]

3. THE PRINCIPLE OF EFFECTIVENESS

Under the second part of the *Rewe* test, national rules pertaining to procedure and remedies must not render the exercise of Community rights virtually impossible or excessively difficult. Although this requirement was traditionally understood as one of minimum protection, in fact the standard required by the case-law is high and any national rule of procedure or substance which unduly restricts the protection of Community rights will be struck down.[38] The term "effectiveness" more accurately reflects the state of the law than the term "minimum protection". The principle of effectiveness will be discussed here by reference to two lines of cases: the post-*Emmott* case-law, and recent judgments pertaining to national rules specifically introduced to restrict Community claims.

The post-Emmott case-law

In *Emmott*,[39] decided in 1991, the Court held that so long as a directive has not been properly transposed into national law, individuals are unable to ascertain the full extent of their rights. Consequently, until a directive has been properly transposed, a defaulting Member State may not rely on an individual's delay in initiating proceedings against it in order to protect rights conferred upon him by the directive, and a period laid down by national law within which proceedings must be initiated cannot begin to run before that time. *Emmott* was hailed as introducing a new, more assertive, approach on the part of the Court. In subsequent cases, however, the scope of the ruling was restricted. In *Steenhorst-Neerings*[40] it was held that the failure of a Member State to transpose properly

[36] Compare, for example, Case C–271/91 *Marshall II* [1993] ECR I–4367 with Case C–66/95 *R* v. *Secretary for Social Security, ex parte Sutton* [1997] ECR I–2163, and see further Tridimas, note 13, above, at 347.

[37] See, for example, *IN.CO.GE '90*, note 32, above, para. 26.

[38] See, for example, *Peterbroeck*, note 7, above.

[39] Case C–208/90 [1991] ECR 4269. See, further, Flynn, this volume.

[40] Case C–338/91 *Steenhorst-Neerings* v. *Bestuur van de Bedrijfsvereniging voor Detailhandel, Ambachten en Huisvrouwen* [1993] ECR I–5475.

Article 4(1) of Directive 79/7 [41] did not preclude it from relying on a rule of national law according to which benefits for incapacity for work were payable not earlier than one year before the date when benefit was claimed. The Court held that the national rule in issue applied equally to claims based on national law and claims based on Community law, and did not make virtually impossible the exercise of rights conferred by Community law. *Emmott* was distinguished on the ground that the rule of Irish law in issue in that case fixed a time-limit for bringing actions and made it impossible for the applicant to rely on Article 4(1). By contrast, the rule in issue in *Steenhorst-Neerings* did not affect the right of individuals to rely on Directive 79/7 but restricted the retroactive effect of claims for benefits. That restriction was justified by the need to ensure that the claimant satisfied the conditions for eligibility and the need to preserve the financial balance of the social security system.[42] *Steenhorst-Neerings* was confirmed in *Johnson*[43] where the benefit in issue, unlike that in issue in *Steenhorst-Neerings*, was non-contributory and consequently there was no need to preserve the financial balance of the system.

Thus, in the above cases the Court distinguished between national rules which prescribe time-limits within which proceedings must be brought and national rules which limit the period prior to the bringing of a claim in respect of which arrears of benefit may be claimed. The two types of rules however may lead in practice to the same result. In *Steenhorst-Neerings* and *Johnson* the Court focused on whether the national rules applicable made it impossible to exercise rights based on Community law rather than on whether an individual suffered as a result of late transposition. The judgments do not require that an individual should be put in the same position that he would have been, had a Member State transposed Directive 79/7 properly into national law within the requisite period of implementation. They thus leave open the possibility that a Member State may derive a benefit as a result of its failure to implement a directive in time.[44]

The trend towards a restrictive interpretation of *Emmott* reached its climax in *Fantask A/S and Others* v. *Industriministeriet (Erhvervsministeriet)*.[45] The case concerned charges on the registration of companies levied by the Danish authorities which were found to be contrary to Directive 69/335. Danish law made the recovery of such charges subject to a limitation period of five years but the applicants argued pursuant to *Emmott* that a Member State could not rely on that limitation period as long as Directive 69/335 had not been properly transposed into national law. Confirming *Johnson* and *Steenhorst-Neerings*, the Court stated that the solution adopted in *Emmott* was justified by the particu-

[41] Directive 79/7 on the progressive implementation of the principle of equal treatment between men and women in matters of social security, OJ 1979 L 6, 24.

[42] *Cf.* the "dissenting" opinion of Darmon AG, in *Steenhorst-Neerings*, above, note 40, 5492–3.

[43] Case C–410/92 [1994] ECR I–5483.

[44] But see the judgment in *ex parte Sutton*, note 36, above, according to which the individual concerned may recover any loss suffered by bringing an action for damages against the State.

[45] Case C–188/95 [1997] I–6783.

lar circumstances of that case where the time bar had "the result of depriving the applicant of any opportunity whatever" to rely on her right arising from the directive in issue. The five year limitation period imposed by Danish law was reasonable and applied without distinction to domestic claims and those based on Community law and was therefore compatible with Community law.

Fantask gave a fatal blow to *Emmott* and it is now settled that the latter must be read on its facts. It applies only in relation to directives and only given the specific circumstances of that case.[46] As a general rule, a limitation period imposed by national law starts from the date specified therein rather than the date when national legislation has complied with the Community obligation in issue. This was reiterated more recently in *Edis*, where the Court held that Community law does not prevent a Member State from resisting actions for repayment of charges levied in breach of a directive by relying on a time-limit under national law which begins to run from the day of payment of the charges in question, even if the directive concerned had not yet been properly transposed into national law.[47]

The case-law focuses on whether the time-limit imposed by national law is adequate, in the sense that it offers to the individual the opportunity to protect rights derived from Community law, and whether it complies with the principle of equivalence. An example of the Court's policy of selective deference is provided by *Magorrian* v. *Eastern Health and Social Services Board*.[48] The applicants were women employed as mental health nurses. They were refused additional pension benefits payable under a voluntary contracted-out pension scheme on the ground that they did not have the status of full-time workers at the time of their retirement. The national court held that their exclusion from the additional benefits amounted to indirect sex discrimination. The question then arose from which date their periods of service as part-time workers should be taken into account for the purpose of calculating the additional benefits to which they were entitled. In response to a preliminary reference, the Court held that the appropriate date as from which periods of service of part-time workers who have suffered indirect sex discrimination must be taken into account is 8 April 1976, the date of the judgment in *Defrenne*.[49] The claim of the applicants however encountered an obstacle posed by national law. Regulation 12 of the Northern Ireland Occupational Pension Regulations[50] provides that, in proceedings concerning access to membership of occupational schemes, the right to

[46] See Case C–90/94 *Haahr Petroleum* v. *Åbenrå Havn and Others* [1997] ECR I–4085, paras. 52–3; Joined Cases C–114 and C–115/95 *TexacoA/S* v. *Havn and Others* [1997] ECR I–4263, paras. 48–9; and see also Case C–2/94 *Denkavit International and Others* v. *Kamer van Koophandel en Fabrieken voor Midden-Gelderland and Others* [1996] ECR I–2827, at 2851 *per* Jacobs AG.

[47] *Edis*, note 15, above, paras. 45–8; *Aprile*, note 32, above, paras. 40–5; *SPAC*, note 32, above, paras. 28–32; *Ansaldo Energia*, note 34, above, paras. 19–23.

[48] Case C–246/96, [1997] ECR I–7153.

[49] Case 43/75 *Defrenne* v. *SABENA (Defrenne II)* [1976] ECR 455.

[50] Occupational Pension Schemes (Equal Access to Membership) Regulations (Northern Ireland) 1976 No. 238.

be admitted to the scheme is to have effect from a date no earlier than two years before the institution of proceedings. The Court held that Regulation 12 deprived the applicants of the additional benefits under the scheme to which they were entitled to be affiliated, since those benefits could be calculated only by reference to periods of service completed by them as from 1990, that is to say two years prior to their commencing proceedings. The Court distinguished *Steenhorst-Neerings* and *Johnson* on the following ground. The rules in issue in those cases limited the period, prior to commencement of proceedings, in respect of which backdated benefits could be obtained. By contrast, Regulation 12 prevented the entire record of service completed by those concerned after 8 April 1976 until 1990 from being taken into account for the purposes of calculating the additional benefits which would be payable even after the date of the claim. Consequently, Regulation 12 was such as to strike "at the very essence of the rights conferred by the Community legal order".[51] Also, the effect of the regulation was to limit in time the direct effect of Article 119 of the Treaty in cases where no such limitation has been laid down either in the Court's case-law or in Protocol No. 2 annexed to the Treaty on European Union. The distinct feature of Regulation 12 was that it restricted claims for future benefits based on past service. Are all national rules which have such restrictive effects caught by the ruling in *Magorrian*? Given the generality of the ruling one may venture to suggest that that is so. It is to be noted that in a recent case where the same issue of principle has arisen the House of Lords has made a further reference to the Court of Justice.[52]

Rules specifically introduced to restrict Community claims

The case-law takes a much stricter view with regard to rules which are introduced by a Member State specifically to restrict claims for the recovery of a charge which has been found by the Court of Justice to be incompatible with Community law. In *Barra*[53] it was held that Community law precludes a national provision which restricts repayment of a duty held to be contrary to the Treaty by a judgment of the Court solely to plaintiffs who brought an action for repayment before the delivery of that judgment. Such a provision renders impossible the exercise of the rights conferred by Community law for those persons who initiate proceedings after the Court's judgment. Similarly, in *Deville*[54] it was held that a Member State may not, subsequent to a judgment of the Court from which it follows that certain legislation is incompatible with the Treaty, adopt a procedural rule which specifically reduces the possibilities of bringing proceedings for repayment of charges unduly levied under that legislation. More

[51] *Magorrian*, note 48, above, para. 44.

[52] *Preston* v. *Wolverhampton NHS Trust* [1998] 1 All ER 528. See now Case C–78/98 *Preston* judgment of 16 May 2000 where the Court of Justice followed *Magorrian* and endorsed the view taken in the text.

[53] Case 309/85 *Barra* v. *Belgium and Another* [1988] ECR 355.

[54] Case 240/87 *Deville* v. *Administration des Impôts* [1988] ECR 3513.

recently the Court has had the opportunity to revisit the judgments in *Barra* and *Deville* in a series of cases arising as a result of preliminary references made by Italian courts.

As we saw above, *Edis* v. *Ministero delle Finanze*[55] arose as a result of the imposition by Italian law of an annual fee in respect of the registration of companies in the corporate register. In its judgment in *Ponente Carni*,[56] the Court had held that the payment of such a fee ran counter to Directive 69/335 concerning indirect charges on the raising of capital.[57] Following the judgment in *Ponente Carni*, Edis sought repayment of unduly paid registration charges but a dispute arose as to the applicable limitation period. Under Article 13(2) of Italian Decree No. 641/72, the taxpayer may request repayment of charges wrongly paid within a period of three years from the date of payment. Traditionally, the case-law of Italian courts interpreted that provision as applying only in cases where a sum had been unduly paid owing to an error in the calculation in the tax. Claims for the recovery of unduly paid corporate charges were subject to the ten year limitation period provided for in the Italian Civil Code. In 1996, however, after the judgment in *Ponente Carni* was delivered, the Corte Suprema di Cassazione departed from its previous case-law, holding that repayment of the registration charge was subject to the three year time limit provided for in Decree No. 641/72. The Commission argued that, by departing from its previous case-law, the Corte Suprema di Cassazione specifically curtailed the opportunity for the persons concerned to bring proceedings to secure repayment of charges levied in breach of Community law. The Court rejected that argument, distinguishing the case in issue from *Barra* and *Deville*. It held that a Member State is prohibited from adopting provisions making repayment of a tax held to be contrary to Community law subject to conditions relating specifically to that tax which are less favourable than those which would otherwise be applied.[58] The case in issue was distinguishable on two grounds. First, the interpretation given by the Corte Suprema di Cassazione related to a national provision which had been in force for several years when judgment was delivered in *Ponente Carni*. Secondly, that provision was concerned not only with repayment of corporate registration charges, which were in issue in *Ponente Carni*, but also with all registration charges levied by the Italian Government.[59] The Court expressly left open the issue under what conditions the *Deville* principle might apply to judicial authorities.[60]

In *Aprile Srl* v. *Amministrazione delle Finanze dello Stato*,[61] the applicant sought to recover inspections fees charged by the Italian authorities on the

[55] *Ibid.*

[56] Joined Cases C–71/ and C–178/91 *Ponente Carni and Cispadana Construzioni* [1993] ECR I–1915.

[57] *Ibid.*

[58] *Edis*, note 15, above, para. 24.

[59] *Ibid*, para. 25.

[60] *Op. cit.*

[61] *Aprile*, note 32, above.

importation of goods, which in *Aprile I*,[62] on a previous reference for a preliminary ruling, the Court had found to be incompatible with Community law. The right to reimbursement, however, had become statute-barred by virtue of Article 29 of Italian Decree Law No. 428/1990. That Decree Law introduced a special time-limit of three years for all actions for reimbursement of customs charges instead of the ordinary ten year limitation period laid down for actions for the recovery of sums paid but not due provided for in the Italian Civil Code. The change in the law was prompted by the case-law of the Corte Suprema di Cassazione which had held that an action for sums paid but not due under Community law was subject to the ten year limitation period provided for in the Civil Code and not the shorter period provided for in the customs legislation which applied only to actions for the recovery of sums overpaid as a result of an error of calculation or incorrect application of a tariff.

Recalling *Edis*,[63] the Court held that Community law does not preclude the legislation of a Member State from laying down, alongside a limitation period applicable under the ordinary law to actions between individuals for the recovery of sums paid but not due, special detailed rules, which are less favourable, governing claims and legal proceedings to challenge the imposition of charges and other levies. The position would be different only if those detailed rules applied solely to actions for repayment based on Community law.[64] In the case in issue, the time-limit provided for by Decree Law No. 428/1990 applied without distinction to all actions for recovery of indirect levies and therefore complied with the principle of equivalence. The Commission argued however that by making repayment subject to a three year time-limit rather than the ten year time-limit provided for under ordinary law, Article 29 of Decree Law No. 428/1990 specifically curtailed the opportunity for the persons concerned to bring proceedings thereby disregarding the judgments in *Barra* and *Deville*. The Court did not accept that argument. It stated that, although Article 29 reduced significantly the period within which reimbursement of unduly paid sums could be claimed, it set a time-limit which was sufficient to guarantee the effectiveness of the right to reimbursement. That provision did not have retroactive effect. Also, the time-limit in issue was applicable not solely to a specific kind of charge which had previously been declared incompatible with Community law but to a whole range of internal charges and taxes for which the legislation had standardised the rules on time-limits. The Court also pointed out that the adoption of the contested law preceded its judgment in *Aprile I*.

It appears therefore that a Member State is prohibited from adopting provisions governing the repayment of a tax which has been held to be contrary to Community law where those provisions:

[62] Case C–125/94 [1995] ECR I–2919.
[63] Note 15, above.
[64] *Aprile*, note 32, above, para. 26.

(a) relate specifically to that tax;
(b) are less favourable than those which would otherwise apply.

It remains open whether a Member State may adopt, subsequent to a judgment of the Court declaring a national levy incompatible with Community law, provisions which are less favourable than those which would otherwise apply but which relate not specifically to the recovery of that levy but also to comparable national levies. Arguably, if such provisions are an integral part of a general reform of the regulations governing recovery of sums unduly paid to the national administration, and there is no element of discrimination against Community claims, they could be compatible with Community law.

4. *LEVEZ*: THE INTER-RELATIONSHIP BETWEEN EQUIVALENCE AND EFFECTIVENESS

A case which gave rise to interesting issues concerning the requirements of effectiveness and equivalence was *Levez*.[65] Mrs Levez took up employment as manager of a betting shop replacing a male employee. Her employer falsely told her that she received the same salary as her predecessor although in fact she was paid less. When she found out, she sought to recover arrears of equal pay but her claim to full recovery was obstructed by s. 2(5) of the Equal Pay Act 1970. That provision limits a woman's entitlement to arrears of remuneration or damages for breach of the principle of equal pay to a period of two years prior to the date when proceedings are instituted. The Court examined first the requirement of effectiveness. It held that a national rule under which entitlement to arrears of remuneration is restricted to the two years preceding the date on which the proceedings were instituted is not in itself open to criticism. Mrs Levez, however, was late in bringing proceedings precisely because of the misleading information provided by her employer. The Court held that the application of s.2(5) in the circumstances would be manifestly incompatible with the principle of effectiveness. It would facilitate the breach of Community law by an employer whose deceit caused the employee's delay in bringing proceedings.[66]

It would be difficult to disagree with the ruling of the Court. Basic principles of justice require that a deceitful employer should not deny a remedy to one of his employees nor obtain an unfair advantage over an honest employer, precisely as a result of his deceit.[67] *Levez*, like *Magorrian*, can be seen as an exception to the rule that, in principle, Community law is willing to defer to national time-limits. It is notable that in its judgment in *Levez*, the Court placed emphasis on the deceit of the employer. The Advocate General, by contrast, formulated his response to the question referred in slightly wider terms. Section 2(5) is

[65] *Levez*, note 20, above.
[66] *Ibid*, paras. 31–2.
[67] See C. Barnard and T. Hervey, "European Union Employment and Social Policy Survey" (1998) 18 *YEL* 613.

a strict rule in that it does not grant any discretion to the national court to extend the backdating of payment beyond the two year period in special circumstances. In the view of Advocate General Léger, what ran counter to the principle of effectiveness was not s.2(5) itself but the lack of flexibility in its enforcement. The fact that the national court had no power to extent the time-limit set, and thus mitigate its application in order to take into account special circumstances, made it excessively difficult to enforce a Community law right.[68] The Advocate General therefore appeared to leave the door open to setting aside s.2(5) in other cases where its application would be inequitable.

Levez raised also the issue of inter-relationship of domestic remedies, which so far has not been examined by the case-law in any detail. The UK Government argued that Mrs Levez could have recovered full compensation by bringing proceedings against her employer based on the tort of deceit before the county court. In such proceedings, she could have relied both on the Equal Pay Act and the deceit of her employer and s. 2(5) would not have applied. The Court accepted that, where an employee can rely on the rights derived from Article 119 (now Article 141) of the Treaty and the Equal Pay Directive before another court, s. 2(5) does not compromise the principle of effectiveness.[69] It then turned to examine whether, in the circumstances, proceedings such as those brought before the county court would comply with the principle of equivalence. The order for reference suggested that claims similar to those based on the Equal Pay Act may include those linked to a contract of employment, to pay discrimination on grounds of race, to unlawful deductions from wages, or to sex discrimination in matters other than pay. The Court left the determination of whether any of those forms of action could be considered similar to a claim under the Equal Pay Act brought before the county court to the national court. If any of them were found to be similar, the national court would need to determine whether the claim brought before the county court was governed by procedural rules or other requirements which were less favourable. It would be appropriate to consider whether, in order to assert fully her Community rights before the county court, an employee in the position of Mrs Levez would incur additional costs and delay by comparison with a claimant of a similar right based on national law, who could bring an action before the Industrial Tribunal, which is simpler and, in principle, less costly.[70] Also, it was of relevance that s.2(5) applied solely to claims based on equal pay without discrimination on grounds of sex, whereas claims based on similar rights under domestic law were not limited by such a rule and therefore could be adequately protected by actions brought before the industrial tribunal.[71]

Levez establishes that a rule of national law which makes excessively difficult the protection of Community rights is precluded even where an alternative rem-

[68] Opinion of the Advocate General delivered on 12 May 1998, at paras. 96–7.

[69] *Levez*, note 20, above, para. 38.

[70] *Ibid*, para. 51.

[71] *Ibid*, para. 52.

edy is available, if the latter is likely to entail procedural rules or other conditions which are less favourable than those applicable to similar domestic actions. This illustrates the inter-relationship between the principles of effectiveness and equivalence which, taken together, provide a double shield. However, the Court's apparent readiness to accept that proceedings before the county court based on the tort of deceit could be a viable alternative to proceedings before the Industrial Tribunal (now the Employment Tribunal), and therefore satisfied the principle of effectiveness, may be problematic. The reason why the Court did not enter into that enquiry appears to be twofold, namely, the way the preliminary questions were formulated by the national court and the Court's general tendency not to interfere with the national rules of procedure more than is necessary. Suffice it to say in this context that the natural forum for a claim based on equal pay irrespective of sex is the Employment Tribunal. An action before that specialist tribunal compares favourably both in terms of access to justice and in terms of substance with an action before the county court.[72]

In general, it should be accepted that a rule of domestic law, such as s.2(5), which in certain circumstances makes excessively difficult the protection of Community rights is not incompatible with Community law, if, on the facts, the applicant can have recourse to another remedy before another national court. However, such alternative remedy must be effective and equivalent. That is particularly important where the alternative remedy is a substitute for the remedy specifically introduced by implementing legislation for the protection of a Community right.

5. CONCLUSION

The Court's approach to the national rules of procedure and remedies in recent years can perhaps best be described as being one of selective deference. As Advocate General Jacobs has observed, the case-law in this area seeks to draw a balance between the effectiveness of Community law and the autonomy of the national procedural systems. It may be said that, overall, the case-law has drawn that balance successfully. The requirements of equivalence and effectiveness are inter-related and overlap. They are not to be treated as terms of art but rather as facilitating the judicial enquiry. The Court sees the development of the law in this area as a dialectical process which results from a constant dialogue with the national courts. Indeed, the development of no other area of Community law depends as much on the co-operation of the national courts as the law of remedies. The principles of effectiveness and equivalence force national courts to view the national remedies under the prism of Community law. An incidental effect of their application is to expose possible inconsistencies and lack of

[72] In an action before the county court, the prospective plaintiff would have to overcome the problem of legal aid; she would have to establish the tort of deceit as an independent cause of action but also argue the sex equality point occupying valuable judicial time in an unsuited forum.

coherence in the national system of remedies and, at times, to lead to a rethinking of national remedies as they apply to areas unconnected with Community law.[73] This infusion of Community standards into the national legal systems by the Court of Justice may yet prove the most powerful force towards a *jus communae europeum*.

[73] See, for example, *M* v. *Home Office* [1994] 1 AC 3777.

2

Whatever Happened to Emmott? The Perfecting of Community Rules on National Time-Limits

LEO FLYNN[1]

1. INTRODUCTION

THE DECISION in *Emmott* is one of the most celebrated judgments of the Court of Justice from the past decade.[2] Its notoriety is well-deserved, and for two reasons. First, the ruling in that case, that national authorities were not entitled to rely on national procedural rules relating to time-limits for bringing proceedings in cases based on a directive so long as the Member State had not properly transposed that directive into its domestic legal system, was bold, clear and revolutionary in its implications. Second, that revolution was strangled at birth and the judgment itself was progressively air-brushed by the Court itself from its doctrine so that what remained was presented as little more than an anomaly, at worst as a moment of judicial madness induced by the harsh circumstances involved in the case. This revisionist view is now well-entrenched, and it offers the sole orthodox understanding of the case. However, while the principal part of the *Emmott* judgment is no longer cited by the Court, save where the excessively optimistic arguments of parties to a case are set out and where the ruling is later distinguished and confined to its facts in the Court's reasoning, echoes are still to be detected in the Court's jurisprudence. It is worth asking, therefore, whatever happened to *Emmott*?

The *Emmott* litigation

Emmott was part of a litigation saga which took place in Ireland after the time-limit had expired for the implementation of Directive 79/7/EEC which requires

[1] All views expressed are personal to the author.

[2] Case C–208/90 *Emmott* v. *Minister for Social Welfare and Attorney-General* [1991] ECR I–4629. Twenty-eight comments on the case are recorded in the library of the Court of Justice.

the abolition of sex discrimination in social security.[3] Ireland had let this period end without removing a body of legislation and administrative practice which gave full benefits to unemployed married men while leaving unemployed married women on lower benefits. In particular, married women, unlike married men, were initially deemed to be dependent on their spouses, and so entitled to a lower level of benefit, and subsequently it was deemed that these women could not have adults or children dependent upon them, unlike married men, which again reduced the value of their benefits. The maintenance of these provisions was successfully challenged in *McDermott and Cotter No. 1*, an action in the Irish High Court which involved a reference to the Court of Justice.[4]

In the wake of the Court's judgment, Theresa Emmott, an unemployed married woman in Cork, contacted the Department of Social Security to inquire if she was entitled to a higher rate of benefit as a result of Community legislation. She had been in receipt of disability benefit from 1983 onwards which was paid initially at a reduced rate applicable to all married woman and from 1986 until 1988 she received the benefit at a rate which did not take account of her dependent children. The Department replied that the issue was currently the subject of litigation in the High Court and that no decision could be taken on the matter until such time as that action had been resolved. It stated that once judgment had been handed down, this question would be examined. Subsequent to the eventual High Court judgment, Ms Emmott, whose case had still not been dealt with by the Department, began an action for judicial review of the Department's decision not to give equal benefits. She was met in the High Court by the Department's objection that her action was out of time and that her delay in taking an action constituted a bar to her claim. The High Court then decided to ask the Court of Justice if it was contrary to the general principles of Community law for the national authorities to rely upon national procedural rules, in particular relating to time-limits, in order to oppose claims for equal treatment and compensatory payment for discrimination under Directive 79/7/EEC.

Time-limits on claims are a standard part of any legal system and are specific instantiations of the principle of legal certainty. The applicability of national limitation period rules to directly effective rights derived from directives is a difficult issue. If national rules exclude actions based on such provisions, their practical effect may be so limited as to render the rights conferred illusory; this was the gist of Ms Emmott's argument to the Court. However, in the absence of express EC rules on limitation periods, a full suspension of national time-limits would have far-reaching consequences, as was emphasised by the Governments of Ireland, The Netherlands and the United Kingdom, all of whom submitted written observations to the Court. They argued that the Court should apply its well-established jurisprudence on national procedural rules, and hold that

[3] Council Directive 79/7/EEC of 19 December 1978 on the progressive implementation of the principle of equal treatment for men and women in matters of social security, OJ 1979 L 6/24.

[4] Case 286/85 *McDermott and Cotter* v. *Minister for Social Welfare and Attorney-General (No.1)* [1987] ECR 1465.

provided that the national procedural rules are not less favourable than those which apply to proceedings based on domestic law and provided that they do not make it impossible in practice to exercise rights conferred by Community law, national authorities may rely on the expiry of a limitation period against a litigant in its national courts. The Commission preferred to emphasise the behaviour of the Irish authorities. It proposed that the question be answered by ruling that it is contrary to the requirements of the effectiveness of Community law for national authorities to rely on a national rule relating to time-limits to defeat a claim based on Community law where they have previously acted in such a way as to indicate that the satisfaction of the claim would not depend on complying with the rule in question.

The Court was therefore faced with three options, the first based on the principle of effectiveness, the second based on the principles of legal certainty and of national procedural autonomy, and the third a carefully nuanced solution which combined the two other approaches in a manner closely tailored to the facts of the case before the national court. Its Advocate General, Mr Mischo, proposed a modified version of that intermediate test, albeit one which was broader than that envisaged by the Commission; as well as treating all similar causes of actions in an equivalent fashion, national time-limits "should also be of reasonable length and should begin to run only from the time when the person concerned should reasonably have been aware of his rights and his exercise of those rights must not have been made impossible in practice by the attitude of the competent authorities".[5] However, sitting in a plenary formation,[6] the Court instead embraced the first approach with a whole-hearted enthusiasm.

The Court's judgment was quite short, its reasoning extending over nine paragraphs, including the answer given. It started by recalling its jurisprudence on national procedural autonomy,[7] before going on to speak of the "particular nature of directives". It referred to the discretion enjoyed by Member States in transposing directives and to the obligation to ensure that they are given full legal effect which had been enunciated in *Von Colson*.[8] It then referred to the duty imposed on national authorities to ensure that individuals were certain as to their rights under directives and to the fact that directives are only exceptionally a source of directly effective rights, and even then merely as a minimum guarantee of legal effect which does not displace the basic duty to implement properly and in good time. On this basis the Court then stated that:

> So long as a directive has not been properly transposed into national law, individuals are unable to ascertain the full extent of their rights. That state of uncertainty for individuals subsists even after the Court has delivered a judgment finding that the Member State in question has not fulfilled its obligations under the directive and even if the

[5] *Emmott*, note 2, above, Opinion of Advocate General Mischo, point 38.

[6] The case was decided by a plenum made up of President Due and Judges O'Higgins (rapporteur), Rodríguez Iglesias, Díez de Velasco, Slynn, Kakouris, Joliet, Schockweiler and Kapteyn.

[7] *Emmott*, note 2, above, para. 16.

[8] Case 14/83 *Von Colson and Kamann* v. *Land Nordrhein-Westfalen* [1984] ECR 1891.

> Court has held that a particular provision or provisions of the directive are sufficiently precise and unconditional to be relied upon before a national court.
>
> Only a proper transposition of the directive will bring that state of uncertainty to an end and it is only upon that transposition that the legal certainty which must exist if individuals are to be required to assert their rights is created.

It follows that, until such time as a directive has been properly transposed, a defaulting Member State may not rely on an individual's delay in initiating proceedings against it in order to protect rights conferred upon him by the provisions of the directive and that a period laid down by national law within which proceedings must be initiated cannot begin to run before that time.[9]

The breadth of the Court's ruling immediately engendered doubts in many commentators because of the practical difficulties which it would create if taken at face value. The question of liability in connection with directives which were implemented mistakenly, albeit innocently, seemed particularly difficult. It was unclear if a similar suspension of limitation periods could arise in proceedings between private individuals.[10] The judgment also had the potential for an enormously disruptive effect on the cohesion of national procedural rules. If, for example, a national claim based on a constitutional right was subject to a certain limitation period, it might be considered arbitrary if no such limits applied to claims deriving from Community law. But these issues cannot have been ignored by a Court which had deliberately rejected the traditional approach to national procedural rules as well as the solutions proposed by the Commission and its Advocate General which would have been specific to this case.

2. REVISING *EMMOTT* I: DISTINGUISHING ITS MATERIAL SCOPE

A little more than two years after judgment was delivered in *Emmott*, the process of revision got under way. The first stage in this process did not take issue with the reasoning in the case, but sought instead to confine the impact of that reasoning to one field. It began with *Steenhorst-Neerings*, a preliminary ruling in which the issue of time-limits arose because Dutch law limited to one year the back-payment of disability benefits, thereby denying the applicant the benefits to which she was entitled between 23 December 1984, by when Directive 79/7/EEC should have been implemented, and 17 May 1987, one year before she had submitted her claim.[11] Unsurprisingly, the applicant relied on the ruling in

[9] *Emmott*, note 2, above, paras. 21–3. The answer given to the national court differs slightly from the statement of law at paragraph 23 in that the Court spoke of the national authorities being precluded from assserting national time-limits to bar claims "to protect rights conferred directly" on the applicant.

[10] Advocate General Van Gerven dismissed this possibility at point 31 of his Opinion in Case C–57/93 *Vroege* v. *NCIV Instituut voor Volkshuisvesting BV and Stichting Pensioenfonds NCIV* [1994] ECR I–4541.

[11] Case C–338/91 *Steenhorst-Neerings v. Bestuur van de Bedrijfsvereniging voor Detailhandel, Ambachten en Huisvrouwen* [1993] ECR I–5475.

Emmott in support of her case, and the Commission shared her analysis of that judgment. On the other hand, both the competent authority and the Dutch Government considered that the traditional approach to national procedural autonomy should be followed, with the Dutch Government carefully arguing that the time-limit in this case was constitutive of the right which could be claimed and so differed from that in *Emmott*. Advocate General Darmon robustly rejected such jesuitical niceties; having recalled the essential facts of *Emmott*, which did not include, in his account, the behaviour of the Irish authorities, he quoted the key elements of the Court's reasoning and concluded that:

> The terms of this judgment are very clear and cannot be limited to the category of procedural time-limits. Accordingly, until the "proper transposition" of a directive, a Member State cannot rely on internal procedural rules in order to refuse an individual a right which he derives from a directive.[12]

He then cast a sceptical eye over attempts to distinguish the situation involved in *Emmott* from that before the Court on the basis that in the former case no right could be claimed at all while in the latter the right was merely restricted. Such a distinction was, he considered, untenable because it ignored the unfairness created when an individual had to bear the cost of the State's wrong-doing, because it dwelt on the formal classifications of national legal systems and ignored the effect of the rule on the individual's right, and finally because it overlooked the very general nature of both the question which had been posed by the Irish High Court and the answer given by the Court.[13]

The Court's judgment in *Steenhorst-Neerings* shares only one common element with its judgment in *Emmott*, namely the spectacular distance from the Opinion of its Advocate General in the case. The Court, again sitting in a plenary formation,[14] distinguished both the factual context of the two cases and the material nature of the rules involved. It held that national rules fixing a period for which back payments could be claimed on the basis of Directive 79/7/EEC continued to apply, notwithstanding that the Directive had been incorrectly applied (and therefore been improperly implemented) during the period for which back payments were excluded. The judgment begins to tame *Emmott* at an early stage in the reasoning, citing it for the proposition that national procedural autonomy applies subject to the rules of equivalence and of effectiveness.[15] This proposition of law is correct but is not the first one which might be derived from the ruling, especially as *Emmott*'s restatement referred to *Rewe*[16]

[12] *Ibid*, Opinion of Advocate General Darmon, point 22.

[13] *Ibid*, Opinion of Advocate General Darmon, points 28–32. The Irish Court had referred to national rules which are used to "*restrict* or refuse such compensation". Emphasis added.

[14] The case was decided by a plenum made up of President Due and Judges Mancini, Moitinho de Almedia, Díez de Velasco, Edward, Joliet, Rodríguez Iglesias, Kapteyn (rapporteur), and Murray. Five of the nine judges who sat in *Emmott* also sat in this case.

[15] *Steenhorst-Neerings*, note 11, above, para. 15, citing *Emmott*, para. 16.

[16] Case 33/76 *Rewe-Zentralfinanz eG and Rewe-Zentral AG* v. *Landwirtschaftskammer für das Saarland* [1976] ECR 1989.

and *San Giorgio,*[17]two classic authorities on the point, and was immediately followed by a caution as to its limits.[18]

Having stated that the national rule in question satisfied these criteria, the Court tackled *Emmott* head on. The facts of the earlier case were, it stated, "clearly distinguishable from those of this case",[19] and it summarised these before demonstrating that difference in two ways. In its summary, the Court recalled that Ms Emmott had relied on an earlier ruling of the Court, that the Irish authorities had not dealt with her case while this other action was pending, and that they argued her claim was out of time notwithstanding the incorrect implementation of the directive. In order to differentiate the cases, it first pointed out that the national rule in *Steenhorst-Neerings* did not exclude the right, it merely limited its retroactive vindication.[20] Second, while the Court acknowledged that the judgment in *Emmott* decided that concerns based on legal certainty could not be raised against the directly effective rights derived by an individual from a directive until the directive was properly transposed, it refused to allow the indefinite suspension of a time-bar excluding late challenge to administrative acts.[21] As regards the rule in *Steenhorst-Neerings*, it noted that this time-bar allowed both for sound administration, ensuring that the applicant did satisfy the criteria for the benefit at the relevant time, and for financial balance in the system being administered which met claims made in one financial year from contributions made in that same year.[22] However, as both the sound administration and financial balance aspects of the principle of legal certainty were, at least potentially, equally applicable to *Emmott*, *Steenhorst-Neerings* seemed to leave *Emmott* intact but confined in its scope.

Just over a year later, in *Johnson II*, the Court was asked by the English Court of Appeal to clarify *Emmott* and was therefore given an opportunity to illuminate its now problematic place in the case-law.[23] The parties to the case only had an opportunity to make their observations on *Steenhorst-Neerings* at the oral hearing, and their positions were predictable. Ms Johnson, who had been denied entitlement to a UK non-contributory benefit, Severe Disablement Allowance, in violation of Directive 79/7/EEC, claimed that her case was governed by *Emmott* and that a twelve month limitation on back-payment could not be invoked while the Directive was not correctly transposed. She pointed out that neither sound administration nor financial balance were pertinent here because her entitlement to the benefit had been established as existing between 23 December 1984 and 16 August 1986, the period for which back payments

17 Case 199/82 *Amministrazione delle Finanze dello Stato* v. *SpA San Giorgio* [1983] ECR 3595.

18 However, it can be noted that Advocate General Gulmann prefigured this aspect of *Steenhorst-Neerings*, note 11, above, point 22 in his Opinion delivered on 15 June 1993 in Case C–60/92 *Otto BV* v. *Postbank NV* [1993] ECR I–5683.

19 *Steenhorst-Neerings*, note 11, above.

20 *Ibid*, para. 21.

21 *Ibid*, para. 22.

22 *Ibid*, para. 23.

23 Case C–410/92 *Johnson* v. *Chief Adjudication Officer (No.2)* [1994] ECR I–5483.

were sought, and the financial balance described by the Court in *Steenhorst-Neerings* was inapplicable to a non-contributory scheme. The Irish and UK Governments, as well as the Commission, considered that *Steenhorst-Neerings* was the controlling case because the rules involved had an identical nature and aim.

Advocate General Gulmann took the same position as the intervening governments and the Commission, considering that the purpose, contents and effects of the rules were identical. In his view, there was no need to examine the distinctions between *Steenhorst-Neerings* and *Emmott* because the latter case was simply not pertinent to the reference before the Court. However, he did refer, albeit without comment, to the Commission's attempt to distinguish the cases on the basis that in *Emmott* the national authorities had acted in a way which was liable to mislead the applicant.[24] Notwithstanding his view that the difference between the cases was not significant for *Johnson II*, he acknowledged that "when the Court's judgments in the *Emmott* and *Steenhorst-Neerings* cases are compared on their facts, it might at first glance appear difficult to understand why the national time-limits in question were treated differently under EC law", adding that the rules had the same effect and that the applicants were in the same position.[25] Moreover, he identified "general and fundamental differences" between the two types of rules: *Steenhorst-Neerings*-type administrative time-limits do not preclude individuals from relying on EC law but simply limit the period in respect of which current benefits can be required to be paid with retroactive effect, while *Emmott*-type time-bars in practice preclude reliance on Community Directives which have not been properly transposed into national law, regardless of the type of claim submitted.[26]

The judgment of the Court was on similar lines to the Opinion of its Advocate General. The plenary formation dealing with the case produced a judgment which turned on its assessment that the national rule adversely affecting Ms Johnson was similar in nature to that in *Steenhorst-Neerings*;[27] neither rule constituted a bar to proceedings, and merely limited the period prior to bringing the claim in respect of which arrears of benefit are payable. The arguments that the position of the applicant and the nature of the benefit differed between the two cases was dismissed as not cogent in light of the ultimate similarity of the rules.[28] The Court continued to domesticate the ruling in *Emmott*, referring to it alongside *Steenhorst-Neerings* as authority to show that national procedural rules were to be applied, subject only to the requirements of equivalence and

[24] *Ibid*, Opinion of Advocate General Gulmann, point 36.

[25] *Ibid*, Opinion of Advocate General Gulmann, point 38.

[26] *Ibid*, Opinion of Advocate General Gulmann, point 41.

[27] The case was decided by a plenum made up of President Rodríguez Iglesias (rapporteur) and Judges Joliet, Schockweiler, Kapteyn, Mancini, Kakouris, Moitinho de Almeida, Murray and Edward. Of these nine judges, five had sat in *Emmott*, note 2, above, and seven in *Steenhorst-Neerings*, note 11, above.

[28] *Johnson II*, note 23, above, paras. 31–5.

effectiveness.[29] The Court admitted that it had held in *Emmott* that individuals could not be sure of their rights until transposition occurred and that, as a result, until then the Member State could not raise an individual's delay in bringing an action against them nor would national limitation periods begin to run. However, it stated that it was clear from *Steenhorst-Neerings* that, "the solution adopted in *Emmott* was justified by the particular circumstances of that case, in which a time-bar had the result of depriving the applicant of any opportunity whatever to rely on her right to equal treatment under the directive".[30] This assessment is, in fact, quite different from the approach taken in *Steenhorst-Neerings* which had limited itself to distinguishing the facts of the cases without speaking of the earlier ruling being "justified" by the case's circumstances. The Court went on to rely on a formal distinction between the types of rules involved, the former impermissibly barring proceedings while the latter justifiably determined the period for which arrears can be claimed.[31]

After *Steenhorst-Neerings* and *Johnson II* it was clear that *Emmott* did not apply to all forms of national procedural rules on time-limits. However, its ratio was not overruled, merely confined to limitation periods whose expiry prior to correct implementation of a directive left the applicant without a remedy. Notwithstanding suggestions to the Court to the effect that it was the behaviour of the Irish authorities which was at the root of the ruling, the Court continued to refer to broader statements of principle in *Emmott*. In short, the case had been moved to the back of the group portrait but had not yet been removed.

3. REVISING *EMMOTT* II: A RULING ON ITS FACTS

Certain elements of the judgment in *Emmott* have been cited as examples of the application of general principles of EC law, such as the existence of national procedural autonomy once rules of equivalence and effectiveness are respected,[32] and the obligation of Member States to ensure that directives are put into full effect.[33] However, the central holding of the case, that national

[29] *Johnson II*, note 23, above, para. 21.

[30] *Ibid*, para. 26.

[31] *Ibid*, paras. 28 and 30.

[32] Apart from the judgments in *Steenhorst-Neerings*, note 11, above, *Johnson II*, note 23, above, and Advocate General Gulmann's Opinion in *Otto BV* v. *Postbank BV*, para. 16 of *Emmott* has been cited with approval by Advocates General Jacob (Case C–62/93 *BP Soupergaz* v. *Greek State* [1995] ECR I–1883, point 52; Case C–312/93 *Peterbroeck, Van Campenhout and Cie SCS* v. *Belgian State* [1995] ECR I–4599, point 28; Case C–24/95 *Land Rheinland-Pfalz* v. *Alcan Deutschland GmbH* [1997] ECR I–1591, point 15), Léger (Case C–66/95 *R* v. *Secretary of State for Social Security, ex parte Sutton* [1997] ECR I–2163, point 64; Case C–326/96 *Levez* v. *T.H. Jennings (Harlow Pools) Ltd* [1998] ECR I–7835, point 5), and Cosmas (Case C–261/95 *Palmisani* v. *INPS* [1997] ECR I–4025, point 18).

[33] See Case C–336/97 *Commission* v. *Italy* [1999] ECR I–3771, para. 19; Case C–143/91 *Criminal Proceedings Against Van der Tas* [1992] ECR I–5045, para. 18. Interestingly, in Case C–336/97 this aspect of *Emmott*, note 2, above, is linked with Article 10 EC (ex Article 5), a connection which does not appear to have been made before.

authorities may not invoke time-bars on proceedings to enforce rights derived directly from a directive until the directive has been properly implemented in national law, has withered on the vine. The Advocates General of the Court have not referred to this proposition of law with favour,[34] apart from Advocate General Léger who has used it on two occasions without referring to any limitations on its scope, albeit merely to provide ancillary support for a different proposition.[35] For the most part, however, the references to *Emmott* in the Opinions have increasingly emphasised its exceptional nature, not merely the distinction between different forms of time-limit, and the Court has taken a similar approach in its judgments.

This process began when Advocate General Jacobs suggested that *Emmott* should be seen as confined to its facts. The Advocate General initially noted in *BP Soupergaz* that *Steenhorst-Neerings* and *Johnson II* had suggested that the case rested on its particular circumstances, without elaborating why this analysis was to be preferred.[36] In *Denkavit*, he offered two alternative readings of *Emmott*.[37] The first was that the ruling should be treated, its general language notwithstanding, "as establishing the principle that a Member State may not rely on a limitation period where a Member State is in default both in failing to implement a directive and in obstructing the exercise of a judicial remedy in reliance upon it, or perhaps where the delay in exercising the remedy . . . is in some other way due to the conduct of the national authorities".[38] The second was the case could be seen as a new application of the principle that the exercise of Community rights must not be excessively difficult, and that in the interests of legal certainty this novel application should be confined to wholly exceptional circumstances.[39] He repeated these views in his Opinions in *Haahr Petroleum*[40] and in *Fantask*.[41] In the latter case, while he noted that similar rulings could be found in national legal systems based on the principles of equity and good faith, he did not think it necessary to have recourse to these to explain *Emmott* within the context of the EC legal system.[42]

[34] See Opinion of Advocate General Van Gerven in *Vroege*, note 10, above, point 31.

[35] See Case C–5/94 *R* v. *Ministry of Agriculture, Fisheries and Food, ex parte Hedley Lomas (Ireland) Ltd* [1996] ECR I–2553, Opinion of Advocate General Léger, points 58 and 63; *ex parte Sutton*, note 32, above, Opinion of Advocate General Léger, point 71.

[36] *BP Soupergaz*, note 32, above, Opinion of Advocate General Jacobs, point 56.

[37] Case 2/94 *Denkavit International and Others* v. *Kamer van Koophandel en Fabrieken voor Midden-Gelderland and Others* [1996] ECR I–2827.

[38] *Ibid*, Opinion of Advocate General Jacobs, point 74. The description of this norm as a "principle" is somewhat at odds with its extreme specificity. The Advocate General added, "A further factor in *Emmott* was that the applicant was in the particularly unprotected position of an individual dependent on social welfare".

[39] *Ibid*, Opinion of Advocate General Jacobs, point 76.

[40] Case C–90/94 *Haahr Petroleum Ltd* v. *Åbenrå Havn and Others* [1997] ECR I–4085, Opinion of Advocate General Jacobs, point 159.

[41] Case C–188/95 *Fantask A/S e.a.* v. *Industrieministeriet* [1997] ECR I–6783, Opinion of Advocate General Jacobs, points 85–8.

[42] *Ibid*, Opinion of Advocate General Jacobs, point 87 and cases set out at footnote 60 of his Opinion.

The Court did not directly address *Emmott* again until July 1997 when its Sixth Chamber delivered judgment in *Haahr Petroleum*[43] and *Texaco*,[44] related cases referred to it from Denmark concerning the reimbursement of harbour charges levied in violation of EC law.[45] The charges violated Article 90 (ex Article 95) EC and harbour users sought to recover the monies they had paid despite the existence of a five year limitation period under national law. Their arguments based on *Emmott* were unsuccessful; the Court, having found that the national rules treated all similar causes of action in an equivalent fashion and that they did not render vindication of EC law rights unduly difficult, ruled that *Emmott* was not applicable because this action was based on violation of a Treaty provision and not of a directive.[46] It supported this conclusion by referring back to the parts of its reasoning in the earlier case which set out the special nature of directives and the particular responsibilities they create for Member States, as well as the case's specific circumstances.[47] Thus, not only was *Emmott* excluded from national time rules determining the content of rights but it was also inapplicable where the rules in question restricted or precluded an ability to assert rights based on the Treaty.

While *Haahr Petroleum* involved a provision of the Treaty, allowing some distinction to be drawn with *Emmott*, the Court firmly closed down its scope in *Fantask*, which centred on the limitation periods applicable to an action based on a directive which was not fully implemented on time.[48] The applicants before the national court and the Commission both underlined the similarity of the two cases; until the date of correct implementation of the directive, individuals were unable to ascertain their rights. The Court ruled that Community law does not prevent the Member State which has not properly implemented a directive from resisting actions for the repayment of monies improperly levied in breach of that directive by relying on a limitation period under domestic law running from the date on which the monies were paid.[49] Because the action and the time-limit involved at national level were, in essence, the same as those at issue in *Emmott*, there was no question of the earlier ruling being confined to a particular type of action or to a specific species of time-limits. The judgment of the Court, having recalled its jurisprudence on national procedural rules and having established the acceptability of this kind of national rule, quoted the ruling in *Emmott* but then stated that:

[43] *Haahr Petroleum*, note 40, above.

[44] Joined Cases C–114/95 and C–115/95 *Texaco A/S* v. *Middelfart Havn and Others* [1997] ECR I–4263.

[45] The cases were dealt with by a formation of the Sixth Chamber consisting of Chamber President Mancini and Judges Murray and Kapteyn (rapporteur).

[46] *Haahr Petroleum*, note 40, above, paras. 51–3; *Texaco*, note 44, above, paras. 47–9.

[47] *Haahr Petroleum*, note 40, above, para. 52; *Texaco*, note 44, above, para. 48.

[48] *Fantask*, note 41, above.

[49] The case was decided by a grand plenum made up of President Rodríguez Iglesias, and Judges Gulmann, Ragnemalm, Wathelet, Mancini, Moitinho de Almeida, Kapteyn, Murray, Edward, Puissochet (rapporteur), Hirsch, Jann, and Sevon.

> However, as was confirmed by the judgment in [*Johnson II*], it is clear from [*Steenhorst-Neerings*] that the solution adopted in Emmott was justified by the particular circumstances of that case, in which the time-bar had the result of depriving the applicant of any opportunity whatever to rely on her right to equal treatment under a Community directive (see also [*Haahr Petroleum* and *Texaco*]).[50]

By this re-reading of the case, the Court moves beyond the two already limited versions of *Emmott* resulting from *Johnson II* and *Steenhorst-Neerings*, and from *Haahr Petroleum* and *Texaco*, respectively, to produce a "super-limited, *Emmott* on its facts" version of the judgment. *Emmott* survives this process of re-positioning in the jurisprudential canon, just about, but only in the sense that the decision itself stands even if it has been eviscerated of its reasoning.

The marginal and anomalous position of *Emmott* was confirmed more recently by the Court, sitting in plenary formation, in *Edis*,[51] *Spac*[52] and *Ansaldo*.[53] This group of cases dealt with time-limits applicable to claims based on a directive which was not properly transposed into Italian law. The effect of *Fantask* on these rulings, all of which were handed down on the same day by a plenary formation,[54] was evident. At the hearing the Commission had revised its arguments on *Emmott* to the Court so as to accommodate the case. In his Opinions, Advocate General Ruiz-Jarabo Colomer was extremely frank in his assessment of *Emmott*'s fate, stating that its scope had been "subsequently cut down by the Court of Justice when it emphasised that the rule in the case can be applied only when the same singular circumstances arise as characterised that case".[55] The Advocate General added that in future parties wishing to use the case should identify the similarities between their situation and that of Ms Emmott, rather than seeking to distinguish their situation from those in *Steenhorst-Neerings*, *Johnson II* and *Fantask*. Because the referring courts had expressly raised questions relating to *Emmott* in each of the cases, the Court took the opportunity to reiterate its reasoning in *Fantask* in relation to that judgment, and noted that it did not appear from the case-file that "the conduct of the Italian authorities, in conjunction with the existence of the contested time-limit, had the effect in this case, as it did in *Emmott*, of depriving the plaintiff company of any opportunity of enforcing its rights before the national courts".[56] This statement seems to be a belated acceptance of the views of the

[50] *Fantask*, note 41, above, para. 51.

[51] Case C–231/96 *Edis* v. *Ministero delle Finanze* [1998] ECR I–4951.

[52] Case C–260/96 *Ministero delle Finanze* v. *Spac SpA*[1998] ECR I–4997.

[53] Joined Cases C–279/96, C–280/96 and C–281/96 *Ansaldo Energia SpA* v. *Amministrazione delle Finanze dello Stato* [1998] ECR I–5025.

[54] The cases were decided by a petit plenum made up of President Rodríguez Iglesias and Judges Ragnemalm, Wathelet, Schingten, Mancini, Moitinho de Almeida, Kapteyn, Edward, Puissochet (rapporteur), Sevon and Iaonnou.

[55] *Edis*, note 51, above, Opinion of Advocate General Ruiz-Jarabo Colomer, point 68; *Spac*, note 52, above, Opinion of Advocate General Ruiz-Jarabo Colomer, point 29; *Ansaldo*, note 53, above, Opinion of Advocate General Ruiz-Jarabo Colomer, point 10.

[56] *Edis*, note 51, above, para. 48; *Spac*, note 52, above, para. 31; *Ansaldo*, note 53, above, para. 22.

Commission and Advocate General Mischo in *Emmott* that the case's outcome should be linked explicitly to the national authorities' behaviour.

The plenary formation had another opportunity to affirm this diminished view of *Emmott* two months later when giving judgment in *Aprile II*, another Italian reference involving the use of national procedural time-limits to resist the recovery of monies paid but not due under EC law.[57] The judgment of the Court seems somewhat less assured than those in *Fantask*, *Edis*, *Spac* and *Ansaldo*. While it repeated the line established in these cases that *Emmott* is only applicable in very exceptional circumstances,[58] having established that these were not present in the case before the referring court, the judgment then identified a secondary argument for excluding the application of *Emmott*:

> Moreover, it is clear from the case-law of the Court . . . that the solution adopted in *Emmott* is not applicable to claims for repayment not based on the direct effect of a directive. Even though the Court, in *Aprile I*, gave a ruling as to the scope of Directive 87/53, it is clear from the documents now before the Court that the incompatibility of the charges at issue with Community law derives not from a failure to implement, or incorrect transposition of, that directive but from infringement of the provisions of the Treaty or of other directly applicable Community instruments.[59]

Given the absence of exceptional circumstances in the case which could have triggered an *Emmott*-type suspension of time-limits, this additional observation obviously was unnecessary. However, it sends an unambiguous message; even in exceptional circumstances, national time-bars may still be invoked unless a directive is involved. Thus, even though the comment is superogatory, it squeezes *Emmott* still further.

4. FINAL THOUGHTS: HOW WRONG? HOW DEAD? HOW NECESSARY?

Notwithstanding the clarity of the judgment in *Emmott* and, in particular, its considered and robust use of basic constitutional principles, the decision in that case now seems, at best, an aberration in the Court's jurisprudence. Certainly the judgment did not give rise to any new lines of case-law based on it, although it can claim credit for a small cottage industry of judgments dedicated to limiting and, ultimately, refuting it. However, while *Emmott* did not give rise to a distinct doctrinal line of its own, it is worth asking if the Court had really taken the wrong direction in that case. In this respect, two issues are worth examining: first, whether the return to a traditional analysis of national procedural time-limits governing actions based on incorrectly transposed directives was facilitated by the development of the state liability doctrine; and second,

[57] Case C–228/96 *Aprile Srl (in liquidation)* v. *Amministrazione delle Finanze dello Stato (No.2)* [1998] ECR I–7141.

[58] *Ibid*, para. 41.

[59] *Ibid*, para. 44.

whether anything remains of *Emmott* in the case-law of the Court where it is not cited.

The Court of Justice began its recent odyssey into the doctrine of state liability for violation of EC law in *Francovich*, a judgment delivered four months after that in *Emmott*.[60] While many questions remain open as to the precise details of this doctrine, its broad parameters have been clarified, notably by a series of judgments delivered in 1996.[61] These cases establish that it is for national law to determine the procedural rules to which such actions are subject, so that national limitation periods apply in the usual way to state liability actions based on EC law.[62] Returning to the specific setting of Ms Emmott's situation, the failure of the Irish authorities to pay her a full rate of disability benefit in violation of Directive 79/7EEC is reminiscent of the situation in *Sutton*, where the Court held that once the conditions of state liability were fulfilled, national authorities are obliged to make reparation for loss and damage caused by an individual as a result of the breach of a directive.[63] It is probable that were the same situation to emerge now, the action against the Irish authorities would involve proceedings, not for judicial review, but for damages for breach of EC law, a form of action which involves a more generous limitation period in Ireland, and in most other jurisdictions.

Of course, to postulate a functional displacement of the pressure created by the absence of a remedy from the doctrinal dead-end of *Emmott*'s absolute bar on the use of national limitation periods to the fruitful doctrine of State liability does not lead to firm proof of such a connection. However, these developments do overlap in time and are, in their effect, congruent. Moreover, the state liability doctrine had the advantage, in terms of maintaining the delicate balance between national procedural autonomy and effective enforcement of EC law rights, of being less overtly radical than the judgment in *Emmott* because of its symbiotic relationship to existing features of national law.

It is true that the jurisprudence shows little indication of any link. Several Advocates General have, however, offered some reflections on the relations between these doctrinal strands in their Opinions. Advocate General Léger, setting out the general principles which ensure effective protection of individuals' rights, in *Hedley Lomas*, considered that *Emmott* and State liability formed part of "the same line of reasoning".[64] In *Denkavit*, Advocate General Jacobs rejected a link proposed by the UK and Dutch Governments between the

[60] Case C–6/90 *Francovich and Bonifaci and Others* v. *Italian State* [1991] ECR I–5357.

[61] Joined Cases C–46/93 and C–48/93 *Brasserie du Pêcheur SA* v. *Bundesrepublik Deutschland* and *R* v. *Secretary of State for Tranport, ex parte Factortame Ltd and Others* [1996] ECR I–1029; Case C–392/93 *R* v. *HM Treasury, ex parte British Telecommunications plc* [1996] ECR I–1631; *ex parte Hedley Lomas*, note 35, above; Case C–178/94 *Dillenkofer and Others* v. *Bundesrepublik Deutschland* [1996] ECR I–4845.

[62] *Francovich*, note 60, above, paras. 41–3; *Palmisani*, note 32, above, paras. 28–39.

[63] *Ex parte Sutton*, note 32, above.

[64] *Ex parte Sutton*, note 32, above, Opinion of Advocate General Léger, points 54–74, especially point 71.

conditions for state liability and those for the setting aside of ordinary time-limits, on the grounds that this involved a misunderstanding of the state liability remedy and that it would undermine legal certainty.[65] However, in a comment which supports the idea of a functional, if not a doctrinal, similarity between these responses to state non-compliance, he spoke of State liability's "exceptional character as a remedy which goes beyond ordinary administrative remedies by providing compensation for loss or damage arising from flagrant legislative or administrative misconduct".[66] In *Fantask* Advocate General Jacobs again warned against conflating the *Emmott* principle with State liability, stating that the former:

> continues to provide an important safeguard notwithstanding the more recent developments in the case-law [on state liability]. An individual must be allowed to make use of all available remedies. The existence of another claim, for example a claim for damages in the competent courts, cannot justify the obstruction of a repayment or entitlement claim which an individual was seeking to exercise.[67]

It seems, therefore, that Advocate General Jacobs sees *Emmott* as lying in reserve should exceptional circumstances arise in relation to a particular form of action, and that the presence of an alternative remedy does not suffice to displace it. Advocate General Fennelly did not disagree with this view expressly when he commented in his *EvoBus* Opinion on the possibility of Community law requiring the exceptional non-application of national time-limits for the commencement of proceedings in respect of rights contained in an unimplemented directive.[68] However, he indicated that from a practical point of view a state liability action would make more sense for the claimant than attempting to use *Emmott*. He noted that *Emmott* might have been pertinent were the applicant before the national court deprived of any opportunity whatsoever to rely on its rights under the Utilities Directive[69] because:

> pending the implementation of the Utilities Review Directive,[70] no national court had competence to enforce the provisions of the Utilities Directive, whether as transposed by [national law] or by virtue of the principle of the direct effect of directive, or [because] a competent national court did not provide adequate remedies to ensure the protection of rights under the Utilities Directive, despite its Community-law obligation to do so. In that case, however, the most appropriate response might be the initiation of proceedings for state liability . . .[71]

[65] *Denkavit International*, note 37, above, Opinion of Advocate General Jacobs, points 77–9.

[66] *Ibid*, Opinion of Advocate General Jacobs, point 78.

[67] *Fantask*, note 41, above, Opinion of Advocate General Jacobs, point 88.

[68] Case C–111/97 *EvoBus Austria GmbH* v. *Niederösterreichische Verkehrsorganisations GmbH (Növog)* [1998] ECR I–5411.

[69] Council Directive 93/38/EEC of 14 June 1993 co-ordinating the procurement procedures of entities operating in the water, energy, transport and telecommunications sectors, OJ 1993 L 199/84.

[70] Council Directive 92/13/EEC of 25 February 1992 co-ordinating the laws, regulations and administrative provisions relating to the application of Community rules on the procurement procedures of entities operating in the water, energy, transport and telecommunications sectors, OJ 1992 L 76/14.

[71] *EvoBus*, note 68, above, Opinion of Advocate General Fennelly, point 25.

When *Emmott* is placed in the line of the state liability jurisprudence and is seen, therefore, as a response to the same concerns, namely the need to ensure that the effective protection of EC law rights is not frustrated by the particularity of national procedural rules, the judgment appears less a wrong turning than a premature and possibly ill-considered step, but nevertheless one in the right direction.

The remarks of Advocates General Jacobs and Fennelly make it clear that, even allowing for the retrenchment of *Emmott* in the later jurisprudence, it can still be legitimately invoked, albeit in exceptional circumstances. These might have been thought to exist in *Magorrian*, a reference by the Industrial Tribunal, Belfast, concerning the exclusion of part-time mental health officers from an occupational pension scheme.[72] While, *Emmott* would not, in line with *Haahr Petroleum*, have been applicable, given that the case concerned an exclusion which constituted indirect discrimination in violation not only of Directive 75/117/EEC[73] but also of former Article 119 EC,[74] its echoes can be detected in the judgment. The period in respect of which membership rights could be claimed was limited by national law to two years prior to the date of the introduction of an action. The UK Government argued that this rule satisfied the *Rewe* conditions and that it fell within the scope of *Johnson II*. However, in its judgment the Court, sitting as the Sixth Chamber, distinguished both *Johnson II* and *Steenhorst-Neerings* on the basis that this rule concerned the admission of employees to a special status under an occupational pension scheme, not their right to claim pension benefits retroactively:

> Consequently, unlike the rules at issue in the judgments cited above, which in the interests of legal certainty merely limited the retroactive scope of a claim for certain benefits and did not therefore strike at the very essence of the rights conferred by the Community legal order, a rule such as that before the national court in this case is such as to render any action by individuals relying on Community law impossible in practice.[75]

This approach confirms that the logic in *Emmott*, even in its reduced form, remains viable and potentially applicable, although quite how this ruling is to be reconciled with *Aprile II* is less clear. Moreover, *Magorrian* indicates that misleading conduct on the part of national authorities is not necessary to bar the application of a national time-limit.

[72] Case C–246/96 *Magorrian and Cunningham* v. *Eastern Health and Social Services Board and Department of Health and Social Services* [1997] ECR I–7153. The case was dealt with by a formation of the Sixth Chamber consisting of Chamber President Schintgen and Judges Mancini (rapporteur), Kapteyn, Murray and Hirsch.

[73] Council Directive 75/117/EEC of 10 February 1975 on the approximation of the laws of the Member States relating to the application of the principle of equal pay for men and women, OJ 1975 L 45/19.

[74] *Magorrian*, note 72, above, Opinion of Advocate General Cosmas, footnote 50.

[75] *Ibid*, para. 44. The Court also ruled that such a national rule would limit the direct effect of former Article 119 EC in cases where this had no Treaty basis, and that this rule could not encourage legal certainty by requiring applicants to be diligent. *Ibid*, paras. 45 and 46.

The full Court found another national time-bar inapplicable one year later, in *Levez*, a UK reference involving remedies for violation of Directive 75/117/EEC and former Article 119 EC.[76] The situation it faced was reminiscent of *Emmott*; while Ms Levez had suffered direct sex discrimination, she had not been able to bring judicial proceedings in respect of the entirety of wages unlawfully withheld from her; the two year arrears period laid down by national law applied and precluded a claim in respect of that period because her employer had withheld from her information which would have enabled her to take an action. Both Ms Levez and the Commission drew the Court's attention to the combination of the employer's deceit and the national court's inability to extend the deadline to take this circumstance into account, while the employer and the UK Government concentrated on her alleged ability to take an action without having this information. The Court, having recalled the established case-law relating to national procedural autonomy and its limitations, then ruled, using the national court's findings, that inaccurate information provided gave the employee no way of determining whether she was being discriminated against in violation of Directive 75/117/EEC. It concluded:

> In short, to allow an employer to rely on a national rule such as the rule at issue would, in the circumstances of the case before the national court, be manifestly incompatible with the principle of effectiveness referred to above. Application of the rule at issue is likely, in the circumstances of the present case, to make it virtually impossible or excessively difficult to obtain arrears of remuneration in respect of sex discrimination. It is plain that the ultimate effect of this rule would be to facilitate the breach of Community law by an employer whose deceit caused the employee's delay in bringing proceedings for enforcement of the principle of equal pay.
>
> Furthermore, it does not appear that application of the rule at issue in the circumstances of the case before the national court can reasonably be justified by principles such as legal certainty or the proper conduct of proceedings.[77]

Given the judgment focuses on rights derived from a directive and not a treaty provision, it would not have been impossible to invoke *Emmott*, although it would have gone against the view expressed by Advocate General Van Gerven in *Vroege* that *Emmott* was not pertinent to legal relations between individuals. Clearly the material facts of this case are very like that of *Emmott*, but it is a measure of how dangerous that judgment now seems that it is conspicuously absent here. It may be, however, that at some point in the future *Levez* and *Emmott* will be synthesised and seen as applications of the broader principle of effectiveness of remedies.

If, therefore, *Emmott* is not entirely wrong, nor indeed entirely dead, it seems somewhat churlish to ask if the judgment was entirely necessary. Given its extensive judicial rewriting since it was originally delivered, clearly the judg-

[76] *Levez*, note 32, above. The case was decided by a petit plenum made up of President Rodríguez Iglesias and Judges Puissochet, Hirsch, Jann, Mancini (rapporteur), Moitinho de Almeida, Murray, Edward, Ragnemalm, Schingten and Ioannou.

[77] *Ibid*, paras. 32 and 33.

ment could have used more cautious language and have avoided the suggestion that new principles of Community law were being declared. However, was the reference itself necessary, strictly speaking? When the Irish rule at issue in the case is examined again, it proves not to be a rigid limitation period. Order 84, Rule 21(1) of the Rules of the Superior Court 1986 provided that:

> An application for leave to apply for judicial review shall be made promptly and in any event within three months from the date when grounds for the application first arose . . . , unless the Court considers that there is good reason for extending the period within which the application shall be made.

While delay in applying for relief may be taken into account when the courts exercise their discretion to invalidate an administrative decision, the Irish Supreme Court had stated that there was no reason "why delay, however long, should of itself, disentitle to certiorari any applicant for that remedy who can demonstrate that a public wrong has been done to him – that, for instance, a conviction has been obtained without jurisdiction, or that otherwise, the State has wronged him and that wrong continues to mark or mar his life".[78] Rather than exercising its discretion to disregard the delay, the High Court took the opportunity presented by the invocation of delay by the State to make a reference, with the consequent dramatic results. That reference has given rise to a lengthy construction and reconstruction of authority in the Court's case-law but one is entitled to ask, in the light of the official's behaviour and Irish courts' usually equitable attitude towards such situations, whether the *Emmott* ruling was really necessary.

[78] *State (Furey)* v. *Minister for Defence* [1988] ILRM 89, *per* McCarthy J.

3

A Common European Law of Remedies?

CAROL HARLOW

1. IN SUPPORT OF UNIFORMITY

The European Parliament once declared that the:

> uniform, complete and simultaneous application of Community law in all Member States is a fundamental prerequisite for the existence of a Community governed by the rule of law,[1]

a large claim. The statement finds an echo, however, in a passage from a report of the European Court of Justice (ECJ) where it is maintained that:

> Any weakening, even if only potential, of the uniform application and interpretation of Community law throughout the Union would be liable to give rise to distortions of competition and discrimination between economic operators, thus jeopardising equality of opportunity between economic operators and consequently the proper functioning of the internal market.[2]

Here the Court is clearly referring to *substantive* law. The passage continues that preliminary reference forms:

> the veritable cornerstone of the operation of the internal market, since it plays a fundamental role in ensuring that the law established by the Treaties retains its Community character with a view to guaranteeing that that law has the same effect in all circumstances in all the Member States of the European Union.[3]

Here the market objective as well as the contribution of the Community courts towards securing the single market is flagged up, as are two further points. First, the introduction of the phrase "the same effect" suggests that real uniformity, at least of interpretation, is the aim; second, the Court places its faith in the procedural device of reference under Article 234 EC (ex Article 177) to secure that uniformity.

[1] [1983] OJ C68/32–34.
[2] *The Future of the Judicial System of the European Union (Proposals and Reflections)* (1999).
[3] *Ibid.*

Thus far we find no mention of procedural law, nor should we expect to, since EC law recognises the procedural autonomy of the national jurisdictions. Yet for many reasons, it might seem appropriate to harmonise procedural as well as substantive law. Professor Jolowicz is only one among many to share this view:

> If a market is to flourish, disputes arising out of business conducted in the market must be resolved consistently with one another, and that requires more than a uniform substantive law. Distortion is bound to occur if the mode of litigation, with all that that implies both by way of procedural techniques and by way of their implications for costs, delays, appeals, enforcement of judgements and so on, varies substantially from one place to another. The idea of a single "internal market" requires for its complete realisation a single system for the judicial resolution of disputes.[4]

Implausible as it seems, procedural differentiation is here presented in terms of a manufacturing cost and legal remedies become yet another readily transferable technology required to complete the market and make it more effective. Does it perhaps follow that the more remedies a court has at its disposal for the purpose of effective enforcement of EC law the better? Is it then permissible to suggest that, if a court does not have appropriate remedies at their disposal, it should simply supply them?

These are the assumptions to be tested in this chapter.

2. EFFECTIVE REMEDY

Procedure and substance

For reasons discussed later, questions of procedure have been left in practice to the courts. The division of jurisdictional competence devised by the ECJ depended from early days on a substantive/procedural distinction. At least in theory, the governing principle remains that established in the early *Saarland* ruling, which confirms the procedural autonomy of the national jurisdictions:

> [I]n the absence of Community rules on this subject, it is for the domestic legal system of each Member State to designate the courts having jurisdiction and to determine the protection of the rights which citizens have from the direct effect of Community law.[5]

Autonomy was, however, always subject to two overriding provisos: (i) that national jurisdictions must offer an effective remedy for breach of EC law; and

[4] T. Jolowicz, "Introduction" in M. Storme (ed.), *Approximation of Judiciary Law in the European Union* (The Storme Report) (Dordrecht; London: Kluwer and Martinus Nijhoff, 1994), xiii. See also W. van Gerven, "Bridging the Gap Between Community and National Laws: Towards a Principle of Homogeneity in the Field of Legal Remedies?" (1995) 32 *CMLRev* 679 and (more critically), R. Caranta, "Judicial Protection Against Member States: A New *Jus Commune* Takes Shape" (1995) 32 *CMLRev* 703.

[5] Case 33/76 *Rewe* v. *Landwirtschaftskammer Saarland* [1976] ECR 1989 at 1997. See also Case 158/80 *Rewe-Handellgesellschaft Nord mbll and Another* v. *Hauptzollamt Kiel* [1981] ECR 1805.

(ii) that the conditions of exercise must be no less favourable than those governing domestic cases.

In practice we find that the jurisprudence has often departed considerably from the spirit of its *Saarland* ruling, from time to time trenching considerably on national procedural autonomy. The procedural rights of defendants have even been described as "principles of higher rank which prevail over all other rules".[6] The insistence that national procedural rules must give way:

> whenever it is essential . . . to ensure the proper implementation of Community law and correct, effective protection of the rights claimed by individuals under Community law[7]

is a clear subversion of the *Saarland* principle, turning the provisos on their head.[8]

Two recent cases seem, however, to take a step back in the name of subsidiarity. A passage from the Opinion of Advocate General Jacobs in *van Schijndel*[9] in particular strongly reinforces the principle of procedural autonomy:

> What the primacy of Community law requires in the first place is a general rule that, when a national court is confronted with a conflict between a substantive provision of national law and a substantive provision of Community law, the Community provision should prevail. It is easy to see that, in the absence of such a general rule, Community law would be a dead letter.
>
> But as regards procedural rules, the primacy of Community law does not require that they should be overridden in all circumstances so as to allow Community law to enter the arena at any stage in the proceedings. As the Court's case law has shown, it is sufficient that individuals are given, by the national procedural rules, an effective opportunity of enforcing their rights. . . .
>
> Moreover, if the view were taken that national procedural rules must always yield to Community law, that would . . . unduly subvert established principles underlying the legal systems of the Member States. It would go further than is necessary for effective judicial protection. It could be regarded as infringing the principle of proportionality and, in a broad sense, the principle of subsidiarity, which reflects precisely the balance which the Court has sought to attain in this area for many years. It would also give rise to widespread anomalies, since the effect would be to afford greater protection to rights which are not, by virtue of being Community rights, inherently of greater importance than rights recognized by national law.[10]

This passage reinstates a clear distinction between substantive and procedural rules. In the event, however, the Court's final ruling that a point of EC law

[6] Joined Cases 6, 9/90 *Francovich and Bonafaci* v. *Italy* [1991] ECR I–5357, 5385–6 (A-G Mischo).

[7] *Ibid.*

[8] P. Craig and G. de Búrca, *EU Law. Text, Cases and Materials*, 2nd edn. (Oxford: Oxford University Press, 1998) at 236.

[9] Joined Cases C–430, 431/93 *Van Schijndel & van Veen* v. *Stichting Pensioenfonds voor Fysiotherapeuten* [1995] I–4705.

[10] *Ibid*, paras. 24, 25, 27.

based on new *facts* cannot be raised on appeal, was less clear than that of their Advocate General. The matter was hardly clarified by the ruling in the parallel case of *Peterbroeck*.[11] Here the Court rejected the advice of the same Advocate General, to rule that a Belgian Cour d'Appel must raise a point of EC law of its own motion where appeal is the first opportunity on which the point can be raised. EC law, in short, required modification of national procedures.

These cases, which clearly demonstrate the extent to which procedure may dictate substantive outcome, recall the earlier procedural quagmire of *Bourgoin*,[12] where French turkey producers sued in the English courts for damages in respect of a refusal to allow import of their produce on grounds of public health. This decision had been ruled illegal by the ECJ.[13] By a majority, the English Court of Appeal ruled that challenge was confined to public law proceedings, rendering attack impossible because the applicants were out of time.

On no occasion has the ECJ ever departed in principle from the division of competences established in *Saarland*. Yet commentators are generally agreed that the rule of national procedural autonomy has been seriously eroded. The jurisprudence is best described as cryptic or "highly complex with some perplexing inconsistencies".[14] What has been happening? The Court has simply benefited from semantic ambiguities latent in their imprecise formulation.

Widening and deepening

Although the discussion in the previous section turns on a distinction between substance and procedure, in practice it is hard to differentiate between the two. This is especially true of common law systems, where substantive law was once classically described as "secreted in the interstices of procedure"[15] and where remedies often fill the place filled in civilian systems by rights.[16] To put this differently, not only may procedure often affect or dictate outcome but the boundary between procedure and substance is blurred. In *Marshall (No. 2)*,[17] for example, it was held that an award of damages:

[11] Case C 312/93 *Peterbroeck, Van Campenhout et Cie* v. *Belgium* [1995] ECR I–4599. For discussion of the drastic impact on the French conception of justice, see J. Delicostopolous, "L'Influence du droit européen quant aux pouvoirs du juge judiciare national sur le fait et le droit" (1997) 6 *Justices* 117.

[12] *Bourgoin* v. *Ministry of Agriculture and Fisheries* [1986] QB 716. Note that this very dubious decision, which seems to fall squarely within the first limb of the *Saarland* proviso, was neither appealed to the House of Lords nor referred to the ECJ but settled out of court.

[13] Case 40182 *Commission* v. *United Kingdom* [1982] ECR 2793.

[14] R. Craufurd Smith, "Remedies for Breaches of EU Law in National Courts: Legal Variation and Selection" in P. Craig and G. de Búrca (eds.), *The Evolution of EU Law* (Oxford: Oxford University Press, 1999) at 318.

[15] Maine, *Early Law and Custom*, famously cited by W.H. Maitland, *The Forms of Action at Common Law* (Cambridge: Cambridge University Press, 1968), 1.

[16] P. Legrand, "European Legal Systems Are Not Converging" (1996) 45 *ICLQ* 52, 56.

[17] Case C–271/91 *Marshall* v. *Southampton and SW Area Health Authority* [1993] ECR I–4367, para. 26. But see now Case C–180/95 *Nils Draehmpaehl* v. *Urania Immobilienservice ohG* [1997]

must be adequate, in that it must enable the loss and damage actually sustained . . . to be made good in full in accordance with the applicable national rules.

This had the effect of outlawing a statutory cap on damages applicable to sex discrimination cases in national law.

This ruling clearly deals with "remedy" in the narrow sense of reparation. It deals with "procedure", in which sense it can be seen as an incursion across the border of procedural autonomy. But because it defines a "right", the statutory cap on damages is also substantive in character. We have here a useful illustration of the way in which remedies, rights, procedure and substantive law can converge.

Osman,[18] a more recent case from the European Court of Human Rights, makes the same point still more clearly. This time the Court is interpreting the requirement of access to court protected by Article 6(1) of the European Convention on Human Rights (ECHR). The applicant had contested an order to strike out his negligence action against the police, arguing that this effectively denied access to the court "in the determination of his civil rights". The concept of duty of care in English law requires both proximity and foreseeability. In addition, a court is required to assess whether it is "fair, just and reasonable" to impose the duty. The Court of Appeal ruled against a duty on grounds of public policy; it was not fair, just and reasonable to impose on the police investigating crime the added burden of liability for negligence. The action was struck out.

How was this ruling to be interpreted? The European Court of Human Rights held that the policy ruling had created an absolute immunity which had the effect of barring any action. This can of course be interpreted as a procedural ruling. It outlaws the practice of striking out without consideration of the facts of the *immediate* case. It can, on the other hand, be seen as an intrusion into substantive law, requiring the English courts to reshape the law of tortious liability. This is certainly how an irritated House of Lords chose to see it![19]

The word "remedy" is also capable of slippage. A treatise on legal "remedies" would deal normally with the orders a court can award to a successful litigant. The term can, however, be widened out to cover the judicial process in its entirety. Time-limits and standing, as well as interim and final orders, then come within its purview.[20] Remedy becomes synonymous with redress, subsuming the preponderance of procedural law. When the ECJ talks of "effective remedy", it gives the term a broad meaning. Just as the Court of Human Rights

ECR I–2195 and Case C–66/95 *R* v. *Social Security Secretary, ex parte Sutton* [1997] ECR I–2163, noted Ward, "New Frontiers in Private Enforcement of EC Directives" (1998) 23 *ELRev* 65.

[18] *Osman* v. *United Kingdom* (1998) 5 BHRC 293.

[19] *Barrett* v. *Enfield LBC* [1999] 3 WLR 79. But see L. Hoyano, "Policing Flawed Police Investigations: Unravelling the Blanket" (1999) 62 *MLR* 912.

[20] P. Oliver, "State Liability in Damages following *Factortame III*: A Remedy Seen in Context" in J. Beatson and T. Tridimas (eds.), *New Directions in European Public Law* (Oxford: Hart Publishing, 1998); T. Bingham, "Should Public Law Remedies be Discretionary?" [1991] *PL* 64.

in *Osman* read access forward to include outcome, so the ECJ reads remedy backward to include access. Thus it has ruled decisively on the right of access to court. *Johnston*[21] famously prohibited an ouster clause which barred effective remedy. *Emmott*[22] dealt with time-limits, normally a threshold requirement in national legal system. Perhaps only its own restrictive rights of standing, laid down at Treaty level by Article 230 EC (ex Article 173) inhibits the Court from seeking, under the guise of approximation of national standing rights, a "levelling up" to the most generous national standard.

Alongside, the ECJ is widening the ambit of judicial remedy. By constantly adding to the requirements of due process inside the administrative process,[23] it allows a deep penetration of the terrain of the administration. This again mirrors the practice of the Court of Human Rights, where we have seen a similar widening of the reach of Article 6(1) ECHR.

The impact of this approach has been felt by the French Conseil d'État, threatened by both lines of development.[24] Not only are we touching here on a procedure respected for its impartiality and probity but also on a distinction between inquisitorial and adversarial procedures of which the Storme Report said that it was "so deeply enshrined in the respective legal cultures as to make harmonisation practically unfeasible".[25] Abraham strongly contends[26] that cultural uniformity precludes experiment and creates a real danger of stultification. Minority practices are not always wrong, they are just different.

In addition, the direction taken to date by both courts adds creates pressure for *judicial* resolution of every problem and denies its rightful place to the extra-legal tradition.[27] Yet the comparativist, John Bell, describes the common law countries of Britain and Ireland as possessing, in common with The Netherlands, "a strong tradition of administrative *non-law*".[28] The same point could be made of Scandinavian countries, where legal redress often takes second

[21] Case 222/84 *Johnston* v. *Chief Constable of the Royal Ulster Constabulary* [1986] ECR 1651.

[22] Case C–208/90 *Emmott* v. *Minister for Social Welfare* [1991] ECR I–4629. But see now Case C–188/95 *Fantask A/S and Others* v. *Industriministeriet (Ehrvervsministeriet)* [1997] ECR I–6783 noted A.Ward, "Indirect Taxes and National Remedies" (1999) 58 *Cambridge Law Journal* 36.

[23] C 222/86 *UNECTEF* v. *Heylens* [1987] ECR 4097. And see generally, H.P. Nehl, *Principles of Administrative Procedure in EC Law* (Oxford: Hart Publishing, 1998).

[24] The practice of allowing members of administrative formation of a Conseil d'État to participate in adjudication was challenged in *Procola* 28 Sep 1995, Series A 326, noted R. Drago, "Un nouveau juge administratif" in *Ecrits en hommage à Jean Foyer* (Presses universitaires de France) at 454–5.

[25] M. Storme, "General Introductory Report" in Storme (1994) note 4, above, at 63.

[26] R. Abraham, "Les principes généraux de la protection juridictionnelle administrative en Europe: L'influence des jurisprudences européennes", (1997) 9 *ERPL* 577.

[27] See generally M. Palmer and S. Roberts, *Dispute Processes: ADR and the Primary Forms of Decision Making* (London: Butterworths, 1998). For the contribution of ADR to public law, see C. Harlow and R.W. Rawlings, *Law and Administration*, 2nd edn. (London: Butterworths, 1997), chapter 12; C. Glasser and C. Harlow, "Legal Services and the Alternatives: The LSE Tradition" in R. Rawlings (ed.), *Law, Society and Economy* (Oxford: Oxford University Press, 1996).

[28] J. Bell, "Mechanisms for Cross-Fertilisation of Administrative Law in Europe" in J. Beatson and T. Tridimas (eds.), *New Directions in European Public Law* (Oxford: Hart Publishing, 1998) at 150.

place to the ombudsman. In an era when every European jurisdiction is suffering a dangerous degree of overload and consequential delay, for which several have been castigated before the Court of Human Rights, this is foolishness. There has been an enormous increase in the ECJ's docket, leaving an unacceptably large backlog of cases.[29] National courts face the same dilemma.

A double enlargement is under way. On the one hand, the ambit of legal redress is being extended; on the other, it is being deepened. Procedure is being tailored, piecemeal and haphazardly, to suit the convenience of transnational courts.

Standardising the toolkit

Before we explore this point further, we might ask what remedies judges actually have at their disposal. The answer is variable. A definition limited to outcome will think first in terms of a declaratory order to clarify the law or quash illegal administrative action, rendering it null and void. Most courts possess such orders. Most also possess a power to award compensatory damages; damages may on occasion also be penal in character. Some, but by no means all, possess mandatory or injunctive orders. The wide definition of remedy calls for additions to the toolkit at earlier stages of the action, such as suspensive orders or interim injunctions, clearly necessary to ensure the integrity of the legal process. Other possibilities, such as the common law order for discovery of documents, can be envisaged.

The point to make is that these remedies are neither common nor universal. This emerges clearly from the Report of the Storme Commission, an unofficial body of academic experts from every Member State which, with some encouragement and financial assistance from the European Commission, set out to provide Europe with a "European Judicial Code" of procedural law.[30] Consensus was achieved only on relatively minor aspects of procedure and codification proved impossible. Storme did press for some common remedies. In particular, they thought interim measures so fundamental that they recommended endowing *all* European courts with wide, discretionary powers to award them.[31] This, as Professor Lindblom points out,[32] would add to the existing complexity, since it would graft on to the national system a new, universal remedy, creating an additional problem of horizontal divergence. Similarly, Storme thought access to documents so essential that it proposed the approximation of discovery procedures

[29] The caseload rose from 384 cases in 1990 to 485 in 1998, negating the creation of the CFI, whose own caseload soared in the same period from 59 to 238 cases. This left a pending backlog in the ECJ of 748 and in the CFI of 1008: Annex, *The Future of the Judicial System of the European Union (Proposals and Reflections)* (Luxembourg: ECJ, 1999).

[30] Storme (1994), note 4, above.

[31] *Ibid*, chapter 10.

[32] P. Lindblom, "Harmony of the legal spheres" (1997) 5 *European Review of Private Law* 11, 42.

across Europe, even though this meant introducing the order to systems where it was previously unknown.[33]

The product of Storme was a draft Directive of 127 articles, never implemented though it could be used like American Restatements. Storme concluded that it was best to leave the main issues to national bodies; approximation was "rather complicated and would mean a radical change in the formal structure of court proceedings in some Member States".[34] As to the key civilian/common law divide between adversarial and inquisitorial procedure, the Storme Commission felt that this was "so deeply enshrined in the respective legal cultures as to make harmonisation practically unfeasible".[35] Lindblom adds[36] that civil procedure "presents an extremely disrupted image" across the continent; "the Member States have their own procedural orders, which differ considerably". He sees the divergences as likely to be semi-permanent given the "weak and slow trend towards decreasing differences". This is probably correct. The European Commission, reputedly disenchanted with large-scale harmonisation, prefers to work on a small scale. Substantive directives sometimes contain specific requirements as to remedies,[37] binding on Member States. It has to be admitted, however, that harmonisation of national procedural law is not high on anyone's political agenda.[38]

What is really in issue is an extension of the process of piecemeal convergence through judge-made law, discussed in the last section. This, however, adds to the practical problems experienced by Storme, a serious issue of legitimacy.[39] Metaphorically, the EC legal order is a parasitic construction; it fastens itself to the branches of the national legal orders. The national courts of Member States fill a dual role. First and foremost, they act as national courts; they also act as agents of the Community for the enforcement of EC law. Despite the claims implicit in the doctrine of legal supremacy, the EC legal order ultimately derives its legitimacy from national legal orders.[40] The EC legal system is not holistic. National courts have not metamorphosed into Community courts. This simple

[33] Storme (1994) note 4, above, chapter 4. Discovery is essentially a common law procedure, contested by civilian systems: see Case 155/79 *AM &S* v. *Commission* [1982] ECR 1575.

[34] Storme (1994) note 4, above.

[35] *Ibid* at 63.

[36] Lindblom (1997) note 32, above, at 12.

[37] For example, Council Directive 92/13/EEC co-ordinating the laws, regulations and administrative provisions relating to public procurement 1992 OJ L 76/14.

[38] The same is probably true of substantive civil law. See A. Hartkamp. E. Hondius, C. du Perron and J. Vranken (eds.), *Towards a European Civil Code*, 2 vols (Nijmegen: Ars Aequi Libri Dordrecht, 1994: London: Martinus Nijhoff, 1997), of which H. Kötz remarks that codification is "not a live issue yet". H. Kötz, "Towards a European Civil Code" in P. Cane and J. Stapleton (eds.), *The Law of Obligations, Essays in Honour of John Fleming* (Oxford: Oxford University Press, 1998), at 257.

[39] The legitimacy issue of whether procedural law falls within existing EU competence is tackled by Lindblom (1997) note 32, above, at 21–2.

[40] P. Kirchhof, "The Balance of Powers Between National and European Institutions" (1999) 5 *ELJ* 221. And see B. de Witte, "Sovereignty and European Integration: the Weight of Legal Tradition" in A.-M. Slaughter, A. Stone Sweet, J. Weiler (eds.), *The European Courts and National Courts – Doctrine and Jurisprudence* (Oxford: Hart Publishing, 1998).

truth is demonstrated by the way national courts have behaved in case of conflict.[41] The EU legal order is a plural community of legal systems, of which the EC system is merely one.[42] The integrationist explanation is fictional.

The toolkit set out in the EC Treaty is fairly limited. By Article 231 EC (ex Article 174) the ECJ, where an action is well founded, is empowered "to declare the act concerned to be void". Direct actions are severely restricted by the standing rules of EC Article 230 (ex Article 173), notably narrow and old-fashioned. There is, however, compensation in the power of Commission and Member States to bring infringement proceedings under Articles 226 and 227 EC (ex Articles 169 and 170) before the ECJ. The possibility of disobedience was dealt with by Articles 228 and 233 EC (ex Articles 171 and 176), which exhorts states found in breach to "take the necessary measures to comply with the judgement of the Court of Justice" – an Article 10 EC (ex Article 5) fidelity obligation.

The Treaties do envisage compensation, but in what circumstances was left vague. Article 288 EC (ex Article 215) provides for the Community to "make good any damage caused by its institutions or its servants in the performance of their duties". This non-contractual liability was to be based on "general principles common to the laws of the Member States". In practice therefore the Court had considerable discretion to fashion rules of compensation for the Community on a case-to-case basis. The so-called *Schöppenstedt* formula,[43] which emerged as one of the main vehicles for Community liability, is generally admitted to be restrictive. In practice, it has not proved easy to get compensation from the Community institutions for the use of its discretionary or rule-making powers.[44]

Well-suited to the Court's function of seeing the law "observed", the remedies could be viewed as defective if the ECJ construed its function as one of law enforcement. The concept of "effective remedy" suggests enforceability and a system which professes to provide protection for "individuals" – as the EC legal system did[45] – may persuade itself of the need for enforceable remedies. Many courts have at their disposal injunctive or mandatory orders; before Maastricht, the ECJ did not. Not until Maastricht was a punitive edge added to the Court's declaratory remedies when the Council agreed to amend Article 228 EC (ex Article 171) to allow the Court to "impose a lump sum or penalty payment" on a Member State which defaulted. Nor could it supply the void by an award of damages, partly because of narrow standing requirements, partly because

[41] See the German *Solange* cases, fully discussed by J. Kokott, "Report on Germany", in A.-M. Slaughter, A. Stone Sweet, J. Weiler (eds.), *The European Courts and National Courts – Doctrine and Jurisprudence* (Oxford: Hart Publishing, 1998).

[42] N. MacCormick, "The *Maastricht-Urteil*: Sovereignty Now" (1995) 1 *ELJ* 259 and "Beyond the Sovereign State" (1993) 56 *MLR* 1.

[43] C 5/71 *Zuckerfabrik Schöppenstedt* v. *Council* [1971] ECR 975.

[44] F. Fines, "Etude de la Responsabilité extra-contractuelle de la Communauté" (1990) *LGDJ*; T.C. Hartley, *The Foundations of European Community Law* 4th edn. (Oxford: Clarendon Press, 1998) at 465–76.

[45] E. Szyszczak, "Making Europe More Relevant to its Citizens" (1996) 21 *ELRev* 351.

Article 288 EC (ex Article 215) covers only the Community and its institutions. Without a drastic structural reform of the Community legal order,[46] new judicial remedies would have to develop *inside* national systems. This meant manoeuvring within the restrictive parameters of *Saarland*.

A further obstacle to harmonisation lies in the fact that remedies in national legal systems differ considerably. Storme established that not even the minimal toolkit of remedies is common to every national system: we saw this illustrated with discovery and interim orders. Again, not every national court possesses mandatory remedies or the power to award exemplary damages. Perhaps more surprising, national courts do not necessarily covet the complete toolkit. Why should this be?

3. CONSTITUTIONAL CONSEQUENCES

Writing specifically about the redress afforded by English judicial review, Richard Rawlings and I argued that models had emerged which were consonant with the system's main objectives.[47] These models were not static; not only could they change incrementally over time but they were capable of being moved by the judiciary in a particular direction. We described the classic English model as a model of legal interests, in which the court's primary function was to protect the legal rights of individuals. We noted, and later tracked, the emergence of new models of administrative law, reflected in changed standing rules and a more flexible law of remedies. A "public interest" action has gradually evolved, widely used by social action groups. In this model, there is a new leniency to third party standing and interventions and "public interest" arguments are beginning to be invited in actions between third parties.[48] Significantly, this development, pioneered without thought for the consequences by the judiciary, met a setback in the recent *Pinochet* proceedings.[49]

A further point of significance with regard to the English law of remedies is that the courts have for long at their disposal powerful mandatory remedies. This advantage has recently been described as a principal characteristic of judicial review proceedings by a leading member of the judiciary: judicial review is "coercive" in character, rather than based on "trust and co-operation"[50] – one

[46] Along the lines of that envisaged by J.-P. Jacque and J. Weiler, "On the Road to European Union – A New Judicial Architecture. An Agenda for the Intergovernmental Conference" (1990) 27 *CMLRev* 185, before Maastricht.

[47] C. Harlow and R. Rawlings, *Pressure Through Law* (London: Routledge, 1992), chapter 7.

[48] C. Harlow, and R. W. Rawlings, *Law and Administration* 2nd edn, (London: Butterworths, 1997) 540–52. See also C. Harlow, "A Special Relationship? The American Influence on English Public Law", in I. Loveland (ed.), *A Special Relationship? American Influences on Public Law in the UK* (Oxford: Clarendon Press, 1995).

[49] *R* v. *Bow Street Magistrate, ex parte Pinochet Ugarte (No. 2)* [1999] 2 WLR 272.

[50] *M* v. *Home Office* [1993] 3 WLR 445.

reason perhaps for the comparative weakness of the action for damages in cases involving the State.[51]

French administrative law offers an alternative model which deals almost wholly in declarations of nullity. The French Conseil d'État consciously deprived itself of the power to grant mandatory remedies and the power both to award penal damages and grant injunctive relief has only lately been restored by legislative initiative. This is one reason why French administrative law, in contrast to English, *has* developed a sophisticated law of administrative liability.[52]

It is perhaps unkind to remark that the boasted English "mandatory model" was actually completed by the very case in which Lord Woolf was speaking. Whether the change could have been achieved without the aid of EC law is questionable. In *Factortame (No. 1)*,[53] the House of Lords had ruled that injunctive and suspensive relief against the Crown was not available in civil proceedings, because of s. 21 of the Crown Proceedings Act 1947. Famously, in *Factortame (No. 2)*,[54] the ECJ insisted that interim injunctive relief must be available *pendente lite*:

> [T]he full effectiveness of Community law would be . . . impaired if a rule of national law could prevent a court seised of a dispute governed by Community law from granting interim relief in order to ensure the full effectiveness of the judgement to be given on the existence of the rights claimed under Community law. It follows that a court which in those circumstances would grant interim relief, if it were not for a rule of national law, is obliged to set aside that rule.

Now this is a very contested ruling; it has been argued both that the ECJ misunderstood the real position of English law, that courts had never had power to grant injunctive relief against the Crown,[55] and that it failed to give adequate consideration to the issue of subsidiarity.[56] Of the national level, it has been argued that an unorthodox twist was given to the doctrine of parliamentary sovereignty.[57]

These judgments on the surface involved a narrow point of procedural law. Even at this level, they had an unexpected "spillover effect", allowing the step taken in *M* v. *Home Office* to be justified on the ground of disparity in the protection afforded to rights protected under EC law and those grounded in the

[51] The view of the action for damages as a subsidiary or collateral model is compounded by the emergence of the (arguably inappropriate) "exclusivity rule": C. Harlow and R. Rawlings, *Law and Administration* 2nd edn. (London: Butterworths, 1997), 619–28.

[52] D. Lochak, "Réflexions sur les fonctions sociales de la responsabilité administrative" in J. Chevallier (ed.), *Le droit administratif en mutation* (Presses universitaires de France, 1993).

[53] *R* v. *Transport Secretary, ex parte Factortame (No. 1)* [1990] 2 AC 85.

[54] Case C213/89 *R* v. *Secretary of State for Transport, ex parte Factortame (No. 3)* [1990] ECR I–2433.

[55] A. Barav, "Omnipotent Courts", in D. Curtin and T. Heukels (eds.), *Institutional Dynamics of European Integration* (Dordrecht: Martinus Nijhoff, 1994), Vol. II, 265.

[56] G. de Búrca, "The Quest for Legitimacy in the European Union" (1996) 59 *MLR* 349. Contrast A. Arnull, "Rights and Remedies: Restraint or Activism?" in J. Lonbay and A. Biondi (eds.), *Remedies for Breach of EC Law* (Chichester: Wiley, 1997).

[57] P. Craig, "United Kingdom Report" in Slaughter *et al.* (1998), above note 41.

domestic legal system ("levelling up"). The judgment was thus "a crucial development along the road to interim relief in public law proceedings".[58] The constitutional impact was, however, considerably greater. At least theoretically, the new power to issue mandatory remedies greatly affected the balance of power between executive and judiciary. The cases also seriously undercut the doctrine of parliamentary sovereignty, the keystone of the British constitution.[59] Surely this was more than a question of "transferable technology"!

Factortame involved a system in which injunctive relief was normal and the ECJ probably did not see the ruling as compelling the introduction of mandatory interim remedies into a system where these were not available. Though it might encourage convergence, the effect of *Factortame* was not to harmonise nor to introduce a new remedy into national law. In *Francovich*,[60] however, there could be no such doubt.[61] Here the ECJ clearly authorised the creation of a novel remedy in damages and one, moreover, which was intended to apply in every Member State.[62] This piece of judicial activism was justified on grounds of effectiveness:

> The full effectiveness of Community rules would be impaired and the protection of the rights which they grant would be weakened if individuals were unable to obtain redress when their rights are infringed by a breach of Community law for which a Member State can be held responsible.[63]

Even in those national systems which – like France – possess a doctrine of state liability, this judgment was problematic, requiring modification of substantive law.[64] In those which, like the United Kingdom, possessed no such doctrine, the intrusion into substantive law was monumental.[65] Nor are the "spillover effects" confined to the purely legal. State liability – as I have argued at greater length elsewhere[66] – always has serious implications for resource allocation. This again affects judicial relationships with the executive – a point recognised by the ECJ in *Schöppenstedt*[67] and its subsequent parsimonious jurisprudence. Legal procedures are not merely pathways to the court nor are

[58] J. Jowell and P. Birkinshaw, "English Report" in J. Schwarze (ed.), *Administrative Law under European Influence* (London: Sweet & Maxwell/Nomos, 1996), at 304.

[59] See Lord Woolf of Barnes, "Droit Public – English Style" [1995] *PL* 57.

[60] Joined Cases 6, 9/90 *Francovich and Bonafaci* v. *Italy* [1991] ECR I–5357.

[61] F. Jacobs, "The Right to a Fair Trial in European Law" [1999] 2 *EHRLR*, 141, 152.

[62] *Francovich* involved Italy. For Germany and the UK, see Joined Cases C 46/93 and C 48/93 *Brasserie du Pecheur SA* v. *Germany* and *R* v. *Transport Secretary, ex parte Factortame (No. 4)* [1996] ECR I–1029.

[63] At para. 33.

[64] See R. Caranta, "Judicial Protection Against Member States: A New *Jus Commune* Takes Shape" (1995) 32 *CMLRev* 703; N. Green and A. Barav, "National Damages in the National Courts for Breach of Community Law" (1986) 6 *YEL* 55.

[65] See now *Factortame*.

[66] C. Harlow, "State Liability: Problem Without Solution" (1995) 6 *National Journal of Constitutional Law* 67; C. Harlow and R. Rawlings (1997), note 48, above, chapter 18.

[67] Note 43, above.

they easily transferable technology. Procedure tells us much about the character and objectives of a given legal system, to which it is intimately related. More important still, they exist in the context of a constitution and in a given cultural context. Legal procedures may reflect and signify important relationships between the executive and judiciary.

4. CONCLUSION: EMPOWERING NATIONAL COURTS

We set out to examine the case for common judicial remedies on the assumption that it is market-driven. As Martin Shapiro has observed:

> the stability and predictability that legal-political, as opposed to purely political, institutions have to offer are peculiarly attractive to economic enterprise. Legalization, and thus judicialization, fits an "economic community" particularly well.[68]

This in turn suggests that the beneficiaries of procedural equality will be in the main restricted to a handful of multi-national corporations and firms which trade regularly across international boundaries – big players, well able to protect themselves against the transaction costs of divergence through in-house lawyers.[69] Forum shopping and other ills that law is prone to, are also normally the preserve of international commerce and the transnational consumer groups which spring up to oppose them.

The general lesson of this chapter is that the "level playing field" of procedural rights is illusory. Limited competence and limited interest combine to inhibit harmonisation through codification. The curious structure of the EC legal order prevents sensible judicial approximation. Uniformity is a largely symbolic concept, part of a wider integrationist project to "make Europe more relevant to its citizens".

Symbolism is, of course, important, as Snyder remarks of the Court's "judicial liability system":

> Symbolic action is significant, but it may fail to make any real impact on the effectiveness of Community law, especially if by "effectiveness" we refer to effects in addition to the elaboration of legal doctrine.[70]

While this helps to explain the Court's search for enforceable remedies to transform symbolism into action, Snyder correctly argues that judicial remedies will never be:

[68] M. Shapiro, "The European Court of Justice" in P. Craig and G. de Búrca, *The Evolution of EU Law*, (Oxford: Oxford University Press, 1999), 328, 330. See also H. Schermers, "The Role of the European Court of Justice in the Free Movement of Goods" in T. Sandalow and E. Stein, *Courts and Free Markets* (Oxford: Clarendon Press, 1982).

[69] M. Galanter, "Predators and Parasites: Lawyer-Bashing and Civil Justice" (1994) 28 *Georgia Law Review* 633.

[70] F. Snyder, "The Effectiveness of European Community Law: Institutions, Processes, Tools and Techniques" (1993) 56 *MLR* 19, 52.

> sufficient alone to ensure the effectiveness of Community law in the broader social sense, in particular in so far as it entails the commitment of citizens, popular participation and political legitimacy. For this purpose, it may be suggested, other institutions, processes, tools and techniques are also required.[71]

Is this merely a feature of EC law, a legal system set in a vacuum, where no obedient administration directly executes its commands and remedy is left to national institutions? National judicial systems rely for their effect on "the habit of obedience". This habit has complex origins. There are very "obvious connections and overlaps between procedural law, constitutional law, administrative law, and legal philosophy".[72] The standing of the judiciary derives from the place of the legal system in the constitution and the political culture which surrounds it. The danger of the *Factortame* saga lies in the way in which national courts were pushed into the position of subordinate, threatening their authority in the domestic arena. Only by the subterfuge of resort to a purely fictional conception of parliamentary sovereignty, was prestige preserved intact.[73]

The integrity of the legal system lies in the care of the judiciary. The divergence which occurs whenever there is variance between EC principles and procedures of the Member States faces the ECJ with the problem of inequality. The "spillover effect" which occurs when a change to some of the rules of the national legal system is commanded by EC law creates a quandary for the national judiciary. Supposedly, Article 234 EC (ex Article 177) acts as a mediating device, the problem being that, after the doctrine of supremacy became established, supremacy replaced parity as the guiding presumption.[74] The *Saarland* division of competences was accordingly undercut. De la Mare sees steady slippage from the initial choice of a model of arbitration by the Treaty's framers, to a supremacist focus "as the ECJ became more assertive and developed legally supranationalist doctrines such as direct effect and supremacy".[75] This needs to be reversed.

The way forward is to trust national courts, best fitted to understand the national context, to decide routine points of EC law for themselves, as the ECJ is currently encouraging them to do.[76] The more radical suggestion of allowing national courts to give judgment on points of EC law *before* reference to the ECJ,[77]

[71] F. Snyder, "The Effectiveness of European Community Law: Institutions, Processes, Tools and Techniques" (1993) 56 *MLR* 19, 52. See also C. Harding, "Member State Enforcement of European Community Measures: The Chimera of Effective Enforcement" (1997) 4 *Maastricht J. of International and European Law* 5.

[72] Lindblom (1997) note 32, above, at 13.

[73] This point was understood and expounded by Hoffmann J in *Stoke-on-Trent CC and Norwich CC* v. *B & Q plc* [1991] chapter 48 at 56, 69–71 during the Sunday Trading Saga: see R. Rawlings, "The Euro-law Game: Some Deductions from a Saga" (1993) 20 *JLS* 309.

[74] See R. Dehousse, "Comparing National and EC Law: The Problem of the Level of Analysis" (1994) 42 *Am. J. of Comp Law* 761.

[75] T. de la Mare, "Article 177 and Legal Integration" in Craig and de Búrca (1998), note 68, above.

[76] Note 2, above, at 24.

[77] *Ibid*, at 26–7.

is also worth considering. This would enhance judicial co-operation, providing an opening for national courts to indicate potential impact of decisions on the national legal system; forcing them to articulate their reasoning in the language of that system; reinforcing domestic accountability by submitting judgments to scrutiny in the national arena where their impact needs to be weighed and tested. The basic *Saarland* rule of national procedural autonomy must be reinstated and incursions subjected to a formal proportionality test, rigorously applied, requiring them to be overwhelmingly justified.

Judicial remedies and legal procedure are not readily transferable technology, safely left in the care and custody of judges and lawyers. Law fulfils particular functions in different societies which:

> are detected and made evident when Community law and its impact on domestic procedural law are discussed. Here, one is confronted by big and far-reaching questions on the role of the courts and the limits of litigation, all seen in relation to the Community institutions and their competence.[78]

Law and legal procedure is part of our distinctive cultural heritage and deserves as much of our care and attention as does democracy. National culture is protected by the Preamble to the Treaty on European Union, which confirms the desire of the Masters of the Treaties "to deepen the solidarity between their peoples *while respecting their history, their culture and their traditions*" (my emphasis). Given the integrationist history of EC law, it is not surprising to find in the Treaty of Amsterdam specific reference to *legal* culture. A Protocol requires "care [to] be taken to respect well established national arrangements and the organisation and working of Member States' legal systems".[79] This ought to put paid to the idea of judge-made approximation of the law of remedies.

[78] Lindblom (1997) note 32, above, 13.

[79] Treaty of Amsterdam, Protocol on the Application of the Principle of Subsidiarity and Proportionality, para. 7.

PART II
Sectoral Approaches to EC Remedies

4

Addressing Problems of Imbalanced Implementation in EC Law: Remedies in an Institutional Perspective

STEPHEN WEATHERILL

1. INTRODUCTION

THE PURSUIT of the even and effective application of European Community law across the territory of all fifteen Member States presents an intuitively appealing, even economically indispensable, ambition for the integration process in Europe. It cannot be perfectly realised. This may not, of itself, provide any serious cause for anxiety. Laws typically exert impacts which vary from those planned for them on paper. But gaps in the even and effective application of Community law apply unequally across the system. The concern which underpins this chapter is that in the EC there are imbalances in the application of the law which tend to favour those seeking to assert market freedoms when contrasted with those concerned to secure enforcement of rules of market regulation. But even this perception, if shown to be accurate, does not suffice to make the EC a special case. Other legal systems would recognise an imbalance between the vigour of the commercial sector in exploiting the law and the more limited scope for legal redress where, for example, environmental damage is at stake. However, the case is made that the imbalance, though not unique to the EC, has peculiarly acute features in the context of European market-building and, moreover, that it is an imbalance that is widening. Inquiry into the possible routes for addressing this perceived flaw in the post-1992 evolution of the EC draws necessarily on a range of institutional mechanisms.

2. AN ILLUSTRATION: *HEDLEY LOMAS*

I have elaborated my analysis of the relative imbalance in the enforcement of different strands of EC law elsewhere[1] in connection with the ruling in

[1] S. Weatherill, "Reflections on EC law's 'implementation imbalance' in the light of the ruling in *Hedley Lomas*" in L. Krämer, H. Micklitz and K. Tonner, (eds.), *Law and Diffuse Interests in the*

R v. *MAFF, ex parte Hedley Lomas (Ireland) Ltd.*[2] This is a decision that remains unusually instructive. Beginning in April 1990 the British authorities had systematically refused to issue licences for the export to Spain of live animals for slaughter. The British authorities considered that exported animals would suffer a substantial risk of treatment in Spanish slaughterhouses falling short of the requirements of stunning before slaughter imposed by Directive 74/577. The ban was lifted only from the start of 1993 after bilateral talks between the two governments. Litigation before the English courts was initiated by Hedley Lomas, a trader refused a licence in 1992, and reached the European Court by way of a preliminary reference.

The Court found the United Kingdom to have violated Article 29 EC (ex Article 34) by refusing to issue export licences. The UK's allegation that Spain was in breach of Directive 74/577 provided no justification. The Court was not prepared to accept the UK's attempted reliance on Article 30 EC (ex Article 36). The UK had pointed out that Directive 74/577 made no reference to enforcement mechanisms. But the Court stated that the absence of provisions in the Directive harmonising procedures for monitoring compliance simply meant that Member States were obliged under Articles 10 and 249 EC (ex Articles 5 and 189) to "to take all measures necessary to guarantee the application and effectiveness of Community law". It added that "Member States must rely on trust in each other to carry out inspections on their respective territories".

There are a number of distinct issues that may arise in Community law when one Member State attempts to export its regulatory standards to others.[3] But at stake here was not an attempt by the UK to apply stricter standards than those mandated by the EC measure. Rather it sought to subordinate free trade to its desire to remedy perceived Spanish failings in observing agreed EC rules. In *Hedley Lomas* the Court opted for a clean-cut solution based on occupation of the field achieved by Community legislative intervention and an expectation of enforcement by all Member States on their own territory supervised by the Commission (and, in appropriate cases, by national courts). Recourse to Article 30 EC (ex Article 36) was excluded and the UK had acted unlawfully in blocking export trade in response to perceived inadequacy in law enforcement elsewhere.

The Court's ruling conforms to the orthodox constitutional assumptions of EC law that self-help is impermissible as a remedy.[4] Mr Léger's Opinion in

European Legal Order: Liber Amicorum Norbert Reich (VIEW/Nomos Verlagsgesellschaft, 1997), 31–53.

[2] Case C–5/94 [1996] ECR I–2553.

[3] For discussion see J. Scott, "On Kith and Kin and Crustaceans: Trade and Environment in the EU and WTO" (Harvard Law School: Jean Monnet Working Papers 3/99 (available via http://www.law.harvard.edu/Programs/JeanMonnet)), which takes the discussion beyond the EC onto the plane of international economic law.

[4] It cited both Cases 90/63 and 91/63 *Commission* v. *Luxembourg and Belgium* [1964] ECR 625 and Case 232/78 *Commission* v. *France* [1979] ECR 2729. See, subsequent to *Lomas*, Case C–11/95 *Commission* v. *Belgium* [1996] ECR I–4115.

Hedley Lomas gravely asserts that "nothing is more alien to Community law" than retaliation. The explanation for this exclusion lies in the relatively sophisticated enforcement mechanisms contained within the Treaty itself. Indeed, the injection of retaliation into the EC system would shatter the structure of "constitutionalism" built around alliance between national and European courts in controlling state action. This supplies an insight into the powerful appeal of clinging hard to the assumption that EC law enforcement belongs in the hands of national officials, and that it will be performed effectively. This is "indirect rule".[5] It lies at the heart of the European Court's remarkably skilful mission to embed the enforcement of EC law within a national legal and administrative context. Yet how could such (alleged) under-implementation of EC law really have been addressed? The Commission had chosen not to proceed under Article 226 EC (ex Article 169); Article 227 EC (ex Article 170) is virtually a dead letter for obvious political reasons; and pursuit at national level is sorely impeded both by the jurisprudential difficulties in identifying a right either of a directly effective nature or apt to fit the *Francovich* mould and by the practical obstacles to access to justice before Spanish courts. Who would really have an incentive to sue? And would they have the necessary resources? This is not to suggest that Spain escaped punishment for under-implementation of EC law as a result of the Court's exclusion of the British trade blockage as a lawful response, for there was no adequate evidence in the case that any such default had actually occurred. But the fact pattern of the case is instructive. *Had* there been neglect in Spain, how would it have been effectively addressed? One may conclude: not readily through the orthodox expectations of the "dual vigilance" model of EC law enforcement via "supranational" Commission enforcement and/or private enforcement before national courts.

3. THE IMPLEMENTATION IMBALANCE IN CONTEXT

The point which I am anxious to make is that there are weaknesses in the enforcement of some species of EC law *relative* to those which apply to the enforcement of others. In particular, "negative law" requires a less sophisticated system of enforcement than does "positive law".

Negative law refers to the body of Community norms that prevent States from acting in a manner inconsistent with the Community's objectives. In this vein, the rules governing the free movement of goods and services provide classic illustrations of negative law; States are forbidden from maintaining or introducing measures that may impede cross-border trade, with the result that the market is deregulated in pursuit of the Community objective of market

[5] T. Daintith (ed.), *Implementing EC Law in the UK: Structures for Indirect Rule* (Chichester: Wiley, 1995). *Cf.* in the Dutch context J. Vervaele, (ed.), *Administrative Law Application and Enforcement of Community Law in the Netherlands* (Deventer: Kluwer, 1994) and, more generally, J. Vervaele *et al.* (eds.), *Compliance and Enforcement of EC Law* (Hague/London: Kluwer, 1999).

integration. By contrast, positive law makes deeper demands of the Community's capacity to develop its own autonomous regulatory strategies. Positive law refers to the body of rules establishing standards at Community level in the fields of, for example, consumer, environmental or social policy. Whereas negative law involves appraisal of national rules in a Community context, positive law creates a body of Community rules. Positive law is regulatory in nature or, perhaps more accurately in the terms preferred in this paper, *re*-regulatory in nature, in the light of the perception that the Community is rarely engaged in *de novo* regulatory intervention but rather operative in total or partial replacement for national measures in the field subject to regulatory intervention. There is, however, a peril attached to the beguilingly neat classification of measures into the deceptively distinct folders of negative or positive law. Harmonisation policy, for example, which owes its constitutional basis to Article 94 EC (ex Article 100) and, since the entry into force of the Single European Act in 1987, Article 95 EC (ex Article 100a), is dual-functional. In so far as harmonisation of laws reduces fifteen different national norms to one Community norm, it is essentially deregulatory in impact and serves to iron out competitive distortions caused by discrepancies between national laws, thereby advancing integration. This is the pursuit of a "level playing field" for commercial activity in the EC. Yet that process, though, in converting "fifteen to one", deregulatory in nature, is also re-regulatory. The Community has to make a choice about the content of the harmonised regime. There will typically be debate, often fierce, about the intensity of the level of regulation that ought to be set at Community-level, which may plausibly range from permissive no-regulation to rigorous regulation perhaps even involving the suppression of particular practices.[6] The complete bargain struck in a particular sector may encompass both rules of trade liberalisation and also rules establishing protection at Community level. Broadcasting, for example, is the subject of a regime established by Directive 89/552 which situates control of unacceptable practices in an overall framework designed to promote the "Europeanisation" of commercial activity in the sector. Naturally, this reflects the complexity of the process of integrating and (re-)regulating the market at a European level against a background of accumulated national choices which differ, often enormously, state-by-state. Accordingly, I embrace the negative law/positive law dichotomy as a useful analytical tool, but I caution against inflating it into an unquestioned basis for examining the modern Community which has developed a pattern that is far more complex and sophisticated than anything imaginable at the time that Tinbergen introduced his framework in the context of international economic law.[7]

[6] A. McGee and S. Weatherill, "The Evolution of the Single Market – Harmonisation or Liberalisation" (1990) 53 *MLR* 578; J. Sun and J. Pelkmans, "Regulatory Competition and the Single Market" (1995) 33 *JCMS* 67.

[7] P. Tinbergen, *International Economic Integration* (Amsterdam: Elsevier, 1965).

Nevertheless, with that *caveat*, this paper is concerned to demonstrate that strategies for implementing negative law are significantly more mature than those relevant to positive law. This is true both with regard to "supranational" and to national enforcement. The Commission is – generally – more likely to identify and more likely to pursue blockages to integration and free movement than deviations from effective (re-)regulation of the market. The Court's construction of an enforcement pattern based on individual rights is also more likely to produce active policing of rights apt to drive the integration of markets than rights to secure the (re-)regulation of markets. The risk is that States will be tempted to cut costs by skimping on their duty to enforce agreed EC rules of market (re-)regulation. The problem lies not so much in the inadequacies associated with the enforcement of the law of market (re-)regulation (which, far from being unique to the EC framework, are identifiable as features of most systems of law) as the *relative* inadequacy of its enforcement in the EC when compared with the law of market integration. Moreover, in the EC context, there is a particular risk that perceptions of one State's slippage on commitments in the realms of laws of (re-)regulation may generate retaliatory laxity among other Member States. This threatens a corrosive downward spiral of "competitive under-implementation". Perhaps the message of the *Hedley Lomas* ruling itself is: a State would be astute to respond to perceived evasion of enforcement responsibilities in other Member States by subtle under-implementation of its own in the relevant sector, if it wishes to counter the competitive disadvantage flowing from its own perceived relatively rigorous enforcement. This type of laxity in the enforcement of laws of market (re-)regulation is very hard to track, in sharp contrast to the retaliatory denial of export licences preferred by the British authorities which is clearly visible and rapidly caught the attention of litigious commercial interests wielding the sharp blade of negative law.

A reliably comprehensive survey of the empirical truth of the phenomenon of "competitive under-implementation" would demand investment of huge resources. In its absence, the analysis presented in this paper is ostentatiously modest in its ambition. This is work-in-progress. It is, however, work which examines, though without yet doing justice to, some formidably important issues. European rule-making is well developed, under the influence of many pressures which vary sector by sector. European rule-enforcement is much less sophisticated. Aside from pockets of real "supranational" control such as that conferred on the Commission in the field of competition policy, the normal assumption is that it is national authorities which secure the enforcement of Community rules, under the broad supervision of the Commission and, in appropriate cases, private parties seeking to vindicate Community law rights before national courts. The spread of EC law and policy over the past four decades has been remarkable and has constrained the capacity of Member States to act free of the influence of EC policies in many areas. However, administration in the EC remains largely not the direct concern of the EC institutions. This is "indirect rule";[8] this is the EC as a "regulatory state" with a relatively meagre budget and therefore forced to avoid policies requiring direct expenditure in favour of the making of regulatory policies the costs of which largely fall on the parties subject to the obligation to comply with them.[9] Of course, this is a division of function with much to commend it. It allows the Community to draw on the established strengths of domestic systems for the execution of its policy choices. In cementing the application of EC rules into domestic judicial and bureaucratic frameworks, the risk that Community rules may be pushed to one side as unwanted alien intruders is minimised. But as the density of Community rule-making increases, so the potential weaknesses of expecting faithful, even and effective compliance among national public officials across the whole territory of the Union becomes ever more visible. Thus far the dominant response within the Community has been to load a greater expectation on to the established system of "dual vigilance". So State infractions remain subject to a general supervisory jurisdiction exercised by the Commission – but the Commission's teeth are sharpened by the addition at Maastricht of a power to fine recalcitrant Member States, now found in Article 228 EC, subject ultimately to the jurisdiction of the European Court. At national level, Community legislation has cautiously begun to interfere with domestic remedies law, most strikingly in the realms of public procurement law, and, more dramatically, the European Court has raised the stakes for States that default on their Treaty obligations, *inter alia*, by developing a remedy in damages mandated by Community law but to be awarded in appropriate cases of loss caused by breach of EC obligations by national judges. These adjustments represent progress towards firmer control over faulty implementation and application of EC law. But they suggest a persisting nervousness about bigger institutional steps. The awkward, evaded question is: will European-level enforcement become accepted? This is more than tinkering with dual vigilance. It concerns the very nature of the Community. The debate about improving the enforcement of EC law is accordingly intensely political.

4. FEATURES OF THE IMPLEMENTATION IMBALANCE

With the constitutional background in place, it is now appropriate to explore more closely the pattern of enforcement of EC law in order to make good the submission that particular types of EC law are less readily susceptible to effective enforcement than others. It is basically in the realms of laws concerning market (re-)regulation where shortcomings are identified, although I here take the opportunity to repeat the point that the negative law/positive law divide should not be thought to be watertight. There are a number of elements which constitute the implementation imbalance which I diagnose.

[8] Daintith (1995), note 5, above.
[9] G. Majone,*Regulating Europe* (London: Routledge, 1996).

Infringement proceedings

The Article 226 (ex Article 169) infringement procedure is a blunt instrument. It is slow. It was toothless until the insertion at Maastricht of the power to impose fines on persistently defaulting Member States. Even this power will be sparingly used, although that is not to deny its potential function as a deterrent. The procedure is subject to politicisation as Member States seek to exert influence over the exercise of the Commission's discretion, a process more prominent in some sectors than others.[10] In line with the thesis advanced in this paper, it is alleged violations of requirements to (re-)regulate national markets in line with Community measures have proved especially susceptible to perceived politicisation. Environmental policy has an unusually chequered history.[11] However, it should be made clear that the thesis presented here is not directed at the pollution of politicisation, although of course such incidents occur, but rather at the general cumbersome and intransparent nature of the Article 226 (ex Article 169) procedure. Individual access to challenge the Commission's allocation of priorities in infringement proceedings is confined by the fundamentally important decision in *Star Fruit* v. *Commission* in which the Court insisted on "a discretion which excludes the right for individuals to require . . . the Commission to adopt a specific position".[12] There has been a partial erosion of the Commission's imperviousness to any duty to explain its priorities in the field of competition policy where, on rare occasions, the Commission's refusal to pursue a complaint has been challenged and shown to be legally flawed.[13] But this is a special case, apparently developed because of the explicit status of complainants recognised in Regulation 17/62, the relevant secondary legislation in the field of competition law, and even here this concession does not mean that the Commission can be forced to come to a conclusion on the substance of a complaint,[14] only that it must consider the complaint with due care. Moreover, the Court of First Instance has ruled that the Commission is entitled to choose not to pursue a complaint if it concludes that there is no "Community interest" in doing so,[15] a nebulous concept which requires elucidation and which has

[10] See generally G. Ross, *Jacques Delors and European Integration* (New York: Polity Press, 1995).

[11] R. Williams, "The European Commission and the Enforcement of Environmental Law: an Invidious Position" (1994) 14 *YEL* 351; P. Kunzlik, "Environmental Impact Assessment: the British Cases"(1995) *EELR* 336; L. Krämer, "Public Interest Litigation in Environmental Matters before European Courts" in H. Micklitz and N. Reich (eds.), *Public Interest Litigation before European Courts* (Nomos Verlagsgesellschaft, 1996), 297–318.

[12] Case 247/87 [1989] ECR 291, para. 11 of the ruling.

[13] For example, Case T–37/92 *BEUC* v. *Commission* [1994] ECR II–285. For discussion see S. Weatherill, "Public Interest Litigation in EC Competition Law", in Micklitz and Reich (1996), note 11, above, 169–89; C. Kerse, "The Complainant in Competition Cases: a Progress Report"(1997) 34 *CMLRev* 213.

[14] Case 125/78 *GEMA* v. *Commission* [1979] ECR 3173 and confirmed frequently since. See S. Weatherill and P. Beaumont, *EU Law* (London: Penguin, 1999), 3rd edn., 885–90.

[15] Case T–24/90 *Automec srl* v. *Commission* [1992] ECR II–2223.

accordingly formed the basis of a Commission Notice directed at improving decentralisation of enforcement in the sphere, a matter in respect of which the Commission is naturally anxious given its own resource constraints.[16] The requirement imposed on the Commission to respond to a complainant in the competition sphere could usefully be expanded to other areas of enforcement activity. However, despite numerous invitations, the Courts have so far declined to abandon the general resistance evident in *Star Fruit* to imposing duties on the Commission to adopt a more formal approach to complaint-handling under Article 226 (ex Article 169) and it is probably realistic to suppose now that legislative reform is the only way to defeat the Court's obstinacy on this point. Admittedly, there may be avenues for securing greater transparency in the Commission's handling of infringement procedures which fall short of the setting aside of *Star Fruit*. An intriguing new method for securing scrutiny of the exercise of the Commission's discretion under Article 226 (ex Article 169) is offered by complaint to the European Ombudsman and by petitioning the European Parliament.[17] And it is possible that the release of documentation may be secured. In the judgment of the Court of First Instance in *The Bavarian Lager Company Ltd* v. *Commission*[18] the applicant sought to rely on the Code of Conduct concerning public access to documents in order to secure the release of a reasoned opinion sent by the Commission to the UK. It failed. The Court of First Instance considered the document concerned was mis-classified as a reasoned opinion, even though the Commission itself had not disputed that label during the proceedings. The document was treated by the Court as preparatory to the production of a reasoned opinion, and access to it could properly be refused in order to preserve confidentiality during State/Commission negotiation. This leaves open the possibility in future that an applicant may gain access to a true reasoned opinion. In the case the Commission was anxious to deny even this possibility, but the Court's ruling suggests that in at least some circumstances where the process of negotiation has come to an end the documents should be produced.[19] However, as a general observation, one must conclude that the Article 226 (ex Article 169) procedure is surrounded by strong assumptions of Commission discretion in the allocation of scarce enforcement resources. Review at the behest of the individual is limited.

Monitoring compliance

Some of the comments above apply to the deployment of the infringement procedure in all cases of violation of Community law, but, as already suggested, the

[16] OJ 1993 C39/6.

[17] See P. Kunzlik, "The Enforcement of EU Environmental Law: Article 169, the Ombudsman and the Parliament"(1997) 6 *EELR* 46.

[18] Case T–309/97, Judgment of 14 October 1999.

[19] See also Article 255 EC, an Amsterdam innovation.

problems are especially acute in relation to alleged violation of the law of market (re-)regulation. Instances of delinquency tend to be harder to monitor, for they involve less visible or clear-cut violations than typically arise in the field of negative law. Consider rules requiring air or water quality; or standards of health and safety in the workplace. The standard of "effective enforcement", expected of an implementing Member State drawn from Article 10 EC (ex Article 5), is disturbingly imprecise, thereby diminishing effective application of the rule. It is, moreover, a continuing obligation which is costly to monitor. Article 10 (ex Article 5) itself, as an obligation of fidelity to the Community, is appealingly malleable and has been employed by the Court to achieve some surprising results, but if offers nothing concrete on the nature of the responsibility of Member States to enforce EC law.[20] Snyder has expressed a general anxiety about over-reliance on the symbol rather than the reality of Article 10 (ex Article 5) EC; there is, at least, a risk that the expectations of loyalty to the Community system are placing a load on Article 10 (ex Article 5) which it cannot easily bear. "Effectiveness" is being over-worked, its range of meanings blurred.[21] For the Court, it is required that penalties must be fixed with reference to analogous situations under national law and must in any event secure an effect that is "effective, proportionate and dissuasive". This may be regarded as a minimum standard of effective enforcement.[22] Separating the lawful supply of a prudently limited budget for the enforcement of particular rules of market (re-)regulation from the unlawful allocation of a budget that is simply inadequate to ensure effective enforcement is fiendishly difficult, and, given the imprecision surrounding such an issue, incentives to pursue national choices through litigation will be small. This goes not only for the Commission, equipped with a finite budget, but also for potential litigants wishing to vindicate EC law rights at national level.

Regulatory reform and enforcement

There are features of recent regulatory initiatives which may contribute to making this problem still more severe, further weakening the possibility of effective supervision. The Community exercises an increasing preference in favour of Framework Directives over more detailed measures as part of its process of regulatory renovation. This is written into the Protocol on the Application of the Principles of Subsidiarity and Proportionality, one of the major innovations of

[20] On drawing up a code, see J. Temple Lang, "The Duties of National Authorities under Community Constitutional Law" (1998) 23 *ELRev* 109.

[21] F. Snyder, "General Course on Constitutional Law of the EU" in Academy of European Law (ed.), *Collected Courses of the Academy of European Law 1995* (Hague/London: Kluwer, 1998), especially Part III.

[22] Case C–341/94 *André Allain and Stecl Trading France SARL* [1996] ECR I–4631. See also for example, Case C–382/92 *Commission* v. *UK* [1994] ECR I–2435; Case 326/88 *Anklagemyndigheden* v. *Hansen & Soen I/S* [1990] ECR I–2911.

the Amsterdam Treaty. The risk is that as agreed rules begin to assume a less precise character under the influence of this policy adaptation, so too the attached obligation of effective enforcement becomes still harder to track. For example, in connection with Community rules on health and safety regulation Vos has identified the wide discretion necessarily left to the Member States in order to permit nuanced application in the light of local conditions as likely to prejudice evenness in the impact of Community law as a result of "ample leeway for divergent and probably self-interested implementation". The same anxiety attaches to use of "vague and open-ended terms" in directives in the field, generated by the search for political compromise but sowing the seeds of divergent local application.[23] Use of the subsidiarity principle to justify the elimination of detail from directives may prove an approach likely to yield "fictitious harmonisation", for basic disagreement on the shape of the Community's regime may be finessed into agreement on a compromise framework measure which allows Member States to pursue fundamentally divergent approaches under the camouflage of a platitudinous framework measure. If this criticism is valid, anxiety about the consequences for the viability and integrity of a workable Community legal order must inevitably spill over into the scope for effective enforcement, whether by Commission or by private litigation. Indeed, the purpose of such measures is that effective enforcement will be defied, and local choices preserved. Much the same comment may be persuasively directed at derogations and options allowed to Member States in Community measures. This is an increasingly common feature of Community legislative activity and it reflects the inevitable pressure for permissible differentiation within the Community system which is created by the geographical and functional expansion of the system in recent years.[24] The notorious Working Time Directive provides an illustration. The measure survived the UK's challenge to its validity[25] but its text supplies a number of very awkward questions about its intended impact which will inevitably, and perhaps deliberately, undermine its even and effective application across the territory of the EU.[26] Here too the fragmentation of the law tends to impede effective enforcement. As in the case of Framework Directives, there are here too advantages in adopting such strategies for they improve the chances of getting rules agreed in the first place. Moreover, regimes including derogations and options are also valuable for other perfectly good reasons of

[23] E. Vos, *Institutional Frameworks of Community Health and Safety Regulation: Committees, Agencies and Private Bodies* (Oxford: Hart Publishing, 1999), 66–67. *Cf.* in another sector, J. Scott, *EC Environmental Law* (London: Longman, 1998) especially chapter 6.

[24] Generally see S. Weatherill, "Flexibility or Fragmentation? Trends in European Integration" in J. Usher (ed.), *The State of the European Union* (London: Longman, forthcoming); N. Walker, "Sovereignty and Differentiated Integration" (1998) 4 *ELJ* 355.

[25] Case C–84/94 *United Kingdom* v. *Council* [1996] ECR I–5755.

[26] See from the UK perspective C. Barnard, "The Working Time Regulations 1998" (1998) 28 *ILJ* 61. Imprecision is also a gift to critics of the EU; see, for example, the mischief made by the Conservative Party about whether the Directive covers newspaper delivery boys and girls ("Labour attacked over EU rules", *Financial Times* 12 February 1999, 8). The cost to the EU of such bickering is hard to quantify but not trivial.

nuanced regulatory strategy, for example to avoid the inefficient rigidities of a broad framework which is locally ill-fitting. But there are costs involved. Rules on paper may have a very different impact on the ground, which will be difficult to track, and, in addition and a specifically EC anxiety, this may damage the evenness of application state-by-state, in turn breeding risks of competitive under-implementation as States suspect that "their" firms are facing higher compliance costs than competitors based in other, less rigorous States. Firms will not be slow to draw such suspicions to the attention of the bureaucrats with which they deal.

There is, of course, no Commission inspectorate with powers to pursue examination of state practice in the application of Community rules governing environmental or labour standards. It is highly unlikely to be granted such powers. In any event, even an enhanced Commission competence to investigate the grass roots would be of limited value without a major increase in its resources, which seems politically unfeasible in the short- or medium-term. To an extent, part of the underlying pattern is that these Community laws are deliberately fed through the national process. This is the familiar pattern of "indirect rule". This has much appeal and its virtues are sung in the Amsterdam Treaty's Protocol on Subsidiarity and Proportionality:

> Regarding the nature and the extent of Community action, Community measures should leave as much scope for national decision as possible, consistent with securing the aim of the measure and observing the requirements of the Treaty. While respecting Community law, care should be taken to respect well established national arrangements and the organisation and working of Member States' legal systems. Where appropriate and subject to the need for proper enforcement, Community measures should provide Member States with alternative ways to achieve the objectives of the measures.

In a sense this is not new. Directives are not designed to breed uniformity, but rather to undergo transmission via tried and trusted but varying local structures. A directive may "be applied by the Member States in different ways", especially where it grants the Member States a wide discretion in a field involving complex assessments.[27] Naturally, administrative tradition varies among the Member States and this affects the practical patterns of application of EC policies across the territory of the Union. Accordingly, for reasons of both a constitutional and a practical nature, the Commission's scope of inquiry is inevitably shallow and largely limited to inspection of "paper transposition" of directives. It can do little more than focus on the legally verifiable formal point of transposition,[28] rather than delving into deeper patterns of implementation practice. The

[27] Case C–293/97 *R* v. *Secretary of State for the Environment, Minister of Agriculture, Fisheries and Food,ex parte H.A. Standley and Others and D.G.D. Metson and Others*, Judgment of 29 April 1999.

[28] Although even paper transposition itself attracts very different approaches state-by-state; see reports prepared for XVIII FIDE Congress on "Les Directives Communautaires: Effets, Efficacité, Justiciabilité" (Stockholm, 1998).

Community is not concerned to re-allocate functions as between central and local organs of a Member State, but rather to leave such choices about absorption to the internal process of the Member States.[29] The Commission's "Scoreboards" which display percentages of directives duly transposed by each Member State contribute to publicising the importance of implementation fidelity to agreed rules,[30] but they cannot capture deeper phenomena within the implementation process such as budgetary allocation and genuine will among local officials to take Community-derived rules seriously. By contrast, an obstruction to the free movement of goods tends to be more concrete and clearly recognisable.[31] It attracts whistle blowers more readily. Apart from a naked failure to transpose a directive at all, mishandling of EC (re-)regulatory laws is typically less definite, requires enduring monitoring to uncover and may not involve a victim able or willing to blow the whistle. Moreover, the problem becomes increasingly severe under the pressures of geographical and functional expansion which have dominated the EU in recent years. One may conclude with Rasmussen that "the panoply of technically illegal means of evasion of obligations under Community law of a Member State is impressive".[32] Especially, I add, as far as the rules of market (re-)regulation are concerned.

The Court is not unaware of the risk that legislative compromises might enfeeble the possibilities for individual policing of agreed Community measures. Judge Mancini, writing in 1989, stated explicitly that directives have a "dangerously elastic quality", which might lead to States agreeing to their adoption "knowing that the price to pay for possible failure to transpose it is non-existent or minimal".[33] He presented this as part of the background to the Court's willingness to attribute direct effect to unimplemented directives. The Court has gone further as that "elastic" quality has itself been stretched further. The famous *Francovich* ruling[34] opened up the possibility for an action in damages brought by an individual suffering loss caused by mis-implementation of Community law, but, in a less remarked upon feature of the judgment, the Court also appears to have widened the potential scope of directly effective rights by holding that there existed a justiciable minimum guarantee for payment of unpaid remuneration in the event of employer insolvency even though the Directive allowed a discretion to fix a ceiling to the amount guaranteed. By definition, since the Directive had been left wholly untransposed, Italy had failed to make a choice on location of the ceiling but the Court did not allow this

[29] Although it is certainly the case that Community law may act as a catalyst for change within national legal and administrative systems. See Daintith (1995), note 5, above, and Snyder (1998), note 21, above.

[30] These are available via the Commission web pages; http://europa.eu.int.

[31] To emphasise: the point is relative. I do not suggest that the law of free movement is definitionally problem-free (*cf.* Joined Cases C–267 and C–268/91 *Keck and Mithouard* [1993] ECR I–6097), rather that it tends to throw up more easily identifiable and remediable violations than those which arise in the law of market (re-)regulation.

[32] H. Rasmussen, *European Court of Justice* (Copenhagen: Gad Jura, 1998), 106.

[33] F. Mancini, "The Making of a Constitution for Europe" (1989) 26 *CMLRev* 595.

[34] Cases C–6, C–9/90 [1991] ECR I–5357.

to defeat the direct effect of the provisions. It was only the absence of an identifiable guarantor under the Directive, not the flexible content of the guarantee, that was treated as fatal to direct effect. Private control of faulty implementation is thereby enhanced. Frequently, however, even a minimum guarantee will be impossible to discern. As a general proposition, the rise of derogations and options in Community secondary legislation and of Framework Directives militates against effective enforcement.

"Rights" and the limits of individual enforcement in EC law

Even the remarkable ruling in *Francovich* impinges on the implementation and enforcement imbalance. The great genius of the European Court has been to lure national courts into doing its bidding.[35] They enforce rights arising under Community law as directly effective within national systems and as supreme in the event of conflict with national law. In this way EC law has become part of the fabric of national law and its policing has been rendered immeasurably more rigorous than is normal of international treaties.[36] "Compliance problems" are capable of being dealt with much more energetically than might be the case were the focus to rest solely on the Commission's discretion and its limited resources.[37] The Court's orthodox treatment of this pattern has been to insist that the procedures and remedies made available within the national system for the vindication of Community law rights remain within the preserve of the national legal order, subject only to the insistence that, first, Community law-derived claims be treated no less favourably than similar domestic clams and, second, it should not be practically impossible to secure the vindication of Community law rights.[38] This concession to national autonomy, suggesting a sharp division between rights (fixed by Community law) and remedies and procedures (shaped according to local preference) has become blurred. It is the influence of the Court's rather interventionist reading of the qualification that the national system prevails *provided* it supplies a remedy that is not empty of practical value that is especially significant in eroding the shelter of national procedural autonomy. In demanding that effective protection be available to Community law-based litigants pursuing the national route, the Court has increasingly felt able to specify remedies that a national court must be regarded

[35] On how and why, see J. Weiler, "A Quiet Revolution: the European Court of Justice and its Interlocutors" (1994) 26 *Comparative Political Studies* 510. See also B. de Witte, "Direct Effect, Supremacy and the Nature of the Legal Order", chapter 5 in P. Craig and G. de Búrca, *The Evolution of EU Law* (Oxford: Oxford University Press,1999).

[36] For an interesting discussion of circumstances in which such absorption may be counter-productive to effective enforcement see A. Cassese, "Reflections on International Criminal Justice"(1998) 61 *MLR* 1 at 6–8.

[37] *Cf.* the narrative provided by Rasmussen, note 32, above, chapters 4 and 5. See also, with distinct points of emphasis, R. Dehousse, *The European Court of Justice* (London: Macmillan, 1998), chapter 5; S. Hix, *The Political System of the EU* (London: Macmillan, 1999), chapter 4.

[38] For a very early statement, see Case 45/76 *Comet* v. *Produktschap* [1976] ECR 2043.

as competent to award as a matter of Community law.[39] In such circumstances it is not open to the national court to limit its search for an appropriate remedy to orthodox national law alone. So in *Factortame* the House of Lords determined that it had no competence under English law to grant the remedy sought (interim relief against the Crown) but once the European Court had ruled that as a matter of EC law, itself a part of English law, such a remedy had to be available within the domestic system in order to ensure an effective remedy,[40] the House of Lords accepted its obligations in this respect and, after examining the circumstances of the case, decided the matter was apt for such an interim award.[41] In *Francovich* the Court ruled that rights to reparation for loss caused by breach of Community law might arise as a matter of EC law within the national legal order. This operates even outside the sphere of directly effective law. The Court felt able to specify a remedy to be granted by national courts despite the absence of any explicit textual support in the Treaty for such an instruction. The Court's inspiration lay in its determination to secure an effective remedy. Since *Francovich* the Court has taken opportunities to elaborate the conditions which should govern the award of this Community law remedy placed in the hands of national judges. Most prominently, in *Brasserie du Pecheur SA* v. *Germany* and *R* v. *Secretary of State for Transport, ex parte Factortame Ltd and others*,[42] the Court confirmed its bold view that a right to reparation in cases of loss caused to individuals as a result of breaches of Community law was "inherent in the system of the Treaty". It then made plain that the right to reparation might arise in cases of violation of primary Treaty Articles concerning the law of free movement and explained more fully than it had previously the manner in which national judges should approach such claims.

Nothing that follows should be read as detracting from this author's admiration for the Court's subtle and astutely judged construction of a system of individual rights protection under EC law. But we should not be blind to the limitations of this pattern of enforceable rights. Here too the "implementation imbalance" is a feature of the landscape. Legal and practical obstacles that confront the agent of the law of market (re)-regulation are much higher than those faced by the party seeking to insist on compliance with the law of market integration. The notion of "rights" is an intriguing one in EC law. As is well known, one of the European Court's first and momentous choices was to adopt a language of "individual rights" in a new legal order which was doubtless designed to propel European Community law, though originating in the treaty-based realms of public international law, into distinctive *sui generis* territory. This was, of course, a vibrant success story. The principle of direct effect places the

[39] See T. Tridimas, *The General Principles of EC Law* (Oxford/New York: Oxford University Press, 1999), chapter 8; R. Craufurd Smith, "Remedies for Breach of EU Law in National Courts", chapter 8 in Craig and de Búrca, note 35, above.

[40] Case C–213/89 [1990] ECR I–2433.

[41] [1990] 3 CMLR 375.

[42] Cases C–46/93 and C–48/93 [1996] ECR I–1029.

policing of Community law in the hands of individual right holders throughout the Member States, converting national courts into protectors of EC law rights. *Francovich* and its progeny nudge the devices of control beyond directly effective rights. But, put simply, for present purposes, it is jurisprudentially far easier to identify rights to integration than rights to (re-)regulation. For example, Articles 28 (ex Article 30) and 49 (ex Article 59) are, of course, directly effective. There is a (non-absolute) right to trade which has been the subject of hundreds of decisions of the European Court driven by commercial parties' readiness to litigate and the willingness of national courts to make references to Luxembourg. This has allowed the Court to develop a framework within which to redistribute functions between the Community's judicial and legislative institutions and to develop its own function of adjudicating on the validity of national choices about market regulation in so far as they impact on the market-building process. By contrast, establishing justiciable rights to, for example, a clean environment or a safe workplace even in accordance with a particular EC Directive is an enterprise that is a great deal more elusive. *Comitato di Coordinamento per la Difesa della Cava and Others* v. *Regione Lombardia and Others* provides an example of the Court's refusal to find provisions of a directive dealing with shaping of a programme governing treatment of waste apt to create rights relating to environmental protection susceptible to safeguard by a national court.[43] So too in *Enichem Base* the Court found that direct effect did not attach to an obligation to inform the Commission in advance of draft rules relating to waste.[44] Breach of the obligation to notify did not render unlawful the rules adopted. Individual enforcement in a case of plain non-compliance by public authorities in a Member State was thereby excluded, leaving the matter in the hands of the Commission. For all the ingenuity of the techniques of direct and indirect effect plus the use of EC law as a basis for a claim for damages against a Member State, there remain significant defects in the capacity of EC law to equip individuals with the means to improve compliance. "Rights" protection goes only so far in the system crafted by the European Court.[45] The Court's identification of the possibility of a violation of Article 28 (ex Article 30) – not merely of Article 10 (ex Article 5) – in cases of unsuppressed civil disturbance is of the highest significance in improving individual enforcement of obstructions to trade caused by indolence among the public authorities,[46] but persistent failure (for example) to protect wild birds or regulate rigorously the

[43] Case C–236/92 [1994] ECR I–483. See generally J. Jans, "Legal Protection in European Environmental Law" and L. Kramer, "Direct Effect of EC Environmental Law", chapters 5 and 6 in H. Somsen (ed.), *Protecting the European Environment* (London: Blackstone Press, 1996); Scott (1998), note 23, above, chapter 8.

[44] Case 380/87 [1989] ECR 2491.

[45] See C. Boch, "The Iroquois at the Kirchberg; or some naive remarks on the status and relevance of direct effect" in Usher (forthcoming), note 24, above; C. Hilson and A. Downes, "Making Sense of Rights: Community Rights in EC Law"(1999) 24 *ELRev* 121.

[46] Case C–265/95 *Commission* v. *France* [1997] ECR I–6959 (which spurred the adoption of Reg 2679/98 OJ 1998 L337/8).

market for doorstep selling in accordance with relevant EC Directives would not readily create rights against the defaulting public authorities capable of being vindicated by private parties.

This is not to say that rights to regulation do not arise, nor that the European Court is not adept at extending the reach of effective individual protection in the EC legal order. *Francovich* was, after all, a case concerned with Community rules governing worker protection. It represented an important step towards a notion of enforceable rights which transcends direct effect. The Court in that case placed rights in the hands of individuals in respect of a directive which it had determined was *not* directly effective. In doing so, it empowered individuals to protect their rights to markets (re-)regulated in line with EC law. Incidentally, those same litigants' actions for compensation were apt (though not on the facts[47]) to prevent the Italian State (though not Italian firms) from enjoying a competitive advantage consequent on non-implementation at the expense of firms located in States which had faithfully accepted the regulatory burden agreed at Community level by duly implementing the Directive. And in both *Paola Faccini Dori*[48] and *Dillenkofer*[49] the Court was not deterred from identifying consumer rights to a regulated market by the constitutional point that the directives at stake were, in formal terms, measures of harmonisation designed to promote the process of market integration adopted under Articles 100 and 100a EC respectively, and in doing so the Court offered further confirmation of the indissociable link between integration and protective (re-)regulation in the context of harmonisation policy. Here too rights to regulation (in conformity with EC Directives) serve as individual protection and, equally, as methods for stripping States of costs saved through mis-implementation. More generally, Reich has attempted to show the progress, albeit limited, that may be made in the current state of EC law beyond economic rights in the direction of citizens' rights.[50] But the task is arduous. Most of all, it is a harder struggle than that faced by parties wishing to establish rights based on the Treaty provisions governing free movement.

An attempt to portray EC laws of market (re-)regulation as potential dead letters would be over-dramatic and would represent an impoverished view of the subtlety of the process of EC law-making and law-enforcing. This does not defeat the point that these elements notwithstanding, commercial interests wishing to take up legal arms to combat restrictions on trade are in a far stronger position in law than proponents of properly regulated markets. The way in which the EC legal system has chosen to channel access to the courts falls well short of allowing a general right to secure the observance of EC Law. And

[47] Case C–479/93 *Francovich* v. *Italian State* [1995] ECR I–3843.

[48] Case C–91/92 [1994] ECR I–3325.

[49] Case C–178/94 *et al.* [1996] ECR I–4845.

[50] N. Reich, "System der subjectiven offentlichen Rechte in the Union: A European Constitution for Citizens of Bits and Pieces", in Academy of European Law (ed.), *Collected Courses of the Academy of European Law 1996* (Hague/London: Kluwer, 1998), 157–236; more fully, *Burgerrechte in der Europaischen Union* (Nomos Verlagsgesellschaft, 1999).

one should not over-estimate the vitality even of *Francovich*. It remains uncertain quite how far beyond orthodox direct effect the rights protection envisaged by the Court truly stretches. Showing a causal link between breach and loss will frequently prove awkward. More generally, not the least of concerns should be access to justice. Harlow has expressed anxiety that:

> [I]n locking the Community into national systems of liability, the ECJ may be creating an illusion of remedy where few remedies are in practice found.[51]

In practice, once cannot realistically suppose that a litigant in the position of Ms Dori, faced by a relatively small loss flowing from entry into a contract from which she could not elect to withdraw because Italy had failed to transpose the relevant EC Directive which envisaged the grant of such a right of withdrawal,[52] could normally sue the State even if one is able to classify her right as one which, when infringed, yields an action against the State in principle. What she needed was the opportunity to rely on the Directive to defeat a breach of contract action brought by a private party, the supplier of goods, but this would involve the horizontal application of an unimplemented Directive which the Court confirmed in *Dori* lies beyond the EC constitutional pale. The gains made by Italy from non-implementation will not be clawed back. Here one sees again a constitutional deficiency in the EC system. Denial of the attribution of horizontal direct effect to directives causes a significant gap in the system of individual rights protection for which the creation of a right enforceable against the State cannot fully compensate. Union citizens might expect more in order to preclude inequality before the law resulting from differences in implementation of Directives state-by-state,[53] but the Court is unreceptive to such appeals.

Generally, then, there are huge advantages in converting national courts into the loyal lieutenants of the European Court in the enforcement of Community law. But, even assuming that fidelity, the tools with which national courts are equipped operate in a way which causes imbalance. The point embraces not only the jurisprudential difficulty in identifying legal rights to re-regulation, which looms larger than the task of traders seeking to exploit rights to trade. It also involves essentially practical aspects of access to justice. Repeat-playing commercial interests are not slow to exploit Community law as even a cursory inspection of the European Court Reports will reveal. But who will litigate to secure effective market (re-)regulation? Costs are high. These are "diffuse interests", where individual losses are small, but aggregate losses big. On occasion, interest group representation may bridge the gap. The work of the Equal Opportunities Commission in the UK provides an example.[54] But such

[51] C. Harlow, "Francovich and the Problem of the Disobedient State"(1996) 2 *ELJ* 199 at 222, commenting on the "largely negative" contribution of *Francovich*.

[52] Case C–91/92, note 48, above.

[53] The Opinion of A-G Lenz in *Dori* develops this argument but it failed to persuade the Court.

[54] C. Barnard, "A European Litigation Strategy: the Case of the EOC" in J. Shaw and G. More, *New Legal Dynamics of European Union* (Oxford: Clarendon Press, 1995). See generally Dehousse (1998), note 37, above, chapter 4; Micklitz and Reich (1996), note 11, above.

intervention is patchy, sector by sector, state-by-state, and as a general observation private enforcement is less likely to be efficient than public enforcement where loss is spread thinly among a wide range of victims.

In general, the phenomenon of "creative compliance" becomes a much more credible option in the sphere of laws of market (re-)regulation than that of laws of market integration. That is to say, evasion of the full responsibilities of Community membership is less likely to provoke challenge by the Commission or private parties. As already suggested above, the message of the *Hedley Lomas* ruling itself is: a State would be astute to respond to perceived evasion of enforcement responsibilities in other Member States by subtle under-implementation of its own in the relevant sector, if it wishes to counter the competitive disadvantage flowing from its own perceived relatively rigorous enforcement. Blocking trade is by contrast clearly visible and apt to prompt rapid whistle-blowing.

5. MARKET TRANSPARENCY: DEEPENING THE IMBALANCE?

My contention is not that the law of market (re-)regulation allows States comfortable leeway in marginalising the costs undertaken on paper under Community law, nor that the law of market integration/deregulation operates a dogged and inescapable control over state action antagonistic to cross-border commercial freedom. Neither extreme is remotely realistic. Rather, I point to the imbalance in comparative ease of enforcement tools which favours the effective application of negative law over that of positive law. Moreover, there is a risk that this imbalance is deepening. The Commission is wisely searching for techniques for moving away from over-reliance on the ad hoc, *ex post facto* control of the Article 226 (ex Article 169) infringement procedure. A more comprehensive strategy than litigation alone is required if the post-1992 market is to be stabilised in order to provide a reliable commercial environment in which to secure the perceived advantages of the restructured European market. The law governing the free movement of goods exhibits trends away from a predominant focus on control by (reactive) litigation towards control by management and notification – in short, transparency. In the context of observations made above about the potentially corrupting influence on the EU of mistrust of the reliability of effective law enforcement across the territory of all the Member States, it is important to appreciate that the Commission's evolving post-1992 strategy of market management heavily emphasises confidence in the operation of the market. Not only commercial interests but also consumers should be given confidence that cross-border activity is viable. For example, in its Twelfth Annual Report on Monitoring the Application of Community law, the Commission asserted that:

> The removal of barriers between Member States gives rise to a new situation in which Community law, and the way in which it is applied in other Member States, takes on greater importance for individuals and business in the Union. They need to feel confi-

dent that administration of the law is as reliable and effective as it is for their own national regulations.[55]

Emphasis on the practice of market management remains central to Commission thinking. In the 1997 "Action Plan for the Single Market", endorsed at the Amsterdam European Council, it is asserted amid insistence on transparency as a basis for creating a reliable environment for commercial activity that "The Single Market stands or falls on confidence".[56] It is plain that such trust needs to be built and sustained, and cannot simply be assumed.

Obligations of notification are central to the quest for transparency. Directive 83/189 required prior notification to the Commission of draft technical standards and regulations. The regime was consolidated in Directive 98/34.[57] A "standstill" period allows the Commission to examine draft measures with a view to halting their introduction at national level should it conclude that a violation of Article 28 (ex 30) would follow. It is a form of "early warning system". The drive to improve transparency and to establish supervisory mechanisms that are more sensitive than *ad hoc*, *ex post facto* litigation was extended by Decision 3052/95,[58] which has operated since the start of 1997 at the more detailed level of control exercised by national authorities over the marketing of a particular model or type of product lawfully produced or marketed in another Member State. Action taken must be notified to the Commission. These devices may be expected to deepen administrative co-operation in the EC both vertically (Commission/national authorities) and horizontally (national/national) in order to improve effective, transparent market management, although statistics reveal that patterns of notification vary state-by-state and sector by sector.[59] Administrative heterogeneity among the Member States operates as a persisting barrier to the "Europeanisation" of networks of information gathering and sharing.[60] This is a disadvantage inherent in "indirect rule".

Prevention is better than cure and this is reflected in the efforts of the Commission to develop networks which will forestall the introduction of initiatives at national level that destabilise the integrated market. Moreover, the Commission has been able to recruit the Court to support its strategy of improved transparency. In *CIA Security International SA* v. *Signalson SA and Securitel SPRL* the Court ruled that a national technical regulation which is not notified to the Commission in default of the obligations laid down by Directive 83/189 is unenforceable against third parties before the courts of the Member

55 COM (95) 500, OJ 1995 C254, report covering 1994; see also Council Resolution, OJ 1996 C224/3.

56 CSE (97)1 final, 4 June 1997.

57 OJ 1998 L204/37 amended by Directive 98/48 OJ 1998 L217/18.

58 OJ 1995 L321/1.

59 See S. Weatherill, "Compulsory notification of draft technical standards: the contribution of Directive 83/189 to the management of the internal market" (1996) 16 *YEL* 129.

60 For examples drawn from the area of product safety, see H. Micklitz, S. Weatherill and T. Roethe, *Federalism and Responsibility* (London: Graham and Trotman, 1994); on health and safety regulation, see Vos (1999), note 23, above, especially chapter 2.

State which is in breach of its notification obligation.[61] This penalty, which is not provided for in the Directive itself, greatly increases the incentive for Member States to co-operate actively with the Commission in support of its mission to improve the flow of information about proposed regulatory activity in the Member States.[62] Quite how far this dramatic penalty of unenforceability in proceedings involving third parties extends into other Community regimes requiring notification of national acts is not yet fully clear,[63] but it represents a significant enhancement of the vitality of a system designed to improve transparency, dialogue and *ex ante* Commission control. Yet here too lurks the imbalance in implementation. The penalty of unenforceability in proceedings involving third parties attaches neatly to acts introduced at national level. There is no counterpart with regard to omissions to regulate in accordance with Community law. Failure properly to enforce, for example, environmental protection laws or, more basic still, to notify what has not been done that should have been requires a response that is more sophisticated. Moreover, the construction of networks between administrative agencies is hard enough in pursuit of integration, it is more problematic still in the world of laws of (re-)regulation, where administrative heterogeneity dominates. The imbalance deepens. The underlying question remains whether the required goal of "market confidence", on which the Commission astutely places such emphasis, can be delivered with these instruments.

Imminent enlargement of the Union may deepen the problem yet further. It is appropriate to question whether applicant States possess the infrastructure required to take seriously their obligations of faithful and effective enforcement. This should not be an inquiry aimed at exposing the failings of applicant States contrasted with the virtues of existing members, but rather a more even-handed examination inspired by the patchy track record even of long-term Member States. The Commission is alert to the problems of compliance which will follow enlargement. In the "Agenda 2000" documentation, it observes that:

> It is vital that Union legislation be transposed into national law. But this is not sufficient to ensure its correct application. It is equally important for the applicants' administrations to be modernized so that they can implement and enforce the *acquis*.[64]

In its 1998 report on competition policy it emphasises that applicant States are expected to equip their newly formed competition authorities with real powers

[61] Case C–194/94 [1996] ECR I–2201. The regime was treated as more complete than that held incapable of direct effect in Case 380/87, note 44, above.

[62] This compares closely to the Court's approach to unnotified State Aid in Case C–354/90 *Fédération Nationale du commerce extérieur des produits alimentaires* v. *France* [1991] ECR I–5523.

[63] See J. Jans, "National Legislative Autonomy? The Procedural Constraints of European Law" *LIEI* [1998/1] 25; S. Weatherill, "A case study in judicial activism in the 1990s: The status before national courts of measures wrongfully un-notified to the Commission" in D. O'Keeffe (ed.), *Liber Amicorum Gordon Slynn* (forthcoming).

[64] Bull Supp 5/97, 46.

of investigation and resources.[65] While it is pleasing to observe the Commission's emphasis on a world beyond "paper transposition", it is hard to believe the Commission's words extend much beyond lip-service to the role of enforcement patterns, and in any event monitoring is likely to prove beyond it. Creative compliance is probable. But here too the aspects of the Community legal order with which conformity is likely to prove especially difficult to track are those concerned with market re-regulation, rather than integration.

My purpose is not to criticise the advances made in the direction of opening up national practices to transparent inspection alongside improved administrative co-operation. Rather, I wish to observe that one species of EC law is underprivileged. In general the problem is that enforcing negative law is easier than enforcing positive law, whether through public or private policing, but that the current emphasis is on improvement of the already privileged branch. This risks "indirect rule" causing a double inefficiency. The areas in which private policing is ineffective should be the main focus of public enforcement, and vice versa. But the very opposite is emerging.

6. WHAT MIGHT BE DONE?

The purpose of this paper has been to explain the features of an "implementation imbalance" in EC law; that the law of integration is privileged over the law of market (re-)regulation for many reasons, the majority of which are associated with the very nature of the system and which defy simple solutions. I do not at all advocate that self-help should be permitted in a case such as *Hedley Lomas*, for that would require the unpicking of vital constitutional principles on which the EC legal order depends. Nor do I find workable a general right to bring an action to enforce EC law before a national court (although I favour the attribution of horizontal direct effect to unimplemented Directives). However, I do note the distance the system remains from one on which even and effective law enforcement may be relied throughout the territory of the EU. On several levels, under-implementation of laws of market (re-)regulation is less likely to generate direct challenge than misapplication of laws of integration. A further anxiety is that this may breed deepening suspicion and covert retaliation, causing a downward spiral in respect for agreed laws of market (re-)regulation. So a preliminary conclusion is that enforcement via the familiar structure of "dual vigilance" is flawed.

This remains the case even though Commission control has been enhanced by the addition at Maastricht of a power to impose fines on recalcitrant Member States, found in Article 228 EC (ex Article 171). It remains the case notwithstanding the adjustments made to the second limb of dual vigilance, enforcement before national courts. The notion of national procedural autonomy must

[65] SEC (1999) 743, para. 299.

today be read in the light of interventionist trends directed both by the Court and by the Community's legislature, which have added a thickening veneer of EC requirements attached to domestic law of remedies and procedure. The Court's contribution to trimming national procedural autonomy is discussed above. Legislative incursion is piecemeal. Public procurement provides the most spectacular example of the capacity of the Community legislature to establish procedures and remedies to be available for pursuit of the vindication of Community law rights at national level. Directives 89/665 and 92/13 deal with matters such as interim relief and the award of damages.[66] There is also a batch of EC measures which stipulate the need for types of public enforcement of the agreed rules, such as Directive 84/450 on misleading advertising and Directive 93/13 on unfair terms in consumer contracts.[67] In the consumer field, Directive 98/27 on cross-border injunctions has been adopted.[68] A key question is whether a more radical break with assumptions of dual vigilance might be appropriate. What of European agencies with direct enforcement powers? This, of course, invites a need to address fundamental constitutional questions.[69] This might be taken as a nudge towards the choice between what Dehousse has identified as the tension between two paradigms for the EU's evolution, that of the "regulatory model" and the "parliamentary model", both of which strains may be traced in the arrangements agreed at Amsterdam, reminding us of how fundamental these apparently technical choices about market management become in the context of polity-building.[70]

It far escapes this paper to look in any depth at the adjustments occurring in structures for rule-making and (the predominant current concern) rule-enforcing within the Community. This section merely surveys the pattern of incentives to address these problems. There are clues to the circumstances in which a coalition of interests may generate conditions in which there is receptivity to breakthroughs beyond the limits of "indirect rule". Just as pressures for rule-making at European level vary sector by sector[71] so too it is here assumed that in the area of rule enforcement different sectors attract very different responses, and that generalisations are potentially misleading. Indeed agencies that have thus far been created display very different characteristics. It escapes the reach of this paper to do more than provide glimpses of a future research

[66] OJ 1989 L395/33, OJ 1992 L76/14 respectively.

[67] OJ 1984 L250/17, OJ 1993 L95/29 respectively.

[68] OJ 1998 L166/51.

[69] On current limits to agency creation, underpinned but not exhaustively dealt with by the Court's ruling in Case 10/56 *Meroni* [1957–58] ECR 157, see Vos (1999), note 23, above.

[70] R. Dehousse, "European Institutional Architecture after Amsterdam: Parliamentary System or Regulatory Structure?"(1998) 35 *CMLRev* 595. See also, with particular reference to agencies, M. Everson, "Independent Agencies: Hierarchy Beaters?" (1995) 1 *ELJ* 180; A. Kreher and Y. Meny (eds.), Special Issue, "European Agencies"(1997) 4/2 *JEPP*. Also G. de Búrca, "The Institutional Development of the EU: a Constitutional Analysis" in Craig and de Búrca (1999), note 35, above.

[71] See F. Scharpf (ed.), Special Issue, "Governance in the Internal Market"(1997) 4/4 *JEPP*; K. Armstrong and S. Bulmer, *The Governance of the Single European Market* (Manchester/New York: MUP, 1998).

agenda. But, nevertheless, it is intriguing at least to begin to examine how there may be pressures not simply for rule-making at the European level but also for effective enforcement of those rules at European level.

Traders may want "Euro-rules", in order to level the commercial playing field fragmented by diverse national choices. So trans-frontier regulation is generated by perceived inefficiencies in a trans-frontier market resulting from the fragmenting effect of rules and decisions limited to national territories. The establishment of a medicines agency in the EC reflects the strength of incentives to develop regulatory and institutional structures at European level to avoid multi-state authorisations.[72] A shade more subtly, levelling the playing field may be especially attractive to operators in States which are relatively intensive regulators. Such interests may wish to see their comparatively costly regimes imposed on competitors elsewhere. This appreciation of patterns of commercial demand for rule-making offers a reminder that the cleavage between negative law and positive law dichotomy should not be accorded inflated importance and, in particular, that it misleads simply to equate positive law with diffuse interests in market regulation and negative law with commercial operators seeking unhindered cross-border market access. Both serve as methods for building the market. External factors form part of the landscape too. Insulation of the Community market from external competition may appeal and it may be achieved by demands for regulation. Anti-dumping provides the most spectacular setting for examining such trends, but more subtly the general practice of standards setting may involve the erection of non-tariff barriers to trade from outside the EU. Such intervention may be challengeable via the deregulatory, "negative law" of the World Trade Organisation.

These are not perceptions about pressures for trade regulation that are unique to the EC, though they are unusually fully developed within the EC because of the rapid progress it has made towards trade integration and beyond. But international trade generally is also increasingly characterised by pressures for co-operation as a means to resist a race to the bottom.[73] Relatively heavy regulators may aim to export their practices. For example, States that ban bribery by their own nationals may have an interest in securing international agreements mirroring their stance or else they find themselves at a competitive disadvantage.[74] One could assess attempts to secure international rules forbidding use of child labour in this vein; so too the thorny question of the inter-relation between trade and the environment. In this sense, protective laws (broadly understood) generate an inevitable wider dynamic of reform in an open trading system, leading, in the most high profile example of these trends, to questions about the appropriate

[72] For examination see Vos (1999), note 23, above; also D. Vogel, "The Globalization of Pharmaceutical Regulation" (1998) 11 *Governance* 1.

[73] P. Genschel and T. Plumper, "Regulatory competition and International co-operation" (1997) 4 *JEPP* 626; D. Vogel, *Barriers or Benefits? Regulation in Transatlantic Trade* (Washington: Brookings Institution Press, 1997).

[74] "US presses drive against business bribery", *Financial Times*, 24 February 1999.

place of demands for respect for human rights as a condition of trade engagement. Trade policy spills over.

Once agreement is secured that there should be transnational rule-making, whatever the motivation, attention will then be devoted to debating the more detailed patterns of the quality and intensity of that regulation.[75]

But do traders want in addition Euro-enforcement? Not if they can capture national agencies and depress "their" costs! In that case, European-level rule-making conceals new post-agreement strategies for acquiring competitive advantage, lost on paper to harmonisation. But this in turn – at least for the losers in this game, saddled with relatively high costs – may generate fresh incentives to level the enforcement playing field by developing something more than an expectation of national-level enforcement. Credibility of effective enforcement assumes a high priority. This is significant because it suggest a breakdown in the division of function which sees the Community as a rather well-developed rule-maker but as dependent on authorities in the Member States for execution of its policies, instead suggesting the growth of incentives for European-level intervention. The discourse of reliable enforcement and confidence in the market is highly visible in the Commission's post-1992 strategies for managing the market, examined above. Yet it finds itself confined to pressing the case for transparency and administrative co-operation, both vertical and horizontal, rather than seeking more direct powers of supervision. As explained, my anxiety is that the inadequacies in this pattern which I have identified tend to generate competitive under-implementation. It is nurtured by the EC's relative institutional weaknesses and it is especially harmful to laws of market (re-) regulation.

Competition policy is the sector in which the argument in favour of European-level supervision as a basis for even and effective law enforcement has been most conspicuously won. Merger control in particular provides a powerful illustration of pressures for European-level regulation to avoid the inefficiencies of requiring clearance from several national authorities. For big mergers – as defined by governing Regulation 4064/89 – competence to examine the deal rests exclusively with the Commission, subject only to limited and rarely invoked exceptional circumstances in which national control may be re-asserted.[76] The success of this regime in reducing the weight of regulatory burdens may be gauged by the fact that in 1997 the Member States agreed in Regulation 1310/97 to lower the thresholds, allowing a greater number of mergers to fall into the EC's exclusive grip. In competition policy generally, the Commission has always held exclusive competence over the grant of exemption under the third paragraph of Article 81 of

[75] Although, of course, the two stages are not wholly divorced; as discussed above, concession that the regime may be flexible and subject on implementation to local variation may condition readiness to accept agreement in the first place.

[76] See Weatherill and Beaumont (1999), note 14, above, chapter 25. On the pressures that led to adoption of the regime, see S. Bulmer, "Institutions and Policy Change in the EC; the case of merger control" (1994) 72 *Public Administration* 423.

restrictive agreements falling within the first paragraph. The Commission's dominance of the process combined with its strong powers of investigation and sanction ensure credibility for the even application of the regime across the territory of the Union. But this may change. Appreciation of the political mood may be gleaned from the Commission's current proposals that it should surrender that exclusivity over the grant of exemption and instead share control with national courts and competition authorities.[77] Allowing local-level exemption imperils uniformity and, in particular, raises the prospect of over-generous grant of exemption to local firms, especially where anti-competitive effects may be expected to be felt out-of-state. Emphasis on national-level application will also heighten the impact of diverse approaches between national jurisdictions to matters such as the burden of proof, discovery of documents and availability of damages. Although the Commission promises that it will perform a supervisory role to prevent divergent practice, there are practical limits to what it can do. These proposals are doubtless part of a much broader Commission strategy in all fields to aim to do less but to try and do it better in recognition that its responsibilities may have outstripped its resources, but the detail of this form of "modernisation" raises the spectre of fragmentation and allows room for competitive under-implementation.

Given the possible diminution in the "Europeanised" nature of even competition law enforcement, it is doubtless politically realistic not to anticipate much movement towards sharper European-level enforcement in other sectors. Such steps as have been taken are illuminatingly tentative. The Copenhagen-based Environment Agency possesses very limited powers. Its role is essentially information-gathering, which is doubtless important, but it in no sense operates as an inspectorate.[78] It seems that neither Member States nor indeed the Commission would wish it to. In the field of product safety, Directive 92/59[79] confers only a heavily qualified power of action on the Commission in cases of emergencies and even that very limited Europeanisation of the administration of product safety policy proved sufficiently controversial to provoke Germany to seek annulment of the relevant provisions before the European Court. The legal challenge failed,[80] but it serves to emphasise the disquiet at national level about such institutional change. "Indirect rule" remains heavily preferred.

7. ARE THESE PROBLEMS UNIQUE TO THE EC?

Even if one accepts that the present system is flawed this does not mean that an alternative would be superior. It is not merely facetious in the first instance to

[77] OJ 1999 C132, White Paper on Modernisation.

[78] See P. Davies, "The European Environment Agency" (1994) 14 *YEL* 313.

[79] OJ 1992 L228/24.

[80] Case C–359/92 *Germany* v. *Council* [1994] ECR I–3681. See generally S. Weatherill, *EC Consumer Law and Policy* (London: Longman, 1997), chapter 7.

propose that nothing need be done. These are, after all, not unique problems. A national lawyer may advise that all systems contain these imbalances between economic rights which are relatively accessible and "diffuse interests" which are less readily justiciable. It is not news to an environmental lawyer working in a domestic context that securing access to the courts to seek remedies against the failings of public authorities is difficult. And a national lawyer might point to, for example, laws of consumer protection and observe that laws have different impacts in different parts of the country, depending on the approach of local enforcement agencies and on judicial sentencing policy. So why should one worry if the same brand of problem operates at Community level? I submit that the problem at Community level is qualitatively more severe. The distance between rule-maker and rule-enforcer is all the greater at transnational level. On top of imbalanced implementation, the EU suffers from unevenness between States which hinders the ironing out of competitive inequalities caused by regulatory divergence. And, relative to national systems, the EC legal order is truly less institutionally sophisticated. I would therefore find it difficult to accept the thesis that these problems should be treated as no different from those confronting a national legal order. But the pertinent suggestion that the weaknesses of the EC system should not be taken out of their context as necessarily unique may also be made from a different direction. The international lawyer inspecting these perceived problems might also advise, do nothing. Planning the control of non-compliance in international law has become progressively more sophisticated in recent years. For example, in the context of international environmental Treaties, non-compliance procedures are increasingly being considered as apt for inclusion in relevant agreements in preference to leaving infractions of the regime to be addressed through orthodox general rules governing treaty breach and state responsibility. Less confrontational methods are sought in order to ease participants in the regime back to compliance with agreed rules.[81] There is a growing literature concerned with general questions of improving the credibility of compliance with Treaty obligations through patterns of dialogue and management rather than coercion.[82] But it remains true that treaties are substantially dependent on state structures for implementation. Impacts vary. This is not novel. And so the same may be thought unsurprising in the EC context. But it has become commonplace that the scope of the EC's activities and ambitions are more profound than those of an orthodox international organisation. "Market without a State" it might be,[83] but more is expected of the EC's penetration into the fabric of national legal and political systems than is standard under an international treaty system, not least in the

[81] For example C. Redgwell, "Non-compliance Procedures and the Climate Change Convention" in W. Bradnee Chambers (ed.), *Global Climate Governance* (Tokyo: United Nations University, 1999).

[82] See A. Chayes and A. Chayes, *The New Sovereignty: Compliance with International Regulatory Agreements* (Cambridge, Mass./London: Harvard University Press, 1995).

[83] C. Joerges, "European Economic Law, the Nation-State and the Maastricht Treaty" chap. 3 in R. Dehousse (ed.), *Europe after Maastricht* (München: Law Books in Europe, 1994).

depth and breadth of direct individual participation in law enforcement. The Court's ruling in *Hedley Lomas*, examined above, reveals some of the assumptions about the "constitutionalised" nature of the EC legal order, which prompted the Court to go so far as to require Member States to trust each other in enforcing agreed rules. On a different note, the observer attuned to the realities of international treaty-making might also caution that in so far as agreement on the international plane is facilitated by the security felt by States in controlling processes of implementation on their territory and, to some extent, in softening the impact of the agreement according to local tastes, then the elaboration of a more intrusive regime of enforcement might deter or at least diminish willingness to sign up to the agreement in the first place. This too would be an anxiety within the EC system, although it would not be a novel phenomenon because EC rules too may be agreed in anticipation of local control and space for creative compliance,[84] but, even if the risk of greater reluctance pre-agreement consequent on tighter control post-agreement is real, I consider this to be a price worth paying in order to inject real meaning into the pursuit of the Commission's stated post-1992 and post-Delors goal of "better lawmaking", a notion which should be taken to encompass both laws on paper and laws enforced on the ground.[85]

My anxiety lies in the risk that relative neglect of under-implementation of EC laws which establish protective standards affecting, *inter alia*, workers, the environment and consumers is not indefinitely tolerable. There is a corrosive dynamic inherent in turning a blind-eye to the mishandling at national level of agreed Community laws of this nature. As suggested above, the Court, by refusing in *Hedley Lomas* to contemplate blockages to trade as a permissible form of response to perceived under-implementation of laws of market (re-)regulation elsewhere, may have defended the constitutional orthodoxy of an EC system which has transcended retaliation as a remedy, but unwittingly it may have given incentives to pursuit of a more subtle form of retaliation based on reduction in domestic costs of compliance. If there is any truth in this hypothesis about state practice, then a downward spiral in rigour of even and effective enforcement is the consequence.[86]

In the EC, States may formally agree to measures which they would prefer not to sign up to, because to do so is part of the "package" which, overall, they wish to see adopted. It takes little imagination to suppose that there is a temptation

[84] For example V. Eichener, "Effective European problem-solving: lessons from the regulation of occupational safety and environmental protection"(1997) 4 *JEPP* 591 at 605.

[85] See generally C. Timmermans, "How can one improve the quality of Community legislation?" (1997) 34 *CMLRev* 1229.

[86] Competitive under-implementation is not necessarily the preserve of the administration alone. It is not without interest in this context to observe the close similarities between the reasoning of the Bundesverfassungsgericht on how and why EC acts may be reviewed at national level and that subsequently offered by the Danish Supreme Court. There is a form of horizontal co-operation between national courts which may generate an expanding challenge to EC law as understood in Luxembourg. See Weatherill and Beaumont (1999), note 14, above, chap. 12.

to dilute the consequences of the downside of that package in the post-agreement phase. This need not be a treacherous tale of agreement given in the full knowledge that compliance will be selective. One must take care not to overestimate the strategy of "States" as monolithic structures, for the post-agreement phase may be remote from the agreement phase, and it may be that the arm of the State which agrees a measure will have a quite different agenda from that which comes subsequently to enforce it. The enforcement agency may plausibly have been wholly uninvolved in the decision-making process, and, when presented with an EC *fait accompli*, may find its absorption into domestic practice, at best, awkward. Budgetary constraints will typically loom large. This is of course poor regulatory practice; efficient rule-making demands close connection between the policy-making phase and the policy-enforcement phase lest the former underestimate or misunderstand the practical problems and in consequence design an inapt system.[87] But such a lack of co-ordination is frequent in any system of governance and especially common in a transnational system such as the EU. Moreover, variation in administrative tradition among the Member States makes it improbable that a regime can be shaped at EC level that is suitable for effective enforcement in all or even most Member States. There is a temporal aspect too. The national government which finds itself responsible for enforcing agreed EC rules might be a newly elected administration which never would have agreed to the rule in the first place, and which is accordingly tempted to diminish its domestic impact. Or governments may have agreed to rules for short-term electoral gain even if the rule is costly in the long term. It is overstating the coherence of policy making to posit a direct chain between tactical acceptance of rules at EC level and their subsequent under-implementation at national level, although that does not mean that it never happens. The broad conclusion is that improving compliance rates in the EC is a multi-faceted non-trivial task.[88]

8. CONCLUSION

The EC is ripe for "competitive under-implementation". The risk is especially severe where any damage felt as a result of such laxity is likely to be felt by out-of-state interests, for example in the shape of environmental harm suffered elsewhere or by consumers resident in other Member States. Why would a Member State strive scrupulously to regulate "its" providers if the parties who will benefit are out-of-state consumers?[89] This suggests an agenda for a race to the

[87] R. Baldwin, "Why rules don't work"(1990) 53 *MLR* 321; more generally, R. Baldwin and M. Cave *Understanding Regulation* (Oxford: Oxford University Press, 1999); A. Ogus, *Regulation* (Oxford: Clarendon Press, 1994).

[88] *Cf.* P. Van den Bossche, "In search of remedies for non-compliance: the Experience of the EC" (1996) 3 *MJ* 371.

[89] On legal and practical obstacles to control of misleading practices directed at French consumers by traders based in Germany, see H. Micklitz, "Cross-Border Consumer Conflicts – a French–German Experience" (1993) 16 *JCP* 411. See now Directive 98/27, note 68, above.

bottom not in rule-setting – for which there is negligible evidence in Europe and indeed it has been explained above that there is frequently a powerful coalition of interest in surpassing the unpredictability of a market based on fragmented national regimes[90] – but rather in applying agreed Community rules. The political conditions of mature democracies make racing to the bottom in regulatory protection unpalatable, at least other than in niche areas, but this may be less true in relation to rule-applying. Part of the perceived appeal of competitive under-implementation is the point that it is hard to track, which ought to make its examination much more problematic than the more concrete phenomenon of racing to the bottom in rule-setting. Moreover, the nature of competitive under-implementation is that it may occur at many different points and via many different actors. It is a complex, subtle and only partially visible phenomenon. It is the absence of comprehensive data that places limits on the ambition of the analysis here presented. There is some evidence. Jordan, for example, finds elements of "post-decisional" attempts by the UK to reduce the costs of implementing EC rules on bathing water although he also demonstrates that policing of such tactics was rather effective.[91] Part of the intriguingly complex story of "competitive under-implementation" is that States may seek to offset costs of agreed rules but it may also emerge that there are unintended effects of the bargain struck which alter, and deepen, the impact of EC rules, a pattern which implicates questions of how short the leash held by Member States over the EC's influence really is.

The purpose of this inquiry, of course, has not been simply to point to aspects of under-implementation in EC law of market (re-)regulation. It is hardly a new phenomenon in any legal system that there are impediments to the effective enforcement of diffuse interests. The purpose of this inquiry is to identify distinctive aspects of the issue in the EC context; and to explore incentives for improvement in effective enforcement. I write from the standpoint that without attention being paid to the phenomena of actual and/or perceived under-implementation there is a corrosive dynamic at work in the EC. Enlargement may deepen the problem. As yet, however, the emphasis remains on "indirect rule" supplemented by greater transparency and administrative co-ordination as a basis for securing the even and effective enforcement of EC law in the Member States. There may be space for imaginative elision of the two limbs of "dual vigilance", for example involving greater access by not only national bodies but also Community entities to national judicial and administrative procedures in pursuit of better compliance through complementary supervisory activity. The Court's refusal to allow horizontal direct effect to directives deserves re-visiting, at least in circumstances where acceptance of the possibility would contribute to righting the implementation imbalance against laws of

[90] See Hix (1999), note 37, above, chapter 8, including survey of the literature.

[91] A. Jordan, "European Community Water Policy Standards: Locked in or Watered Down?" (1999) 37 *JCMS* 13 . See also D. Noble, "Enforcing EC Environmental Law: the National Dimension" in Somsen (1996), note 43, above.

market (re-)regulation. But at present the Member States, though anxious to minimise the potential for post-agreement defection which robs Community-level bargains of their potency and credibility, remain even more anxious about the institutional and constitutional consequences of moving beyond reliance on Commission supervision and the role of the European Court and its national judicial allies.

5

The Scope of European Remedies: The Case of Purely Internal Situations and Reverse Discrimination

MIGUEL POIARES MADURO

1. INTRODUCTION

THE EUROPEAN COURT of Justice has consistently refused to award EC law protection to cases it defines as purely internal to a Member State. Purely internal situations fall outside the scope of EC law and the Court refuses to intervene. This approach, which on its face appears a simple logical deduction from the scope of EC law, is in reality embedded in numerous problems and criticisms. In fact, the concept of purely internal situations has been used mainly to justify the lack of protection granted by EC law to numerous cases of reverse discrimination where a State does not extend to its own nationals the same treatment it is required by EC law to award to nationals of Member States. In other words, reverse discrimination occurs when the remedies granted by EC law are not available to nationals in their own State. Reverse discrimination has been treated mainly as a problem for Member States, whose legislation discriminates against their own nationals. The fact that reverse discrimination may originate from a more favourable treatment conferred by EC law on nationals of other Member States is usually ignored, as is the fact that the EC law dimension of this problem means that it can only be properly addressed at that level. Moreover, as we will see there are frequently no remedies available in national law.

In this chapter I will review the judicial treatment of purely internal situations and reverse discrimination in order to highlight the institutional dimension of the question of European remedies. In doing this, I will suggest that a sophisticated comparative institutional analysis may offer us valuable new insights into the question of remedies and lead us to some counter-intuitive proposals; notably, I will argue that national institutions may provide better European remedies and vice-versa. Section 2 looks at the approach of the Court regarding the concept of purely internal situations and the scope of EU remedies, it presents logical and normative problems which are aggravated in the light of recent developments in EC law. Section 3 will show the relevance of EC law to the problems posed by reverse discrimination and purely internal situations. Section 4 suggests a new approach to deal with purely internal situations and reverse discrimination and the remedies available at national and European level. It will be argued that reverse discrimination is within the jurisdiction of EC law, but that the consequence of this should not be the extension of the judicial remedies awarded by the Court of Justice to cases of reverse discrimination. However, as national law may often not provide sufficient protection in such cases, EC law should empower national courts to review cases of reverse discrimination: since the interests affected are exclusively domestic, national courts are the ideal institution to perform that role.

2. PURELY INTERNAL SITUATIONS AND REVERSE DISCRIMINATION

The concept of purely internal situations was developed in parallel with the treatment given by the Court of Justice to cases of reverse discrimination. The latter occurs when a Member State is required by EC law to confer rights on nationals of other Member States which it does not extend to its own nationals, therefore giving rise to discrimination against the latter. The three paradigmatic cases where the Court of Justice established the core of its approach to reverse discrimination and purely internal situations are *Knoors*,[1] *Auer*,[2] and *Saunders*.[3] Since these cases have already been the subject of detailed analysis in legal writing I will limit myself to note the main conclusions that can and have been drawn from them.

Mr Knoors was a Dutch national, residing in Belgium where he had been working as a central heating and sanitary contractor. He applied for authorisation to carry on the same trade in his country of origin. The Dutch authorities, however, refused to grant him such permission on the grounds that he did not possess the necessary qualifications. According to the Dutch authorities, he could not rely on Directive 64/427, which obliges Member States to accept as sufficient proof of qualification the actual practice of the activity in question in another Member State. Being a Dutch national, they argued, he could not be considered a beneficiary within the meaning of Article 4(1) of the Directive.

The question to be answered by the Court was thus whether a national could be considered as a beneficiary of the Directive *vis-à-vis* his own State? The Court reached the conclusion that Directive 64/427 was based on a broad notion of "beneficiaries" covering nationals of all Member States independently of their residence or nationality "*provided that they come objectively within one of the situations provided for by the directive*".[4] The situations which "come objec-

[1] Case 115/78 *Knoors* v. *Secretary of State for Economic Affairs* [1979] ECR 399. See also Case 246/80 *Broekmeulen* v. *Huisarts Registratie Commissie* [1981] ECR 2311.

[2] Case 136/78 *Criminal proceedings against Auer* [1979] ECR 437.

[3] Case 175/78 *R* v. *Saunders* [1979] ECR 1129.

[4] *Saunders*, note 3, above, para. 17, emphasis added.

tively within one of the situations provided for" either by the Directive or by EC law in general came to be established as *those situations which are not purely internal to a Member State*. This is not the case when nationals of a Member State "owing to the fact that they have lawfully resided on the territory of another Member State and have there acquired a trade qualification which is recognised by the provisions of EC law, are, with regard to their State of origin, in a situation, which may be assimilated to that of any other persons enjoying the rights and liberties guaranteed by the Treaty".[5]

The concept of a "purely internal situation" mentioned in *Knoors*, was applied for the first time in *Saunders*. Ms Saunders, a British national, had been released by Bristol Crown Court on the condition, which she accepted, that she go back to Northern Ireland and not return to England or Wales for three years. She did not however comply with this order and was later arrested. The problem before the Court concerned the extent to which nationals could rely on Article 39 EC (ex Article 48) against their own State. Although Article 39 makes no distinction between nationals in their own or in other Member States and although (as emphasised by Advocate General Warner) the exact wording is: "to move freely within the territory of Member States" and not "to move freely from one Member State to another", the Court interpreted the aim of the Article as being "to abolish the legislation of the Member States provisions (. . .) according to which *a worker who is a national of another Member State* is subject to more severe treatment or is placed in an unfavourable situation in law or in fact as compared with the situation of a national in the same circumstances".[6] It conceded that Article 39 could give rights to nationals against their own State but, according to the Court, the provisions of the Treaty do not concern "situations which are wholly internal to a Member State".[7] The closest it came to a definition of this was in stating that they were situations "where there is no factor connecting them to any of the situations envisaged by Community Law".[8]

The use of the concept of "purely internal situations" to define the scope of the protection granted by EC law against reverse discrimination has been, albeit in different words, progressively extended to other areas, especially, the free movement of goods. In cases dealing with free movement of goods and the principle of non-discrimination on the basis of nationality the Court developed an approach on reverse discrimination which although based – at least in part – on different arguments from those used in *Knoors* and *Saunders*, comes to the same result. This policy, first suggested in *Cognet*[9] and *Edah*,[10] was made explicit in

[5] *Ibid*, para. 24. This has been restated by the Court in the field of freedom to provide services, see Case 292/86 *Gullung* v. *Conseil de l'ordre des avocats du barreau de Colmar et de Saverne* [1988] ECR 111, para. 11.

[6] *Saunders*, note 3, above, para. 9, emphasis added.

[7] *Ibid*, para. 11.

[8] *Ibid*.

[9] Case 355/85 *Commissioner of Police, Thouars* v. *Cognet* [1986] ECR 3231, para. 11.

[10] Joined Cases 80 and 159/85 *Nederlands Bakkerij Stichting and Others* v. *Edah BV* [1986] ECR 3359, para. 23.

Mathot[11] where the Court stated that "treatment which works to the detriment of national products as compared with imported products and which is put into effect by a Member State in a sector which is not subject to Community rules or in relation to which there has been no harmonization of national laws does not come within the scope of Community Law."[12] Since, according to the Court, the purpose of Article 28 EC (ex Article 30) "is to eliminate obstacles to the importation of goods and not to ensure that goods of national origin always enjoy the same treatment as imported goods",[13] cases of reverse discrimination over the free movement of goods are outside the scope of EC law. The only exception is for re-imported goods.[14] This interpretation of Article 28 is settled case-law[15] and it is now commonplace for the Court to phrase its decisions on Article 28 so that they cover the treatment of imported products alone.[16] In cases of reverse discrimination there are no remedies available for home nationals who cannot prove a cross-border link. The logic of the Court's reasoning is, *prima facie*, straightforward: no remedy is available under EC law because those cases are not within the scope of EC law. But the important question then arises: what brings a situation within the scope of EC law? The case-law of the Court gives us two main criteria to ascertain the connection of a particular fact with the Community legal order: the degree of legal integration and the existence of a cross-border element.

The notion of purely internal situations

The notion of purely internal situations varies depending on the area of EC law which is invoked. A given situation may or may not come under EC law depending on the rule applicable and on the degree of legal integration in that area.

[11] Case 98/86 *Criminal proceedings against Mathot* [1987] ECR 809.

[12] *Ibid*, para. 9.

[13] *Ibid*, para. 7. See also *Cognet*, note 9, above, para. 10, and *Edah*, note 10, above, para. 18.

[14] See Case 229/83 *Association des Centres distributeurs Édouard Leclerc and Others* v. *SARL "Au blé vert"and Others (Prix du Libre)* [1985] ECR 1, para. 26, and *Cognet*, note 9, above, para.10.

[15] See also Joined Cases 314 to 316/81 and 83/82 *Procureur de la République* v. *Waterkeyn* [1982] ECR 4337.

[16] See, among others: Case 94/82 *Criminal proceedings against De Kikvorsch Groothandel-Import-Export BV* [1983] ECR 947, para. 13; Case 176/84 *Commission* v. *Greece (Greek beer purity law)* [1987] ECR 1193, para. 46; Case 298/87 *Proceedings against Smanor* [1988] ECR 4489, para. 25; Case 302/86 *Commission* v. *Denmark (Danish bottles)* [1988] ECR 4607, para. 22; Case C–362/88 *GB-INNO-BM* v. *Confédération du commerce luxembourgeois* [1990] ECR I–667, para. 20. See, however, the decision in *Lancry*, a case concerning Article 23 EC (ex Article 9) and a regional levy of charges exhibiting the features of dock dues from a French overseas department. The Court stated: "It is not disputed that dock dues apply to all products entering the overseas department concerned, irrespective of their origin. It would accordingly be inconsistent to hold, on the one hand, that dock dues constitute charges having equivalent effect in so far as they are levied on goods from other Member States and to concede, on the other, that those dues do not constitute charges having equivalent effect where they are levied on goods from metropolitan France": Joined Cases C–363/93, C–407/93, C–409/93, C–410/93, C–411/93 *Lancry* v. *Direction Generale des Douanes* [1994] ECR I–3957, at para. 30. This decision raises the question as to whether or not the same reasoning can be applied to Article 28.

There are rules of Community law which the Court interprets as applicable to situations in which all elements are situated within one State; thus, situations which the Court would normally consider as "purely internal" and outside the scope of EC law. There are also different degrees of legal integration, which extend or restrict the scope of the remedies awarded by EC law and the way in which it encroaches upon national legal systems. An example of a rule which applies to situations whose facts may be wholly internal to a Member State is Article 141 EC (ex Article 119).[17] The same is generally the case where there is a common organisation of the market.[18] The reason for this is either an intention to prevent competition based on factors such as low pay for women;[19] or the existence of EU aims and policies which treat individuals as the "peoples of Europe" without reference to their nationality[20] or both.[21] Hence, there are EC rules which apply even in the "absence of any element going beyond a purely national setting".[22] In these areas, remedies against reverse discrimination are available at the EU level. The core of EC law – including the four freedoms and competition rules[23] – is not subject to that broader application but secondary legislation may extend the scope of application of these EC rules and prevent reverse discrimination. Community legislation regarding market integration may apply to purely internal situations, covering national persons and products in circumstances which would otherwise have no link with EC law.[24]

This linking of the remedies available for reverse discrimination to the degree of legal integration already highlights the fact that the treatment given by the Court to cases of reverse discrimination does not depend upon the principle of equality but upon the specific EU goals of each area of the EU legal order. Therefore, EC law is only applicable if, apart from any violation of the principle of equality and non-discrimination, the individual can claim that the specific

[17] The wording leaves no doubt in this respect. The Court has confirmed the scope and the aims of Article 141 in Case 43/75 *Defrenne* v. *Sabena (No. 2)* [1976] ECR 455.

[18] See Case 207/86 *Apesco* v. *Commission* [1988] ECR 2151, para. 23 and Case C–370/88 *Procurator Fiscal* v. *Marshall* [1990] ECR I–4071. In the latter case, the Court also stated that: ". . . such a difference in treatment is capable of constituting discrimination contrary to Article 40(3) of the Treaty [now Article 34(3) EC] only if it is arbitrary, that is to say, lacking sufficient justification and not based on objective criteria". See paras. 24 to 26.

[19] See *Defrenne (No. 2)*, note 17, above, para. 9.

[20] *Ibid*, para. 10.

[21] Note however that fundamental rights in the EC do not generally enjoy this status. There is no incorporation of Community fundamental rights (including those of non-discrimination) into the national legal orders.

[22] An expression used by the Court to define purely internal situations outside the scope of Community law on free movement: Case 20/87 *Ministère Public* v. *Gauchard* [1987] ECR 4879, para. 12.

[23] In *Michelin* the Court considered that competition rules are applicable to cases limited to the territory of a Member State. However, such situations must still be capable of affecting trade between Member States in order to fall within the scope of Community law. See Case 322/81 *Michelin* v. *Commission* [1983] ECR 3461. Nevertheless, the criterion which must be met to prove a link with Community law under the competition rules appear to be less rigorous than in other areas. See Case C–41/90 *Höfner* v. *Macrotron GmbH* [1991] ECR I–1979: compare paras. 33 and 39.

[24] For an example see Case C–241/89 *SARPP* v. *Chambre syndicale des raffineurs et conditionneurs de sucre de France and others* [1990] ECR I–4695, at para. 16.

EC law goal dominating that area of the law is affected. Discrimination arising from the different treatment given by national and EC law to similar situations is not, in itself, sufficient to claim the application of the Community legal order. As a consequence, the protection afforded in cases of reverse discrimination in the area of free movement will be a function of the need to protect free movement and not the principle of equality. The rationale for the more limited scope of European remedies available in the area of free movement becomes clearer if we review the construction of the concept of purely internal situations by the Court. At the same time, this will allow us to note the present instability and incoherence of the purely internal criterion as developed by the Court, which relies strongly on the existence of a cross-border element.

The Court of Justice has made repeated use of the concept of "purely internal situations" in determining whether a situation has a link with EC law.[25] In *Moser*[26] the Court considered that the situation was purely internal even if by reason of the rules imposed by a State on its nationals their freedom of movement to another Member State was restricted (at least, where this restriction was linked with a purely hypothetical perspective of a job in another Member State). Similarly, a *remote possibility* of restriction on the importation of goods arising from limitations imposed by a State on the freedom of establishment of its own nationals does not provide a sufficient link with EC law.[27] The same is the case if by the restriction imposed on nationals the *mere possibility* of these to provide services to nationals of other Member States is diminished.[28] Finally, the fact that a national may be "forced" to leave his/her State and move to another Member State in order to enjoy the same treatment as nationals of other

[25] For recent examples see for example Joined Cases C–225 to 227/95 *Anestis Kapasakalis and others* v. *Greek state* [1998] ECR I–4239; Case C–152/94 *Criminal proceedings against Van Buynder* [1995] ECR I–3981; Case C–60/91 *Criminal proceedings against Batista Morais* [1992] ECR I–2085; Case C–132/93 *Volker Steen* v. *Deutsche Bundespost (No. 2)* [1994] ECR I–2715; Case C–294/89 *Commission* v. *France (lawyers services)* [1991] I–3591; *Höfner*, note 23, above; Joined cases C–297/88 and C–197/89 *Dzodzi* v. *Belgium* [1990] ECR I–3763; Case C–61/89 *Criminal proceedings against Bouchoucha* [1990] ECR I–3551; Joined Cases C–54/88, C–91/88 and C–14/89 *Criminal proceedings against Eleanora Nino* [1990] ECR I–3537; Case 204/87 *Criminal proceedings against Guy Bekaert* [1988] ECR 2029.

[26] Case 180/83 *Moser* v. *Land Baden-Württemberg* [1984] ECR 2539.

[27] See *Gauchard*, note 22, above, and *Bekaert*, note 25, above. The facts of these two cases are identical.

[28] In paragraph 39 of *Höfner*, note 23, above, when referring to the possible application of Articles 12 and 43 EC to this case, the Court stated: "Such a situation displays no link with any of the situations envisaged by Community law. That finding cannot be invalidated by the fact that a contract concluded between the recruitment consultants and the undertaking concerned includes the theoretical possibility of seeking German candidates resident in other Member States or nationals of other Member States". But this seems in contradiction to the position of the Court, interestingly restated in this case and first revealed in *Michelin*, note 23, above, that competition rules are applicable to cases limited to the territory of one Member State, this being susceptible to constituting a "substantial part" of the Common Market. These must be applied on condition that trade between Member States may be affected. This reasoning should also be valid for other areas, such as Article 49 EC, or at least when competition is indirectly at stake as often occurs with reverse discrimination, especially in the free movement of goods.

Member States have within his/her own State does not constitute a sufficient link with EC law.[29]

This last decision expressly stated an idea which was already present in the previous cases: that for a national to be able to invoke EC law against his/her own State, he/she must previously have exercised freedom of movement within the European Union (meaning from one State to another).[30] The same occurs in free movement of goods where national goods exported and then re-imported are the only national goods to which Article 28 applies.[31] The exercise of free movement or the nationality of another Member State provide the necessary link for a connection to EC law to be recognised by the Court. Only if a cross-border element exists does the situation fall within the scope of EC law. Where this is the case, the Court may protect home nationals against reverse discrimination. If no such element exists, the situation is purely internal and outside the scope of EC law.

Problems and inconsistencies in the definition of purely internal situations

Protection granted by EC law also covers nationals against their home State *but only to the extent considered necessary to protect EU free movement and the construction of the internal market*. Protection of home-nationals by EC law is a result of free movement rules, not of the principle of equality.[32] As the Court stated in *Knoors*:

> these liberties, which are fundamental in the Community system, could not be fully realized if the Member States were in a position to refuse to grant the benefit of the provisions of Community law to those of their nationals who have taken advantage of the facilities existing in the matter of freedom of movement and establishment and who have acquired, by virtue of such facilities, the trade qualifications referred to by the directive in a Member State other than that whose nationality they possess.[33]

Free movement *to another State*[34] would be limited if individuals could not make use of the qualifications which they had acquired there when returning to

[29] As suggested by the referring national court in Case C–332/90 *Volker Steen* v. *Deutsche Bundepost (No. 1)* [1992] ECR I–341.

[30] *Ibid*, para. 12. See also Joined Cases 35 and 36/82 *Morson and Jhanjan*,v. *The Netherlands* [1982] ECR 3723, para. 17.

[31] *Leclerc (Prix du Libre)*, note 14, above; and *Cognet*, note 9, above.

[32] Lenaerts has already noted this: ". . . the prohibition of reverse discrimination, where it exists, is, in reality, a functional extension of the economic freedoms that underlie the community market, more than an application in direct line of the principle of equality" (author's translation). K. Lenaerts, *L'égalité de traitement en droit communautaire: un principe unique aux apparences multiples*' (1991) 27 *CDE* 3 at 19. For Benedettelli, "it is evident that the prohibition of discrimination on grounds of nationality is applied only in circumstances relevant to the aims of the integration process . . ." (author's translation). A. Benedettelli, *Il giudizio di eguaglianza nell'ordinamento giuridico delle Communità europee* (Padova: CEDAM, 1989), at 222.

[33] *Knoors*, note 1, above, para. 20.

[34] *Ibid*. The Commission (in accordance with a view already expressed in Case 71/76 *Thieffry* v. *Conseil de l'ordre des avocats à la Cour de Paris* [1977] ECR 765) seemed to have a broader

their home State or if they were, in any way, disadvantaged by the fact they had gone to live in another Member State. However, the confusion between the aim of protecting free movement and the exercise of free movement as the element ascertaining a connection with EC law may lead the Court to apply EC rules even when that goal is not at stake. In other words, once a cross-border element exists EC law will apply even if there is no impact on free movement. In *Singh*, decided on the basis of a cross-border element, the Court concluded that a national could be *deterred from leaving* his country of origin if a State would apply to him/her the same national law it would have applied had he/she remained.[35]

In this case, the spouse of a British national argued that the rights of residence given by Community law to the spouse and children of a national of a Member State who resides in the territory of another Member State in order to pursue an economic activity, should also apply when the national returns to her/his home State after having pursued an economic activity in another Member State. This right was recognised by the Court, not as a right of free movement *to one's own Member State*, nor by reason of the principle of equality. The right to accompany a spouse on his return to his home State arose from the need to protect the original freedom of movement *to another State*. In the words of the Court:

> A national of a Member State might be deterred from leaving his country of origin in order to pursue an activity as an employed or self-employed person as envisaged by the Treaty in the territory of another Member State if, on returning to the Member State of which he is a national in order to pursue an activity there as an employed or self-employed person, the conditions of his entry and residence were not at least equivalent to those which he would enjoy under the Treaty or secondary law in the territory of another Member State.
>
> He would in particular be deterred from so doing if his spouse and children were not also permitted to enter and reside in the territory of his Member State of origin under conditions at least equivalent to those granted them by Community law in the territory of another Member State.[36]

This argument raises serious doubts. How can a national be *deterred from leaving* his country of origin if a State applies to him the same law it would have applied had he remained? He may be *deterred from leaving* if he knows that the rights of residence which his spouse has under Community law are not applica-

understanding of free movement of persons as granting "all nationals of each of the Member States (. . .) the opportunity to carry on their livelihoods by establishing themselves or providing services in any place within the Community". A similar reasoning, not requiring a cross-frontier link, was also made by Advocate General Reischl in *Knoors*, at 415: "the first paragraph of Article 52 [new Article 43 EC], which moreover in no way precludes a guarantee of freedom of establishment going beyond its wording must in any case not be interpreted as meaning that it permits discrimination against nationals of the Member States no matter what circumstances". The Commission however came to limit its position in future cases, following the Court's requirement of a cross-frontier or international element.

[35] Case C–370/90 *R* v. *Immigration Appeal Tribunal and Surinder Singh, ex parte Secretary of State for Home Department* [1992] ECR I–4265].

[36] *Ibid*, paras. 19 and 20.

ble in his own State. But that is not an obstacle to the freedom of movement *to another Member State* since he would be treated exactly the same way whether or not he had exercised free movement. Nationals are deterred from moving *to another Member State* in two cases: if upon their return their position is worse off than if they had remained; or if they were prevented from enjoying any goods or qualification obtained during their stay in the other Member State. That was not the case in *Singh*.

The right to take one's family with one when moving to another Member State exists so that nationals are not deterred from moving, and so that they enjoy the advantages (whether economic, social, cultural or legal) provided by that Member State. The right is given to allow people to choose among States with different rules, i.e. is instrumental to the freedom of movement, but not a reason for free movement itself. The cross-border element in *Singh* led the Court to give some nationals *vis-à-vis* their home State a "bonus" right that is in no way linked with the protection of their freedom of movement to another Member State.

These inconsistencies are the result of an approach that d'Oliveira has characterised as geographical not juridical.[37] D'Oliveira notes that in private international law there are two approaches to the distinction between internal and international cases:[38] the "geographical" and the "juridical" approaches. The first focuses on the facts of the cases; the second on a claim of application of the legal system.[39] The "juridical" approach, advocated by d'Oliveira, will "catch the Community cases with the net of Community norms and principles that, given their purposes and policies, claim application to certain categories of cases".[40] The geographical approach, on the other hand, concentrates on the legal relationship in order to ascertain the existence of a fact connecting it with the Community legal order. D'Oliveira says that "whether or not the Community legal system is brought in cannot depend, at any rate not exclusively, on some sort of catalogue of contacts or factual points of reference".[41] For example, as in *Singh*, why should a UK citizen who has lived in another Member State be given the right to bring his/her third-country spouse into the UK while the same is denied to a UK citizen who is also married to a third-country national but has always lived in the UK? As argued by Pickup the present need for a "linking factor" operates as an arbitrary distinction.[42] The

[37] H.U.J. d'Oliveira, "Is reverse discrimination still possible under the Single European Act?" in *Forty years on: the evolution of postwar private international law in Europe: symposium in celebration of the 40th anniversary of the Centre of Foreign Law and Private International Law, University of Amsterdam, on 27 October 1989* (Deventer: Kluwer, 1990), at 73*ff*.

[38] *Ibid*, at 73, referring to the work of L. Strikwerda, *Inleiding tot het Nederlandse internationaal privaatrecht* (Groningen: Wolters-Noordhoff, 1988).

[39] *Ibid*, 73–4.

[40] *Ibid*, at 74.

[41] He adds that "it depends partly, perhaps even predominantly, on the very teleology and dynamics of the Community legal system". D'Oliveira (1990), note 37, above, at 75.

[42] D.M.W. Pickup, "Reverse Discrimination and Freedom of Movement for Workers" (1986) 23 *CMLRev* 135 at 154.

present approach raises problems of consistency between the aims of EC law and the scope of its remedies (coming down either to a more restrictive or expansive application).[43]

The current approach is also difficult to sustain in light of the dynamics of the legal integration process. European legal integration is expanding. This means that fewer and fewer situations can remain insulated from EC law, claiming not to have a European connection. The higher degree of integration will mean that it will no longer be sustainable to make the availability of European remedies dependent on an arbitrary factual connection given the principle of non-discrimination between European citizens in an internal market. The creation of a European Union citizenship, the expansion of the principle of equality and the ever growing importance given to the protection of fundamental rights by the European Union will require a substantive and not a formal solution to the problem of reverse discrimination. The European Union is no longer directed to economic agents but to European Union citizens. Reverse discrimination will therefore be re-proposed as a problem of discrimination among the citizens of the Union.

Discriminatory treatment with the consequent competitive distortions can no longer be dependent on incidental facts related to the crossing of frontiers (which by now should not exist) but on its compatibility with the aims and efficiency of the internal market and the principle of equality. As stressed by d'Oliveira, "aiming at an internal market, or completing it, while at the same time continuing to attach importance to the crossing of national frontiers is self-contradictory".[44] This means that the Court will have, sooner or later, either to prohibit all cases of reverse discrimination or to find a new basis to distinguish acceptable and non-acceptable reverse discrimination under EC law. The underlying idea of purely internal situations (that there are rights and remedies better left to national legal orders) should not be abandoned but it must be grounded in different criteria.

Moreover, when secondary legislation exists the problem of reverse discrimination becomes a problem of the treatment given or authorised by EC law with regard to nationals of different Member States. In spite of this, the Court has always limited itself to identifying the scope and the degree of harmonisation sought by Community secondary legislation without reviewing the validity of the provisions that either apply exclusively to nationals in other Member States or allow Member States to impose stricter requirements on their own nationals.[45] In *Gallaher*, the Court expressly recognised that the exclusion of national

[43] For examples of situations in which the present criterion can lead to the application of Community law, independently of any connection with the protection of free movement or other Community aim, see the hypothetical cases raised by C. Greenwood, "Limits on free movement of persons in EEC law" (1987) 7 *YEL* 185, 202–3.

[44] D'Oliveira (1990), note 37, above, at 84.

[45] See *Knoors*, note 1, above, and the Dutch Government's argument that Directive 64/427 established a discriminatory treatment between home and foreign nationals. Although the Court seemed to consider, rightly from my point of view, that in the present case equal treatment was guaranteed

products from the scope of application of Directive 73/173 created reverse discrimination:

> Admittedly, as the applicants in the main proceedings have pointed out, this interpretation of the provisions may imply less favourable treatment for national products in comparison with imported products and leaves in existence some inequalities in conditions of competition. However, those consequences are attributable to the degree of harmonization sought by the provisions in question, which lay down minimum requirements.[46]

The logical question which should have followed such a statement would concern the validity of the Directive (or of that interpretation made of it) under the principle of equality in EC law. When it is Community secondary legislation which discriminates or authorises discrimination among home nationals or products and foreign nationals or imports, the issue is no longer a "purely internal" one, and the relevant question is the validity and acceptability of that discrimination. The non-availability of remedies to home nationals in these cases is a consequence of the discrimination inserted in those EU rights. This can no longer be ignored by the Court.

The European character of the question of remedies in purely internal situations and reverse discrimination becomes obvious if we compare the scope of protection granted by EC law with the origins of reverse discrimination and the problems in providing national remedies for these cases.

3. REVERSING REVERSE DISCRIMINATION

Contrary to first appearances, reverse discrimination is not so much a problem of the less favourable treatment given by States to their own nationals as of the more favourable treatment granted by EC law to nationals of other Member States. Pickup hinted at this when he said that "reverse discrimination arises when a national of a Member State is disadvantaged because he or she may not rely on a protective provision of EC law when a national of another Member State, in otherwise, identical circumstances may rely on that same provision".[47] States do not, in general, want to discriminate against their own nationals. Reverse discrimination normally occurs because EC law obliges States to treat nationals of other Member States in a way which – by reasons of their own policies and aims – they did not originally intend to treat their own nationals. Where

by the conditions set out in Article 3 of the Directive (see para. 26 of the judgment), the statement in para. 25 appears to admit that Community provisions can place home nationals in a disadvantageous position *vis-à-vis* nationals of other Member States. Subsequent decisions confirm the idea that this entire issue is reduced by the Court to the interpretation of the scope of Directives: see, for instance, *Morson and Jhanjan*, note 30, above; *SARPP*, note 24, above, and Joined Cases C–251/90 and C–252/90 *Procurator Fiscal, Elgin* v. *Wood and Cowie* [1992] ECR I–2873.

[46] Case C–11/92 *R* v. *Secretary of State for Health, ex parte Gallaher Ltd and Others* [1993] ECR I–3545, para. 22.

[47] Pickup (1986), note 42, above, at 137.

States still consider it worthwhile to pursue these policies and aims by continuing to impose this treatment on their own nationals, reverse discrimination arises. If the Court of Justice does not find any factual connection with another State and in the absence of an explicit application of EC law to nationals against their own State, it considers those cases of discrimination as purely internal situations for which no European remedies are available.

But this "Pilate-solution" does not fit well with the European dimension of reverse discrimination. In fact, most cases of reverse discrimination are a result of EC law and no remedies may be available under national law. First, Community secondary legislation may apply only to nationals of other Member States and confer on them rights that are not given to nationals in their own State. Secondly, EC rules are often interpreted as requiring more than equal treatment: they are taken as demanding *with regard to foreign products and nationals only* the abolition of measures which, in spite of being non-discriminatory, affect free movement and economic integration. Thirdly, even when EC law is interpreted as only requiring equal treatment, the standard of comparison used to determine that equal treatment may, in fact, lead to a more favourable treatment for nationals or products of other Member States.

The criteria for the allocation of rights and determination of the applicable norms to home nationals and nationals of other Member States by EC law has been dominated by the concept of mutual recognition. Two visions of mutual recognition are present in European market integration. The first applies a test of equivalence among national rules: if, in spite of their "different forms [these rules] essentially come down to the same thing, [then they] should normally be accorded recognition in all Member States".[48] The second, acknowledges that some essential requirements must be guaranteed by all national rules but holds that in all places where these essential requirements do not apply, mutual recognition will be applied, even where different national rules are not equivalent, in order to create "competition among rules". While the latter clearly embodies the idea of reverse discrimination, the former may also give rise to cases of reverse discrimination. In theory, that should not be so with the first, but in practice, equivalence among national rules may be deemed to exist when in fact the conditions imposed by the different national rules or the circumstances of nationals subject to those rules are not the same or similar. This is the case even when mutual recognition is established by Community legislation. The aim of directives has been defined as to "establish broad criteria of comparability for the different activities so as to render the assimilation to the national effective".[49] However, these criteria of comparability may be defined in such a way that they benefit nationals of other Member States. Moreover, directives (and regulations) are concerned with increasing free movement beyond the considerations

[48] *Completing the Internal Market*, White Paper from the Commission to the European Council, COM (85) 310,final.

[49] S.D. Kon, "Aspects of Reverse Discrimination in Community Law", 6 *European Law Review* 75 at 80.

of non-discrimination. Fundamentally, harmonisation is not a process of declaring equivalence between national legislation: it is above all a process of independent legislation, in which all States may contribute, but the outcome of which may be a legal regime different (in both form and substance) from the regimes in all or some of the Member States. If this legal regime is restricted to the aim of ensuring free movement (if it applies exclusively to nationals and products of one Member State when they move to another State) reverse discrimination will arise if the legal regime applicable to nationals in their own State is stricter than the Community legal regime established in the Directives or Regulations.[50] A short analysis of these types of mutual recognition in the context of market integration rules will make even more clear the different forms of Community creation of reverse discrimination.

Mutual recognition as equivalence: the production of reverse discrimination and the principle of non-discrimination

Even in areas where non-discrimination has been portrayed as the controlling rationale behind EC law, reverse discrimination has come about as a side-effect of EC law. The general rule in free movement of persons and freedom to provide services has been, for a long period,[51] the principle of national treatment. It may therefore seem highly improbable that situations of reverse discrimination could have resulted from the application of those rules. If what EC law determines, according to the principle of national treatment, is that a State should treat nationals of other Member States in the same way that it treats its own, the latter will never be discriminated against in favour of the former. However, the principle of national treatment contains more than an obligation for States to apply the same legislation to its own nationals and to nationals of other Member States. The principle of national treatment dependent upon the principle of non-discrimination determines that nationals of other Member States should be treated the same as home nationals, which does not mean that they should be subject to the same rules. In reality, equal treatment may mean different treatment. It is well known that the principle of equality implies a criterion for ascertaining which are identical situations deserving similar treatment and which are different situations deserving different treatment. The principle of national treatment also requires such a criterion. The way in which this criterion is defined may, however, be responsible for situations of reverse discrimination.

[50] With respect to the free movement of persons and the freedom to provide services, Greenwood, note 43, above, at 195 writes that: "much of the secondary legislation which gives effect to Article 48 [new Article 39] and certain aspects of Article 52 [new Article 43] and 59 [new Article 49], however, is stated to apply only to cases in which a national of one Member State works, or seeks to work, in the territory of another Member State".

[51] On the relatively recent changes see Luigi Daniele, "Non-Discriminatory Restrictions to the Free Movement of Persons" (1997) 22 *ELRev* 191 and M.P. Maduro, "The Saga of Article 30 EC Treaty: To Be Continued" (1998) 5 *MJ* 298.

When applying a material notion of non-discrimination the Court may indeed use "questionable" standards of comparison, and in this way give rise not to equal treatment for nationals of other Member States but in fact to more favourable treatment, which Member States may not want to extend to their own nationals.

To determine what equal treatment in the field of the free movement of persons should consist of, the Court has elaborated what has been called the "principle of equivalence"[52] in parallel with its development in Community legislation as the initial face of mutual recognition. In *Webb*,[53] a case on the provision of services, the Court stated that the principle of equivalence imposes on States the obligation to "take into account the evidence and guarantees already furnished by the provider of the services for the pursuit of his activities in the Member State of his establishment".[54] In this way, it would seem that the principle of equivalence is the basis for a substantive or material principle of non-discrimination, which imposes on States the obligation to take into consideration the specific elements of each situation (and qualifications of each person) in order to determine which are identical situations deserving similar treatment and which are different situations deserving different treatment. A Member State must take into account the qualifications obtained by a national of another Member State in his country of origin since, although the requirements made in both Member States may be formally distinct, they can in substance be identical. Defined in this way, the principle of equivalence would not be likely to result in reverse discrimination. Home nationals could be subject to a different regime from that imposed on nationals of other Member States, but only to the extent to which this corresponds to distinct situations of fact capable of justifying the difference in treatment: formal reverse discrimination would correspond to material non-discrimination. Nevertheless, situations of reverse discrimination have resulted from the application of the principle of equivalence. A good example of this are those cases concerning the limits posed on the right of establishment and the freedom to provide services of lawyers by the principle of territoriality applicable in some States to the exercise of that profession. In *Klopp*[55] a German lawyer already established at a German Bar was denied admission to a French Bar as an "avocat" by the Paris Bar on the grounds that French law and the internal rules of the Paris Bar only allowed a principal and secondary set of chambers within the territorial jurisdiction of the *Tribunal de grande instance* in which he had registered. The Court rejected this restriction: "the existence of a second set of chambers in another Member State

[52] The first application of this principle was in *Thieffry*, note 34, above. See further P. Watson, "Freedom of Establishment and Freedom to Provide Services:Some Recent Developments" (1983) 20 *CMLRev*, 767.

[53] Case 279/80 *Criminal proceedings against Webb* [1981] ECR 3305.

[54] *Ibid*, para. 20. See also Joined cases 110 and 111/78 *Ministère public and "Chambre syndicale des agents artistiques et impresarii de Belgique"* ASBL v. *Willy van Wesemael and Others* [1979] ECR 35.

[55] Case 107/83 *Ordre des avocats au Barreau de Paris* v. *Klopp* [1984] ECR 2971.

does not prevent the application of the rules of ethics in the host Member State . . . (and) modern methods of transport and telecommunications facilitate proper contact with clients and the judicial authorities".[56] In this way the Court rejected the French authorities' denial of the right of establishment to *a national of another Member State* "on the grounds that he maintains chambers in another Member State".[57] The French Bar can still, however, refuse admission to a French lawyer solely on the grounds that he maintains chambers in another region of France.[58]

Mutual recognition as competition among rules: the production of reverse discrimination and the principle of free movement

Reverse discrimination can be conceived as a form of preserving some autonomy for States in defining their own goals and policies while, at the same time, promoting the free movement of nationals and products conforming with the minimum European standard. This underlies the new approach to harmonisation and its trust in minimum requirements and mutual recognition of national rules independently of an equivalence between those rules. One of the main characteristics of this approach was the transformation of reverse discrimination from a side-effect of integration into an instrument of integration. The new approach to harmonisation saw mutual recognition, essential or minimum requirements and reverse discrimination as the basis for Community legislation. Reverse discrimination and mutual recognition are, in this case, two sides of the same coin: the creation of a competitive process among different national rules. They lead to the possibility of States having different degrees and forms of regulation. Mutual recognition and minimum requirements provides an assurance to States with less strict regulations and/or conforming with the minimum requirements that these rules will be recognised by all Member States. Reverse discrimination recognises the right of States with stricter regulations to continue

[56] *Ibid*, para. 21.

[57] *Ibid*, para. 22.

[58] A similar result was reached in a case concerning the freedom of lawyers to provide services in Germany (Case 427/85 *Commission* v. *Germany* [1988] ECR 1123). Paragraphs 52(1) and (2) of the *Bundesrechtsanwaltsordnung* (Federal Law on the Legal Profession) determined the cases in which lawyers providing services were required to work under the authority of an authorised lawyer. The situations requiring the participation of, and dependence upon, an authorised lawyer were some civil cases occurring in the *Landgerichte*, matters of family law in the *Familiengerichte* and in the high courts (the *Oberlandesgerichte*, the *Bayerisches Oberstes Landesgericht* and the *Bundesgerichtshof*). This was justified by the German Government in the interest of the proper administration of justice. The Court of Justice prohibited the application of these rules to lawyers of other Member States providing services in Germany, making an exception only in the case of the *Bundesgerichtshof*. In all other cases the Court did not accept the "locality" principle. However, as questioned by the Advocate General Cruz Vilaça in his Opinion: is there any relevant difference between a lawyer of another Member State providing a service in Germany and a lawyer of one *Länder* providing a service in another *Länder*? The Court repeated its case law on the principle of territoriality in *Commission* v. *France (lawyers services)*, note 25, above.

to impose them but only with respect to their own nationals. This approach risks increasing the number of situations of reverse discrimination.[59] At the same time, it demonstrates that reverse discrimination is a European Union problem and not one "purely internal to a Member State". The extent to which EC law can accept reverse discrimination in order to promote economic integration under a system of competition among rules is a question the Court can no longer ignore. On the one hand, there are the values of market integration and the project of "competition among rules";[60] on the other, there is the principle of equality, and the risks of both distorted competition and of a "race to the bottom".

The same problem arises in the case of Community rules which are interpreted as requiring more than non-discrimination from States in order to promote free movement and the free exercise of economic activities. In these cases, the standard of treatment imposed by Community rules applicable to nationals and products from other Member States may often be more favourable than that to which domestic products and home nationals may be subject. That was traditionally the case with free movement of goods. The *Dassonville*[61] and *Cassis de Dijon*[62] case-law on measures having equivalent effect to quantitative restrictions on imports (which was valid for all national measures touching upon free movement of goods until *Keck*)[63] meant that national measures may be caught by the prohibition in Article 28 even if they do not discriminate in law or in fact against imported products. If a measure restricts the importation of goods it would have to be subject to a test of proportionality with regard to the aims of Article 30 and the mandatory requirements exception in *Cassis de Dijon*. After *Keck*, measures regulating the marketing of goods are no longer subject to such a close review. Nevertheless, we still have to observe what interpretation is made of the test of discrimination in law or in fact, in order to see if, as happened for the other freedoms, the assessment of *de facto* (material) discrimination will not result in fact in a more favourable treatment being accorded to imports. In the case of rules on product characteristics however the *Cassis de Dijon* doctrine is still applicable: if national rules do not pass the proportionality test they will not be acceptable, but only with respect to their application to imported or re-

[59] However, reverse discrimination as a consequence of the new approach to harmonisation has so far been limited by the fact that the implementation of the approach has not corresponded to its abstract definition.

[60] The fact that different rules will be recognised as valid under mutual recognition and reverse discrimination gives individuals and economic agents the possibility to choose under which rules to live or operate, and creates a competitive process that is expected to end with the victory of the better rules (harmonization ex-post). See, for example, the Padoa-Schioppa report from 1987 in T. Padoa-Schioppa *et al.*, *Efficiency, Stability and Equity* (Oxford: Oxford University Press, 1987) at 61; or G. Majone, *Market Integration and Regulation: Europe After 1992*, Working Papers, SPS 91/10 (European University Institute: Florence, 1991), 17*ff*.

[61] Case 8/74 *Procureur du Roi* v. *Dassonville* [1974] ECR 837.

[62] Case 120/78 *Rewe-Zentral AG* v. *Bundesmonopolverwaltung für Branntwein (Cassis de Dijon)* [1979] ECR 649.

[63] Joined Cases C–267/91 and C–268/91 *Criminal proceedings against Keck and Mithouard* [1993] ECR I–6097.

imported goods. This gives rise to situations of reverse discrimination. When a non-discriminatory national measure is struck down by the Court because it is capable of restricting free movement, but only with respect to imported products, its application to national products alone will discriminate against the latter. As the Court recognised in *Mathot*: "with regard to Article 30 of the EEC Treaty (new Article 28), it must be emphasized that the purpose of that provision is to eliminate obstacles to the importation of goods and not to ensure that goods of national origin always enjoy the same treatment as imported goods".[64] Thus, imported books in France cannot be subject to minimum prices but national books can;[65] beer imported to Germany may contain some additives that German beer may not;[66] and Italian pasta will still have to be made from durum wheat though Italian consumers can buy pasta not made from durum wheat imported into Italy from other Member States.[67] These are only some well known examples of reverse discrimination arising from the partial striking down of national rules under EC law. Following the idea of mutual recognition in *Cassis de Dijon*, national and imported products may compete under different rules in the same national market. The fact that national and imported products are subject to different requirements may generate competitive disadvantages burdening those producers subject to stricter and more costly standards. However, the Court accepts this, so that States may still pursue different policies. As stated in *Jongeneel Kaas*, "a Member State may legitimately pursue a policy based on quality in order to promote sales even if that policy exposes its producers to the risk of price competition from the producers of other Member States who are not bound by the same standards of quality".[68] The extent to which that State's policy will still be feasible in a context of competition of its producers with low cost products from other States is a key issue of reverse discrimination to be addressed below.

Recently, the Court has shifted the broad interpretation traditionally given to free movement of goods to the other free movement rules. Therefore, cases of reverse discrimination are bound to multiply themselves, reinforcing the calls for the ECJ to put an end to this type of discrimination. The issue was raised, for example, as a consequence of the *Bosman* decision which, according to the Court, only applies to the transfer of players between Member States. It, therefore, continued to allow the application of the old rules in the cases of players whose transfer takes place between two clubs of the same State. Should the Court have accorded a remedy for these cases?

[64] *Mathot*, above, note 11, para. 7.

[65] See *Leclerc (Prix du Libre)*, note 14, above, and *Cognet*, note 9, above.

[66] According to the *Reinheitsgebot*. See Case 178/84 *Commission* v. *Germany* (*German beer purity law*) [1987] ECR 1227.

[67] See Case 407/85 *3 Glocken* v. *USL* [1988] ECR 4233 and the follow up by the Italian Constitutional Court: *Corte costituzionale, Sentenza del gennaio* 1994, n. 27, *Ditta Punto e Pasta c. Sindaco di Vicenza*.

[68] Case 237/82 *Jongeneel Kaas* v. *The Netherlands* [1984] ECR 483, para. 23. See also Case 155/80 *Summary proceedings against Oebel* [1981] ECR 1993, paras. 9 and 10.

4. THE CHOICE OF REMEDIES AND THE CHOICE OF INSTITUTIONS

The analysis made was intended to highlight the European dimension of reverse discrimination. Reverse discrimination in EC law is a European problem but does it deserve or require European remedies? Should the Court of Justice extend to purely internal situations the more favourable treatment often granted by EC law to situations with a cross-national link? In my view, that depends upon an institutional analysis of the origins of reverse discrimination and the remedies which can be available to prevent it. First, one must distinguish between *ex-ante* and *ex-post* analyses of reverse discrimination. An *ex-post* perspective focuses on a State's discrimination against home nationals. An *ex-ante* perspective will review the role of EC law in the creation of reverse discrimination. An *ex-ante* approach addresses reverse discrimination at its origin (linked to the two forms of mutual recognition described above). An *ex-post* approach has to do with the national response to the favourable treatment granted by EC law to nationals or products of other Member States (does the State extend that treatment to its own nationals or does it continue to apply to them its more restrictive rules?). Both approaches are required in order to fully address the problem of reverse discrimination and its different legal questions. The criteria developed by the Court to address both sides of reverse discrimination reveals a predominantly hands-off approach. The Court relies on alternative institutions to solve the problems of reverse discrimination. Those alternative institutions are the market and the national political process.

Entrusting reverse discrimination to the market and national political processes

The problem of reverse discrimination must be taken into account by the Court either when it considers the application of mutual recognition in reviewing national measures or when it reviews Community legislation authorising Member States to impose rules different from Community rules on their own nationals. To take reverse discrimination into consideration means that the Court should look at the discriminatory effects EC rules may have by excluding purely internal situations. The decision on whether or not to uphold reverse discrimination at the EU level is dependent on a balance to be made between free trade and competition among rules (subjecting different nationals and companies to different rules) on the one hand and regulatory and equality concerns on the other. Both the Court (when it interprets EC rules) and the EU political process (when it enacts legislation) have to decide on the scope of application of those EC rules and what may be the alternative remedies available for nationals not benefiting from those rules.

The Court of Justice is aware of the discrimination and distorted competition which may arise from the limitation of the scope of EC rules under the concept of purely internal situations. However, the Court accepts this. The Court believes that the market will correct the discrimination which operates against home nationals. This can be seen in the *3 Glocken* case. The case concerned the obligation arising from Italian legislation requiring all pasta to be made exclusively from durum wheat. The Court did not accept that such an obligation could be imposed on imports. However, it expressly stated:

> (. . .) it is the extension of the law on pasta products to imported products which is at issue, and that Community Law does not require the legislature to repeal the law as far as pasta producers established on Italian territory are concerned.[69]

The result is a discrimination between the rules to which Italian and imported products are subject. However, the Court trusted that such a discrimination would work in favour of those discriminated against:

> (. . .) it should be observed that trends in the export markets demonstrate that competition based on quality operates in favour of durum wheat. The statistics supplied to the Court show a steady increase in the market share held by pasta products made exclusively from durum wheat in other Member States in which they already face competition from pasta made from common wheat or from mixture of common wheat and durum wheat. In those circumstances, it is clear that the fears expressed by the Italian Government as to the disappearance of durum wheat growing are unfounded.[70]

This entrusts, in the first place, to the market the correction of reverse discrimination and the provision of remedies for those discriminated against by being subject to stricter rules. However, the market may suffer from problems such as information costs and externalities which prevent consumers from rewarding individuals and products whose qualifications or characteristics are subject to stricter requirements. In these cases, national political processes may still intervene in order to prevent their nationals from continuing to be subject to stricter rules (reverse discrimination). But even here problems arise. First, Member States may only prevent discrimination by extending the less strict rules applicable to foreign nationals and products to their home nationals and domestic products. In this case, the remedy provided by the national political process may differ from that originally intended by the Court of Justice: instead of a competition among rules which may operate in favour of quality the consequence will be a uniform application of the less strict requirements. Therefore, the Court of Justice should review the ability of the market to provide viable and transparent competition among rules before authorising EC legislation based on competition among rules with its inherent discriminatory effects.

There is a second problem which may occur in entrusting to the national political process a decision on the admissibility of reverse discrimination. National political processes may be dominated by some national interests which

[69] *3 Glocken*, note 67, above, para. 25.
[70] *Ibid*, para. 27.

would gain by the maintenance of reverse discrimination, at the expense of other national interests. In these cases, national political processes may not be an appropriate institution to assess the reasonableness of reverse discrimination and to determine the need to remedy the situation of discrimination against some of its nationals.

Waterkeyn[71] is a case which clearly demonstrates the problems and choices involved. It concerned the French legislation on the advertising of alcoholic beverages determining which types of alcoholic beverages could be advertised and which could not. In a first judgment, the Court found that imported alcoholic beverages were in law or in fact subject to more stringent provisions than competing national products.[72] This was because alcoholic beverages were divided in groups for which permission to advertise was either granted or denied. According to the Court these groups were drafted in such a way that French alcoholic beverages tended to be placed in the groups benefiting from less stringent rules or no restrictive rules at all, whereas imported alcoholic beverages tended to be placed in groups to which the restrictions did apply. However, the Court also stated that its judgment applied exclusively to imports. This meant that reverse discrimination arose with regard to the (probably few) French products included in the same groups as imported products. The Court of Justice may have rightly conceived that it would be more appropriate for the French State to decide whether discrimination against some French nationals is justified. The French Government had itself argued that Member States should retain the power to regulate the advertising of national alcoholic beverages and to subject them to more stringent, and therefore discriminatory rules if it saw fit.[73] For the Court, EC law should not interfere in the regulation of domestic alcoholic beverages since it could be expected that States would not unjustifiably discriminate against their own nationals. National legislators were a preferable institution to the Court in dealing with reverse discrimination and purely internal situations.

One must however note that the decision of the French Government to accept reverse discrimination may also indicate some type of bias against some of the French producers. A bias for which no remedy may be available in the national political system. French nationals affected by reverse discrimination in this case were a clear and discrete minority of French nationals. Most French alcoholic beverages were already inserted in the groups benefiting from a more favourable treatment, into which the ECJ decision inserted imported products. The few French alcoholic beverages of the same type as imported ones were not however inserted into those more favourable categories and, as a consequence, remained the only products to be subject to more stringent rules. The few French producers involved were side-lined in the French political process by the interests of the majority producers (their competitors), and also by consumer pressure groups.[74] This may have led the French Government to maintain the legislation

[71] *Waterkeyn*, note 15, above.

[72] Case 152/78 *Commission* v. *French Republic* [1980] ECR 2299.

[73] *Waterkeyn*, note 15, above, at 4352.

with regard to the minority of French producers of alcoholic beverages, to the advantage of both consumers and the great majority of French producers of alcoholic beverages.[75] Reverse discrimination has thus occurred, and consideration should be given to whether the burden placed on a minority of French nationals, to the advantage of other French nationals, is acceptable. In this case, the national political process will not provide an adequate remedy for the few French nationals discriminated against.

Exploring different institutional alternatives

The evidence so far presented clearly demonstrates that reverse discrimination is an EU issue. But should we automatically assume that it requires an EU-level remedy? In other words, what remedial institutional conclusions should be drawn from the fact that reverse discrimination is an EU issue? I do not believe that it should be an EU institution which decides whether nationals of a particular State should or should not be subjected to stricter rules imposed by that State. Since this judgment implies a balancing of different national interests, national institutions are usually (though not always)[76] better suited to make that decision. Those arguing for the Court of Justice to put an end to reverse discrimination ignore both the values of diversity and competition it promotes and the institutional comparison necessary to determine who should decide the issue. *Ex-post*, it is for the institutions of Member States to decide whether to compete by creating reverse discrimination. Another question is which national institution should make these decisions and the role that the ECJ should continue to play in this context.

Although national institutions should be competent to assess cases of reverse discrimination, the strong risks of majoritarian bias (under-representation of minority interests) existing in the national political process regarding a decision establishing reverse discrimination require that national courts be empowered to review the initial assessment of reverse discrimination made by the national political process. In such a case, national courts should be empowered to decide when reverse discrimination is acceptable taking into account the broader public interests and the burden placed on the home nationals discriminated against. They are at the appropriate level (national) and better equipped to balance the majority interest with the rights of the minority.[77]

National courts have already been faced with challenges to reverse discrimi-

[74] The "*Comité national de défense contre l'alcoolisme*".

[75] For another example involving a similar minority see Drago in a comment on the French Conseil d'État decision *Syndicat national des fabricants de spiritueux consommés à l'eau* (27 July 1979): R. Drago, "Note de Jurisprudence" *Revue du Droit Public* 1-1980, 214, at 218.

[76] The explanation of why, in some circumstances, European institutions may be more adequate to solve national problems would require another paper . . .

[77] Although courts may in these cases suffer from the alternative institutional malfunction (minoritarian bias) I believe this risk will be lower due to the mobilisation of the national political process and the majority interests behind the existent legislation.

nation on the grounds that it violates the principles of equality and undistorted competition. However, when reverse discrimination is authorised by Community legislation (following the policy of minimum requirements and mutual recognition) it will be difficult for national courts to prohibit national rules which take advantage of that authorisation and impose stricter rules on home nationals. Furthermore, in some national legal systems, courts are simply not empowered to review the validity of national legislation, even with respect to the principle of equality. That is the case, for example, in France, where there is only *a priori* review of constitutionality of the laws by the *Conseil Constitutionnel*. As a result, if a national law is, *a posteriori*, struck down by the European Court of Justice only with regard to nationals of other Member States, reverse discrimination could arise without any way being open for the French courts to review the conformity of the new legislative situation with the principle of equality. This consequence has appeared so absurd to some French courts that they have decided to review reverse discrimination under EC law themselves, even if expressly contradicting the ECJ case-law. The principle of supremacy of EC law gives them the power, which they do not have under national law, to review the validity of reverse discrimination. This resulted in the development of a body of case-law in France which contradicts the consistent ECJ case-law on reverse discrimination.[78]

The best solution to the problems raised by the fact that some national legal systems are not prepared to deal with question of reverse discrimination arising from the European integration process, is the empowering of national courts through EC law. I have argued that reverse discrimination should not be approached as a question of jurisdiction. National judgments on reverse discrimination have a clear EU dimension in that the issue is almost always a comparison between the treatment by national law of all or some nationals, and the rights granted in EC law to nationals of other Member States. If EC law gives rise to the problem, it should also give national courts the means to provide the adequate remedies. This is an area of EC law where the ECJ could improve its policy of co-operation with national courts. In *Debauve*,[79] the Court recognised a potential role for national courts in the assessment of purely internal situations:

[78] Reviewing reverse discrimination under Community law: Cour de cassation, chambre criminelle *Comité national de défense contre l'alcoolisme* c. *Rossi de Montalera et autres*, 16 June 1983, reported in (1983) 19 *RTDE*, 468; Tribunal d'instance de Bressuire (greffe de Thouars) *Commissaire de police de Thouars* c. *M.Cognet (Centre Leclerc)*, 10 April 1987, reported in (1987) 23 *RTDE*, 553. Denying the application of Community law, thus in agreement with the ECJ: Conseil d'État, *Aufaure*, 3 November 1976, [1976] Recueil des décisions du Conseil d'État 465; Conseil d'État, *Association des centres distributeurs Edouard Leclerc*, 8 February 1985, [1985] Recueil des décisions du Conseil d'État 25; Conseil d'Etat, *Association professionnelle des guides interprétes*, 3 June 1987 [1987] Recueil des décisions du Conseil d'État 910.

[79] Case 52/79 *Procureur du Roi* v. *Debauve* [1980] ECR 833. Restated in *Volker Steen (No. 2)*, note 25, above, para. 9.

> (. . .) it should be observed that the provisions of the Treaty on freedom to provide services cannot apply to activities whose relevant elements are confined within a single Member State. Whether that is the case depends on findings of fact which are for the national court to establish. Since the Tribunal Correctionnel has concluded that in the given circumstances of this case the services out of which the prosecutions brought before it arose are as such as to come under the provisions of the Treaty relating to services, the questions referred to the Court should be examined from the same point of view.[80]

This does not imply that the ECJ has no role to play. On the contrary, it is demonstrative of the general necessity for the Court of Justice to fine-tune and develop a more conscious and coherent understanding of what co-operation with national courts means in tackling specific issues. This area of remedies could provide a good testing ground. The Court should abandon the "geographical" test and instead entrust to national courts the EC law judgment on the validity of national rules which impose on home nationals stricter requirements than those imposed by European rules. The Court should simply state that it is for national courts, having regard to the facts of the case, to assess whether the discrimination found in national rules against home nationals can be justified in light of specific national interests. Reverse discrimination is a matter of EC law that national courts can better deal with in most cases, since it involves the interests of home nationals alone. Abandoning the present "geographical" test will also focus the attention of the Court to the *ex-ante* problem of reverse discrimination: European rules and interpretation thereof which can create reverse discrimination in the first place. The question of reverse discrimination and the discrimination it entails among European citizens should not be conceived in light of a formal application of the scope of European remedies but as a question of institutional choice which requires due attention to be paid to different institutions in providing remedies for European problems.

This area may serve as an appropriate starting point for the European Court of Justice in developing a better allocation of tasks between national courts and other institutions in the field of remedies. There are many areas in which the Court already allocates to other institutions the provision of European remedies but these developments appear more a consequence of *ad hoc* circumstances and pragmatic constraints than a result of solid and thought through institutional choice and comparison. The present status quo on the horizontal direct effect of directives, for example, constitutes, to a great extent, a delegation to national courts on the choice of remedies: state liability, indirect effect or, possibly, even *contra legem* interpretation. This is an area where the Court could also clarify the impact of European law and its allocation of tasks to national courts. A possible solution to the old dilemma of the horizontal direct effect of directives would be openly to entrust to national courts the definition of the extent of remedies available. It should be for national courts, taking into account their

[80] *Debauve*, note 79 above, para. 9.

national legal system and the principle that national law should be applied and interpreted in order to give the fullest effect possible to the Community directives, to determine whether the provisions of a not yet transposed directive can be invoked between individuals. In most of the cases of horizontal direct effect of directives conflicts do not tend to occur between nationals of different Member States. It can therefore be expected that national courts will decide on the question of horizontal direct effect independently of any national bias. The lack of uniformity that may arise in consequence of the allocation of this decision to national courts already occurs. The only difference would be a greater empowerment of national courts to decide on a broader scope of remedies without requiring the Court of Justice to totally abandon the distinction between the legal effects of regulations and directives.

I have tried to highlight the institutional choices involved in the question of remedies while paying particular attention to the problem of reverse discrimination in European Union law. Fundamentally, I wanted to note that the provision of European remedies does not have to be ECJ centred. National courts and other institutional alternatives, such as the market, may, in some instances, provide better remedies to some European legal problems. Some allocation of remedies to alternative institutions is already taking place but we need to start complementing these hidden institutional choices with proper institutional criteria. Only this will allow us to make the right institutional choices and take full advantage of the different institutional alternatives available in the field of European remedies.

6

The Private Enforcement of European Union Labour Laws

BERNARD RYAN

1. INTRODUCTION

THE GRADUAL strengthening by the Court of Justice of the status of European Community (EC) law within national legal systems evokes a variety of responses.[1] One view questions the desirability of strengthening EC law both because it may disrupt the specific social, political and legal cultures of the Member States and because of doubts as to the democratic legitimacy of the Court of Justice. Carol Harlow has for example observed, in criticism of the principle of state liability for breaches of Community law, that:

> law is a cultural artifact rooted in shared community experience and reflecting the community's cultural identity and ethical values. Unhappy law reform can jar with societal and constitutional arrangements. Law also embodies political beliefs – views on distributive justice or property expropriation – and structures – the welfare state or constitutional adjudication. EC law, however, is particularly the culture of an elite group.[2]

For others, however, the central question is whether the authority and uniformity of EC law are secured. From that perspective, the Court of Justice's initiatives in relation to enforcement are welcomed, but are instead open to criticism for not going far enough.[3]

This essay is concerned with the enforcement of European Union labour law (EU labour law) by individuals.[4] It accepts that cultural and democratic

[1] Note that the policy area examined in this essay is termed "EU labour law" as it has been developed by the institutions (now) of the European Union. The rules governing the enforcement of those laws are however referred to as relating to "EC law" as they exclusively concern provisions of, or instruments adopted under, the European Community Treaty.

[2] C. Harlow, "*Francovich* and the Problem of the Disobedient State" (1996) 2 *ELJ* 199 at 222.

[3] See, for example, D. Curtin, "The Decentralised Enforcement of Community Law Rights. Judicial Snakes and Ladders", in D. Curtin and D. O'Keeffe (eds.), *Constitutional Adjudication in European Community and National Law* (Dublin: Butterworths, 1992).

[4] This is not to deny the potential rôle of Commission action under Article 226 EC (ex Article 169) in securing compliance by Member States with their EC law obligations. The essay focuses upon individual enforcement because of its potential advantages in terms of speed and comprehensiveness.

criticisms of legal integration in the European Union establish a presumption against attempts to maximise the effectiveness of EC law within the national legal order. Accordingly, the starting-point here is that, if there is a case for further strengthening of the rules relating to the enforcement of EC law, it must follow, not from general notions of respect for EC law, but rather from an examination of its underlying purposes. In that vein, the essay assesses the legal regime governing the enforcement of EC law by individuals in terms of the objectives of EU labour law.

The first section of the essay considers the possible objectives of EU labour law in general terms. Three kinds of argument are outlined in turn – that EU labour law can resolve transnational regulatory problems, that it upholds fundamental rights, and that it overcomes the tension between competition and national labour law.[5] The second, third and fourth sections then examine three issues in the enforcement of EU labour law in the light of its possible objectives – whether all employees have a remedy, whether state liability is an adequate substitute for employer liability, and the desirability of Member State discretion in relation to procedures and sanctions. It will be argued that, from the perspective of EU labour law, significant deficiencies in the current rules relating to the enforcement of EC law can be identified, but that those deficiencies differ with the presumed purposes of EU labour laws. The essay concludes by identifying its wider implications, both for the enforcement of EC law, and for EU labour law.

2. THREE THEORIES OF EUROPEAN UNION LABOUR LAW

Three of the principal approaches to the justification of the setting of labour law standards at the European Union level are outlined in this section. In so doing, reference will be made to content of EU labour laws and to the opinions of EU institutions and of academic commentators. This section is not however concerned with the more complex question of the *explanation* of EU labour laws, either in general or in particular cases. Nor does it seek to address the *persuasiveness* of the different accounts of EU labour law which are outlined. Instead, these theories of EU labour law are outlined in order to provide the basis for a detailed critique of the rules governing the enforcement of EC law in subsequent sections.

[5] Note that it is not being suggested that these are the only possible rationales for European Union labour law, but rather that the most common arguments can be categorised in this way. For a classification similar to that used here, see the distinction between "physical", "psychic" and "economic" spillovers in the context of EC environmental policy in W. Wils, "Subsidiarity and EC Environmental Policy: Taking People's Concerns Seriously" (1994) 6 *Journal of Environmental Law* 85.

Transnational regulation

A first argument for European Union intervention in the field of labour law is that there are transnational regulatory problems in the European Union labour market which cannot satisfactorily be left to national solutions. This may occur whenever labour market processes and events have a connection with more than one Member State. In those circumstances, EU labour law intervention may be desirable in order to co-ordinate the laws of the different Member States.

This "transnational" interpretation of EU labour law has typically been explored in the context of collective labour law. In that sphere, attention has focused in particular upon the possibility of a right to take transnational industrial action[6] and of a right to organise across national boundaries.[7] The one concrete achievement in relation to collective labour law is the European Works Councils Directive, which requires the establishment of a European Works Council or transnational information and consultation mechanism in certain multinationals in the European Economic Area (EEA).[8] Legislation of this kind may be thought indispensable if legal rights of representation in EU multinationals are to be effectively guaranteed.

Other cases of "transnational" EU labour law can be identified in the field of individual labour law. The Posted Workers Directive[9] applies to workers who are employed in one Member State but temporarily posted to another, and requires that the "host" State's labour law provisions specified in the Directive apply to the worker. Where employment relationships have a connection with more than one Member State, European Union action to resolve choice of law problems may be preferable to reliance upon the unilateral action of Member States, or international agreements. The advantage of European Union legislation is precisely that it may enhance the enforceability of choice of law rules within national legal systems.[10]

A further, more speculative, example is the possible application of free movement of workers principles to individual employers. Article 39 EC (the former

[6] See K. Wedderburn, "Multi-National Enterprise and National Labour Law" (1972) 1 *ILJ* 12 at 18–19; A. Jacobs, "Towards Community Action on Strike Law?" (1978) 15 *CMLRev* 133; and N. Bruun and B. Veneziani, "The Right or Freedom to Transnational Industrial Action in the European Union" in *A Legal Framework for European Industrial Relations* (Brussels: European Trade Union Institute, 1999).

[7] See B. Ryan, "Pay, Trade Union Rights and European Community Law" (1997) 13 *IJCLLIR* 305 at 323–4.

[8] Council Directive 94/45 on the establishment of a European Works Council, 1994 OJ L 254/64, extended to United Kingdom by Directive 97/74, 1998 OJ L 10/22. It applies to employers with more than 1,000 employees in the EEA and more than 150 employees in each of two EEA States.

[9] Council Directive 96/71 concerning the posting of workers in the framework of the provision of services, 1997 OJ L 18/1.

[10] Note that the adoption of the Posted Workers Directive in 1996 also had the effect of permitting Member States to extend parts of their labour laws to the employees of service-providers based in other Member States. That possibility had however already been accepted by the Court of Justice in Case C–113/89 *Rush Portugesa* v. *Office National d'Immigration* [1990] ECR I–1417.

Article 48) and parts of Regulation 1612/68[11] require employers to permit workers to take up employment in Member States other than their own, to give due recognition to their qualifications and experience, and not to discriminate on grounds of nationality against them.[12] These principles may be thought essential to the construction of a functioning European Union labour market. If so, then it may be necessary to require them at the European Union level, because Member States might be reluctant to take unilateral action to prohibit the giving of preference to their own nationals.

Fundamental rights

A second interpretation of the role of EU labour law is that it guarantees the fundamental rights of individual workers. The free movement of workers offers one possible example. Since its judgment in *Sotgiu* in 1974, the Court of Justice has recognised that the free movement of workers is a "fundamental principle" of Community law.[13] Among the consequences of that approach to the free movement of workers have been that the concept of "worker" has been given a broad interpretation,[14] and that exceptions to it have been narrowly construed.[15] To the extent that free movement of workers principles are part of EU labour law, they may therefore be thought to uphold a fundamental right of personal movement.

A second example is provided by the law relating to the equal treatment of men and women in the employment sphere. In the Court of Justice's view "the elimination of discrimination based on sex forms part of [the] fundamental rights" which are to be respected as general principles of Community law.[16] The core labour law provisions which require equal treatment as between men and women – Article 141 EC (ex Article 119), the Equal Pay Directive and the Equal Treatment Directive[17] – are therefore taken to reflect that fundamental right.[18] The conceptualisation of the legal rules on equal treatment between men and women in "fundamental rights" terms has proven especially important in recent

[11] Council Regulation 1612/68 on freedom of movement for workers within the Community, 1968 OJ Sp. Ed. L 257/2. In particular, Article 6(1) of the Regulation prohibits recruitment criteria which are discriminatory on grounds of nationality, and Article 7(1) prohibits discrimination on grounds of nationality "in respect of any conditions of employment and work".

[12] Note that the scope of application of these principles is considered in section 3, below.

[13] See Case 152/73 *Sotgiu* v. *Deutsche Bundespost* [1974] ECR 153, paras. 4 and 11.

[14] See Case 53/81 *Levin* v. *Staatsecretaris van Justitutie* [1982] ECR 1035, para. 13.

[15] See *Sotgiu*, note 13, above, para. 4 and Case 41/74, *Van Duyn* v. *Home Office* [1974] ECR 1337, paras. 13 and 18.

[16] Case 149/77 *Defrenne* v. *SABENA (No. 3)* [1978] ECR 1365, para. 27.

[17] Council Directive 75/117 on the principle of equal pay for men and women, [1975] OJ L 45/19 and Council Directive 76/207 on the principle of equal treatment for men and women, [1976] OJ L 39/40.

[18] See C. Docksey, "The Principle of Equality between Men and Women as a Fundamental Right under Community Law" (1991) 20 *ILJ* 258.

years. In *Kalanke*, decided in 1995, the fundamental nature of the principle of equal treatment contributed to the Court of Justice's conclusion that rigid systems of positive action were contrary to the Equal Treatment Directive.[19] Then, in *P* v. *S*, decided in 1996, the Court of Justice observed that "the right not to be discriminated against on grounds of sex is one of the fundamental human rights whose observance the Court has a duty to ensure", and accordingly concluded that discrimination arising out of gender reassignment was prohibited by the Equal Treatment Directive.[20]

The notion that EU labour law may uphold "fundamental rights" can also be applied in other contexts. Article 13 EC, introduced by the Treaty of Amsterdam, gives the Community power to legislate "to combat discrimination based on sex, racial or ethnic origin, religion or belief, disability, age or sexual orientation". If legislation of this kind were adopted in relation to the employment relationship, it too would provide an example of the expression of fundamental rights through EU labour law.[21] Finally, reference may be made here to the various proposals for the codification of fundamental social rights in the European Union.[22] These too reflect a conceptualisation of EU labour law as having the capacity to express fundamental rights.

Labour law and competition

A third approach to EU labour law is concerned with the tension between national labour laws and competition in the European Union market.[23] One

[19] See in particular the comments of Advocate General Tesauro in Case C–450/93, *Kalanke* v. *Freie Hansestadt Bremen* [1995] ECR I–3051, at para. 7 of the Opinion, where he refers to the "fundamental right" "not to be discriminated against on grounds of sex". The Court of Justice used different language, and instead limited the scope of permissible positive action because it was "a derogation from an individual right": see para. 21 of the judgment. The effect of the *Kalanke* decision was subsequently reduced by the acceptance of the legality of a flexible approach to positive action in Case C–409/95, *Marshall* v. *Land Nordrhein-Westfalen* [1997] ECR I–6363.

[20] Case C–13/94 *P* v. *S and Cornwall County Council* [1996] ECR I–2143, para.19. Note however that in Case C–249/96 *Grant* v. *South-West Trains* [1998] ECR I–621, the Court of Justice declined to extend the Equal Treatment Directive to cover cases of sexual orientation discrimination. It reached that decision despite the view of Advocate General Elmer that the Court's approach in *P* v. *S* meant that the protection of the Directive should also be available in such cases: see paras. 13–17 of the Opinion.

[21] See, for example, the report of the Commission's "Expert Group on Fundamental Rights", which offers Article 13 as an example of a "procedure intended to secure [the] protection" of fundamental rights: European Commission, *Affirming Fundamental Rights in the European Union: Time to Act* (Brussels: European Commission, 1999), 7.

[22] See *Comité des Sages: For a Europe of Civic and Social Rights* (Brussels: European Commission, 1996); R. Blanpain, B. Hepple, S. Sciarra and M. Weiss, *Fundamental Social Rights: Proposals for the European Union* (Leuven: Peeters, 1996); and B. Bercusson, S. Deakin, P. Koistinen, Y. Kravaritou, U. Mückenberger, A. Supriot and B. Veneziani, "A Manifesto for Social Europe" (1997) 3 *ELJ* 189 at 196–200.

[23] Note that this "tension" is distinct from the potential conflict between EC competition law and national labour laws, as illustrated by the related judgments of the Court of Justice of 21 September 1999 in Case C–67/96 *Albany International* v. *Stichting Bedrijfspensionenfonds Textielindustrie;* Joined Cases C–115/97, C–116/97 and C–117/97 *Brentjens' Handelsonderneming* v. *Stichting*

version of this general analysis may be termed the "competition policy" argument. On that view, differences in the costs associated with labour laws in the Member States may undermine the competitive process within the European Union. This will occur if more efficient producers in a more onerous labour law environment do not prevail over less efficient producers in a less onerous labour law environment. If the "distortion of competition" consequent upon differences in national labour laws is a real possibility, then the solution is to promote the equalisation of the costs faced by different employers through EU labour law. That objective may be advanced either by the harmonisation of labour laws or, more pragmatically, by laying down minimum standards so as to reduce differences in national labour laws.

The "competition policy" approach to EU labour law has a long history. It was initially set out in the Ohlin and Spaak Reports of 1956,[24] which were the background to the social policy provisions of the 1957 EEC Treaty, and in particular to the requirement of equal pay between men and women in what is now Article 141 EC. This "competition policy" background to Article 141 was moreover endorsed by the Court of Justice in its judgment in *Defrenne (No. 2)*.[25] The "competition policy" argument has also been used for example to justify the 1975 Collective Redundancies Directive[26] and the 1977 Transfer of Undertakings Directive.[27] The Court of Justice concluded in its *Commission* v. *United Kingdom* judgments in 1994 that the purpose of each of these Directives was to "harmonize the costs" of protective labour laws in different Member States.[28]

A second, and distinct, interpretation of the tension between labour law and competition in the European Union context argues that competitive pressures may constrain the development of national labour law. The fear is that Member States may fail to introduce new laws, and may pursue strategies of "competitive deregulation" in the field of labour law in order to obtain a competitive advantage for employers within their jurisdiction. On this second account, the role of labour laws at the European Union level is essentially to limit the extent

Bedrijfspensionenfonds voor de Handel in Bouwmaterialen; and Case C–219/97 *Maatschappij Drijvende Bokken* v. *Stichting Pensioenfonds voor de Vervoer-en Havenbedrijven.*

[24] The Ohlin Report is published as International Labour Office, "Social Aspects of European Economic Co-operation" (1956) 74 *International Labour Review* 99. The Spaak Report is summarised in Political and Economic Planning, *Planning*, No. 405 (1956). For an extended discussion of the Ohlin and Spaak Reports, see S. Deakin, "Labour Law as Market Regulation: the Economic Foundations of European Social Policy" in P. Davies, A. Lyon-Caen, S. Sciarra and S. Simitis (eds.), *European Community Labour Law: Principles and Perspectives* (Oxford: Clarendon Press, 1996), 65–70.

[25] See Case 43/75 *Defrenne* v. *SABENA (No. 2)* [1976] ECR 455, para. 9.

[26] Council Directive 75/129 on the Approximation of the Laws of the Member States relating to Collective Redundancies [1975] OJ L 48/29, as amended by Directive 92/56 [1992] OJ L 245/3 and consolidated by Council Directive 98/59/EC [1998] OJ L 225/16.

[27] Council Directive 77/187 on the Safeguarding of Employees' Rights in the Event of Transfers of Undertakings [1977] OJ L 61/26, as amended by Council Directive 98/50/EC [1998] OJ L 201/88.

[28] For essentially identical formulations, see Case C–383/92 *Commission* v. *United Kingdom* [1994] ECR I–2479, para. 16, in relation to the Collective Redundancies Directive; and Case C–382/92 *Commission* v. *United Kingdom* [1994] ECR I–2435, para. 15 in relation to the Transfer of Undertakings Directive.

to which competitive pressures undermine national labour laws by ensuring that labour law standards on a given subject are not unacceptably low in some Member States. It does not matter to this argument what the purposes of national labour laws are. As long as labour laws impose significant costs upon businesses, then they may be vulnerable to competitive pressures, and the possibility of protecting national labour law through EU labour law will arise.[29]

This second account of the tension between national labour law and competition in the European Union market is frequently to be found in the Commission's accounts of EU labour law. Typically, it is expressed in the notion of "unfair competition", which competition through the weakening of national labour law is taken to entail. In that vein, for example, the Commission argued in its 1994 White Paper on social policy that "the establishment of a framework of basic minimum standards . . . provides a bulwark against using low social standards as an instrument of unfair economic competition".[30]

This is not the place to consider the important differences between accounts of EU labour law which seek to uphold the logic of competition, and those which seek to protect national labour law from competitive pressures, or to speculate on the credibility of these accounts as a justification for EU labour law as it has developed historically. For present purposes, it is sufficient that, on either account of the tension between national labour law and competition, the role of EU labour law is to ensure greater equivalence in the *costs* associated with labour laws in the Member States. The significance of that emphasis upon costs for the enforcement of EC law will become apparent in the sections which follow.

3. COMPREHENSIVENESS

Having outlined these three approaches to the justification of EU labour law, their implications for central questions in the enforcement of EC law are examined in the rest of the essay. This section is concerned with the comprehensiveness of the mechanisms for the enforcement of EU labour law by individual employees. In which circumstances are employees who are intended to benefit from EU labour law left without a cause of action? Is it desirable in terms of the objectives of EU labour law for any gaps in protection to be remedied?

The starting-point for a discussion of the comprehensiveness of remedies is that most EU labour laws have vertical effect, but not horizontal effect. In other words, EU labour laws can usually be enforced against public employers but not private ones. To date, the only part of EU labour law which *has* been accorded

[29] For an account within which labour laws are costly and potentially efficiency-enhancing and accordingly require protection at the European Union level, see S. Deakin and F. Wilkinson, "Rights v Efficiency? The Economic Case for Transnational Labour Standards" (1994) 23 *ILJ* 289; and Deakin (1996), note 23, above, at 77–92.

[30] European Commission, *European Social Policy – A Way Forward for the Union* COM (94) 333, 5.

horizontal effect is the requirement of equal pay as between men and women in Article 141 EC.[31] The only other part of EU labour law which is a candidate for horizontal effect is the free movement of workers principles which are relevant to the employment sphere (discussed in section 1, above). The Court of Justice has stated in general terms that it is "clear . . . that Article 48 [now Article 39] and Regulation 1612/ 68 are directly applicable".[32] What is unclear however is the scope of the obligations contained in these provisions. Free movement of workers principles have been held to be binding upon both public and private regulatory bodies.[33] The requirement of equal treatment on grounds of nationality has also frequently been relied upon against public employers.[34] The Court of Justice has not however definitively decided whether the free movement of workers principles in Article 39 and Regulation 1612/ 68 can *apply* to individual private employers. Indeed, the Court of Justice in *Bosman* appeared to distance itself from the notion that the former Article 48 EC was applicable to private employers. Advocate General Lenz had proposed that Article 48 prevented individual clubs from demanding a fee for the transfer of out-of-contract players.[35] By contrast, the Court limited its ruling on Article 48 to "rules laid down by sporting associations", and made no reference to the position of individual clubs.[36]

These cases apart, EU labour law is not enforceable against private employers, as it is contained in Directives, which the Court of Justice has only allowed to be enforced against public bodies.[37] The Court's argument for this position is essentially that Article 249 EC (ex Article 189) provides that a directive is "binding upon each Member State to which it is addressed". In the Court's opinion, its extension of direct effect "to the sphere of relations between individuals [that] would be to recognize a power in the Community to enact obligations for individuals with immediate effect, whereas it has competence to do so only where it is empowered to adopt regulations".[38] Since the use of directives is necessitated by the principal

[31] The horizontal effect of that Article was first decided upon in *Defrenne (No. 2)*, note 25, above. It was subsequently extended to "all forms of discrimination which may be identified solely with the aid of the criteria of equal work and equal pay . . . without national or Community measures being required to define them with greater precision": see Case 69/80 *Worringham and Humphreys* v. *Lloyds Bank Ltd* [1981] ECR 767, para. 23.

[32] Case 167/73 *Commission* v. *France* [1974] ECR 359, para. 41.

[33] See Case 36/74 *Walrave and Koch* v. *Union Cycliste International* [1974] ECR 1405; Case 13/76 *Donà* v. *Mantero* [1976] ECR 1333; and Case C–415/93 *Union Royale Belge des Sociétés de Football Association* v. *Bosman* [1995] ECR I–4921.

[34] See in particular *Sotgiu*, note 13, above, in relation to Articles 7(1) and 7(4) of Regulation 1612/68.

[35] See para. 287 of the Opinion.

[36] For a similar observation, see D. O'Keeffe and P. Osborne, "The European Court Scores a Goal" (1996) 12 *IJCLLIR* 111 at 116. For an account of the arguments for and against the "horizontal" application of free movement of workers principles, see S. Weatherill, "Discrimination on Grounds of Nationality in Sport" (1989) 9 *YEL* 55, at 63–6 and 89–92.

[37] See Case 152/84 *Marshall* v. *Southampton and South-West Hampshire Area Health Authority (No. 1)* [1986] ECR 723; and Case C–91/92 *Dori* v. *Recreb Srl* [1994] ECR I–3325.

[38] Para. 24 of the judgment in *Dori*.

legislative powers of relevance to labour law,[39] it follows that most EU labour laws will continue to lack horizontal effect for the foreseeable future.

The lack of horizontal effect for directives is however mitigated to a significant extent by three other legal developments which respect the fact that directives are addressed to States.[40] As the content of these principles is well-known, they need be considered here only in outline. The Court of Justice has firstly insisted upon a broad approach to the state bodies against which directives may be directly effective. This has been seen most recently in *Kampelmann*, where the Court stated that directives could be enforced against "organizations or bodies which are subject to the authority or control of the State or have special powers beyond those which result from the normal rules applicable to relations between individuals, such as local or regional authorities or other bodies which . . . have been given responsibility, by the public authorities and under their supervision, for providing a public service".[41] The breadth of this approach lies in the fact that *either* state control *or* special powers will be sufficient for a body to be deemed part of the "State" for the purposes of the enforcement of directives.

Secondly, the Court of Justice has introduced the requirement that, as far as possible, national courts should give a sympathetic interpretation to national law, so as to give effect to a Member State's obligations under Community law.[42] It may therefore be possible for directives to be enforced "indirectly" against private employers if national law is capable of being interpreted to achieve that result.[43]

Thirdly, the Court of Justice has developed the principle of state liability, according to which a Member State is liable in damages for losses suffered by individuals because of its breach of EC law.[44] A right to compensation will in general arise where three conditions are satisfied: "the rule of law must be

[39] See in particular Article 94 EC (ex Article 100) and Article 137 EC (ex Article 2 of the Social Policy Agreement). Note that Article 94 may continue to have a role in relation to labour law because of the substantive limitations upon the scope of Article 137 contained in its paragraph 6.

[40] The argument in the rest of the section refers to directives only. With suitable modifications it could be extended to the special case of the free movement of workers principles in Article 39 and Regulation 1612/68, if these were found to have implications for private employers which Member States were required to implement in national law.

[41] Cases C–253/96 to C–258/96 *Kamplemann and others* v. *Landschaftsverbund Westfalen-Lippe*, [1997] ECR I–6907, para. 46. See too its earlier formulation in Case C–188/89 *Foster* v. *British Gas* [1990] ECR I–3313, paras. 18–20.

[42] Case 14/83 *Von Colson and Kamann* v. *Land Nordrhein-Westfalen* [1984] ECR 1891. It does not matter for these purposes whether the national law in question was itself introduced or retained in order to comply with the Community obligation: see Case C–106/89 *Marleasing SA* v. *La Comercial Internacionale de Alimentacion* [1990] ECR I–4135.

[43] Note that some doubt has been cast upon the use of sympathetic interpretation to impose obligations upon individuals by the Judgment in Case C–168/95 *Arcaro* [1996] ECR I–4705, at para. 42. For a discussion of the possible interpretations of that Judgment, see P. Craig, "Directives: Direct Effect, Indirect Effect and the Construction of National Legislation" (1997) 22 *ELRev* 519 at 526–8. In the present author's view, the judgment in *Arcaro* ought to be interpreted as precluding the use of sympathetic interpretation where the result is to enhance the criminal or administrative liability of individuals. It is not obvious that the Court was contemplating any limitation in civil law cases.

[44] See Case C–6/90 *Francovich* v. *Italy* [1991] ECR I–5357.

intended to confer rights on individuals; the breach must be sufficiently serious; and there must be a direct causal link between the breach of the obligation resting on the State and the damage sustained".[45] For our purposes, the meaning of a "sufficiently serious" breach is especially important. It seems clear that it includes situations where a Member State has entirely failed to translate a directive into national law[46] and where it has failed to alter national law so as to reflect developments in the Court of Justice's jurisprudence.[47] The notion of a "sufficiently serious breach" does not however include reasonable errors in the interpretation of EC law by a Member State.[48]

The analysis here of these principles on the enforcement of EC law in the national legal order is in two stages. Consideration is first given to whether these principles, taken as a whole, give a remedy to *all* employees who are the intended beneficiaries of a right set out in a directive. The discussion then moves on to examine whether any gaps in protection which can be identified are problematic on the accounts of EU labour law outlined in section 1.

In general, a gap in the availability of a remedy will arise only in circumstances where neither the principle of sympathetic interpretation nor the fall-back of state liability is applicable. This will occur when (i) a Member State has introduced legislation in order to comply with a directive's requirements, (ii) the legislation cannot be interpreted in line with the directive, and (iii) the Member State could not have been expected to realise that its implementation of the directive was erroneous. In practice, it is the evolving nature of EU labour laws which opens up the possibility that all of these conditions will be satisfied at once. A directive may be found to have a meaning which the Member State could not have anticipated, so that state liability does not arise, and which is at the same time incapable of being read into national legislation.

A number of examples may serve to illustrate the general point. One case is the development of the concept of indirect discrimination in the law on equal treatment between men and women. In Britain, the prohibition of indirect sex discrimination in EU labour law has been held to invalidate the exclusion of certain part-time workers, and older workers from protection against unfair dismissal and the right to redundancy payments.[49] However, it is only more

[45] Cases C–46/93 and C–48/93 *Brasserie du Pêcheur SA* v. *Germany and R* v. *Secretary of State for Transport, ex parte Factortame (No. 3)* [1996] ECR I–1029, para. 51.

[46] See, for example, Cases C–178, 179, 188, 189 and 190/94 *Dillenkofer* v. *Germany* [1996] ECR I–4845.

[47] See, for example, the judgment in *Brasserie du Pêcheur*, note 45, above, at para.59.

[48] For examples, see Case C–392/93 *R* v. *HM Treasury, ex parte British Telecommunications plc* [1996] ECR I–1631; and Cases C–283/94, C–291/94 and C–292/94 *Denkavit International BV and others* v. *Bundesamt für Finanzen* [1996] ECR I–5063.

[49] In *R* v. *Secretary of State for Employment, ex parte Equal Opportunities Commission* [1995] 1 AC 1, the House of Lords found that the exclusion of certain part-time workers from the right to statutory redundancy payments was inconsistent with what is now Article 141 EC. It also held that the exclusion of those part-time workers from the right to claim unfair dismissal was contrary to the Equal Treatment Directive. The exclusion of workers over 65 from claiming unfair dismissal or statutory redundancy payments was held by the London South Industrial Tribunal to breach what is now Article 141 EC in *Nash* v. *Mash/Roe Group* [1998] IRLR 168.

recently, as a result of the Court of Justice's decision in *Seymour-Smith*, that it has been settled that employees denied the right to claim unfair dismissal compensation by statutory rules can use Article 141 EC to bring an action against a private employer.[50] But for that outcome, this would arguably have been a situation in which private sector employees were left without a remedy. That is because the breaches of EC equal treatment law in each case were not obvious ones, given that Member States have the possibility to use social policy arguments to justify indirectly discriminatory measures. As a result, Britain was probably not guilty of a "sufficiently serious" breach for state liability to have arisen.[51]

A second example is provided by the British failure to provide an acceptable mechanism for the designation of worker representatives for the purposes of consultation upon collective redundancies and transfers of undertakings. The British legislation had provided for a right of consultation with employee representatives only where the employer recognised a trade union. That approach was found to breach the Collective Redundancies Directive and the Transfer of Undertakings Directive in the twin judgments in *Commission* v. *United Kingdom* in 1994, where the Court of Justice held that consultation with representatives was required for *all* employees. Nevertheless, it is arguable that the British approach was based upon a reading of the Directives which was sufficiently plausible for state liability not to have been available. Specifically, the British Government's argument was that giving rights only where there was a recognised union was consistent with the Directives because they defined "representatives of employees" to mean "the representatives of the employees provided for by the laws or practices of the Member States".[52]

A third and more recent example concerns the definition of "working time" in the Working Time Directive as "any period during which the worker is working, at the employer's disposal and carrying-out his activity or duties".[53] There is uncertainty as to whether these criteria are disjunctive or cumulative.[54] The result of this uncertainty may well be that, although the Directive requires

[50] Case C–167/97 *R* v. *Secretary of State for Employment, ex parte Seymour-Smith and Perez* [1999] ECR I–623.

[51] For a discussion of the *EOC* and *Seymour-Smith* litigation which reaches this conclusion, see T.Hervey and P.Rostant, "State Liability and British Employment Law" (1996) 25 *ILJ* 259 at 263–6 and 278–9. The *Seymour-Smith* litigation concerned the claim that the increase of the qualifying-period for unfair dismissal actions from one year to two years in 1985 was indirect sex discrimination. The claim was eventually rejected by the House of Lords in *R.* v. *Secretary of State for Employment, ex parte Seymour-Smith* and *Perez* (No. 2), [2000] ICR 244.

[52] See Article 1(1)(b) of the Collective Redundancies Directive and Article 2(c) of the original version of the Transfer of Undertakings Directive. For the judgments in the *Commission* v. *United Kingdom* cases, see note 28, above.

[53] See Article 2(1) of Council Directive 93/104 concerning certain aspects of the organisation of working time, [1993] OJ L 307/18.

[54] See Case C–303/98 *SIMAP* v. *Cancelleria de Sanidad y Consumo de la Generalidad Valenciana*, and the judgment in *Cawley* v. *Hammersmith Hospital NHS Trust* (EAT, 25 January 1999) discussed in J.Fairhurst, "The Working Time Directive: A Spanish Inquisition" [1999] *Web Journal of Current Legal Issues* (http://webjcli.ncl.ac.uk/1999/issue3/fairhurst3.html).

a broad (disjunctive) definition of working time, where a Member State has adopted a narrow (cumulative) definition, neither indirect effect nor state liability will give a remedy to an employee whose working time rights depend upon the broad construction.

These examples illustrate that some employees may be unable, in some situations, to rely upon the fallback of state liability to give them a remedy for the enforcement of EC law. In those circumstances, private sector employees will be left without any remedy under EC law. Public sector employees will meanwhile be without a remedy if they are also unable to rely upon the notion of vertical effect, because the relevant provision of a directive is insufficiently clear, precise and unconditional to be directly effective. That seems especially likely where positive action by the Member State is necessary to give substance to the EC rights. That might for example include the second and third cases discussed in the previous paragraph, where Member State action was needed to set out a procedure for designating employee representatives,[55] and to define "working time", respectively.

The next question is whether it is significant that some employees may, in some circumstances, have no remedy for the enforcement of EU labour law. If so, then it follows that it is desirable for the system of remedies to be completed, presumably by giving horizontal effect to EC law or by the imposition of strict liability upon Member States for non-compliance.

Within the approach here, the answer to that question depends upon the presumed purpose of EU labour laws. Where its purpose is to solve transnational regulatory problems, then it is arguable that every employee ought indeed to have a remedy, because the integration of national labour law regimes into a coherent whole by EU labour law means that full compliance by the law of each Member State is strongly desirable. An example would be the failure of a Member State to provide for the election or appointment of employee representatives to the "special negotiating body" which negotiates the establishment of a European Works Council or equivalent procedure. A failure of this kind would arguably have the knock-on effect of preventing the formation of these bodies in multinationals with employees in the Member State in question, even if the majority of their employees are in States which have complied with the Directive.[56] The general argument is that, because transnational regulation is concerned with the co-ordination of national systems, compliance is at a pre-

[55] See in particular the judgment of Blackburne J in *Griffin and others* v. *South-West Water Services Ltd* [1995] IRLR 15, High Court. In his view, because the Collective Redundancies Directive "gives to the member States. . . . a wide discretion in designating who the 'workers' representatives' are to be, the obligation to consult with workers' representatives was not 'unconditional and sufficiently precise' so as to be enforceable against a public body". (See the judgment at 32.)

[56] For a discussion of problems of this kind in the implementation of the European Works Councils Directive, see T. Blanke, "European Works Councils as an Institution of European Employee Co-Determination" in *A Legal Framework for European Industrial Relations*, note 6, above, at 42–3.

mium, so that the remedies for the enforcement of EC law ought to be as comprehensive as possible.

The same conclusion is suggested where the purpose of the labour law is to express the fundamental rights of employees. On that approach, it can be argued in general that a remedy ought to be available to each and every employee, as anything less would seem inconsistent with the right's presumed fundamental quality. As far as possible, *all* individuals who are the intended beneficiaries of a right should have some remedy to enforce it.[57] More particularly, the inequality between public and private sectors when it comes to the enforcement of EU labour law appears objectionable in fundamental rights terms.[58]

By contrast, however, it is arguable that, if the purpose of EU labour law is to reconcile competition and national labour laws by equalising the costs of labour law, then a fully comprehensive system of remedies is not absolutely necessary. This follows from the essentially systemic nature of the argument that European Union action is needed where there is tension between labour law and competition. As long as there is a broad equalisation of costs, this is likely to be sufficient to reduce that tension. Competition-based arguments for EU labour law need not require that every individual employee has a legal remedy, as long as the vast majority of employees do.

4. EMPLOYER OR STATE LIABILITY?

The discussion in the previous section assumed for the sake of argument that state liability for failure to implement EU labour law was an acceptable substitute for compliance by employers, and considered whether the combination of the two left any gaps in remedies. There are however reasons, of both principle and practice, to doubt the adequacy of state liability as an alternative to employer liability, achieved through direct effect where the Member State has failed to implement EC law correctly. These doubts about state liability from the perspective of EU labour law, and the corollary that horizontal effect may be desirable even where Member States are liable in damages for non-compliance with EC law, are the subject of this section.[59]

[57] See W. Van Gerven, "The Horizontal Effect of Directives Revisited: the Reality of Catchwords" in D. Curtin and T. Heukels (eds.), *Institutional Dynamics of European Integration* (Dordrecht: Martinus Nijhoff, 1994) at 350: "acknowledging horizontal direct effect would . . . complete, and improve, the judicial protection of individual rights".

[58] See Van Gerven, *loc.cit.*, at 349; and R. Mastroianni, "On the distinction between Vertical and Horizontal Direct Effects of Community Directives: What Role for the Principle of Equality?" (1995) 5 *EPL*, 417 at 433–4.

[59] Note that the analysis of this section could also be used to doubt the adequacy of Commission enforcement actions directed at the Member States under Article 226 EC as an alternative to direct effect in the context of EU labour law.

Arguments of principle in favour of employer liability follow from a consideration of the arguments for EU labour law set out in section 1. One argument is that, as we saw in the previous section, where the purpose of EU labour law is to remedy transnational regulatory problems, compliance within Member State law is likely to be indispensable. While state liability may encourage Member States to impose the relevant legal obligations upon employers, it remains at best an indirect route to this result. It is inherently preferable to achieve the result directly through the horizontal effect of Directives.

A second argument of principle follows from the "fundamental rights" account of EU labour law. It is increasingly argued that human rights standards ought in appropriate circumstances to be protected in the private sphere, including private employment relationships.[60] Support for this view may also be found in the case-law of the European Court of Human Rights.[61] If a significant element of the purpose of the EU labour law is to uphold individuals' fundamental rights against private employers, then it arguably follows that corresponding obligations ought ideally to be borne by the employer. Equal treatment standards provide an obvious example. If an individual is protected against discrimination, then it may be thought that liability for an act of discrimination ought to lie with the discriminating employer. The general point is that imposition of liability on the non-compliant Member State may be considered insufficient from the perspective of the protection of fundamental rights.

A third argument of principle derives from the account of EU labour law as a means to resolve the tension between competitive pressures and national labour law. That argument for EU labour law necessarily requires that the costs of EU labour laws are borne by employers. It is not enough that a Member State which fails in implementation is penalised through state liability. Indeed, the State's acceptance of state liability appears, on this approach, as precisely the kind of subsidy to employers which EU labour law is intended to prevent. The non-implementation of the Working Time Directive in Britain between November 1996 and October 1998, when average working hours in Britain were the longest in the European Union, offers a real-life example of a Member State running the risk of damages claims in order to preserve a competitive advantage enjoyed by employers on its territory.[62] The general argument was forcefully put by

[60] On the application of fundamental rights standards to private bodies and individuals, see, generally, A. Clapham, *Human Rights in the Private Sphere* (Oxford: Clarendon Press, 1993), especially chapter 5; and M. Hunt, "The 'Horizontal Effect' of the Human Rights Act" [1998] *PL* 423 at 424–34. In the context of labour law, see S. Deakin, "The Utility of 'Rights Talk': Employees' Personal Rights" in C. Gearty and A. Tomkins (eds.), *Understanding Human Rights* (London: Mansell, 1996); and K. Ewing, "Social Rights and Constitutional Law" [1999] *PL* 104 at 119–21.

[61] For a discussion of the European Court of Human Rights' case-law on the obligation of States under the European Convention to take positive steps to protect human rights as between private individuals, see D. Harris, M. O'Boyle and C. Warbrick, *Law of the European Convention on Human Rights* (London: Butterworths, 1995) at 19–22.

[62] Eurostat figures show that in 1996, Britain had the longest average working hours among full-time employees of any Member State for both men and women: see "Europe Cuts its Working Hours" *Labour Research*, July 1998, 13.

Advocate General Van Gerven in his Opinion in *Marshall (No. 2)*, when he observed of the principle of state liability that "that – in principle favourable – development does not remedy the fact that individuals who are operating in a Member State which implemented the directive correctly and are therefore bound by the obligations . . . are disadvantaged in comparison with individuals (perhaps their competitors) who are in a Member State which has not yet correctly implemented the directive".[63] The claim that state liability is inferior to direct effect is perhaps strongest on this approach to EU labour law.

In addition to these arguments of principle, practical considerations also suggest that the remedy of state liability is inferior to employer liability through direct effect. One practical argument is that employees may strongly prefer employers to respect the substance of the given legal right, rather than receive monetary compensation from the State. This may be thought especially likely where a legal entitlement cannot be readily given a monetary value. Within existing legislation, examples might include the limitations on working time under the Working Time Directive and the rights to information and consultation set out in the Collective Redundancies Directive, the Transfer of Undertakings Directive and the European Works Councils Directive. This argument could also apply to hypothetical future initiatives in EU labour law recognising civil liberties in the employment sphere or rights of collective action. In all of these cases, it is inherently difficult to attribute a monetary value to the rights of employees.[64]

A second practical argument for employer liability through direct effect is that it may be preferable on procedural grounds. The British case can serve as an illustration here. It is established that directly effective rights can be enforced through employment tribunals where they are analogous to a right over which the tribunals have jurisdiction.[65] By contrast, state liability claims must be brought before the ordinary courts, either as part of an action for judicial review, or as a claim in tort.[66] It is true that recourse to employment tribunals has the potential drawback of a presumptive three or six month time-limit[67] as

[63] See para. 73 of the Opinion in *Marshall* v. *Southampton and South-West Hampshire Area Health Authority* (No. 2), Case C–271/91, [1993] ECR I–4367.

[64] For a similar observation, see Mastroianni (1995), note 58, above, at 419.

[65] See the comments of Mummery J in the Employment Appeal Tribunal in *Biggs* v. *Somerset County Council* [1995] ICR 811, 830, endorsed by the Court of Appeal in *Barber* v. *Staffordshire County Council* [1996] 2 All ER 748, 753–4.

[66] For a discussion of state liability in British law, see J. Convery, "State Liability in the United Kingdom after *Brasserie du Pêcheur*" (1997) 34 *CMLRev* 603. For rejection of suggestions that employment tribunals might have jurisdiction over state liability claims, see Neill LJ in the Court of Appeal in *Secretary of State for Employment* v. *Mann and Others* [1997] ICR 209, 229.

[67] A presumption of three months is the norm. For example, the Sex Discrimination Act 1975, s. 76, has a time-limit of three months or such longer period as appears "just and equitable" to the employment tribunal, while the Employment Rights Act 1996, s. 111 requires claims of unfair dismissal to be brought within three months or "such further period as the tribunal considers reasonable" if it is not "reasonably practicable" to bring the claim within three months. The Equal Pay Act 1970, s. 2(4) is exceptional in requiring that claims be brought during an employment relationship or within six months of its termination.

against the six year time-limit for tort claims.[68] However, the *raison d'être* of the employment tribunals is their accessibility to employees. This is reflected, among other things, in the comparative informality of their proceedings, the absence of an application fee and the rarity with which costs are awarded to the winning side. The accessibility of the employment tribunals is moreover probably reflected in their extensive use by employees in Britain.[69] Employees may therefore be thought likely to have a strong preference that rights be enforceable before employment tribunals and their equivalents in other jurisdictions.

In conclusion, it can be seen that there are a number of reasons to doubt the adequacy of state liability as an alternative to employer liability and direct effect in the context of EU labour law. In reaching that conclusion, the analysis here differs from most judicial and academic commentary on the subject. The predominant view is that state liability is an acceptable substitute for the direct effect of EC law,[70] and that it is preferable on constitutional grounds, in that it focuses legal obligations on the non-compliant state, rather than upon "innocent" private individuals and public bodies.[71] By contrast, the analysis here offers support, by reference to the purposes of EU labour law, for the suggestions that the horizontal effect of Directives may still have a role in the era of state liability.[72]

5. NATIONAL PROCEDURES AND SANCTIONS

A third aspect of the enforcement of EC law by individuals which requires scrutiny in the context of labour law is the discretion retained by Member States in relation to remedies.[73] The Court of Justice has made it clear that it is for the

[68] Limitation Act 1980, s. 2.

[69] ACAS figures show that approximately 136,000 claims were taken to employment tribunals between July 1998 and July 1999: see*The Guardian*, 18 September 1999. It may be thought unlikely that litigation would occur to this extent if the same rights were enforceable before the ordinary courts.

[70] This view is implicit in *Francovich* itself in the Court of Justice's argument that "the full effectiveness of Community rules would be impaired and the protection of the rights which they grant would be weakened" if state liability were not introduced: see para. 33 of the judgment. Similarly, academic commentators have presented the introduction of state liability as "one of the remaining pieces of the jigsaw of judicial protection of individuals under Community law": see D. Curtin, "State Liability under Community Law: A New Remedy for Private Parties" (1993) 56 *MLR* 55 at 55.

[71] Support for that view is found in the Court of Justice's judgment in *Dori*, in which it offered the principle of state liability as an argument for rejecting the horizontal effect of Directives: see para. 27 of the judgment. See too H. Schermers, "No Direct Effect for Directives" (1997) 3 *EPL* 527.

[72] In addition to the remarks of Advocate General Van Gerven quoted in the text, see too the comments of Advocate General Jacobs in Case C–316/92 *Veneetveld* v. *Le Foyer SA* [1994] ECR I–763 at para. 30; and of T. Tridimas, "Horizontal Effect: A Missed Opportunity?" (1994) 19 *ELRev* 621 at 634–5.

[73] Note that the term "remedies" is used here to refer to national provisions which relate to the enforcement of legal rights. The text distinguishes between "procedural rules", which govern the manner in which a claim is made, and "sanctions", which are the orders which may be made once a legal obligation has been found to have been breached. It is not claimed that the distinctions between rights and remedies, or between procedures and sanctions, are easy to draw in every concrete case.

Member States to determine the courts and tribunals which are responsible for upholding EC law rights.[74] Member States also have significant latitude in relation to the procedural rules which govern an action for the enforcement of the EC law and the sanctions for non-compliance with EC law obligations.[75] This national discretion over remedies is a consequence of the absence of a harmonised system of procedures and sanctions in the European Union. It may also be thought to reflect more particularly the nature of directives which, according to Article 249 EC (ex Article 189) "leave to the national authorities the choice of form and methods" in achieving a given result.

It is unnecessary here to provide a detailed account of the Court of Justice's case-law on national procedures and sanctions, or of the intricacies of the evolution of its principles over time.[76] For our purposes, it is sufficient to observe that the Court of Justice has imposed two kinds of requirement upon Member States in exercising their discretion over remedies. First, there is a requirement of *equivalence*: that is, the procedural conditions and sanctions applying to the exercise of EC law rights "cannot be less favourable than those relating to similar actions of a domestic nature".[77] Secondly, there are requirements as to the *effectiveness* of national rules on procedures and sanctions. National procedural rules must not make it "impossible in practice" or "excessively difficult" to exercise the rights which the national courts are obliged to protect".[78] With respect to sanctions, where EC law does not lay down more specific requirements, there is a minimum requirement that Member States "take all measures necessary to guarantee the application and effectiveness of Community law".[79]

The case-law of the Court of Justice shows the relevance of these principles in the labour law field. The Court of Justice has for example twice in recent years doubted British *procedural* rules governing claims for equal pay. The first case was *Magorrian*, which concerned part-time workers who sought to claim that the reservation of a retirement benefit to full-time workers was indirectly discriminatory on grounds of sex. The difficulty they faced was that the value of the benefit depended upon the length of their period of employment, but there

[74] Case C–54/96 *Dorsch Consult Ingenieurgesellschaft mbH* v. *Bundesbaugesellschaft Berlin mbH* [1997] ECR I–4961, para. 40.

[75] In relation to procedural rules, see Case 33/76,*Rewe-Zentralfinanz eG* v. *Landwirtschaftskammer für das Saarland* [1976] ECR 1989, para. 5; and Case 45/76 *Comet BV* v. *Produktschap voor Siergewassen* [1976] ECR 2043, para. 13. In relation to sanctions, see for example para. 18 of the judgment in *Von Colson* in relation to the Equal Treatment Directive: "the Directive does not prescribe a specific sanction; it leaves member States free to choose between the different solutions for achieving its objective".

[76] For a thorough review, see R. Craufurd Smith, "Remedies for Breaches of EU Law in National Courts: Legal Variation and Selection", in P. Craig and G. de Búrca, (eds.), *The Evolution of EU Law* (Oxford: Oxford University Press, 1999).

[77] In relation to procedural rules, see *Rewe-Zentralfinanz eG*, note 75, above, para. 5. In relation to sanctions, see Case 68/88 *Commission* v. *Greece* [1989] ECR 2965.

[78] For the "impossible in practice" formulation, see *Rewe-Zentralfinanz eG*, *ibid*. For the "excessively difficult" formulation, see Case 199/82 *Amministrazione delle Finanze dello Stato* v. *San Giorgio* [1983] ECR 3595, para. 14.

[79] *Commission* v. *Greece*, note 77, above, para. 23.

was a statutory rule that an equal pay claim for admission to an occupational pension scheme could not have effect in respect of a period more than two years before the initiation of proceedings.[80] In the Court's view, that rule rendered the applicants' claim of equal treatment "impossible in practice", as it prevented most of their period of employment from being taken into account for the purposes of their claim.[81]

The second case was *Levez*, which concerned the rule in s. 2(5) of the Equal Pay Act 1970 that a claim for equal pay could not lead to an award of "any payment by way of arrears of remuneration or damages in respect of a time earlier than two years before the date on which proceedings were instituted". One peculiarity in the case was that part of the employee's claim fell outside the two year period because the employer had misled her as to the existence of a situation of unequal pay In those circumstances, the Court firstly held that the principle of effectiveness was likely to be breached. In its words, it was "plain that the ultimate effect of this rule would be to facilitate a breach of Community law by an employer where deceit caused the employee's delay".[82] The British Government had however argued that the effectiveness principle might not have been breached, as the employee could have successfully brought a claim for the tort of deceit, with respect to which there was a six year time-limit. The Court of Justice therefore went on to consider whether the principle of equivalence was respected by section 2(5) of the 1970 Act. In the event, the only guidance which it gave was that all aspects of a procedure had to be taken into account in deciding whether the given rule was less favourable.[83] Nevertheless, when the case returned to the Employment Appeal Tribunal, it concluded that the principle of equivalence had indeed been breached. In its view, the absolute limit on arrears in equal pay claims was more restrictive than the rules governing claims for breach of contract, unlawful deductions from wages, and discrimination on grounds of race and disability, which permitted up to six years' arrears to be claimed in each case.[84]

[80] Case C–246/96 *Magorrian* v. *Eastern Health and Social Services Board* [1997] ECR I–7153. The rule in question was the Occupational Pension Scheme (Equal Access to Membership) Regulations (Northern Ireland) 1976, SI 1976/238, Reg. 12. Note that this rule provides an example of the difficulties of classification in this area. A limitation on the retrospective effect of an award could be classified as a rule about sanctions. It is however treated here as a procedural rule because in many cases its effect will be to prevent claims being brought.

[81] See para. 41 of the judgment. Similar questions were considered by the Court of Justice in Case C–78/98 *Preston and Others* v. *Wolverhampton Healthcare NHS Trust and Others*, [2000] 2 CMLR 837 which concerned claims by part-time workers for retroactive membership of occupational pension schemes. In *Preston*, the applicants were confronted by effectively the same two-year limitations as in *Magorrian*, on this occasion Regulation 12 of the Occupational Pension Schemes (Equal Access to Membership Regulations) 1976 (SI 1976/142). In its judgment, the Court followed *Magorrian* and found the two-year limit contrary to the requirement of effectiveness.

[82] Case C–326/96 *Levez* v. *T.H. Jennings (Harlow Pools) Ltd* [1998] ECR I–7835, para. 32.

[83] *Ibid*, paras. 49–53.

[84] *Levez* v. *T.H. Jennings (Harlow Pools) Ltd* (No. 2), EAT [2000] ICR 58. Note that the outcome in *Levez* has implications for the requirement in section 2(4) of the Equal Pay Act 1970 (above, note 65) that equal pay claims must be brought within six months of the termination of an employment relationship. In *Preston*, the Court of Justice concluded that that rule was consistent in general with the requirement of effectiveness, but did not offer a view as to whether it was consistent with

Other cases have found the *sanctions* in national law for the breach of EU labour laws to be inadequate. The first of these decisions was *Von Colson*, which concerned the sanctions in German law for sex discrimination. Under paragraph 611a(2) of the *Bürgerliches Gesetzbuch* ("BGB"), an individual who was discriminated against in a job application was only entitled to compensation for their expenses in making the application. In that context, the Court of Justice held that the sanctions in national law which gave effect to the Equal Treatment Directive must have "a real deterrent effect on the employer".[85] Moreover, where the compensation of individuals was the method of enforcement chosen, then "that compensation must in any event be adequate in relation to the damage sustained".[86] The implication of the *Von Colson* judgment was that the sanctions for sex discrimination in German law were contrary to the requirement of effectiveness and the Equal Treatment Directive.

A second case on the Equal Treatment Directive was *Marshall (No. 2)*. It concerned the upper limit on sex discrimination cases in s. 65(2) of the Sex Discrimination Act 1975 and the possible absence of a power to award interest as an element of compensation in such cases. In giving judgment, the Court of Justice reiterated its general statements about sanctions in *Von Colson*. It went on to state more particularly that where sanctions took the form of compensation, then the compensation "must enable the loss and damage actually sustained . . . to be made good in full".[87] It followed that neither the ceiling on compensation nor the absence of interest on awards was consistent with the requirement of effectiveness in the context of the Equal Treatment Directive.

The German law developments which followed *Von Colson* and the first substantive issue in *Marshall (No. 2)* came together in *Draehmpaehl*.[88] After *Von Colson*, paragraph 611a(2) BGB was amended to allow "appropriate financial compensation", up to a maximum of three months' earnings, of individuals discriminated against in applications for employment. It was also provided in paragraph 61b(2) of the *Arbeitsgerichtgesetz* ("ArbGG") that, where more than one person had been discriminated against, an employer could apply for the total compensation not to exceed six months' earnings.[89] Where a job applicant would have been hired but for the discrimination by the employer, the Court of Justice held that the three month ceiling which had been introduced into

the requirement of equivalence. After the EAT's decision in *Levez*, however, it is arguable that the fact that time limits in other areas of labour law are longer than six months (six years in the case of breach of contract claims to a county court), or can be extended by a tribunal, means that s. 2(4) fails the test of equivalence.

[85] See Article 6 of the Directive, which provides that "Member States shall introduce into their national legal systems such measures as are necessary to enable all persons who consider themselves wronged . . . to pursue their claims by judicial process".

[86] *Von Colson*, note 42, above, para. 23.

[87] Case C–271/91 *Marshall* v. *Southampton and South-West Hampshire Area Health Authority (No. 2)* [1993] ECR I–4367, para. 26.

[88] Case C–180/95 *Draempaehl* v. *Urania Immobilienservice* [1997] ECR I–2195.

[89] For a discussion of the post-*Von Colson* developments, see E. Steindorff, Note on *Draempaehl* (1997) 34 *CMLRev* 1259 at 1260–2.

paragraph 611a(2) BGB was contrary to the Equal Treatment Directive. This was because the compensation might be inadequate in individual cases and because no equivalent limitation was to be found elsewhere in German civil and labour law. However, the Court of Justice added that the three months' ceiling was acceptable where the applicant would not have got the post even if there had not been discrimination.[90] The Court of Justice also held that the global maximum of six months' earnings in paragraph 61b(2) ArbGG was contrary to the Directive because it would not have a dissuasive effect upon employers and because no similar provisions were to be found elsewhere in German law.

A final example of Court of Justice scrutiny of national sanctions in the context of EU labour law is to be found in its twin judgments in *Commission* v. *United Kingdom* in 1994. In each judgment, the Court of Justice stated that any penalty for employer non-compliance with the consultation obligation by an employer had to be "effective, proportionate and dissuasive".[91] It accordingly found that the "protective award" which served as the sanction for failure to consult upon collective redundancies was inadequate because it could be set off against any amounts paid to the redundant employees under their contracts of employment.[92] It also held that the sanction for failure to consult upon the transfer of undertakings was inadequate, because it could be set off against a protective award.[93]

It can be seen therefore that the Court of Justice has been willing both to question, and to encourage national courts to question, the manner in which Member States exercise their discretion over remedies in the field of EU labour law. Nevertheless, the adequacy of the Court of Justice's approach as a solution to the dilemmas posed by national discretion over remedies is to some extent open to doubt from the perspective of EU labour law.

The Court of Justice's approach fits most readily with the account of EU labour laws as concerned with transnational regulation. From that perspective, it is arguable that the present approach to remedies is acceptable. Within a "transnational" approach, compliance within Member State law is crucial, but the precise means by which it is secured is less important. If national remedial rules are *effective*, then it may be thought unnecessary to invoke the principle of equivalence, or to go further in the direction of the harmonisation of the rules on remedies.

[90] This part of the Court's judgment is not especially convincing. Compensation of more than three months' earnings *might* be necessary in some unusual cases (e.g. a long-term contract) even though it could not be said that the applicant would have got the job in the absence of discrimination. Moreover, it is far from clear that the ceiling of three months' compensation passed the "equivalence" test: see paras. 28 and 54 of Advocate General Léger's Opinion.

[91] See para. 40 of the judgment in Case C–383/92 *Commission* v. *United Kingdom*, on the Collective Redundancies Directive, and pars. 55 of the judgment in Case C–383/92, note 28, above, on the Transfer of Undertakings Directive.

[92] See paras. 41–2 of the judgment in Case C–383/92. The set-off rule was in s.102(3) of the Employment Protection Act 1975.

[93] See paras. 57–8 of the judgment in Case C–182/92. The set-off rule was in Regulation 11(7) of the Transfer of Undertakings (Protection of Employment) Regulations, SI 1981 No. 1794.

Within a "fundamental rights" account of EU labour law, by contrast, there is room for disagreement as to the adequacy of the Court of Justice's approach in relation to remedies. One view is that, if EC law is concerned with fundamental rights, then uniformity in remedies in different Member States is unnecessary. Instead, as Szyszczak argues, the priority is to ensure that "Citizenship is not devalued in some parts of the European Union" and that "Community rights are not undervalued in relation to the enforcement of rights within the national systems".[94] That line of argument is consistent with the emphasis upon equivalence and effectiveness in the Court of Justice's case-law. Conversely, however, it can be argued that the expression of fundamental rights in EC law requires uniformity of protection across the Member States. This follows from Curtin's view that "national differences bring with them a risk of inequality and unfairness in the protection of individual rights conferred by Community law and inevitably have a disintegrating effect".[95] That approach implies that it is unacceptable that Member States differ in practice in the extent of their protection of fundamental rights recognised at the European Union level.

Accounts of European Union intervention as necessary for the resolution of the tension between competition and national labour laws imply a more robust conclusion however. Even if the principles of equivalence and effectiveness are respected, there may still be significant variation in the costs associated with the enforcement of labour laws in the different Member States. There may for example be important differences concerning the enforcement of labour laws – whether in the role of inspection authorities or because the courts and tribunals charged with upholding labour laws are significantly more accessible in some Member States than others.[96] There may also be differences in sanctions, for example if some Member States place a greater emphasis upon punitive awards than others. It is arguable that, on a competition-based approach to EU labour law, actual and potential variations in national approaches to the enforcement of labour law ought to be minimised.

If greater intervention in relation to national remedies is desirable, then that objective might be advanced through Court of Justice jurisprudence. A more comprehensive solution however would be for the development of European Union standards in relation to the enforcement of labour laws within Member States. This is a course of action which has from time to time been suggested by commentators in other contexts.[97] It has also been pursued in specific sectors,

[94] E. Szyszczak, "Making Europe More Relevant to its Citizens: Effective Judicial Process" (1996) 21 *ELRev* 351 at 352.

[95] Curtin (1992), note 3, above, at 35.

[96] For a summary of the non-judicial and judicial mechanisms for the enforcement of employment rights in the twelve pre-1995 Member States, see C. Barnard, J. Clark and R. Lewis, *The Exercise of Individual Employment Rights in the Member States of the European Community* (London: Department of Employment, 1995), chapters 3 and 4.

[97] See, for example, the Court of Justice's reference in a case concerning Common Agricultural Policy levies to the "regrettable absence of Community provisions harmonizing procedures and time-limits": Case 130/79 *Express Dairy Foods Ltd* v. *Intervention Board for Agricultural Produce*, [1980] ECR 1887, at para. 12. More generally, see J. Bridge, "Procedural Aspects of the Enforcement

most notably that of public procurement.[98] Its seems reasonable to expect that these precedents could be extended to the field of labour law.

6. CONCLUSION

This essay has shown that a consideration of the purposes of EU labour law argues for the strengthening of the regime governing the enforcement of EC law by individuals. If the purpose of European Union legislation is transnational regulation or the protection of the fundamental rights of workers, then any gaps in the comprehensiveness of remedies ought to be removed. State liability is an inadequate substitute for direct effect and employer liability, both in principle and in practice, on any account of the purposes of EU labour law. Finally, a case can be made for greater intervention with respect to national procedures and sanctions – arguably, if EU labour law is concerned with the protection of fundamental rights, and definitely if its purpose is to reconcile competitive pressures and national labour laws.

It remains to indicate the wider implications of the analysis developed in this essay. On the one hand, it is straightforward that the arguments set out here are not specific to labour law. Suitably modified, they could be extended to other policy areas where transnational regulation, fundamental rights or the tension between competition and national regulation are relevant.[99] In any of the spheres where the analysis here is of relevance, it will provide a counterweight to the cultural and democratic arguments against the strengthened enforcement of EC law referred to in the introduction to the essay.

At the same time, the criticisms offered here of the rules relating to the enforcement by individuals of EC law may be thought to cast doubt on the adequacy of the institutional framework governing EU labour law. The arguments developed here support suggestions elsewhere that the regime governing the enforcement of EC law may be inadequate in the context of labour law.[100] They also complement suggestions that the legislative powers in the field of labour

of European Community Law through the Legal Systems of the Member States", (1984) 9 *ELRev* 28; and Curtin, note 3, above, at 49.

[98] See Article 2 of Council Directive 89/665 on the application of review procedures to the award of public supply and public works contracts [1989] OJ L 395/33, and Article 2 of Council Directive 92/13 on the procurement procedures of entities operating in the water, energy, transport and telecommunications sectors [1992] OJ L 76/14.

[99] For a discussion of the effective enforcement of EC public procurement laws, see S. Weatherill, "National Remedies and Equal Access to Public Procurement" (1990) 10 *YEL* 243. The adequacy of the rules relating to the private enforcement of EC law have also been of particular concern in the field of environmental law. See, for example J. Holder, "A Dead End for Direct Effect? Prospects for Enforcement of European Community Environmental Laws by Individuals" (1996) 8 *Journal of Environmental Law* 322.

[100] See, for example, C. McCrudden, "The Effectiveness of European Equality Law: National Mechanisms for Enforcing Gender Equality Law in the Light of European Requirements" (1993) 13 *OJLS* 320; and P. Davies, "The European Court of Justice, National Courts and the Member States", in Davies, Lyon-Caen, Sciarra and Simitis (1996), note 23, above, particularly at 101–14.

law under the European Community Treaty remain too weak.[101] The general argument is ultimately that the institutional framework leaves too much room for variation in EU labour laws in practice in the Member States. The minimisation of such variation appears essential if there is to be an effective common system of labour law within the European Union.

[101] See P. Davies, "The Emergence of European Labour Law" in W. McCarthy (ed.), *Legal Intervention in Industrial Relations*, (Oxford: Blackwell, 1992), 313 at 348–51; and Ryan (1997), note 7, above.

PART III

Co-Existence and Interaction with Other European Legal Orders

7

Interplay of Private International Law and European Community Law

PAUL BEAUMONT

1. INTRODUCTION

PRIVATE INTERNATIONAL law can be regarded as an area of interest only to a few specialists which should not excite any political arguments or be of interest to those building a European Union. However, this writer has first hand experience of how politically relevant private international law is on the European and world stage at the moment. It is when one ceases to view private international law as primarily about choice of law in disputes between private parties, and instead views it as primarily about determining the courts of which country can decide civil and commercial disputes, that one realises its political significance. It is a matter of considerable importance to the sovereignty of a State to place limitations on when its courts can hear and decide cases. It also places limits on the earning capacities of lawyers and how much can be earned by a State in providing this form of service industry. So the negotiations at the Hague Conference on Private International Law on a new Jurisdiction and Judgments Convention due to conclude in 2001/2 are predicated on the assumption that States will be forced to give up some of their jurisdictional power. It would appear that this is something that a significant number of those consulted in the United States of America on the partial draft Convention agreed in June 1999 find hard to accept.[1] At the European level such constraints on sovereignty are an accepted

[1] Some enlightened academics who would like to see some reduction in US jurisdiction are sceptical about whether the Hague negotiations will succeed and if so how widely ratified the Hague Convention will be. See R. Weintraub, "How Substantial is our need for a Judgments-Recognition Convention and What should we Bargain Away to get it?" (1998) XXIV *Brooklyn J.Int.L.* 167 at 220; F. Juenger, "A Hague Judgments Convention?" (1998) XXIV *Brooklyn J.Int.L.* 111 at 121; and A. Lowenfeld, *International Litigation and the Quest for Reasonableness: essays in private international law* (Oxford: Clarendon Press, 1996) at 129. Juenger, at 121–3, suggested it would be preferable for the US and the EU to negotiate a bilateral treaty. At present the EU does not have the competence to negotiate such a bilateral treaty but this is likely to change when the Brussels Regulation is adopted under Title IV of the EC Treaty post-Amsterdam, see below. This adoption will take place, at the earliest, in 2000 – perhaps prior to the diplomatic conference in The Hague in June 2001. However, the US might not find it that easy doing business with the Commission and the bilateral Treaty might exclude its long time ally, the UK, because it may not opt in to the Brussels Regulation. The advantage of the Hague negotiations is that it contains several States that

part of the juridical picture since the entry into force in the 1970s of the Brussels Convention. Here the politically contentious issue is whether or not the Member States of the European Union should retain their external competence in these matters of jurisdiction or whether by transforming the Convention into a Community Regulation they create Community external competence and thereby give the European Commission the power to negotiate on behalf of some or all of the Member States of the European Union at the Hague Conference on Private International Law and in bilateral negotiations with third States. So this is an area which not only throws up questions about loss of state sovereignty but also about institutional politics within the European Union.

The fact that the European Commission may gain competence to speak for "some or all" of the Member States of the European Union is indicative of the fact that this is an area where variable geometry operates in the brave new world of Title IV of the EC Treaty after the entry into force of the Treaty of Amsterdam (1 May 1999). It is highly unlikely that the Commission will speak for all the Member States because Denmark has an opt-out from Title IV which does not permit them to opt back in selectively and Ireland and the UK are opted out of Title IV but can opt in to individual legislative acts.[2] So private international law gains political attention as one of the testbeds of differential integration within the European Union.

However, this is a collection on remedies. The reader may well be wondering what possible relevance jurisdiction and variable geometry have to remedies. The reason is that judicial remedies are only available if the court concerned has jurisdiction over the dispute. Jurisdiction is the key to unlocking the remedies provided in that national legal system. How far can and should the European and international communities go in regulating jurisdiction over final and interim remedies? Clearly one objective is to prevent jurisdiction being taken by a court which has no real connection with the person who is defending the action or with the subject matter of the action. Thus the notorious French rule whereby a French national can bring an action against anyone in France and the Anglo-American rule whereby serving a writ on a person passing through the country is sufficient to found jurisdiction in an action against that person and other "exorbitant jurisdictions" can be eliminated.

One of the most vexed areas in the worldwide negotiations is the problem of conflicts of jurisdiction and of whether or not a court with an accepted basis of jurisdiction should have the power in the individual case to say that it is an inappropriate forum and decline to exercise jurisdiction. Apart from the cases where the courts of one legal system have exclusive jurisdiction (itself something which

can act as a bridge between the EU and the USA, e.g. Australia, Canada, Denmark, Japan, Switzerland, and the UK. Of course, if the Hague negotiations fail to produce a Convention that the USA is able to ratify, or that the core EU States are able to ratify then bilateral negotiations between the EU and USA can be tried but the present writer is very sceptical about the chance of success.

[2] See P. Beaumont, "Treaty of Amsterdam – Community Competence in Private International Law" (1999) 48 *ICLQ* 225–9.

takes careful defining) it is normal to give the party initiating the case some choice of jurisdiction. Therefore that person has the chance to select the jurisdiction with the best remedies (e.g. the one that has a rigorous pre-trial discovery or has very high damages awards). Should that person's choice be determinative or should the court selected have the discretion to decline to exercise jurisdiction?[3] Here the legal certainty in knowing which court will exercise jurisdiction is weighed against the risks of injustice in giving the person initiating proceedings too big an advantage in the litigation. In the context of interim remedies this problem is potentially even greater because the person initiating the proceedings usually has even wider choices as to where to seek interim relief and it is not normal to try and prevent multiple actions because the person is often seeking to find and freeze some assets that could fulfil a final judgment. However, the person against which the action is brought is often in an adverse position because the interim relief may be granted in the first instance in that person's absence and without the person having been informed of the legal action (*ex parte*).

The next issue which the private international law negotiations in The Hague and in Brussels have focused on is the extent to which the judgments of a competent jurisdiction should be recognised and enforced in other Contracting States. Free movement of judgments, the idea that the decisions of courts which have jurisdiction on the basis of a jurisdiction rule which is one of the approved rules under the Convention should be recognised and enforced in all the Contracting States, is a fine ideal but has to be subject to some limits. It is a great example of subsidiarity that the substantive remedies available in each Contracting State are a matter for that State but that each State then agrees to recognise that judgment (even if it has no such equivalent substantive remedy) subject in the case of the EU to very few exceptions and, probably, to a small list of exceptions in the Hague negotiations. In the context of both Conventions what gives some limited protection to state sovereignty is the much discussed but little used "public policy" exception.[4] Both Conventions protect the person

[3] For background on how a discretion to decline to exercise jurisdiction can be controlled by the development of case-law separating out relevant from irrelevant factors and helping to give more weight to some factors than others see the various annexes, including Annex D by the United Kingdom (written by P. Beaumont), to the "Note on the Question of "Forum non Conveniens" in the perspective of a Convention on jurisdiction and the enforcement of Decisions" (Hague Conference on Private International Law, Prel. Doc. No. 3, 1996). By June 1999 the Hague Conference Special Commission had negotiated Article 24 on "Exceptional circumstances for declining jurisdiction", an example of a fairly closely structured and limited discretion, as part of a package with Article 23 on "Lis pendens" (see Working Doc. No. 241 of June 1999, the Preliminary Draft Convention on Jurisdiction and the effects of judgments in civil and commercial matters – hereinafter "the Hague Prel. draft").

[4] Article 27(1) of the Brussels and Lugano Conventions and Article 27 *bis* (1) (f) of the Hague Prel. draft. For a fascinating account of the internationalism of the English courts in making very limited use of public policy, also seen in the United States and increasingly so in France, and yet the need to preserve some notion of forum public policy, see N. Enonchong, "Public Policy in the Conflict of Laws: A Chinese Wall Around Little England?" (1996) 45 *ICLQ* 633–61. The Scottish position on public policy is also internationalist, see A. Anton with P. Beaumont, *Private International Law*, 2nd edn. (Edinburgh: W. Green/SULI, 1990) 101–06.

against whom enforcement is sought if the original claim was decided against that person without being notified in a way that enabled the person to arrange for a defence.[5] In the worldwide negotiations it is recognised that some greater protection is needed for persons against whom enforcement is sought because the country giving the original judgment could be anywhere in the world and is not part of a sophisticated club of like-minded European States with mutual respect for the integrity of their various legal systems. Therefore recognition or enforcement may be refused if the proceedings in the state of origin were incompatible with "fundamental principles of procedure of the State addressed".[6] Another bone of contention is about the level of damages awards. Much of the anxiety here stems from some spectacularly high jury awards in tort cases in the United States. Although most of these awards are reduced on appeal and are pitched at a high level to take account of the very high costs of medical care in the United States most other countries at The Hague want to have some discretion to reduce "grossly excessive damages".[7]

This introduction suggests an ambitious sweep for this chapter but the reader will find that the sweep is rather superficial and transient. The former is due to the constraints of time and space as to what can be analysed in depth in one book chapter and the latter to the timing of the writing – September 1999 – just before negotiations on a new Brussels Regulation commence in Brussels[8] and just before the Special Commission on the Judgments Convention in The Hague in October 1999[9] which will prepare a draft Convention for the diplomatic conference in the Hague in 2001–2. Particular concentration is given to the area of

[5] Article 27(2) of the Brussels and Lugano Conventions and Article 27 *bis* (1)(d) of the Hague Prel. draft.

[6] Article 27 *bis* (1)(c) of the Hague Prel. draft.

[7] Article 32 of the Hague Prel. draft. This issue has received a lot of attention at the Hague Special Commission as the negotiating history will reveal (much of it is not in the public domain until after the diplomatic conference has been concluded) but has not been as difficult to negotiate as the problems surrounding conflicts of jurisdiction and the extent to which a court that has jurisdiction can validly decline to exercise it whether or not there is a conflict.

[8] The first consideration of the proposal for a Council Regulation on jurisdiction and the enforcement of judgments in civil and commercial matters in 10742/99 JUSTCIV 124 was scheduled for the Council of the European Union Committee on Civil Law (Brussels I) on 20–21 September 1999.

[9] The Special Commission on international jurisdiction and the effects of foreign judgments in civil and commercial matters was scheduled to have its fifth meeting from 25–30 October 1999 in the Academy of International Law, Peace Palace, The Hague. The present writer has been a member of the UK delegation since the meeting of the Special Commission in June 1996. The originator of the concept of a mixed convention – which is what will emerge at the end of these negotiations, is Professor Arthur von Mehren of Harvard University and a leading member of the US delegation at the Hague Conference. For a short and extremely helpful explanation of the concept see his "Enforcing Judgments Abroad: Reflections on the Design of Recognition Conventions" (1998) XXIV *Brooklyn J.Int.L.* 17–29. For insider views of the early part of the Hague negotiations, see in the same symposium volume: P. Pfund, "The Project of the Hague Conference on Private International Law to prepare a Convention on Jurisdiction and the Recognition/Enforcement of judgments in civil and commercial matters", 7–15; L. Lussier, "A Canadian Perspective", 31–73; P. Beaumont, "A United Kingdom Perspective on the Proposed Hague Judgments Convention", 75–109; and R. Brand, "Tort Jurisdiction in a Multilateral Convention: The Lessons of the Due Process Clause and the Brussels Convention", 125–55.

interim remedies because of its difficulty and complexity, of the need for analysis of two of the important and recent decisions of the European Court of Justice and the explicit use in one of those cases of mainstream Community law in developing private international law. Anything said in this chapter is tentative and personal and does not represent the view of the UK in the Brussels or Hague negotiations.

2. EUROPEAN PRIVATE INTERNATIONAL LAW PRE-AMSTERDAM

The Brussels and Lugano Conventions regulate international jurisdiction in eighteen States (the fifteen EU Member States plus Iceland, Norway and Switzerland) and provide for the free movement of judgments. They carve the Single Market up into legal units which include legal systems that exist at or below the level of the Member States (e.g. Scotland).[10]

Legal basis

The Brussels Convention is an international treaty for members of the European Communities negotiated under Article 220 of the EEC Treaty (Article 293 EC, post Amsterdam). The Lugano Convention is a parallel international treaty negotiated by the Member States of the European Community and of the European Free Trade Association (EFTA) but open to any State in the world if approved by all of the EU and EFTA States. Negotiations commenced in September 1997 in Lugano to revise the Brussels and Lugano Conventions together.[11]

Jurisdiction over the substance

The Brussels and Lugano Conventions create absolutely uniform rules of jurisdiction for all people domiciled in one of the Contracting States (apart from a

[10] For an exhaustive five volume analysis of the Brussels and Lugano Conventions see P. Kaye, *Law of the European Judgments Convention* (Chichester: Barry Rose Law Publishers, 1999) and for a single volume analysis of the Conventions which includes a treatment of the broad adoption of the Brussels Convention jurisdiction rules in Scotland, unlike England and Wales, for disputes involving persons domiciled outside the Brussels and Lugano Contracting States see P. Beaumont, *Anton & Beaumont's Civil Jurisdiction in Scotland: Brussels and Lugano Conventions*, 2nd edn. (Edinburgh: W. Green/Sweet & Maxwell, 1995).

[11] These negotiations started in the Lugano Standing Committee but really got underway in Brussels as an ad hoc Working Party of the Council of the European Union. The present writer was a member of the UK team in the negotiations which reached their conclusion in an agreement in the *Ad Hoc* Working Party in April 1999 (see Document 7700/99 JUSTCIV 60) and for comment on this see the Twenty Fifth Report of the House of Commons European Scrutiny Committee. For comment on the early stages of the negotiations see P. Beaumont, "A United Kingdom Perspective on the Proposed Hague Judgments Convention" (1998) XXIV *Brooklyn J. Int.L.* 75–109.

few differences between the two Conventions). This is an old fashioned maximum harmonisation route[12] which leaves no room for higher standards (e.g. a rule of *forum non conveniens* whereby a court that has jurisdiction under the Convention could still decline to exercise it on the ground that it is not an appropriate forum in the individual case). The jurisdiction rules operate on a strict first come first served basis (*lis pendens*) and therefore the person initiating the action is in the driving seat in terms of choosing a forum that will provide the best remedy.

Recognition and enforcement of final decisions

All judgments given in a Brussels or Lugano Contracting State must be recognised and enforced in the other Contracting States with very few exceptions (principally public policy and default judgments where the defendant was not duly served). In order to facilitate the free movement of judgments a foreign judgment recognised in another Contracting State "must in principle have the same effects in the State in which enforcement is sought as it does in the State in which the judgment was given".[13] This is a doctrine of equivalent effects which is as familiar in remedies law in other areas of Community law.[14] The scope of free movement of judgments is extremely broad in that it extends to judgments given against people domiciled outside the Contracting States where the jurisdictional basis of the case against them was an exorbitant one (i.e. an unacceptable one in relation to persons domiciled in a Contracting State). Article 59 of the Conventions permits this to be mitigated by agreeing a bilateral Convention with a non-Contracting State ("a protected state") whereby the Contracting State agrees not to recognise or enforce judgments given in another Contracting State based on exorbitant grounds of jurisdiction against domiciliaries from the

[12] For an explanation of the virtues of a move towards a more minimum harmonisation route as it has been adopted even in the core area of EU law – the single market – see Weatherill & Beaumont, *EU Law*, 3rd edn. (London: Penguin, 1999), 556–9.

[13] See the first part of the Court of Justice's ruling in Case 145/86 *Hoffmann* v. *Krieg* [1988] ECR 645. Here the Court was relying on the Jenard Report, the official report on the Brussels Convention, and did so explicitly in para. 10 of the judgment which states: "In that regard it should be recalled that the Convention 'seeks to facilitate as far as possible the free movement of judgments, and should be interpreted in this spirit' ". Recognition must therefore "have the result of conferring on judgments the authority and effectiveness accorded to them in the State in which they were given" (Jenard Report, 42 and 43).

[14] See on supremacy of Community law and recovery of duties imposed in breach of Community law, Joined Cases C–10/97 to C–22/97 *Ministero delle finanze* v. *IN.CO.GE. 90 Srl and Others* [1998] ECR I–6307 discussed in Weatherill and Beaumont (1999), note 12, above, 436–7; on direct effect of directives Case C–246/96 *Magorrian and Cunningham* v. *Eastern Health and Social Services Board* [1997] ECR I–7153, discussed in Weatherill and Beaumont (1999), note 12, above, 405; and on actions for damages against Member States Case C–261/95 *Palmisani* v. *INPS* [1997] ECR I–4025, discussed in Weatherill and Beaumont (1999), note 12, above, 429. For a conclusion as to how far uniformity should go in relation to remedies see Weatherill and Beaumont (1999), note 12, above, 453.

protected state. The UK has such conventions with Australia and Canada,[15] and France has one with Canada.[16]

Jurisdiction to provide interim remedies

Article 24 of the Brussels and Lugano Conventions permits national law to grant provisional, including protective, measures even though the courts of another Contracting State have jurisdiction over the substance of the matter.[17] An important recent thirteen judge decision of the European Court of Justice, *Van Uden*,[18] places some limits on the freedom of national law to grant provisional measures and in doing so refers to a leading case on interim remedies "in the context of Community law" (*Antonissen* v. *Council and Commission*).[19] The *Van Uden* case concerned a Dutch company (Van Uden) seeking interim relief in The Netherlands (in *kort geding* proceedings) against a German company (Deco-Line) relating to the payment of debts arising under a contract containing an arbitration clause. Several conclusions can be drawn from the ECJ's judgment:

(a) The courts which have jurisdiction as to the "substance of the case" under one of the heads of jurisdiction laid down in the Convention (including Article 5(1) on contract) also have unlimited jurisdiction to order provisional or protective measures.[20]

(b) Where a court does not have jurisdiction over the substance of the case, even if the courts of another Contracting State do, Article 24 applies provided that the subject matter of the dispute falls within the scope *ratione materiae* of the Convention.[21] Thus matters excluded from the scope of the Convention (see Article 1) like rights in property arising out of a matrimonial relationship do not fall within the scope of Article 24. The issue of arbitration is more tricky because although it is excluded from the scope of the

[15] See Beaumont (1995), note 10, above, 70–1 and Lussier (1998), note 9, above, at 42–3.

[16] See L. Lussier, *ibid* at 50–1.

[17] For an excellent and up to date analysis of Article 24, including Case C–391/95 *Van Uden Maritime BV, trading as Van Uden Africa Line* v. *Kommanditgesellschaft in Firma Deco-Line and Another* [1998] ECR I–7091 but not Case C–99/96 *Mietz* v. *Intership Yachting Sneek BV* [1999] ECR I–2277, see G. Maher and B. Rodger, "Provisional and Protective Remedies: The British Experience of the Brussels Convention" (1999) 48 *ICLQ* 302–39. For a comparative treatment ranging well beyond the Brussels Convention see the Note on Provisional and Protective Measures in Private International Law and Comparative Law, prepared by C. Kessedjian, Hague Conference on Private International Law, Prel. Doc. No. 10 of October 1998 for the attention of the Special Commission of November 1998 on the jurisdiction and judgments convention.

[18] *Van Uden*, note 17, above.

[19] Case C–393/96P(R) *Antonissen* v. *Council and Commission* [1997] ECR I–441.

[20] *Van Uden*, note 17, above, paras. 19 and 22. This jurisdiction is not derived from Article 24 of the Convention but is inherent in the substantive jurisdiction conferred by Articles 2 and 5 to 18 of the Convention. See the confirmation of this aspect of the *Van Uden* decision in *Mietz*, note 17, above, paras. 40–1.

[21] *Van Uden*, note 17, above, para. 28.

Convention by Article 1(2)(4), and therefore proceedings in courts ancillary to arbitration proceedings are excluded from the scope of the Convention, the Court in *Van Uden* decided that:

> However, it must be noted in that regard that provisional measures are not in principle ancillary to arbitration proceedings but are ordered in parallel to such proceedings and are intended as measures of support. They concern not arbitration as such but the protection of a wide variety of rights. Their place in the scope of the Convention is thus determined not by their own nature but by the nature of the rights which they serve to protect (see Case C–261/90 *Reichert and Kockler* v. *Dresdner Bank* [1992] ECR I–2149, paragraph 32).
>
> It must therefore be concluded that where, as in the case in the main proceedings, the subject-matter of an application for provisional measures relates to a question falling within the scope *ratione materiae* of the Convention, the Convention is applicable and Article 24 thereof may confer jurisdiction on the court hearing that application even where proceedings have already been, or may be, commenced on the substance of the case and even where those proceedings are to be conducted before arbitrators.[22]

(c) The granting of provisional or protective measures on the basis of Article 24 is conditional on, *inter alia*, the "existence of a real connecting link between the subject-matter of the measures sought and the territorial jurisdiction of the Contracting State of the court before which those measures are sought".[23] In addition to the real connecting link the court ordering measures on the basis of Article 24 "must take into consideration the need to impose conditions or stipulations such as to guarantee their provisional or protective character".[24] The idea of the court imposing conditions is not new and can be seen in the much earlier decision of the European Court in *Denilauler*[25] which refers to the court being able to "place a time-limit on its order or, as regards the nature of the assets or good subject to the measures contemplated, require bank guarantees or nominate a sequestration and generally make its authorisation subject to all conditions guaranteeing the provisional or protective character of the measure ordered". One of the most controversial issues in this field is the question of interim payments. In *Van Uden*, Deco-Line, the UK and, to some extent at least, Germany argued against interim payments as being permissible under Article 24 while the Commission and Van Uden argued in favour. The Court's reasoning seems to have something for everybody and involves cross-fertilisation between Community law on interim remedies and the limits on national law of interim remedies imposed by the Brussels Convention:

> Here it must be noted that it is not possible to rule out in advance, in a general and abstract manner, that interim payment of a contractual consideration, even in an

22 *Van Uden*, note 17, above, paras. 33–4.
23 *Ibid* at para. 40.
24 *Ibid* at para. 41.
25 Case 125/79 *Denilauler* v. *Couchet Freres* [1980] ECR 1553, para. 15.

> amount corresponding to that sought as principal relief, may be necessary in order to ensure the practical effect of the decision on the substance of the case and may, in certain cases, appear justified with regard to the interests involved (see, in the context of Community law, Case C–393/96P(R) *Antonissen* v. *Council and Commission* [1997] ECR I–441, paragraph 37).[26]
>
> However, an order for interim payment of a sum of money is, by its very nature, such that it may preempt the decision on the substance of the case. If, moreover, the plaintiff were entitled to secure interim payment of a contractual consideration before the courts of the place where he is himself domiciled, where those courts have no jurisdiction over the substance of the case under Articles 2 to 18 of the Convention, and thereafter to have the order in question recognised and enforced in the defendant's State, the rules of jurisdiction laid down by the Convention could be circumvented.
>
> Consequently, interim payment of a contractual consideration does not constitute a provisional measure within the meaning of Article 24 unless, first, repayment to the defendant of the sum awarded is guaranteed if the plaintiff is unsuccessful as regards the substance of his claim and, second, the measure sought relates only to specific assets of the defendant located or to be located within the confines of the territorial jurisdiction of the court to which application is made.[27]

The interplay of Community law and private international law remedies here is interesting. In the Community context under the *Antonissen* decision the President of the Court of First Instance or the President of the Court of Justice can grant interim payments to applicants. However, the condition imposed is that the applicant's case must not just be a *prima facie* one and an urgent one (normal interim measures tests) but a "particularly strong" *prima facie* case and the urgency of the measures must be "undeniable". The judge is free to impose other conditions such as a guarantee but this is not a requirement. In *Van Uden*, the Court of Justice has drawn from the *Antonissen* reasoning but produced rather different conditions to the award of interim payments. The Court of Justice has left to national law such questions as urgency and the strength of the *prima facie* case and instead made the option of a financial guarantee a precondition. The precondition does not apply if the court has jurisdiction over the

[26] When we examine *Antonissen* we discover that President Rodriguez Iglesias relied on Case C–213/89 *R* v. *Secretary of State for Transport, ex parte Factortame and Others* [1990] ECR I–2433, para. 21, and on Joined Cases C–143/88 and C–92/89 *Zuckerfabrik Süderdithmarschen* v. *Hauptzollamt Itzehoe and Zuckerfabrik Soest GmbH* v. *Hauptzollamt Paderborn* [1991] ECR I–415, paras. 16 to 18, and the order in Case C–399/95R *Germany* v. *Commission* [1996] ECR I–2441, para. 46. He concluded that a denial of a right to interim payment "would not be compatible with the right of individuals to complete and effective judicial protection under Community law" (para. 36) but then takes a further leap of logic and says that one cannot rule out in advance that the interim payment even be "of an amount corresponding to that sought in the main application" (para. 37). But this extension of the scope of interim remedies is counterbalanced in the context of Community law by the requirement that it only applies where the "*prima facie* case is particularly strong and the urgency of the measures sought undeniable" (para. 41) and the "judge dealing with the interim application may still impose any condition or guarantee which he considers necessary when granting that measure, or limit its scope in any other way" (para. 42).

[27] *Van Uden*, note 17, above, paras. 45–7.

substance of the case on the basis of one of the jurisdictional grounds provided by the Brussels Convention in Articles 2 and 5 to 18 because this is not a matter within the scope of Article 24 of the Convention and it is assumed that the final judgment will correct any injustice caused by the interim payment. Therefore the financial guarantee is not required in relation to interim payments granted by the Community courts because those courts only grant interim payments when they have jurisdiction over the substance of the action. The assumption that the final judgment can correct any injustice may not be a wise one if in the meantime the person bringing the action has gone out of business even though they received an interim payment and cannot repay it. If the financial guarantee is a good idea to protect vulnerable defendants why is it imposed only on national courts, and only in some cases, and not on the two Community courts?

This discrepancy between the Community law standard on interim remedies and the national law standard under the Brussels Convention is in sharp contrast to the European Court's insistence on the same legal tests applying to determine the non-contractual liability of the Community institutions as apply to the non-contractual liability of Member States of the EU for damage caused to individuals due to a failure to comply with Community law.[28] One possible explanation for the difference in approach is that unlike actions for damages against Member States for failure to comply with Community law, the European Court did not invent the interim remedies that are available in national law in relation to civil and commercial disputes. The Court's task is to interact with existing national law remedies rather than to force national law to create new remedies to uphold the effectiveness of Community law. Furthermore, the text of Article 24 of the Brussels Convention makes no effort to limit the interim remedies available under national law nor to create a uniform notion of Community interim remedies. So the European Court is to be commended for showing judicial self-restraint and not imposing the Community conditions of a *prima facie* case and urgency on national courts. This is a healthy sign of subsidiarity – let decisions which affect European Union citizens be taken as closely as possible to them – and of the Court implicitly recognising the value of legal pluralism[29] in the varied types of interim remedies available and the conditions on which they are awarded in different legal systems in the European Union. It is a pity that the Court did not show even greater deference to national law in determining the conditions on which, if any, interim

[28] See Weatherill & Beaumont (1999), note 12, above, 426, n. 169.

[29] On the importance of limiting the extent of the Europeanisation of law see P. Legrand, "European Legal Systems are Not Converging" (1996) 45 *ICLQ* 52; P. Legrand, "Against a European Civil Code" (1997) 60 *MLR* 44; P. Legrand, "The Impossibility of 'Legal Transplants'" (1997) 4 *MJ* 111; H. Collins, "European Private Law and the Cultural Identity of States" (1995) *European Review of Private Law* 353; G. Teubner, "Legal Irritants: Good Faith in British Law or How Unifying Law Ends Up in New Divergences" (1998) 61 *MLR* 11; and C. Harlow, elsewhere in this volume.

remedies should be granted.[30] However, its motivation was not to increase its own power. Rather, the imposition by the Court of the requirement of a financial guarantee from the recipient of an interim payment when the national court does not have jurisdiction over the substance of the case is designed to protect the rights of the person defending the action. In the national courts this will usually be a private person, natural or legal, who may be in need of the protection whereas in the Community Courts it will usually be a Community institution which is not in need of the protection. So the difference of treatment may be justified and some restriction on the freedom of national law to decide when interim remedies can be granted is necessary to prevent defendants from suffering at the hands of courts with little or no connection with them or the subject matter of the dispute. However, in the minutiae of the rules on interim remedies we find again the age old tension as to whether the Court of Justice should make the law, no matter how well intentioned and good the outcome may be, or follow the letter of the law and leave it to national law unless there is an amendment to the terms of Article 24 in a revised Brussels Convention or Brussels Regulation.[31]

Recognition and enforcement of interim remedies

Ex parte provisional or protective measures cannot be enforced under the Brussels and Lugano Conventions but *inter partes* measures can.[32]

More recently in *Mietz*,[33] a thirteen judge court had occasion to give further consideration to Article 24 of the Brussels Convention in the context of recognition and enforcement of provisional or protective measures. *Mietz* involved a Netherlands company (Intership Yachting) obtaining interim relief in *kort*

[30] An attitude of deference to national law can be seen in Council Directive 92/13/EEC OJ 1992 L 76/14 on procurement procedures in the water, energy, transport and telecommunications sector. The Directive requires Member States to establish review procedures and to give the reviewing body the power to make an order for the payment of a particular sum. It encourages interlocutory procedures without making them binding (Article 2(1)(a) and (c)). If interim payments are awarded it "may" (Article 2(5)) but not "must" be made to "depend upon a final decision that the infringement has in fact taken place". This is a sign that the Community legislature is reluctant to be prescriptive about national law requiring interim remedies even for the enforcement of Community procurement law. It is rather more prescriptive about final remedies – the payment "must be set at a level high enough to dissuade the contracting entity from committing or persisting in an infringement" (Article 2(5) – this test applies if the Member State chooses to permit the reviewing body to make an interim payment). However, the Court of Justice has pointed out that this still leaves a discretion to the Member State as to whether the payment is fixed or periodic and as to whether the "level high enough to dissuade" is to be determined by the legislature or by the competent court (see Case C–225/97 *Commission* v. *France* [1999] ECR I–3011.

[31] The judicial activism debate has a massive literature but readers should consider H. Rasmussen, *European Court of Justice* (Copenhagen: GadJura, 1998), especially chapters 1 and 10–12; T. Hartley, *Constitutional Problems of the European Union* (Oxford: Hart Publishing, 1999), chapters 2 and 3; Weatherill and Beaumont, note 12, above, chapter 6.

[32] See *Denilauler*, note 25, above.

[33] *Mietz*, note 17, above.

geding proceedings, which were *inter partes*, in The Netherlands against a German domiciliary (Mr Mietz) and seeking to have the interim relief enforced in Germany. The matter was referred to the European Court of Justice which decided that this was not a consumer contract under the Brussels Convention. The Court repeated the part of its judgment from *Van Uden* as to when an interim payment is permitted under the Convention[34] and pointed out that even if Mietz were to be allowed to raise new evidence in Germany before the enforcing court to prove that he was a consumer under the Brussels Convention "the court of origin could still have had jurisdiction to order provisional measures"[35] because Article 24 jurisdiction is not dependent on that court having jurisdiction over the substance of the dispute. The Court noted that in this case "only the provisions of Article 27 and, if appropriate, the first paragraph of Article 28 of the Convention would be capable of preventing recognition and enforcement of the judgment of the court of origin".[36] The Court rejected the view of the Commission and the UK that contesting the interim measures constitutes submission under Article 18 of the Convention and confers unlimited jurisdiction on that court to order any provisional or protective measures which the court might consider appropriate if it had jurisdiction under the Convention as to the substance of the matter.[37]

The Court then took a restrictive view of the enforcement of interim payments from other Contracting States. It is so complex that a long quotation is helpful:

> . . . the Netherlands judgment for the enforcement of which an order is sought in the main proceedings, has the following characteristics:
>
> – it was delivered at the end of proceedings which were not by their very nature, proceedings as to substance, but summary proceedings for the granting of interim measures;
> – the defendant was not domiciled in the Contracting State of the court of origin and it does not appear from the Netherlands judgment that, for other reasons, that court had jurisdiction under the Convention as to the substance of the matter;
> – it does not contain any statement of reasons designed to establish the jurisdiction of the court of origin as to the substance of the matter
>
> and
>
> – it is limited to ordering the payment of a contractual consideration, without, on the one hand, repayment to the defendant of the sum awarded being guaranteed if the plaintiff is unsuccessful as regards the substance of his claim or, on the other, the measure sought relating only to specific assets of the defendant located or to be located within the confines of the territorial jurisdiction of the court to which the application is made [53].[38]

[34] *Ibid* at paras 42–3. See the part of the *Van Uden* judgment quoted at note 27, above.
[35] *Mietz*, note 17, above at para. 45.
[36] *Ibid* at para. 51.
[37] *Ibid* at para. 52.
[38] Is it reasonable to impose this newly created condition from *Van Uden*, note 17, above, to a case where the relevant Dutch judgment was given long before the ECJ's judgment in *Van Uden*?

> . . . if the court of origin had expressly indicated in its judgment that it had based its jurisdiction on its national law in conjunction with Article 24 of the Convention, the court to which application for enforcement was made would have had to conclude that the measure ordered – namely unconditional interim payment – was not a provisional or protective measure within the meaning of that Article and was therefore not capable of being subject to an enforcement order under Title III of the Convention [54].
>
> So, where the court of origin is silent as to the basis of its jurisdiction, the need to ensure that the Convention rules are not circumvented . . . requires that its judgment be construed as meaning that that court founded its jurisdiction to order provisional measures on its national law governing interim measures and not on any jurisdiction as to substance derived from the Convention [55].
>
> It follows that, in a case having the characteristics set out in paragraph 53 of the present judgment, the court to which application for enforcement was made should conclude that the measure ordered is not a provisional measure within the meaning of Article 24 and for that reason cannot be the subject of an enforcement order under Title III of the Convention [56].[39]

So, recognition and enforcement of *inter partes* interim judgments in other Contracting States to the Brussels (and presumably Lugano) Contracting States will only be possible if:

a) the court awarding the interim judgment (measure) has jurisdiction over the substance of the case; or
b) the court awarding the interim judgment ensures that repayment of the interim award is guaranteed if the plaintiff is unsuccessful as regards the substance of his claim and, second, the measure ordered relates only to specific assets of the defendant located *or to be located* within the confines of the territorial jurisdiction of the court granting the interim award.

But the second part of the condition in (b) seems to render the need to enforce an interim award abroad redundant (because the defendant has assets within the jurisdiction and enforcement must be possible there) unless one focuses on the phrase "to be located" which might justify enforcement in another Contracting State where the argument is that the assets were about to be shifted from that third State to the protective state but the existence of the judgment in the protective state will stop the defendant from transferring the assets there and if enforcement is not permitted in that third State of the protective State's judgment the defendant will move the assets to a fourth state (possibly outwith the Brussels and Lugano Contracting States). Clearly the European Court of Justice is going to be asked to decide what it means by "to be located" in some future case. If it gives it a very narrow construction then recognition and enforcement of interim measures based on exorbitant national jurisdiction rules is virtually dead but if it gives it a broad construction it is very much alive and well. Litigants will still be able to protect themselves in the courts of a Contracting

[39] *Mietz*, note 17, above, paras. 53–6.

State offering the best interim remedies and the other States will be obliged to give effect to such judgments pending the outcome on the substance.

Another issue which is bound to come back to the Court is how to apply condition (b) when the interim remedy is an injunction (interdict) or an order for specific performance (i.e. when the remedy is not pecuniary but rather prevents the defendant from doing something or requires the defendant to do something). How can one guarantee the reversal of an act? By some monetary bond which is regarded as equivalent compensation? Why should it matter whether the defendant has assets in the jurisdiction?

The person who initiates legal proceedings, usually a legal person in this context, has significant opportunities to shop for a remedy in the EU and Lugano States at the interim remedies stage although it will have to demonstrate a "real connecting link between the subject-matter of the measures sought and the territorial jurisdiction of the Contracting State of the court before which those measures are sought". Although recognition and enforcement of such interim measures is limited to cases in which the person defending the case has had the opportunity to put its case in adversary proceedings,[40] even if the judgment was given by default, this may not be too significant in cases where the person defending the action has not had such an opportunity because the powers of the court which grants the interim remedies may have the effect of persuading the person defending the action to hand over assets which are located outside the jurisdiction. At the substantive stage shopping for remedies continues (e.g. in a typical contractual dispute the person initiating the action can sue in the courts of the domicile of the person defending the action,[41] in the courts of the place of performance of the obligation in question – the ability to choose which obligation is being sued upon can give the person initiating the action the chance to choose from several jurisdictions in complex contracts ,[42] and where there is more than one person being sued in the courts for the place where any one of them is domiciled).[43] If States want the income generated by foreign litigation there could be a tendency to provide more and more procedures and remedies to entice people to shop in their forum. The virtually automatic recognition and enforcement of foreign judgments (no review of substance and very limited categories of cases where review of jurisdiction is possible)[44] and the doctrine of equivalent effects creates a framework where remedies provided in any one Contracting State must be enforced throughout the Brussels and Lugano zone. There is a real risk that the balance of litigation will be tilted too far in favour of the person initiating legal proceedings. This next section examines the possible impact of developments following the entry into force of the Treaty of Amsterdam.

[40] The phrase "adversary proceedings" is taken from *Denilauler*, note 25 above, paras. 13 and 17.

[41] Article 2 of the Brussels and Lugano Conventions and of the draft Brussels Regulation.

[42] Article 5(1) of the Brussels and Lugano Conventions and of the draft Brussels Regulation.

[43] Article 6(1) of the Brussels and Lugano Conventions and of the draft Brussels Regulation.

[44] See Volume 5 of Kaye (1999), note 10, above and chapter 8 of Beaumont (1995), note 10, above.

3. "REMEDIES SHOPPING" POST-AMSTERDAM

In July 1999 the Commission[45] proposed a new Council Regulation on jurisdiction and the enforcement of judgments in civil and commercial matters (known as Brussels I) which was given its first consideration in the Council of the European Union Committee on Civil Law on 20–21 September 1999.[46] The Amsterdam Treaty came into force on 1 May 1999 and therefore Title IV of the EC Treaty came into force which provides a possible legal basis for a new Regulation, see below. However, there was a political vacuum in the Commission caused by the resignation of the college of Commissioners in March 1999.[47] In an astonishing sign that the disgraced Commission learnt nothing from its forced resignation in March 1999 it ignored its self-imposed and public commitment not to "take fresh political initiatives"[48] until the new Prodi Commission had been appointed. In addition to introducing the proposed Brussels I Regulation it had already, on 4 May 1999, introduced a proposed Regulation based on the content of the Brussels II Convention and a proposed Directive based on the Service Convention.[49] All of this substantiates the view of the Committee of Independent Experts that the Commission does not have a well developed sense of political responsibility.[50] The officials in the Commission should have waited until the Prodi Commission was in place and had time to think about the implications of important new legislative proposals in the field of private international law before introducing them. The college of Commissioners should have considered the merits of the alternative legal basis of Article 293 (ex 220) EC for the revision of the Brussels Convention. The impatience of Commission officials and the old Commission indicates a dangerous lack of political accountability.

Legal basis

Title IV of the EC Treaty, in particular Article 65 of the EC Treaty which requires unanimity in the Council, is the legal basis for new private international law initiatives[51] including the Commission proposals on Brussels I and II and Service. The reasoning in the Commission's explanatory memorandum

45 See COM (1999) 348 final.

46 See Document 10742/99 JUSTCIV 124 which indicates that the Commission proposal was not actually received in the Council until 7 September 1999.

47 See Weatherill & Beaumont (1999), note 12, above, 1059–64.

48 *Ibid* at 1062.

49 COM (1999) 220 and 221.

50 See note 46, above.

51 See Beaumont (1999), note 2, above; C. Kohler, "Interrogations sur les sources du droit international privé européen apres le traité d'Amsterdam" (1999) 88 *Rev. Crit. dr. internat. privé* 1–30.

choosing this legal basis is rather weak. The sound arguments are that there is an advantage in transparency in having a Regulation rather than a Convention because there is no implementing legislation[52] and the Regulation comes into force on the same day in all the Member States bound by it whereas ratification of a Convention amending the Brussels Convention will occur at different times in different Contracting States and may be delayed for a long time in some States.[53] The Commission also argues that opting for a "Regulation enables the Court of Justice to ensure that it is applied uniformly throughout the Member States".[54] The Commission neglects to point out that the Court of Justice is better able to ensure uniformity of the Brussels Convention than the new Brussels I Regulation. The former has a 1971 Protocol which allows all appellate courts to refer cases to the European Court of Justice on the interpretation of the Brussels Convention and requires courts of last resort to refer. On the other hand Article 68(1) of the EC Treaty removes the right of appellate courts to refer cases on the interpretation of any act adopted under Title IV and retains only the mandatory reference for courts of last resort. This unfortunate loss of judicial protection for people domiciled in Member States bound by the Brussels I Regulation could have been avoided if the revision of the Brussels Convention had been concluded on the basis of the original legal basis, i.e. Article 293 EC (ex Article 220). This legal basis, which was the preferred legal basis of the UK, would also have avoided problems of variable geometry which are inevitable if one relies on a legal basis in Title IV. Denmark has an opt-out Protocol from Title IV of the EC Treaty and cannot selectively opt in.[55] Therefore the Commission's proposals, even if adopted, will not apply to all fifteen EU Member States and therefore the Brussels Convention (and the 1971 Protocol allowing references to the ECJ) will remain in place (unamended) for at least Denmark in its relations with the other Member States. The UK and Ireland have an opt-out Protocol from Title IV but can opt in to specific measures.[56] They have a right to take part in the negotiations of the new Brussels I Regulation but whether they opt in or not have no veto over its adoption. A further advantage of using Article 293 as the legal basis would have been to act in good faith[57] with the Lugano States (Iceland, Norway and Switzerland). Those States expected that the long parallel revision negotiations on the Brussels and

[52] But even this argument is two edged because lawyers in individual countries may find a primary statute like the Civil Jurisdiction and Judgments Act 1982 which implemented the Brussels Convention in its own terms in Schedule 1 more accessible and with a higher impact threshold than a Community Regulation. In any case the Regulation will require some implementing legislation – at least by way of rules of court – and Member States are currently asking for at least a gap of six months between the Regulation being agreed and its entry into force.

[53] See pages 4 and 5 of COM (1999) 348 final. This latter point is a definite advantage of a regulation over the Convention but it must be weighed in the scales against the disadvantages.

[54] *Ibid* at 5.

[55] See OJ 1997 C340/101.

[56] See OJ 1997 C340/99.

[57] The relevance of this principle to Community law was confirmed by the Court of First Instance in Case T–115/94 *Opel Austria GmbH* v. *Council* [1997] II–39, paras. 89–94.

Lugano Conventions which began in 1997 would end with the signing of amending treaties for both Conventions at the same time. Instead the Lugano States have ignominiously been told to wait until the Brussels 1 Regulation is concluded and then fresh negotiations with them will be conducted under conditions not yet well established because of the doubts about who will be competent to conduct those negotiations. Clearly the EU Member States not bound by the Regulation will be able to negotiate but will the other Member States be represented by the Commission, or will they be there together with the Commission negotiating on the basis of a mixed competence between the Community and those Member States? A legal basis in Article 293 would also have the advantage of retaining external competence in these matters in the hands of the Member States of the EU rather than creating exclusive competence for the EU or mixed competence between the EU and the Member States bound by the Regulation. If the EU Member States have external competence it preserves the existing balance within the Hague Conference on Private International Law and avoids the common law orientated UK and Ireland being swallowed up in a civil law orientated EU voice. It allows Member States to choose independently whether to ratify a Hague Convention and not to be forced to wait until all the Member States agree, if ever, to ratify.[58] Furthermore, it allows States to reduce the injustice against people not domiciled in a Contracting State of applying the exorbitant rules of jurisdiction and the requirement to recognise judgments from other Member States based on such rules by concluding conventions with one or more third States under Article 59 of the Brussels Convention. There are other external problems generated by creating some Community competence in this area. What do you do about amending all the specialist conventions on maritime, transport and other matters which are given priority over the Brussels Convention by Article 57? The nightmare scenario is that every time one of those conventions is amended in the future there will need to be substantive negotiations in the EU to see if an amendment can be made to the Brussels I Regulation. Whereas under the Brussels Convention the Contracting States were happy not only to recognise existing specialist conventions but to permit the liberty to each other to conclude specialist conventions in the future on "particular matters" which would trump the Brussels Convention rules on jurisdiction and still benefit from that Convention's rules on recognition and enforcement.[59]

[58] This problem might be overcome if the EU were to take an enlightened federal view like that adopted in Canada (where Canada can ratify a Hague Convention on behalf of those provinces and territories who want it) and the UK (where the Convention could be ratified by the UK for Scotland, or Northern Ireland, or England and Wales) and permit the use of the standard federal clause in Hague Conventions to allow those Member States to ratify a Hague Convention who want to rather than wait until the whole of the EU is ready to adopt it. This would require a much less absolutist (and indeed highly centralist) view about things which fall within Community competence having to be agreed by the whole Community or none.

[59] For background on the conventions on particular matters referred to in Article 57 of the Brussels and Lugano Conventions see Beaumont (1995), note 10, above, at 65–9.

The UK and Ireland opted in to the negotiations on Brussels I but the UK will be pressing its concerns on external competence in the hope that provisions like Article 57 and 59 of the Brussels Convention can be incorporated into the Regulation to respect an appropriate degree of subsidiarity by allowing Member States to continue to conclude conventions on particular matters and to contract out of the requirement to recognise judgments from other Member States which are based on exorbitant grounds of jurisdiction.

Thus it is possible that remedy shopping will be enhanced because there will be two slightly (perhaps even significantly) different systems in operation between the hard core twelve (thirteen or fourteen) and the periphery of (one, two or) three. When one adds in the Lugano Convention the opportunities for shopping for remedies will increase. It is likely that the Commission will assert exclusive competence to negotiate a revised Lugano Convention on behalf of the twelve (thirteen or fourteen) EU Member States who are party to the new Regulation once it has been adopted. This raises some very difficult questions of external competence which also arise in relation to how the EU States will be represented at the Hague Conference on Private International Law.[60] However, changes to the Lugano Convention will have to be agreed to unanimously by Iceland, Norway, Switzerland, Denmark, possibly the UK and Ireland, and by the Council for the hardcore EU States. It is possible, though hopefully it will not transpire, that the Lugano Convention will diverge from the substance of the new Regulation.

Jurisdiction over the substance

Likely changes from the Brussels Convention for the new Regulation based on the political agreement reached in the Council Working Party on the Revision of the Brussels and Lugano Conventions in April 1999[61] include a new uniform definition of the domicile of a legal person;[62] a new contract jurisdiction (restricting the place of payment jurisdiction unless it is expressly chosen by the

[60] The Council Legal Service has given an Opinion on 17 March 1999 (Doc. 6683/99 JUR 99 JUSTCIV 48) that the entry into force of the Amsterdam Treaty does not give the Community competence in this area but that once the Brussels I Regulation has been adopted the Community (leaving aside the States not party to the Regulation) will be "exclusively competent to conclude" international agreements "whenever such agreements could affect the internal Community rules" (at 11). A close inspection of the Legal Service Opinion shows that the Hague Convention and any revised Lugano Convention would affect the internal Community rules. However, a strong argument for mixed competence can be made based on Opinion 1/94 *Re the Uruguay Round Treaties* [1994] ECR I–5267 because as with GATS the Brussels Regulation will not "create complete harmonization" (*cf.* para. 96 of Opinion 1/94) of the rules of jurisdiction and recognition and enforcement of civil and commercial matters because of its limited geographical and material scope (e.g. it does not regulate the recognition and enforcement of judgments emanating from non-Contracting States) and its willingness to leave some matters within the control of national law (e.g. Articles 3, 4 and 24 of the Brussels Convention and Articles 3, 4 and 31 of the draft Brussels I Regulation).

[61] See JUSTCIV 60, note 11, above.

[62] Draft Brussels I Regulation, Article 60.

parties as the place of performance and giving a uniform interpretation as to the place of performance for sale of goods contracts and contracts for the provision of services);[63] a tort jurisdiction for threatened wrongs;[64] a codification of the interpretations by the European Court of Justice of the co-defender[65] and submission[66] jurisdictions in the Brussels Convention; minor tidying up of the insurance jurisdictions;[67] extension of the protective jurisdiction for consumers;[68] a new protective section on individual employment contracts;[69] a compromise between the Lugano and Brussels solutions on the exception to the exclusive jurisdiction of the place where the immovable property is situated for short term tenancies of immovable property;[70] a minor change to the exclusive jurisdiction over legal persons;[71] an express statement in the provision on

[63] *Ibid*, Article 5(1). This is the most controversial provision in the revision and a compromise on this provision was the key to securing agreement on the total revision package in the Council Working Party. The new Article 5(1)(c) is included to show that the old rule in Article 5(1) (now 5(1)(a)) that a person domiciled in a Contracting State can be sued in the place of performance of the obligation in question still applies whenever the new rule in Article 5(1)(b) does not apply – i.e. in complex contracts and in contracts where the place of delivery of the goods or the place where the services are provided is in a non-Contracting State.

[64] *Ibid*, Article 5(3).

[65] *Ibid*, Article 6(1), based on Case 189/87 *Kalfelis* v. *Schröder, Münchmeyer, Hengst & Co and others* [1988] ECR 5565.

[66] *Ibid*, Article 24, following the European Court of Justice's interpretation of Article 18 of the Brussels Convention in Case 150/80 *Elefanten Schuh GmbH* v. *Jacqmain* [1981] ECR 1671 by omitting the word "solely" from the English text.

[67] *Ibid*, Articles 9(2) and 14 which depart from the wording in the former Articles 8(2) and 12A of the Brussels Convention. Indeed the Commission's proposal in Article 14 departed from the text agreed by the Council Working Party in April 1999 (see Article 12A of Document 7700/99 JUSTCIV 60 which combined the old Article 12A on large risks with specific references to the definition of large risks in certain Community Insurance Directives) by only referring to the Insurance Directives. This would have had the effect of making it more difficult to enter into an exclusive jurisdiction clause in certain large risks contracts not covered by the Directives (e.g. offshore oil and gas). It is highly surprising that the Commission should attempt to depart from the substance of the agreement in the Council Working Party. It is a regrettable sign of institutional self assertion. Normally a Commission proposal for a regulation or directive can only be amended by the Member States acting unanimously (see Article 250(1) (ex 189a(1)) EC). However, the position is less clear in the context of measures introduced under Title IV of the EC Treaty in the five year period after 1 May 1999 because Article 67(1) does not give the Commission the sole right of initiative. Any Member State could make a counter proposal. So in this situation one of the Member States with voting rights in the Brussels I Regulation might put forward its own proposal based on Article 12A of the Council Working Party agreement and get the support of the other Member States. In fact by the time of the second meeting of the Council Committee on Civil Law (Brussels 1) in November 1999 the Commission put forward two options (the JUSTCIV 60 solution and its own solution which it had put forward in its first draft of the Regulation). The Committee unanimously approved the JUSTCIV 60 version and it will now be retained.

[68] *Ibid*, Articles 15 and 16 (ex Articles 13 and 14 of the Brussels Convention).

[69] *Ibid*, Articles 18–21 (a consolidation and extension of the employment provisions in Article 5(1) and the last paragraph of Article 17 of the Brussels Convention).

[70] *Ibid*, Article 22(1) (ex 16(1) of the Brussels Convention).

[71] *Ibid*, Article 22(2) (ex 16(2) of the Brussels Convention). The minor changes are that the seat of the legal person is to be determined by the private international law rules of the forum and the insertion of the word "of" just before "decisions of their organs". This was to clarify an issue that was contentious in *Newtherapeutics Ltd* v. *Katz* [1991] Ch. 226, 244–5; see Beaumont (1995), note 10, above at 149.

prorogation that parties can choose to give non-exclusive jurisdiction to the courts of a Member State and a statement dealing with agreements entered into by electronic means;[72] a clarification of the meaning of the provision on related actions;[73] and – perhaps most significantly – a new provision providing for a clear date at which a court is first seized for the purpose of *lis pendens*.[74]

Recognition and enforcement of final decisions

The draft Brussels 1 Regulation makes the first stage of enforcement even more of a formality than in the Brussels Convention (it is already conducted without the person against whom enforcement is sought being given the opportunity to contest the enforcement and, therefore, in the UK it is already a formality, but in countries like Denmark, where matters can be raised of their own motion by judges then the scrutiny of the Article 27 exceptions in the Brussels Convention, is not a formality), restructures the Brussels Convention provisions,[75] reduces the protection provided to defendants in default judgments,[76] deletes what was Article 27(4) of the Brussels Convention, and introduces new certificates of enforcement for judicial decisions and authentic instruments.[77]

No equivalent of Article 59 of the Brussels Convention has been retained in the draft Brussels 1 Regulation. The reason being that any deals with a third State or third States would be negotiated by the Commission on behalf of those Member States which are party to the Regulation. This makes it possible for the Commission to assert exclusive external competence in relation to those States which are party to the Regulation. An equivalent of Article 59 of the Brussels Convention would indicate a mixed competence for the Commission and Member States because it permits individual Member States to change the rules of recognition applicable in relation to judgments from other Contracting States by negotiating a convention with a third State. The haste shown by the Commission in proposing the draft Regulation and its omission of an equivalent

[72] *Ibid*, Article 23 (ex 17 of the Brussels Convention). The old Article 17(4) of the Brussels Convention which gave an advantage to the stronger party to a choice of court clause has been deleted.

[73] *Ibid*, Article 28(2) (ex 22(2) of the Brussels Convention) – the Commission's first draft of the Regulation redrafted the French text that had been agreed by the Council Working Party in April 1999.

[74] *Ibid*, Article 30 (not in the Brussels Convention but it was Article 23 *bis* in the Council Working Party agreement of April 1999).

[75] Compare Articles 32–53 of the draft Brussels Regulation with Articles 25–49 of the Brussels Convention (once again the Commission proposed more radical restructuring than was agreed at the Council Working Party in April 1999 – e.g. to reduce the provisions in the recognition section from five – Articles 26–30 – to one – Article 33 but this was rejected at the first meeting of the Committee on Civil Law (Brussels I) in September 1999 and the JUSTCIV 60 structure and text was reverted to).

[76] Compare Article 34(2) of the draft Brussels Regulation with Article 27(2) of the Brussels Convention.

[77] Annex 5 and 6 of the draft Brussels Regulation.

to Article 59 of the Brussels Convention, even for a transitional period,[78] indicates that the Commission would like the Community to have exclusive external competence in matters covered by the Brussels Regulation as quickly as possible so that the Commission can negotiate on behalf of the Community at the Hague Conference on Private International Law and in any future bilateral negotiations. However, one argument for mixed competence, even if Article 59 is scrapped or phased out in the new Regulation, is that the Brussels Regulation will not cover the recognition of judgments from non-Contracting States and this is a matter covered in any negotiation with a third State or States. Although mixed competence would retain a role for the Member States in any negotiations at The Hague and with third States, it would prevent the ratification of any agreement reached in The Hague by individual Member States who are party to the Regulation unless all such Member States agree to ratify the agreement.

Jurisdiction over interim measures

No change is likely and none has been suggested in the Commission's draft Regulation.[79] The Brussels and Lugano Working Party decided not to make changes here because the majority of the group did not think it was either easy or wise to codify the *Van Uden* judgment and preferred to allow more time for judicial development.

Recognition and enforcement of interim measures

In the Brussels and Lugano Working Party there was some significant support for excluding recognition and enforcement of interim measures from the scope of the new Regulation or restricting it to measures awarded *inter partes* in the courts of the state which has jurisdiction over the substance of the matter. However, there was a concern that this matter should be left to judicial development. Perhaps a wise decision in that the meeting ended on 23 April 1999 and the Court gave its judgment on 27 April 1999 in *Mietz*.

Availability of provisional and protective measures at the recognition and enforcement stages

The Council Working Party on the Revision of the Brussels and Lugano Conventions agreed in April 1999 to clarify that provisional or protective

[78] Something held to be legally possible by the Council Legal Service in its Opinion of 17 March 1999, Doc. 6683/99 JUR 99 JUSTCIV 48 at 9.

[79] Article 31 of the draft Brussels Regulation is the same as Article 24 of the Brussels Convention (apart from the inevitable change of terminology from Contracting State to Member State and convention to regulation).

measures should be available, in accordance with the law of the State requested, whenever a judgment must be recognised in accordance with the Convention.[80] Thus a party seeking to enforce a foreign judgment in a Brussels or Lugano Contracting State will be able to get such protective measures as are available in the enforcing state prior to getting the declaration of enforceability (which itself is obtained without notifying the person against whom enforcement is sought). The Working Party then confirmed the existing law as to what happens once a declaration of enforceability has been granted. The person can proceed "directly with protective measures against the property of the party against whom enforcement is sought and is under no obligation to obtain specific authorization . . . and is under no obligation to obtain . . . any confirmatory judgment required by the national law of the court in question" when proceeding to any protective measures.[81] The Commission's draft Brussels Regulation follows the text of the revised Article 39 agreed by the Council Working Party.[82]

4. CONCLUSION

This is a key area where the Treaty of Amsterdam represents a clear step backwards. The Brussels and Lugano Conventions constitute an effective and uniform system of jurisdiction[83] and recognition and enforcement of judgments,

[80] Revised Article 39.

[81] Case 119/84 *Capelloni and Aquilini* v. *Pelkmans* [1985] ECR 3147 in which the Court ignored the advice of the Commission, the UK and Advocate General Slynn in deciding that Article 39 of the Brussels Convention can be relied on notwithstanding the procedural rules of the State where enforcement is sought. At 3152 Slynn had said: "In some Member States such protective measures may be made in precise terms, in respect of specific property and subject to well-established conditions; they may vary according to the circumstances. Some property may not be available for seizure as a matter of national law. I cannot see that the Convention has abolished the power of the national courts to go into these questions by enabling protective measures to be automatically taken merely because an enforcement order has been made".

[82] See Article 47 of the draft Brussels Regulation in JUSTCIV 132, Doc. 11304/99, 15 November 1999. In the original Commission proposal in COM (99) 348 final the provision was numbered Article 44 and the reference in paragraph 1 was to when a judgment must be declared enforceable rather than to when a judgment must be recognised.

[83] Of course there are arguments that the Brussels and Lugano Conventions themselves go too far in creating uniformity of jurisdiction rules in Europe and in not allowing any flexibility for the court first seized to decline to exercise jurisdiction not only where the same cause of action is pending elsewhere but also where a related action is pending elsewhere no matter how much more appropriate a forum the second court seized may be for the particular dispute. In this respect the solution likely to emerge from the Hague negotiations should be more balanced and more in tune with a modern minimum harmonisation pro-subsidiarity solution by allowing the court first seized to decline to exercise jurisdiction. Although efforts were made to reform Article 22 of the Brussels and Lugano Conventions in the Revision Working Party (see the UK Consultation Paper on the revision of the Brussels and Lugano Conventions (1997), prepared by Beaumont and McEleavy at para. 114) to allow the first court seized to decline to exercise jurisdiction in favour of a more appropriate court hearing a related action this was not successful as the necessary unanimity was not forthcoming even for this modest change. The UK made no effort to propose changes to the *lis pendens* rule in Article 21 hoping that its restraint in this area would persuade others to reform the already uncertain Article 22. It was disappointed by the unreasoned intransigence of certain States. This is an example of an area where the UK's late accession to the European Community cost it dear.

guaranteeing effective enforcement of remedies throughout the EU and the three EFTA States (on 1 February 2000 to be extended to Poland and some time thereafter to other Central European States). The 1971 Protocol to the Brussels Convention provides for strong and effective judicial protection from the European Court of Justice for the fifteen Member States of the EU which has a spillover to the other Lugano States because of the parallelism between the Brussels and Lugano Conventions. This system is to be sacrificed at the altar of the aspirations of the Commission and some Member States towards an illusory European judicial space and of the ambitions of the Commission to acquire exclusive external competence in private international law so that it can negotiate on behalf of the Community at the Hague Conference on Private International Law. Variable geometry in this context simply undermines the harmony of the fifteen (actually the harmony of the eighteen) and the *acquis communautaire* for little or no reward in substance for those pressing ahead. The changes to the provisions on jurisdiction and recognition and enforcement now proposed in the draft Brussels I Regulation could already have been agreed by all eighteen States in a diplomatic conference, as revisions of the Brussels Convention under Article 293 (ex 220) EC and of the Lugano Convention under international law. Article 59 of those Conventions could have been retained enabling the worst effects of exorbitant jurisdictions to be reduced by bilateral agreements or by the forthcoming Hague Convention. This would also have the benefit of preserving the viability of the Hague Conference on Private International Law which cannot easily be reformed to cope with the Commission speaking for a block of twelve to fifteen countries, given that it has a small active membership of less than forty States and relies on simple majority voting. For political reasons it is preferred to negotiate everything again in the Council and to scrap Article 59. This is to be done even though the new Regulation will provide less judicial protection for the individual in that fewer courts can refer questions on its interpretation to the European Court; precedents on the meaning of the Regulation will develop at a slower pace than under the Brussels Convention; the changes to the Lugano Convention will be greatly delayed; and the Regulation will differ from the unamended Brussels Convention which will still apply in Denmark, and possibly the UK and Ireland, and between those States and the other Member States of the EU (unless another set of negotiations is successfully conducted to amend the Brussels Convention). In the specific context of remedies the new Regulation will increase the confusion for litigants because of the variety of systems in place and will certainly not significantly reduce the capacity for remedy shopping. It may increase the ease with which decisions on the substance are enforced throughout the twelve, but this could have been achieved for all the Brussels and Lugano States by simply amending both Conventions at the same time (using Article 293 EC as the legal basis for concluding the revised Brussels Convention). The politicians will provide little or no change in the area of interim remedies and at least some will justify this on the basis that there is still room for judicial development. Thus the European

Court of Justice will remain under pressure to cross-fertilise from its own jurisprudence on interim remedies and to develop the law in order to protect the rights of those against whom interim remedies are sought. Such judicial activism, even though tacitly encouraged by the inaction of the politicians, should be confined to cautious gap-filling and should not venture into anything that is contrary to the text of the Brussels Convention or of the future Brussels I Regulation.

8

Remedies in a Multi-Level Legal Order: The Strasbourg Court and the UK

ROBIN WHITE

1. INTRODUCTION

DEBATES ABOUT the relative importance of substantive and procedural law have often proved to be sterile. In truth both are different sides of the same coin. This chapter focuses on one national setting, the United Kingdom, in order to explore some aspects of the relationship between remedial developments at the "supra"-national level and at the national level. United Kingdom accession to what is now the European Union has brought with it important changes to the approach to remedies. Until the incorporation of the European Convention on Human Rights into United Kingdom law, the European Convention had little impact within the United Kingdom on remedies. But the Human Rights Act 1998 requires a re-examination of the remedies provisions of the Convention. Those provisions are not well developed. Article 13 of the Convention requiring Contracting States to provide "an effective remedy before a national authority" has been poorly developed in the case-law of the Court of Human Rights, and analysis of the case-law on just satisfaction under that Court's own power to grant a remedy shows poor reasoning and lack of principles.

With regard to EC law, the Court of Justice began by emphasising national procedural autonomy. There was no obligation to devise new procedures[1] or create new remedies.[2] There was then a move to requiring what Craig and de Búrca describe as proportionality, adequacy and effectiveness of national penalties and remedies for breach of Community law.[3] This inevitably led to a conflict between the principles of proportionality, adequacy and effectiveness and respect for national procedural autonomy. But the signals were mixed as we can

[1] Case 33/76 *Rewe-Zentralfinanz* v. *Landwirtschaftskammer für das Saarland* [1976] ECR 1989; [1977] 1 CMLR 533.

[2] Case 158/80 *Rewe-Handelsgesellschaft Nord mbH* v. *Hauptzollamt Kiel* [1981] ECR 1805; [1982] 1 CMLR 449.

[3] P. Craig and G. de Búrca, *EU Law: Text, Cases and Materials* (Oxford: Oxford University Press, 1998), 217–22. See also R. Craufurd Smith, "Remedies for Breaches of EC Law in National Courts: Legal Variation and Selection" in P. Craig and G. de Búrca (eds.), *The Evolution of EU Law* (Oxford: Oxford University Press, 1999), 287.

see from two UK preliminary references. Hence in *Marshall II*,[4] the Court of Justice ruled that limitations on awards of compensation and the award of interest before the industrial tribunals in sex discrimination cases fell short of the standard required by Community law. But in the *Sutton* case,[5] the Court of Justice upheld a limitation on the award of interest on late-paid social security benefits in the national legal order, on the basis that such payments were not "compensatory in nature".[6]

EC law has subsequently developed a requirement for a uniform remedy for breach of Community law in the line of cases flowing from the *Francovich* case.[7] Where the conditions for liability are met, the Member State is required to make good in full losses suffered as a result of the breach of Community law. In summary, those conditions are that there has been a sufficiently serious breach of a rule of Community law designed to confer rights on individuals, and a clear causal link between the breach by the Member State and the loss sustained by the claimant. The case-law gives some guidance on the factors to be taken into account in determining whether there has been a sufficiently serious breach.

Similar developments mirroring the move away from national procedural autonomy under Community law may not be repeated in the United Kingdom following incorporation of the European Convention because of the different nature of the rights of individuals under Community law and the Convention. But there is overlap where the European Union institutions protect human rights as part of Community law.[8] It may also be the case that, as, and if,[9] Article 13 of the Convention is developed in the case-law of the Court of Human Rights, developments similar to those which have arisen in the European Union may take place.

2. THE RIGHT TO A REMEDY UNDER ARTICLE 13 ECHR

Procedures under the European Convention have always been subsidiary to the protection of human rights within the Contracting States, who guarantee under Article 1 to secure to everyone within their jurisdiction the rights and freedoms defined in Articles 2 to 18 of the Convention. The obligation in Article 13 to provide national processes for determining whether the rights guaranteed in Articles 2 to 18 have been violated is accordingly central to the system of

[4] Case C–271/91 *Marshall* v. *Southampton and South West Area Health Authority (No. 2)* [1993] ECR I–4367; [1993] 3 CMLR 293.

[5] Case C–66/95 *R* v. *Secretary of State for Social Security, ex parte Eunice Sutton* [1997] ECR I–2163; [1997] 2 CMLR 382.

[6] *Ibid*, para. 27 of the Judgment.

[7] Joined Cases C–6/90 and C–9/90 *Francovich and Bonifaci* v. *Italy* [1991] ECR I–5357; [1993] 2 CMLR 66; and see generally P. Craig and G. de Búrca (1998), note 3, above, at 236–54.

[8] See further Schermers, this volume at XX and Ward, this volume at XX.

[9] See also C. Kilpatrick, this volume at XX.

protection required by the Convention.[10] Article 13 is headed "Right to an effective remedy" and provides:

> Everyone whose rights and freedoms as set forth in this Convention are violated shall have an effective remedy before a national authority notwithstanding that the violation has been committed by persons acting in an official capacity.

Given its centrality in the system of protection established by the Convention, it is surprising that the case-law of the Strasbourg organs[11] took so long to focus on the content of the obligation in Article 13, and that, even today, the scope of the Article is obscure. As the partially dissenting opinion of Judges Matscher and Pinheiro Farinha noted in the *Malone* case:

> We recognise that Article 13 constitutes one of the most obscure clauses in the Convention and that its application raises extremely difficult and complicated problems of interpretation. This is probably the reason why, for approximately two decades, the Convention institutions avoided analysing this provision, for the most part advancing barely convincing reasons.[12]

The subsidiary nature of determination by the Strasbourg organs, at least for complaints by individuals, is also demonstrated by the requirement that they must exhaust domestic remedies before they can raise a complaint before the Strasbourg organs.[13]

A number of issues raised by the wording of Article 13 have now been resolved. In its judgment in the *Klass* case, the Court established that it was not necessary for a violation of the Convention to have been established *before* any entitlement to a national process arose; the right to a remedy arises whenever individuals consider that their rights under the Convention have been violated.[14] The threshold where the issue is raised before the Strasbourg organs is that the applicant has an arguable case that his or her rights have been violated. The Court in the *Silver* case declined to offer an abstract definition of the notion of arguability,[15] preferring to decide the issue on a case by case basis.[16] In the *Boyle and Rice* case the Court addressed the relationship of the arguability test

[10] See generally D. Gomien, D. Harris and L. Zwaak, *Law and Practice of the European Convention on Human Rights and the European Social Charter* (Strasbourg: Council of Europe Publishing, 1996), 335–43; D. Harris, M. O'Boyle and C. Warbrick, *Law of the European Convention on Human Rights* (London: Butterworths, 1995), chapter 14; F. Jacobs and R. White, *The European Convention on Human Rights*, 2nd edn. (Oxford: Clarendon Press, 1996), chap. 23; and P. van Dijk and G. van Hoof, *Theory and Practice of the European Convention on Human Rights*, 3rd edn. (The Hague: Kluwer, 1998), 696–710.

[11] The Commission, Court and Committee of Ministers, and, since November 1998, the Court and the Committee of Ministers.

[12] *Malone* v. *United Kingdom*, Judgment of 2 August 1984, A/82; (1985) 7 EHRR 14, at 48.

[13] Article 35(1) ECHR, formerly Article 26 ECHR. See Kilpatrick, *supra*, this volume at XX.

[14] *Klass and others* v. *Germany*, Judgment of 6 September 1978, A/28; (1979–80) 2 EHRR 214.

[15] *Silver and Others* v. *United Kingdom*, Judgment of 25 March 1983, A/61; (1983) 5 EHRR 347. See also F. Hampson, "The concept of an 'arguable claim' under Article 13 of the European Convention on Human Rights" (1990) 39 *ICLQ* 891.

[16] *Boyle and Rice* v. *United Kingdom*, Judgment of 27 April 1988, A/131; (1988) 10 EHRR 425, para. 55 of the Judgment.

with the possibility that a claim might be rejected by the Commission as being "manifestly ill-founded" under Article 27(2) ECHR.[17] The answer would seem to lie in there being two different tests. The Commission in deciding whether a case is manifestly ill-founded will have concluded that the case should proceed no further because the applicant has put forward insufficient evidence upon which the Court (or Committee of Ministers) could find a violation. In determining whether the case is arguable, the issue is whether there are the makings of a *prima facie* case. This means that whenever the Commission admits a case, the arguability threshold must be met, but it would also seem that a case may, nevertheless, be arguable even where the Commission concludes that it is manifestly ill-founded. That being so, it should follow that the test of a claim's being manifestly ill-founded where Article 13 is raised should be different from consideration of the admissibility of the substantive complaints. There have certainly been cases where the Commission has determined the substantive claims to be manifestly ill-founded but has admitted the complaint under Article 13.[18] An example is the *Powell and Rayner* case, in which the Commission had rejected complaints under Articles 6 and 8 as manifestly ill-founded but had admitted the claim under Article 13.[19] The Court said that, in principle, the threshold should be the same,[20] but went on to say that it could still consider whether there had been a violation of Article 13 notwithstanding that the Commission had rejected as manifestly ill-founded claims under Article 6(1) and 8 of the Convention.[21]

Two other Articles of the Convention provide for particular remedies. Article 6 has been read by the Court as giving a right of access to an independent and impartial tribunal established by law in order to determine an individual's civil rights and obligations.[22] Article 5(4) gives those deprived of their liberty by arrest or detention an entitlement to proceedings by which the lawfulness of the detention can be decided speedily by a court with power to order release if the detention is not lawful. Finally, the little-used Article 5(5) of the Convention provides for an enforceable right to compensation for those who have been victims of arrest or detention in contravention of the other provisions of Article 5.

In relation to Article 6, the Court has developed the view that the rights contained in Article 6 are more specific than those in Article 13, and so, when a violation of Article 6 has been found, there is no need to consider the application of

[17] Now Article 35(3) ECHR.

[18] See *Platform "Ärtze für das Leben"* v. *Austria*, Judgment of 21 June 1988, A/139; (1991) 13 EHRR 204, and *Powell and Rayner* v. *United Kingdom*, Judgment of 21 February 1990, A/172; (1990) 12 EHRR 355.

[19] The claim was also admitted under Article 1 of Protocol 1 (property rights), but not pursued after the admissibility phase.

[20] *Powell and Rayner* v. *United Kingdom*, note 18, above, para. 33 of the Judgment.

[21] *Ibid.*

[22] F. Jacobs and R.White (1996), note 10, above, at 126–8, and D. Harris, M. O'Boyle and C. Warbrick (1995), note 10, above, at 196–202.

Article 13.[23] But the view has also been expressed in some minority opinions that the subsumption of Article 13 by Article 6 should not be as complete as the standard approach suggests.[24] The Court has also consistently held,[25] though again subject to reservations expressed in some separate opinions,[26] that the requirements of Article 13 are absorbed into the more detailed system of protection afforded by Article 5(4). A similar view appears to apply to Article 5(5).[27]

The final words of Article 13 referring to the availability of a remedy "notwithstanding that the violation has been committed by persons acting in an official capacity" have been held to exclude the legislature.[28] It has been suggested that the wording may permit the horizontal application of the Convention,[29] but the preferable view is that the wording simply means that the fact that a public official enjoys immunity from suit under national law does not deprive the right to a remedy under Article 13 of its effect.[30]

Now we come to the heart of the requirements of Article 13: what constitutes an "effective remedy"? Some basic propositions can be offered with confidence, but they do not go far in answering the question.

A person within the scope of Article 13 should have a remedy before a national authority in order both to have the claim decided and, if appropriate, to obtain redress.[31] The authority before which the remedy is available need not be a judicial authority. Where it is not, however, the powers and guarantees which it affords must be considered in deciding whether the remedy is effective. The aggregate of remedies should be considered, since this may compensate for a situation in which no single remedy meets all the demands of the Article.[32]

None of this provides much concrete guidance on what constitutes an effective remedy, and certainly provides no guidance on the nature of the redress

[23] See, for example, *Hokkanen* v. *Finland*, Judgment of 23 September 1994, A/ 229–A; (1995) 19 EHRR 139, para. 74 of the Judgment.

[24] See, for example, Joint Separate Opinion of Judges Pinheiro Farinha and De Meyer in *W* v. *United Kingdom*, Judgment of 8 July 1987, A/121; (1988) 10 EHRR 29, at 60.

[25] See, for example, *De Jong, Baljet and van der Brink* v. *The Netherlands*, Judgment of 22 May 1984, A/ 77; (1986) 8 EHRR 20, para. 60 of the Judgment; and *Brannigan and McBride* v. *United Kingdom*, Judgment of 26 May 1993, A/258–B; (1994) 17 EHRR 539, para. 76 of the Judgment.

[26] See, for example, para. 14 of the Dissenting Opinion of Judge Walsh in *Brannigan and McBride*, *ibid*, at 588.

[27] There appears to be no authority from the Court, but this view is expressed by the Commission in para. 69 of its Report in *Brannigan and McBride*, note 25, above, at 563.

[28] *James* v. *United Kingdom*, Judgment of 21 February 1986, A/98; (1986) 8 EHRR 123, para. 85 of the Judgment, re-affirmed in *Leander* v. *Sweden*, Judgment of 26 March 1987, A/116; (1987) 9 EHRR 433, para. 77 of the Judgment.

[29] P. van Dijk and G. van Hoof (1998), note 10, above, at 704, and A. Clapham, *Human Rights in the Private Sphere* (Oxford: Clarendon Press, 1993), 240–4.

[30] D. Gomien, D. Harris and L. Zwaak (1996), note 10, above, at 336.

[31] *Klass and Others* v. *Germany*, note 14, above, para. 64 of the Judgment, affirmed in *Silver and Others*, note 15, above, para. 113 of the Judgment, and in *Leander* v. *Sweden*, note 28, above, para. 77 of the Judgment.

[32] *Klass and Others* v. *Germany*, note 14, above, paras. 67 and 72 of the Judgment, affirmed in *Silver and Others*, note 15, above, para. 113 of the Judgment; (1983) 5 EHRR 347, para. 113 of the Judgment, and in *Leander* v. *Sweden*, note 28, above, para. 77 of the Judgment.

which the national authority must provide. The Court has been extremely coy about this, and has been most reluctant to import into Article 13 entitlement to any particular form of redress. The result has been a case by case consideration of the nature of remedies and their relationship to the substantive provisions of the Convention in issue. The subsidiary nature of the Strasbourg organs and the great variety of remedies available in the national legal systems may account for this. It is, however, surprising not to find statements among the Strasbourg authorities which parallel statements of the Court of Justice of the European Communities recognising national procedural autonomy,[33] though the obligation in Article 13 would not permit a statement that there was no requirement for new remedies where none existed. That is the essence of the obligation in Article 13. Some clues to the content of the redress which must be provided under Article 13 ECHR may be found in the Convention's provisions on just satisfaction.

3. JUST SATISFACTION UNDER ARTICLE 41 ECHR

Article 41 ECHR[34] entitled "Just satisfaction" provides:

> If the Court finds that there has been a violation of the Convention or the protocols thereto, and if the internal law of the High Contracting Party concerned allows only partial reparation to be made, the Court shall, if necessary, afford just satisfaction to the injured party.

Again this is a residual provision, which enables the European Court of Human Rights to afford redress where the internal law of the Contracting Party found to be in violation of the Convention does not allow full redress.[35] It could therefore be expected that the views of the Court[36] on what constitutes just satisfaction would specify with some clarity the approach to be adopted in affording just satisfaction for a violation of the Convention. Unfortunately, that has not happened, and there appears to be little consistency in the Court's approach to

[33] As in, for example, Case 158/80, *Rewe-Handelsgesellschaft*, note 2, above, para. 44 of the Judgment.

[34] Formerly Article 50 ECHR.

[35] See generally M. Mas, "Right to Compensation under Article 50" in R. St J. Macdonald, F. Matscher and H. Petzold (eds.), *The European System for the Protection of Human Rights* (Dordrecht: Martinus Nijhoff, 1993) at 775–90; L. Clements, N. Mole and A. Simmons, *European Human Rights: Taking a Case under the Convention* (London: Sweet & Maxwell, 1999), chap. 6; D. Gomien, D. Harris and L. Zwaak (1996), note 10, above, 82–7; D. Harris, M. O'Boyle and C. Warbrick (1995), note 10, above, 682–8; F. Jacobs and R. White (1996), note 10, above, 388–91; A. Mowbray, "The European Court of Human Rights' Approach to Just Satisfaction" [1997] *PL* 647; K. Reid, *A Practitioner's Guide to the European Convention on Human Rights* (London: Sweet & Maxwell, 1998), 395–426; and P. van Dijk and G. van Hoof (1998), note 10, above, 249–59.

[36] And, prior to the entry into force of Protocol 11, of the Committee of Ministers which had a corresponding power under former Article 32 in those cases where it was the final arbiter of applications. See also r. 9 of the Rules adopted by the Committee of Ministers for the application of Articles 32 and 54 of the European Convention on Human Rights.

the affording of just satisfaction. Many decisions lack convincing reasoning for the awards.

A number of preliminary points can be made. The mandatory language inherent in the phrase "shall . . . afford" is converted to discretionary language by the intervening words "if necessary". The discretionary nature of just satisfaction has been confirmed by the Court.[37] It has been the practice of the Court only to consider just satisfaction where it is requested by the "injured party"[38] a term which is regarded as synonymous with the term "victim" as used in Article 34.[39] The just satisfaction with which the Court is concerned is that to be accorded by reason of the violations found by the Court; there must, accordingly, be some causal link between the finding of violation and the satisfaction the victim is seeking.[40] It is also possible for an award of just satisfaction to include the costs and expenses of bringing the claim. The conditions here are that the costs and expenses were actually and necessarily incurred and that they are reasonable in amount.[41]

Apart from recovery of costs and expenses, the normal heads of just satisfaction are pecuniary loss and non-pecuniary loss. The Court does not award any remedy by way of just satisfaction other than compensation. The Court will not order a Contracting Party to take, or not to take, a particular course of action.[42] However, in many cases the Court regards its own finding of a violation of the Convention as sufficient to constitute just satisfaction.[43]

Pecuniary loss covers actual losses such as loss of earnings, out of pocket expenses (other than sums falling within costs and expenses of lawyers), and the loss of value of an asset arising from the action of the Contracting Party. Non-pecuniary losses have included damages for pain and suffering resulting from ill-treatment, and compensation for anxiety, distress and frustration caused by the action of the Contracting Party. The level of domestic awards can assist the Court in determining the amount of non-pecuniary loss, but it is only a guide.

The overriding consideration by the Court is to exercise its discretion over the award of just satisfaction having regard to what is equitable.[44] This phrase

37 *Guzzardi* v. *Italy*, Judgment of 6 November 1980, A/39; (1981) 3 EHRR 333, para. 114 of the Judgment.

38 *Lombardo* v. *Italy*, Judgment of 26 November 1992, A/249-B, para. 25 of the Judgment

39 Formerly Article 25. *De Wilde, Ooms and Versyp* v. *Belgium (No. 2) (Article 50)*, Judgment of 10 March 1972, A/14; (1979–80) 1 EHRR 438, para. 23 of the Judgment.

40 See, for example, *Quaranta* v. *Switzerland*, Judgment of 24 May 1991, A/205, para. 43 of the Judgment.

41 *The Sunday Times* v. *The United Kingdom (No. 2) (Article 50)*, Judgment of 6 November 1980, A/38; (1981) 3 EHRR 317, para. 23 of the Judgment.

42 *Brozicek* v. *Italy*, Judgment of 19 December 1989, A/167; (1990) 12 EHRR 371, para. 47 of the Judgment (refusal of request by victim to declare a judgment on a trial in the victim's absence void and to be struck from his record); and *Nasri* v. *France*, Judgment of 13 July 1995, A/324; (1996) 21 EHRR 458, para. 50 of the Judgment (refusal of request to require State to annul a deportation order).

43 See, for example, *Fox, Campbell and Hartley* v. *The United Kingdom (Just Satisfaction)*, Judgment of 27 March 1991, A/202; (1992) 14 EHRR 108, para. 11 of the Judgment.

44 *Young, James and Webster* v. *United Kingdom (Article 50)*, Judgment of 18 October 1982, A/55; (1983) 5 EHRR 201, para. 13 of the Judgment. See also r. 54(4) of the Rules of Court "A"

recurs over and over again in the case-law, and frequently covers a complete lack of reasoning in the Court's decision for the award of a particular sum. Reid has analysed the awards of just satisfaction by the Court and concludes:

> The Court has not proved unduly generous in its approach to awarding compensation under any of the heads. The emphasis is not on providing a mechanism for enriching successful applicants but rather its role in making public and binding findings of applicable human rights standards.[45]

The schedules of awards for both pecuniary and non-pecuniary losses in Reid's book[46] demonstrate the lack of consistency in the Court's approach. Nor does a reading of decisions under former Article 50 (now Article 41) provide any insights, since the Court so frequently reverts to the assertion that the sum awarded is justified on equitable grounds. Mowbray's analysis of consideration by the Court of damage claims, "reveals a worrying lack of transparency in reasoning".[47] His analysis of claims also revealed a low level of success in claims for both pecuniary and non-pecuniary losses.

Of course, it is possible to engage in "number-crunching" of the awards made to date, and any lawyer acting for a victim must be familiar with the vagaries of the case-law. But such activity is pointless if the search is for underlying principles where none can be found in the reasoning of the judges beyond a broad appeal to poorly articulated considerations of equity. Two examples will suffice to make the point. A number of property cases have come before the Court in recent years. In the *Papamichalopoulos* case,[48] in which the largest award to date was made, the Court ordered the preparation of a report by three experts on the value of the land in issue. Though this was hotly contested by the Greek Government, the Court relied upon it in determining its award for pecuniary loss. This seems an eminently fair way to proceed where such high value property is in issue. But in a case decided only a few months earlier which involved land with a somewhat lower, but hardly insignificant, value the Court had declined to commission an expert's report on value.[49] This prompted dissenting Judge Martens to note:

> . . . the Court should not shelter behind "equity" but rule on the legal issues and invite experts to provide it with the data which would enable it to assess the value of the land, if need be in equity. Deciding in equity, like any other judicial decision, requires a clear and reliable view of the facts.[50]

adopted on 27 January 1994 and r. 56(4) of the Rules of Court "A" adopted on 27 January 1994 relating to the equitable basis on which the Court approves agreements on just satisfaction. These provisions are now to be found in r. 75(4) of the Rules of the European Court of Human Rights adopted on 4 November 1998.

45 Reid (1998), note 35, above, 398.

46 *Ibid*, 399–401, and 403–20.

47 Mowbray (1997), note 35, above, at 650.

48 *Papamichalopoulos and Others* v. *Greece (Article 50)*, Judgment of 31 October 1995, A/330–B; (1996) 21 EHRR 439.

49 *Hentrich* v. *France (Article 50)*, Judgment of 3 July 1995, A/322; (1996) 21 EHRR 439.

50 *Ibid*, Dissenting Opinion of Judge Martens.

In the *Loizidou* case,[51] the applicant submitted a valuation report which put a value of 621,900 Cypriot pounds on the loss of the use of her land in the Turkish-occupied part of Cyprus. The Delegate of the Commission took an entirely different view of the basis on which pecuniary loss should be calculated. The Turkish Government contested the applicant's entitlement to any compensation for pecuniary loss. The Court, without adducing any contrary evidence, rejected the hypothetical percentage increases in property values which were inherent in the applicant's calculations, and concluded:

> Taking into account the above-mentioned uncertainties, inherent in any attempt to quantify the real losses incurred by the applicant, and making an assessment on an equitable basis the Court decided to award CYP 300,000 under this head.[52]

The very real difficulties in fixing the pecuniary loss in this case must be recognised.[53] However, the Court should have articulated the basis for its calculation of the figure it awarded rather than simply giving the figure and asserting its equitable basis of calculation. As it stands, the determination of figures looks arbitrary in the absence of fuller reasoning.

This criticism is also evident on a reading of the *Schuler-Zgraggen* case.[54] The case concerned a violation of the Convention arising when Switzerland unlawfully discriminated against the applicant in refusing her social security benefits. She sought interest at the rate of five per cent per annum on the late payment of a pension by way of pecuniary loss. Switzerland objected on the basis that national practice was not to pay interest on late payments of social security benefits. The Court's reasoning in reducing the requested sum of 40,933.64 Swiss francs to 25,000 Swiss francs is far from convincing. It accepted that there was an entitlement to "some interest for the period in question", but went on:

> The Court does not, however, agree with the summary and imprecise method of calculation proposed by Mrs Schuler-Zgraggen and in particular with the rate of five per cent. Making its assessment on an equitable basis in accordance with Article 50, it awards the applicant 25,000 Sfr. for the remaining pecuniary damage.[55]

The statement earlier in the judgment on the basis of the applicant's calculation looks far more convincing than the reasoning of the Court. If the objection was that the applicant's calculation was "summary and imprecise", then surely there was an onus on the Court to show that its calculation was neither summary nor imprecise. Why was the rate of five per cent wrong? What rate did the Court use, bearing in mind that it accepted that the applicant was entitled to some interest for the period in question?

[51] *Loizidou* v. *Turkey (Article 50)*, Judgment of 28 July 1998.

[52] *Ibid*, para. 34 of the Judgment.

[53] For the background, see R. White, "Tackling Political Disputes through Individual Applications" [1998] *EHRLR* 61.

[54] *Schuler-Zgraggen* v. *Switzerland (Article 50)*, Judgment of 31 January 1995, A/305–A; (1996) 21 EHRR 404.

[55] *Ibid*, para. 15 of the Judgment.

Overall, one can only conclude that there are a number of propositions for which the case-law on just satisfaction is authority, and these have been summarised above. The main proposition is that when just satisfaction takes the form of compensation, then claims can be made for pecuniary losses, non-pecuniary losses, and for costs and expenses. The Court claims to determine these on an equitable basis, but does not articulate what this means. In short, there are no principles, but the issue is considered on a case by case basis.

4. THE HUMAN RIGHTS ACT 1998 AND REMEDIES

The scheme of the Human Rights Act 1998 is elegant and clever. It sets in place a means of incorporating the European Convention, which preserves the distinct roles of judges and politicians in the constitutional order of the United Kingdom. The substantive rights in Part II of the Convention are included as part of United Kingdom law and, except for Article 13, on the right to a remedy, reproduced in Schedule 1. These substantive rights are called "Convention rights" under the Act.

Under s. 6(1) of the Act, it is unlawful for any public authority to "act in a way which is incompatible with a Convention right". Public authorities include any court or tribunal, and "any person certain of whose functions are functions of a public nature",[56] but does not include the Houses of Parliament. There remains considerable uncertainty as to the ambit of the term "public authority", and elaboration in the case-law will be needed.[57] Under s. 7 any person who claims that a public authority has acted in a manner which is incompatible with a Convention right may bring proceedings against the authority in a court or tribunal as determined by rules to be made under the Act. Equally any party to proceedings can rely on a Convention right in any legal proceedings. Applicants bringing judicial review proceedings will have standing if they are, or would be, considered a victim of a violation under Article 34[58] of the Convention.

Where Convention rights are in issue, new rules of interpretation come into play. First, in determining whether there has been a violation of a Convention right, a court or tribunal must "take into account" case-law of the Commission, Court of Human Rights and Committee of Ministers. Furthermore, in interpreting any primary or secondary legislation whenever enacted, the court or tribunal must "so far as it is possible to do so, read and give effect to that legislation in a way which is compatible with the Convention rights".[59]

[56] s. 6(3)(b) of the 1998 Act.

[57] The concept is reminiscent of, though not identical with, the concept of "emanations of the State" which was developed by the Court of Justice alongside its rulings on direct effect: see generally T. Hartley, *The Foundations of European Community Law*, 4th edn. (Oxford: Oxford University Press, 1998) at 208–11.

[58] Formerly Article 25.

[59] s. 3(1) of the 1998 Act.

If a court or tribunal concludes that there has been a violation of the Convention, s. 8(1) of the 1998 Act provides that "it may grant such relief or remedy, or make such order, within its powers as it considers just and appropriate".[60] This is an enabling provision giving courts and tribunals powers similar to those enjoyed by the Court of Human Rights under Article 41 of the Convention to afford just satisfaction to a victim of a violation. In determining whether to award damages, and if so in what amount, the court or tribunal is required to "take into account the principles applied by the European Court of Human Rights in relation to the award of compensation under Article 41 of the Convention".[61]

The remedies section of the 1998 Act contains both sweeping provisions on the grant of a remedy for a violation of the Convention and sweeping limitations on the powers available, which may not be compliant with the unincorporated Article 13 of the Convention. It also raises questions about the nature and effect of remedies for human rights violations. Hence, s. 8(1) grants a broad competence, but the nature of the remedies available will vary according to the forum. The relief, remedy or order open to the court or tribunal must be one already within its powers. So the Act gives no new competence to decision-making bodies to provide a remedy for a violation of a Convention right. The decision not to extend the powers of all courts and tribunals to include new remedies for violations of Convention rights was apparently motivated by a concern that there would be an explosion of damages awards in this area across a wide range of decision-making bodies. It was this same concern which led to the exclusion of Article 13 of the Convention from the incorporated rights. There are, accordingly, a wide but not unlimited range of remedies available for breaches of Convention rights.

The drafting of s. 8 reveals a concern that damages for violations of Convention rights should be contained. Section 8(2) provides that damages for an unlawful act of a public authority under the Act may be awarded only by a court (or tribunal) which has power to award damages, or to order the payment of compensation, in civil proceedings. Furthermore, damages, though not the remedy of last resort, are circumscribed since they are not to be made unless the court is satisfied that the award is necessary to afford just satisfaction to the person in whose favour the award is made, having regard to all the circumstances of the case, and in particular any other remedy or relief granted and the consequences of any decision in respect of the breach of Convention rights.[62] As noted above, decisions about the award of damages and the amount of damages are to be informed by reference to the case-law of the Court of Human Rights in awarding just satisfaction.

[60] On the availability of damages as a remedy, see M. Amos, "Damages for Breach of the Human Rights Act 1998" [1999] *EHRLR* 178.

[61] s. 8(4) of the 1998 Act.

[62] s. 8(3) of the 1998 Act.

A number of observations need to be made about the structure of s. 8. It assumes that the range of remedies currently available to United Kingdom courts will be adequate to remedy breaches of Convention rights. It seeks to discourage an explosion of damages awards.[63] The Lord Chancellor indicated that the intent was to match the awards victims would get if they received just satisfaction under Article 41.[64] It establishes a system in which the luck of the forum will determine whether duplication of litigation will be needed to secure a money remedy. A good example would be an appeal heard by a unified Social Security Appeal Tribunal, which has no power to award damages, and it has been established that it has no power to award interest on the late payment of benefit.[65] Nor it seems would any other court. Yet, as noted in the discussion of the case-law on just satisfaction above, the Court of Human Rights has awarded just satisfaction referable to interest on the late payment of benefit.[66] In the early days of Community law, an action for a declaration was one means of securing a judicial statement of an entitlement under Community law.[67] This would seem to be the only route open within the national legal order to a victim who had only received social security benefit to which he or she was entitled some years late and who wished to raise the claim for interest on the late payment. Otherwise, such a person would have to raise the complaint that no interest was available before the Court in Strasbourg.

A similar issue seems certain to arise before the criminal courts. Though such courts can make compensation orders against convicted persons,[68] such orders do not arise in civil proceedings[69] and the terms of s. 35 do not, in any event, accommodate orders other than against the convicted party. So, a breach of Convention rights arising before a magistrates' court or the Crown Court could only result in the award of compensation if the victim pursued that remedy through the civil courts as a separate cause of action. There is nothing in the Human Rights Act 1998 that would require the civil court to have regard to the decision of the criminal court which concluded that some aspect of the case before them revealed in their view a breach of Convention rights. Such a scenario gives rise, at least, to an arguable case that the duplication of litigation and the absence of appropriate cross-referencing between judicial authorities constitutes a failure to provide an effective remedy in the national legal order contrary to the unincorporated Article 13 of the Convention.

[63] See the pertinent comments of M. Amos on the effect of the requirement to take into account the "consequences" of a decision to award damages under s. 8(3), note 60, above, at 186.

[64] HL Deb Vol. 582 col. 1232, 3 November 1997.

[65] This undoubtedly follows from the reasoning of the Social Security Commissioner in *R(FC)2/90*; see also the decision of the Court of Justice in *R* v. *Secretary of State for Social Security, ex parte Sutton* [1997] ECR I–2163; [1997] 2 CMLR 382.

[66] *Schuler-Zgraggen*, note 54, above.

[67] One famous example is Case 41/74 *Van Duyn* v. *Home Office* [1974] ECR 1337.

[68] s. 35, Powers of Criminal Courts Act 1973.

[69] s. 8(2) of the 1998 Act.

Perhaps the most pertinent point to make is that the deference to the provisions of the Convention on just satisfaction in the national legislation is misplaced. The provisions in Article 41 of the Convention on affording just satisfaction are a safety net where the national legal order does not offer full compensation for the breach of the Convention. The starting point is that the national legal order should determine what remedies are appropriate for breaches of the Convention. Such an obligation flows from Article 13 of the Convention. Indeed, it could be argued that the effect of s. 8 replicates the failures of earlier years to recognise what was demanded by the Convention. It assumes that the current panoply of remedies available in the national legal order meets the requirements of the Convention. It also reveals a deep anxiety about damages as a remedy for breach of a Convention right.

Ultimately, we may need to ask what is meant, in terms of remedies, by the obligation in Article 13 to provide "an effective remedy before a national authority". I would argue that an effective remedy is not simply the requiring of a process but also an outcome. The Court of Human Rights, in determining whether it should resort to Article 41, appears to proceed on the basis that full compensation[70] is required. But the practice of the Court shows that it does not approach just satisfaction in any principled or scientific way, and has frequently resorted to a broad claim to unarticulated "equitable principles" to justify its awards. If the protection of human rights in the United Kingdom serves a higher interest, then the provision of remedies for violations should, in some way, reflect that.

Despite all this, it may be that national courts in the United Kingdom will over time, and using their skills in adapting the range of remedies within their powers, produce a more coherent national scheme of remedies for violations of Convention rights than can be discerned by examination of the law and practice of the Court of Human Rights in the exercise of its power to award just satisfaction. There is certainly nothing in the Convention which would inhibit this.

5. CONCLUSION

It is hardly surprising that the literature on the European Convention on Human Rights does not answer questions about the nature of remedies for breaches of human rights standards. The principal underlying objective of the Convention is to change the behaviour of States, and not to provide remedies for individuals who are victims of those violations. That is a secondary aim. The problematic Article 13 does not require any particular form of procedure for granting a remedy in the national legal order; national authorities are left with discretion as to how they provide both for a mechanism to examine violations of Convention rights and for the granting of a remedy. The basic philosophy underlying the

[70] *Restitutio in integrum.*

Convention has been described thus by a former Registrar of the Court of Human Rights:

> The object and purpose of the Convention is to achieve the "collective enforcement" – to use the words of the Preamble – of those fundamental freedoms which are enshrined in the Convention itself and in its additional Protocols. Their normative and procedural rules were in no way intended to take the place of national human-rights provisions and machinery, but were clearly designed to add a supplementary and ultimate remedy to those safeguards which the internal law of the Convention States afford to the individual. National protection of human rights and European protection form a couple; they go hand in hand.[71]

The burden is, therefore, placed squarely on the national legal order to develop a scheme of remedies available under an incorporated European Convention, which meets the requirements of Article 13 of the Convention.

Such an obligation brings national authorities up against the requirement for an effective remedy under Article 13 of the Convention. It has been shown that there is little guidance beyond some basic, and largely self-evident, propositions in the case-law of the Strasbourg organs on what makes a remedy effective. The argument in this paper, particularly in relation to the award of damages as a remedy for a violation of Convention rights, is that making the Court of Human Rights' case-law on just satisfaction the starting point for making such decisions will not get national authorities very far. Similarly, just as a gap was revealed in many national legal orders in the scheme of remedies for breach of Community law, so too it is likely that development of Article 13 of the European Convention will reveal a similar gap in United Kingdom law.[72]

Just as national procedural autonomy has been eroded by developments in European Community law, so too, over time, it is likely to be eroded by requirements arising from obligations undertaken under the European Convention.[73] That would have happened whether the Convention had been incorporated or not. The consequence of incorporation is that such issues are likely to emerge somewhat sooner, since there are features of the scheme of incorporation which highlight the issue of remedies. It will be for national authorities to decide whether offering compensation (and other remedies) to victims is to be given at least equal priority to removing aspects of national law and practice which are found not to be Convention compliant. There is certainly an argument that the supplementary nature of European protection demands that national authorities set in place a coherent and compliant system of remedies under the incorporated Convention. Failure to do so may find the United Kingdom on the receiving end of applications to the Court of Human Rights arguing a violation of the unincorporated Article 13 of the Convention.

71 H. Petzold, "The Convention and the Principle of Subsidiarity" in R. St J. Macdonald, F. Matscher and H. Petzold (eds.), *The European System for the Protection of Human Rights* (Dordrecht: Martinus Nijhoff, 1993), 41, at 43.

72 And the law of many other Contracting States to the European Convention.

73 See also C. Harlow, this volume at XX.

9

European Remedies in the Field of Human Rights

HENRY SCHERMERS

1. THE EUROPEAN CONVENTION ON HUMAN RIGHTS AS A SOURCE OF EUROPEAN LAW

THE EUROPEAN Convention on Human Rights and Fundamental Freedoms (the Convention) contains a number of rather vague rights for individuals. The European Court of Human Rights creates more detailed law through its interpretation of the articles of the Convention. As the Convention binds all Member States of the European Union these refined rules of human rights create European law in addition to the legal order of the European Union. Examples are the prohibition of corporal punishment,[1] limits to the use of anonymous witnesses,[2] the prohibition of governments to punish people for homosexual acts between consenting adults[3] and the judgment of the Court that rape is covered by the definition of torture.[4] Rulings on these and many other issues have been given against particular States but they apply to all other participating States as well. Thus these rulings create general European law as much as regulations of the European Community do. Together with European Community law, the law of the Convention creates a European legal order.

2. THE CONVENTION AS PART OF COMMUNITY LAW

The creation of European law through the Convention also affects the legal order of the European Union. It took some time, however, before the two legal orders began to merge. In the original Treaties of the European Communities there were no references to human rights. Neither did the European Court of

[1] See D. Harris, M. O'Boyle and C. Warbrick, *Law of The European Convention on Human Rights* (London: Butterworths, 1995), 84–9.

[2] *Kostovski* v. *the Netherlands*, Judgment of 20 November 1989 , A/166; *Van Mechelen* v. *the Netherlands*, Judgment of 23 April 1997, Reports 1997–III.

[3] *Dudgeon* v. *United Kingdom*, Judgment of 22 October 1981, A/45; *Norris* v. *Ireland*, Judgment of 26 October 1988, A/142; *Modinos* v. *Cyprus*, Judgment of 22 April 1993, A/259.

[4] *Aydin* v. *Turkey*, Judgment of 25 September 1997, Reports 1997–VI.

Justice (ECJ) originally pay attention to them. When in 1960 Mr Nold invoked a fundamental right contained in Article 14 of the German Constitution, the ECJ replied:

> It is not for the Court . . . to ensure that rules of internal law, even constitutional rules, enforced in one or other of the Member States are respected. Therefore the Court may neither interpret nor apply Article 14 of the German basic law in examining the legality of a decision of the High Authority. Moreover Community law, as it arises under the European Coal and Steel Community (ECSC) Treaty, does not contain any general principle, express or otherwise, guaranteeing the maintenance of vested rights.[5]

At that time the ECJ was still so much focused on building the legal order of the Community and persuading national courts to apply that order with priority over domestic legislation that it did not think of expanding the legal order of the Community in any way into the field of human rights. Following extensive academic writing and views expressed by European and domestic constitutional lawyers critical of this stance, the Court referred to human rights in *obiter dictum* in 1969.[6] Finally, in 1974 the Court accepted that the powers of the Community institutions are limited by fundamental human rights. In the second *Nold* Case it held:

> As the Court has already stated, fundamental rights form an integral part of the general principles of law, the observance of which it ensures.
>
> In safeguarding these rights, the Court is bound to draw inspiration from the constitutional traditions common to the Member States, and it cannot therefore uphold measures which are incompatible with fundamental rights recognized and protected by the Constitutions of those States.
>
> Similarly, international treaties for the protection of human rights on which the Member States have collaborated or of which they are signatories, can supply guidelines which should be followed within the framework of Community law.[7]

This second *Nold* case was the first step towards merging the legal order of the Human Rights Convention into the legal order of the Communities, thus creating a larger and stronger European legal order. The incorporation of human rights into the legal order of the Communities was achieved by the ECJ. Formerly, the Communities were never bound by the Convention. Proposals of the Commission to accede to the Convention were not accepted. The possibility to accede was finally rejected by the Court of Justice in its Opinion 2/94 of 28 March 1996.[8]

Notwithstanding the absence of any formal binding Treaty commitments, the Court of Justice in fact considered the Community bound by the Convention. For the interpretation of the Convention it takes the interpretation by the European Court of Human Rights into account, and in fact it follows its case-law wherever possible.

[5] Joined Cases 36, 37, 38 and 40/59 [1960] ECR, 423 at 438.
[6] Case 29/69 *Stauder* v. *City of Ulm* [1969] ECR 419 at 425.
[7] Case 4/73 *Nold KG* v. *Commission* [1974] ECR 491 at 507.
[8] Opinion 2/94 28 March 1996 [1996], ECR I–1759–I–1790.

Through the case-law of the ECJ all Community acts can be challenged to the extent that they contravene the Convention. In fact, therefore, the legal order of the Community is as much controlled by the Convention as any legal order of a Member State. The difference, however, is that, in the case of the domestic legal orders of the Member States, the control by the domestic supreme courts is supervised by the European Court of Human Rights while, in Community law, supervision by the ECJ cannot be followed by any control by the European Court of Human Rights.

Gradually, the protection of human rights in the European Union through the ECJ was further strengthened. In 1977 the Commission, Council and European Parliament issued a declaration supporting the Court's position that the European Convention is part of Community law.[9] In the preamble of the European Act of February 1986 a reference to the European Convention was made. In the Treaty of the Union of February 1992 an Article was incorporated providing that the Union shall respect fundamental rights as guaranteed by the European Convention. The Treaty of Amsterdam further enforced the protection of human rights (though not expressly those of the Convention) by adding the possibility of sanctions against Member States which do not respect fundamental human rights (EU Article 7).

At the summit meeting in Cologne of June 1999 it was decided that a catalogue of human rights should be added to the Treaty of the Union. This catalogue should play the same role in Community law which national constitutional provisions on human rights play in domestic law. This means that a catalogue of human rights in the Treaty of the Union can expand the rights of the citizens but cannot restrict them below the level of the Convention. In *Matthews* the European Court of Human Rights held the Member States of the Union responsible *ratione materiae* under Article 1 of the Convention for the violation of human rights enumerated in the Convention by the Union.[10]

3. THE CONVENTION BEYOND COMMUNITY LAW

From 1989 onwards the ECJ went further than verifying whether Community acts are in conformity with human rights by also requiring that national law executing rules of Community law must be in conformity with the Convention. The Court held:

> 10. Regulation No. 1612/68 must also be interpreted in the light of the requirement of respect for family life set out in Article 8 of the Convention for the Protection of Human Rights and Fundamental Freedoms. That requirement is one of the fundamental rights which, according to the Court's settled case-law, restated in the preamble to the Single European Act, are recognized by Community Law.

[9] Joint Declaration of 5 April 1977, OJ 27 April 1977. No. C–103/1.

[10] *Matthews* case, Application No. 24833/94, Judgment of 8 February 1999.

> . . .
>
> 11. The German legislation is therefore incompatible with the obligations arising under Community law in so far as it provides for non-renewal of a residence permit or a reduction a posteriori of the period of validity of a residence permit for a member of the family of a migrant worker by virtue of the fact that the family's housing can no longer be regarded as suitable according to the criteria applied in that regard in the place of residence, whereas sanctions of comparable severity are not provided for in regard to German nationals.[11]

On the one hand this position of the ECJ should be supported. Of course, national legislation executing Community law should meet the minimum requirements of human rights protection. On the other hand, however, this position leads to a duplication of control. While the legality of Community acts is under the sole control of the ECJ, the legality of national legislation comes under the normal control of the domestic supreme court. When national legislation executing rules of Community law infringes the Convention an injured party may want to bring a complaint before the European Court of Human Rights in Strasbourg. He can do so only after exhausting domestic remedies. Each of the national instances can request a preliminary ruling under Article 234 EC (ex Article 177). The road to Luxembourg is shorter than the road to Strasbourg. This means that human rights violations will come before the ECJ rather than before the Human Rights Court. A good example of this situation is the case of Konstantinidis. Mr Konstantinidis was a Greek national living in Germany. His name in Greek letters was unacceptably changed in Roman letters by the German authorities. Mr Konstantinidis considered that this was an infringement of the German Government's obligation to respect his private life (Article 8 of the Convention). As he was a Community national, established in another country, the German Court of First Instance considered that this transcription of his name concerned the freedom of establishment of a Greek national in Germany and came therefore under Article 52 of the EEC Treaty (now Article 43 EC). It requested the preliminary ruling of the ECJ and that Court found a violation of the freedom of establishment.[12]

The further the control of the ECJ expands in the field of human rights, the more likely it will be that similar overlapping can develop. Most likely conflicts of competence will, in the vast majority of cases, be decided in favour of the Luxembourg Court as Strasbourg can be reached only after exhausting all domestic remedies while Luxembourg can be reached by any court of lower instance. The more human rights protection the Communities offer, the more the Luxembourg Court will replace the Strasbourg Court in the field of human rights. This seems to be an undesirable development, the more so as the individual may still bring his complaint to the Strasbourg Court after the preliminary ruling of the Luxembourg Court.

[11] Case 249/86 *Commission* v. *Germany*[1989] ECR 1263 at 1290–1.

[12] Case C–168/91 *Konstantinidis* v. *Stadt Altensteig, Standesamt, and Landratsamt Calw, Ordnungsamt* [1993] ECR I–1191.

The best way to solve this problem is to permit lower courts also to request preliminary rulings of the European Court of Human Rights. In the past proposals to this effect have been made but they failed. The Second Protocol to the European Convention on the possibility of preliminary rulings (which is now incorporated in Article 47 of the Convention) is so restrictive that it had no practical effect. One of the reasons why the governments did not want preliminary rulings to the European Court of Human Rights was that by this means the European Commission of Human Rights would be shut out, which was considered undesirable as the Commission had an important role of its own. Now that the Commission has disappeared, this argument has lost its value. In former times the inequality of the position of the two European courts never played a role as the two jurisdictions hardly met. The expansion of the jurisdiction of both courts which makes overlapping more likely is another argument for reconsidering the introduction of the same procedure of preliminary rulings for both courts.

4. DEVELOPMENTS UNDER THE CONVENTION

Above, we noticed that initially the Luxembourg Court was reluctant to enter into the field of human rights, but that gradually this reluctance diminished. Similarly, the Strasbourg institutions initially were hesitant to enter into the field of Community law. Complaints against the Community were declared inadmissible on the ground that the Community was not bound by the Convention.[13] As the Community has no executive force of its own, Community acts must be executed by the national authorities. M & Co, convinced that a Community decision was in violation with the Convention, brought a complaint against Germany when the German authorities executed the Community decision. The European Commission of Human Rights declared this case inadmissible on the ground that under Community law the German Government had no discretion and therefore could bear no responsibility for the execution of the decision.[14] The Commission respected the supra-national nature of Community law. Had it held Germany responsible for the execution of a Community act, it would at the same time have established that Member States must verify the legality of Community acts before executing them. This would be a step backwards in European integration, running against the purpose of both the Community and the Convention, which is to establish a European legal system. Holding that the Community sufficiently protected human rights through its own controls Strasbourg could abstain from supervising the execution of Community acts.

[13] See *CFDT* Case (8030/77), 10 July 1978, *Yearbook of the European Convention on Human Rights*, Vol. 21 (1978) 530–8. See also 800, 801.

[14] *M & Co* v. *FRG*, Application No. 13258/87 Decision of the European Commission of Human Rights, 9 February 1990, D & R Vol. 64, 138–46.

This position is not fully satisfactory. If States bound by the Convention create international organisations, then such organisations must also be bound by the Convention. By leaving the control over such binding effect to institutions of subsequently established organizations the Strasbourg institutions fall short of their controlling task. As it is undesirable to force the Member States of the Union to verify the legality of Community acts at the stage of the execution, it is also undesirable to hold the Member States of the Union liable for the execution of Community acts. The proper way to avoid future problems is to bind the Community itself to the Convention and thus to permit applications against the Community whenever a Community act is considered to be in violation of the Convention. This solution was, however, blocked by the Court of Justice in its Opinion 2/94 of 28 March 1996. According to the Court of Justice the Community is not competent to adhere to the Convention. Prior amendment of the Treaty would be required. Also the Convention must be amended as under its present text (Article 59) it is open only to Member States of the Council of Europe. Before 1989 the Member States of the Council of Europe would have been willing to admit the Community as a party to the Convention. Whether that is still the case is unclear. Some more recent Member States might want to use the occasion for requesting concessions in other fields from the European Union.[15]

In the case of *M & Co* the European Commission of Human Rights took the position that it will not accept applications against States for the execution of acts of the Community, as it accepts that the Court of Justice of the Community sufficiently protects the rights enumerated in the Convention. In the case of *Matthews* the European Court of Human Rights held the UK liable for the execution of a Community act which was not controlled by any court as it had the status of a treaty.[16]

Matthews does not expressly refer to the *M & Co* case. However, there are indications that the Strasbourg Court also considers judicial control through the Community to be relevant:

> 32. The Court observes that acts of the EC as such cannot be challenged before the Court because the EC is not a Contracting Party. The Convention does not exclude the transfer of competences to international organisations provided that Convention rights continue to be "secured". Member States' responsibility therefore continues, even after such a transfer.
>
> 33. In the present case, the alleged violation of the Convention flows from an annex to the 1976 Act entered into by the United Kingdom, together with the extension to the European Parliament's competences brought about by the Maastricht Treaty. The Council Decision and the 1976 Act, and the Maastricht Treaty, with its changes to the EEC Treaty, all constituted international instruments which were freely entered into

[15] *Cf.* M. Nowak, "Human Rights 'Conditionality' in Relation to Entry to, and Full Participation in, the EU" in Alston *et al.* (eds.), *The EU and Human Rights* (Oxford: Oxford University Press, 1999).

[16] On this case, see H.G. Schermers, "*Matthews* v. *United Kingdom*" (1999) 36 *CMLRev*, 673–81.

by the United Kingdom. Indeed, the 1976 Act cannot be challenged before the European Court of Justice for the very reason that it is not a "normal" act of the Community, but is a treaty within the Community legal order. The Maastricht Treaty, too, is not an act of the Community, but a treaty by which a revision of the EEC Treaty was brought about. The United Kingdom, together with all the other parties to the Maastricht Treaty is responsible *ratione materiae* under Article 1 of the Convention and, in particular, under Article 3 of Protocol No. 1, for the consequences of that Treaty.

On the same day, the Court of Human Rights also gave judgment in *Waite and Kennedy* v. *Germany*.[17] The case concerned access to judicial proceedings under Article 6 of the Convention, as the European Space Agency (ESA) had immunity of jurisdiction in Germany. The Strasbourg Court unanimously upheld the decision of the Commission, who had found by a majority that there was no violation, since the ESA had its own Appeal Board which offered sufficient judicial protection. "For the Court a material factor in determining whether granting ESA immunity from German jurisdiction is permissible, is whether the applicants had available to them reasonable alternative means to protect effectively their rights under the Convention".[18] Taken together, these two judgments indicate that the Court of Human Rights will be reluctant to hold Contracting Parties to the Convention accountable for acts stemming from participation in another international organisation unless there is no alternative source of judicial control.

5. CONCLUSION

From the developments in the Court of Justice we may safely conclude that in substance the Convention is part of Community law. There are shortcomings with respect to European supervision of the application of the Convention by the Community, but they are not of great practical importance in so far as the Community's own Court carefully applies European human rights law. Developments in the Court of Human Rights indicate the mutual respect and careful demarcation of jurisdiction between the two Courts.

[17] Application No. 26083/94, Judgment of 18 February 1999.
[18] *Ibid*, para. 68.

10

The Limits of the Uniform Application of Community Law and Effective Judicial Review: A Look Post-Amsterdam

ANGELA WARD

1. INTRODUCTION

THE PRIMARY purpose of this paper is to examine the extent to which fragmentation in the scheme of judicial protection of the EC legal system has resulted from amendments introduced by the Amsterdam Treaty. The concept of a Community legal order supplying a system of uniform and coherent remedies[1] was substantially undermined, for the first time, in the Maastricht Treaty on Political Union, in which the Court of Justice was famously excluded from reviewing measures promulgated within the two inter-governmental pillars of Justice and Home Affairs (JHA) and the Common Foreign and Security policy (CFSP). This meant that the impact of these measures, and their influence under national law, was determined almost entirely at Member State level.[2] In addition, no mechanism was provided under Maastricht for co-ordination of the different approaches adopted. The principle of uniformity was additionally compromised by the Maastricht amendments by the inclusion of two country specific opt-outs, one in the hands of the United Kingdom pertaining to Social Policy,[3] and the other held by both the United Kingdom and Denmark concerning Economic and Monetary Union.[4]

[1] Case 314/85 *Foto-Frost* v. *Hauptzollamt Lübeck-Ost* [1987] ECR 4199.

[2] Article 46 (ex Article L) TEU. Under Articles 46 and 31.3(2)(c) (ex Articles L and K.3(2)(c)) TEU of the Court of Justice could be vested with jurisdiction to review conventions passed pursuant to JHA, or to rule on disputes regarding their application. For a detailed discussion on the jurisdiction of the Court after the SEA, Maastricht and Amsterdam revisions, see A. Albors-Llorens, "Changes in the Jurisdiction of the European Court of Justice under the Treaty of Amsterdam" (1998) 35 *CMLRev* 1273.

[3] Protocol 14 of the Maastricht Treaty. Note that under Title XI (Title VIII), Part III of the EC Treaty as amended under Amsterdam, the Agreement on Social Policy will be fully integrated into the EC Treaty.

[4] See Protocols 11 (United Kingdom) and 12 (Denmark) of the Maastricht Treaty. See also

Despite expressions of concern emanating from the Court of Justice over the damage occasioned by the Maastricht Treaty to the imperatives of effective judicial protection and uniformity,[5] the Treaty of Amsterdam accelerated many of the trends of Maastricht. Post-Amsterdam, measures concerning visa, asylum, and immigration policy will no longer be passed under the third pillar, but will now be promulgated under new Title IV of the EC Treaty. The scheme of judicial review, however, that will operate under Title IV will differ in many respects from the system governing the rest of the EC Treaty. In addition, alteration to judicial review in the *Union* legal system has caused further fragmentation and complication of legal remedies. The Court of Justice has been vested with limited, and variegated, jurisdiction to review the remnants of the third pillar, which is now concerned with Police and Judicial Co-operation in Criminal Matters (PJCC).[6]

The genesis of the Title IV amendment lay, at least in part, in a desire to enhance judicial accountability over the *Schengen acquis*, and to improve standards of judicial protection for people subject to the Union's expansive and evolving common immigration policy.[7] However the net result of this development, and the fractious involvement of the Court of Justice in interpretation of PJCC measures (which will be promulgated under the third pillar), may be attenuation of, rather than an improvement in, access to judicial remedies in the EU polity, and further sacrifice of consistency in the application of trans-European rules. The former manifests in the possible exclusion of judicial review with respect to certain Title IV EC, and Title VI TEU measures, and the increase in the length of proceedings entailed by the mechanisms for sending references to the Court of Justice which will operate with respect to these titles.

An assessment will also be made on the role, if any, which might be played by European Human Rights law in overcoming problems in the "effectiveness" of the judicial protection supplied by the Amsterdam Treaty. This takes on particular significance, in the light of the fact that the Court of Justice was granted under Amsterdam with formal authority to review conformity of actions of the EU institutions with fundamental rights in the Community legal order, whether acting in the context of Community or Union policy making.[8] Of additional interest are the recent spate of cases in which the European Court of Human

J.A.Usher, "Economic and Monetary Union – A Model for Flexibility" in A. Dashwood and A. Ward (eds.), *Cambridge Yearbook of Legal Studies* 1 (1998) 39.

[5] "Report on certain aspects of application of the Treaty of European Union", The Report of the Court of Justice (1995) 19, 21.

[6] Article 35 TEU. See generally J. Monar, "Justice and Home Affairs in the Treaty of Amsterdam: Reform at the Price of Fragmentation" (1998) 23 *ELRev* 320.

[7] This point is made, for example, in the context of transfer to the first pillar of visa, asylum and immigration policy in P. Craig, and G. de Búrca, *EU Law: Text, Cases and Materials* (Oxford: Oxford University Press, 1998), 43.

[8] Article 46 TEU (Article L) and Article 6(2) TEU (Article F(2)). See S. Peers, "Human Rights and the Third Pillar" in P. Alston (ed.), *The EU and Human Rights* (Oxford: Oxford University Press, 1999), 167.

Rights was asked to review human rights breaches occasioned within the context of the Community legal system.[9]

2. COMMUNITY *ACQUIS* ON EFFECTIVE REMEDIES AND UNIFORM APPLICATION OF EC RULES

Some thirteen years ago in the landmark case of *Johnston* v. *Chief Constable of the Royal Ulster Constabulary*,[10] the European Court of Justice cast the entitlement of private parties to an effective judicial remedy as a fundamental right in the Community legal order. The Court of Justice, in declaring the relevant national rules incompatible with EC law, stressed the primordial position occupied by judicial review in the Community legal system.

The "effective remedies" principle has burgeoned an enormous body of Court of Justice case-law.[11] It has been characterised by a resolute if not unwavering[12] will on the Court of Justice to ensure that private parties are afforded with tangible means of securing rights derived from the EC Treaty and secondary

[9] See the *Matthews* case, Application No. 24833/94, Judgment of the European Court of Human Rights of 18 February 1999; *Waite and Kennedy* v. *Germany*, Application No. 26083/94, Judgment of 18 February 1999. For a discussion, see H.G. Schermers, "European Remedies in the Field of Human Rights", in C. Kilpatrick, T. Novitz, and P. Skidmore, (eds.), *The Future of Remedies in Europe*; case commentary by Schermers in (1999) 36 *CMLRev* 673. See also *Pafitis and Others* v. *Greece*, Application No. 20323/92 (1998) 27 EHRR 566; *M and Co* v. *FRG*, Application No. 13258/87, Decision of the European Commission of Human Rights, 9 February 1990, D & R, Vol. 64, 138.

[10] Case 222/84 [1986] ECR 1651 (hereafter referred to as *Johnston*). The content of this right was recently considered by the Court of Justice in Case C–120/97 *Upjohn Limited* v. *The Licensing Authority established by the Medicines Act 1968 and Others* [1999] ECR I–223(hereafter referred to as *Upjohn*).

[11] The basic principles of effectiveness and non-discrimination, pursuant to which national remedies are assessed, were laid down in Case 45/76 *Comet BV* [1976] ECR 2043; and Case 33/76 *Rewe* [1976] ECR 1989. See also, for example Case 61/79 *Denkavit Italiana* [1980] ECR 1205; Case 240/87 *Deville* v. *Admistration des Impôts* [1988] ECR 3513 (hereafter referred to as *Deville*); Case 826/79 *Amministrazione delle Finanze dello Stato* v. *Mireco* [1980] ECR 2559; Case C–312/93 *Peterbroeck* [1995] ECR I–4599; Joined Cases C–430/93 and C–432/93 *van Schijndel* [1995] ECR I–4705; Case C–188/95 *Fantask and Others* v. *Industriministeriet* [1997] ECR I–6783 (hereafter referred to as *Fantask*). For a commentary on *Fantask* see A. Ward, "Indirect Taxes and National Remedies" (1999) 58 *Cambridge Law Journal*, 36. Note that the principles of effectiveness and non-discrimination are also applicable to disputes concerning the validity of EC measures, and can be called on to remove an obstructive procedural rule, or to improve sanctions. See Case C–212/94 *FMC plc and Others* v. *Intervention Board for Agricultural Produce, Ministry of Agriculture, Fisheries and Food* [1996] ECR I–389. For a detailed discussion of judicial remedies in the EC system see A. Ward *Judicial Review and the Rights of Private Parties in EC Law* (Oxford, Oxford University Press, 2000).

[12] A principal area in which the Court of Justice rulings on remedies have been fractious concerns national time limits. Compare, for example, Case C–208/90 *Emmott* v. *Minister of Social Welfare and Attorney General* [1991] ECR I–4269 with *Fantask, ibid.* For a detailed commentary on the Court's case-law on national time limits for bringing proceedings, see L. Flynn, "Whatever Happened to Emmott? The Perfecting of Community Rules on National Time Limits" in Kilpatrick, Novitz and Skidmore, note 9, above. The compatibility of retroactive limits on sums due with the principle of "effective enforcement" is also unclear. See, for example, Case C–246/96 *Magorrian and Cunningham* v. *Eastern Health and Social Services Board* [1997] ECR I–7153. See also in this regard, and with respect to national time limits for bringing proceedings Case C–78/98 *Preston and others* v. *Wolverhampton Healthcare Trust and others* and *Fletcher and others* v. *Midland Bank plc*, judgment of 16 May 2000.

legislation. The scale of the Court's incursion into national remedies and procedural rules have been well documented elsewhere,[13] so it is sufficient to recall here that the case-law in this field has stretched to obliging national judges to create new remedies to enforce Community law rights[14] (such as interim relief[15] and damages,[16] even if these sanctions were not otherwise available under national law), and a requirement to set aside national principles that would ordinarily excuse wrongdoers from liability for unlawful conduct.[17]

In addition, Court of Justice rulings have cast an obligation on national judges to ensure that the remedies that attach to claims based on Community law are no less favourable than those that are applicable to analogous claims of a purely domestic nature.[18] This, so-called, principle of non-discrimination has been litigated far less vigorously than its companion rule on effective remedies, but in recent times private parties have been much more willing to argue, and sometimes successfully,[19] that national law affords Community rights with a remedy that falls short of the sanction extended to similar domestic wrongs. Like the principle of effectiveness, therefore, this rule seems destined to play a critical role in the further harmonisation of national remedies and procedural

[13] See, for example, T. Tridimas, *The General Principles of EC Law* (Oxford: Oxford University Press, 1999), 276–438; J. Lonbay and A. Biondi, *Remedies for Breach of EC Law* (Chichester: Wiley, 1997); M. Andenas, and F. Jacobs, *European Community Law in English Courts* (Oxford: Oxford University Press, 1998); S. Prechal, "Community Law in National Courts" (1998) 35 *CMLRev* 681; W. Van Gerven,"Bridging the Gap Between Community and National Laws: Towards a Principle of Homogeneity in the Field of Legal Remedies" (1995) 32 *CMLRev* 679. See also A. Ward, "Effective Sanctions in EC Law: a Moving Boundary in the Division of Competence" (1995) 2 *ELJ* 205; B. Fitzpatrick and E. Szyszczak, "Remedies and Effective Judicial Protection in Community Law" (1994) 57 *MLR* 434; E. Szyszczak, "European Community Law: New Remedies, New Directions?" (1992) 55 *MLR* 215.

[14] Case 158/80 *Rewe-Handelsgesellschaft Nord mbh Rewe-Markt Steffen* v. *Hauptzollamt Kiel* [1981] ECR 1805.

[15] Case C–213/89 *Factortame No. 1* [1990] ECR I–2433.

[16] Joined Cases C–6/90 and C–9/90 *Francovich and Bonifaci and Others* v. *Italian Republic* [1991] ECR 5357; Joined Cases C–46/93 *Brasserie du Pêcheur SA* v. *Germany and the Queen* v. *Secretary of State for Transport, ex parte Factortame and Others* [1996] ECR 1029 (hereafter referred to as *Brasserie du Pêcheur*); Case C–392/93 *The Queen* v. *HM Treasury, ex parte British Telecommunications plc* [1996] ECR 1631; Joined Cases C–178/94, C–179/94, C–188/94, C–189/94 and C–190/94 *The Queen* v. *Ministry of Agriculture, Fisheries and Food, ex parte Heldey Lomas Ireland* [1996] ECR 2553 (hereafter referred to as *Hedley Lomas*). For commentaries on this case-law see, for example, W. Van Gerven, "Bridging the Unbridgeable: Community and National Tort Law after *Francovich* and *Brasserie*" (1996) 45 *ICLQ* 507; J. Convery,"State Liability in the United Kingdom after *Brasserie du Pêcheur*" (1997) 34 *CMLRev* 603; case commentary on state liability cases by P. Olivier in (1997) 34 *CMLRev* 635. The state liability principles were recently considered by the Court of Justice in Case C–319/69 *Brinkmann Tabafabriken GmbH* v. *Skatteministeriet* [1998] ECR I–5255.

[17] See *Fantask*, note 11, above, and the commentary by Ward.

[18] See, for example, cases cited in note 11, above.

[19] For example, Case C–180/95 *Nils Draehmpaehl* v. *Urania* [1997] ECR I–2195. For a discussion, see A. Ward, "New Frontiers in Private Enforcement of EC Directives" (1998) 23 *ELRev* 65. See also Case C–326/96 *Levez* v. *T.H. Jennings (Harlow Pools) Limited* [1998] ECR I–7835 (hereafter referred to as *Levez*). For an example of a case in which the Court of Justice found no breach of the principle on non-discrimination, see Case C–288/96 *Aprile* v. *Amministrazione delle Finanze dello Stato* [1998] ECR I–7141. For recent guidance on the principle of non-discrimination see Case C–78/98 *Preston and others* v. *Wolverhampton Healthcare Trust and others* and *Fletcher and others* v. *Midland Bank plc*, judgment of 16 May 2000.

rules that attach to rights derived from EC law, and in guaranteeing that adequate sanctions are available to protect Community law rights.

3. THE JURISDICTION OF THE COURT OF JUSTICE POST-AMSTERDAM

Court of Justice review of visa, asylum, and immigration policy under Title IV EC

New Title IV of the EC Treaty houses provisions concerning visas, asylum, and immigration policy, which were previously contained in the third pillar. The jurisdiction of the Court of Justice in the context of Title IV references from national courts is not, however, governed by Article 234 EC (ex Article 177). Rather, it is laid out in a separate provision, namely Article 68 EC (ex Article 73p), which supplies domestic judicial authorities with a relatively restricted opportunity to seek guidance from the Court of Justice with respect to disputes arising in this field. Under Article 68(1), references concerning the interpretation and validity of Title IV measures can only emanate from national courts against whose decision there is no judicial remedy under Member State law, leaving no possibility for inferior courts to make a preliminary reference. Courts of last instance, however, are only *obliged* to refer questions if they are necessary for the resolution of the dispute at hand, with Article 234 imposing such a duty with respect to other parts of the EC Treaty.

Further, the Article 68 EC reference mechanism does not extend to all Title IV measures. Under Article 68 (2), measures or decisions relating to the maintenance of law and order and the safeguarding of internal security are excluded from the purview of the Court of Justice.

It is also worth noting that the legal instruments listed in Article 249 EC (ex Article 189) will be deployed to elaborate this policy. This means that they carry the potential to be directly effective, and effect legal relations subsisting on the national plane, even in the absence of implementing legislation. Provided that it is *acte claire*,[20] that the rule in question satisfies the pre-conditions for direct effect, national judges at all levels of the Member State judicial hierarchy will be obliged to apply them over conflicting national measures, despite the absence of a reference facility.

Article 230 of the EC Treaty will apply to new Title IV. This means that the Member States, the Council, the Commission, and private parties who are directly and individually concerned by a Title IV measure, will be entitled to bring judicial review, under EC administrative and constitutional law, seeking its annulment. The European Parliament will enjoy the same, at least for the

[20] Case 283/81 *CILFIT* [1982] ECR 3415. For a commentary on the controversial *CILFIT* doctrine, see, for example, A. Arnull (1985) 34 *ICLQ* 168; H.Rasmussen, "The European Court's *Acte Claire* Strategy in *CILFIT*" (1984) 9 *ELRev* 242. See also C. Barnard and E. Sharpston, "The Changing Face of Article 177 References" (1997) 34 *CMLRev* 1113.

purpose of protecting its prerogatives, which, in the case of Title IV measures, consists of a right to consultation. An entitlement to sue for damages under Article 288 (2) EC (ex Article 215(2)) will also be operative with respect to Part IV measures, as will the Article 232 EC (ex Article 175) action for failure to act. However, the jurisdiction of the Court of Justice under Articles 230 and 288(2) will presumably be subject to the Article 68(2) exclusion of decisions concerning maintenance of law and order and the safeguarding of internal security.

In addition to this, under new Article 68(3) EC, the Commission, Council, or a Member State may request a ruling from the Court of Justice on the *interpretation* of the provisions of Title IV, and of secondary legislation enacted pursuant to it. National courts are partially insulated from the effect of this latter expansion of Court of Justice jurisdiction for Title IV measures. Domestic judgments that have become *res judicata* are not to be affected by Article 68(3) rulings of the Court of Justice.

Express provision has been made for future review, by political actors, of the authority of the Court of Justice under Title IV EC. Under Article 67(2) EC, at the end of the transitional period, the Council, after consulting the Parliament is to take a unanimous decision with a view to adapting the provisions relating to the powers of the Court.

Court of Justice review over the remnants of the third pillar: police and judicial co-operation in criminal matters (PJCC)

Nor was amendment to Article 234 EC (ex Article 177) viewed by the Amsterdam IGC as the appropriate means for extending Court of Justice jurisdiction to the third pillar. Indeed, a solution of abject and inordinate complexity was proposed, and one which will attenuate the relationship of close co-operation between national courts and the Court of Justice. Indeed both the introduction of a reference mechanism, and the manner in which it will operate, lies entirely at the discretion of individual Member States. In addition, the nature of the legal instruments to be passed by Community institutions under this pillar differ from those listed under Article 249 EC (ex Article 189), as does the scheme for challenging these measures, once passed.

Article 34(2) TEU (ex Article K.6) provides that the Council, acting unanimously or at the initiative of either a Member State or the Commission, and after consulting the European Parliament,[21] may adopt common positions, framework decisions and decisions, or establish conventions with respect to PJCC. Article 35(1) TEU (ex Article K.7) vests the Court with authority to rule on the validity and interpretation of framework decisions and decisions, the interpretation of conventions, and the validity and interpretation of measures implementing conventions. However, Article 35(5) TEU (ex Article K.7)

[21] Article 39(1) TEU (ex Article K.11).

prevents the Court of Justice from reviewing the validity or proportionality of operations carried out by police or law enforcement services of a Member State and of decisions relating to the maintenance of law and order and the safeguarding of internal security.

A further provision lays out the effect in national law of framework decisions and decisions, and effectively removes the authority of the Court of Justice to rule on this issue. Article 34 (2) TEU (ex Article K.6) expressly provides that neither framework decisions or decisions will have direct effect.

How then, is the jurisdiction which the Court of Justice enjoys with respect to PJCC measures to be activated ? Under Article 35(2) TEU Member States need to make a declaration accepting the jurisdiction of the Court of Justice to give preliminary rulings, and under Article 35(3) TEU the Member State must state whether any court may refer when a decision on a question of EU law is necessary in order to give a judgment, or whether the *discretion* to refer is confined to courts against whose jurisdiction there is no judicial remedy. This means that there is no *obligation* on any Member State to introduce a reference mechanism, and, even if they do, there will be no *obligation* to refer cast on national courts of last instance. If a Member State decides not to introduce a reference mechanism at all, it seems the jurisdiction here described will be entirely inoperative with respect to that Member State.

The Amsterdam IGC refrained from extending Article 230 EC (ex Article 173) jurisdiction to the third pillar. Rather, it inserted Article 35(6) and (7) into the PJCC pillar, which provide, respectively, for authority in the hands of the Commission and the Member States to bring an action for annulment of framework decisions and decisions, and for Member States to make recourse to the Court of Justice to settle disputes between them regarding the interpretation and application of all the instruments listed under Article 34(2) TEU, provided that the dispute cannot be resolved by the Council within six months. Article 35(7) TEU further lays out a facility for the Court of Justice to adjudicate on disputes between the Member States and the Commission regarding the interpretation and application of conventions.

Conspicuously absent from these procedures are private parties and the European Parliament, who will not be entitled to petition the Court to protect their interests. There would seem, therefore, to be no mechanism through which the European Parliament can protect its Article 39(1) TEU consultation prerogative with respect to framework decisions, decisions and conventions. It might be wondered, therefore, if the Court of Justice will extend the jurisdiction conferred on it by Article 35(6) and (7) of the Treaty on European Union, in order to allow the European Parliament to challenge these measures. This might not be completely implausible, given that the Court of Justice has, in the past, instituted initiatives of this kind in the context of the EC Treaty.[22]

[22] Case 70/88 *European Parliament* v. *Council* (Chernobyl) [1988] ECR I–2041.

In some ways, however, Article 35(6) TEU mirrors Article 230 EC. The action for annulment laid out in Article 35(6), which may be brought by the Commission or by a Member State, expressly provides for grounds of review and time limits for bringing proceedings which are the same as those which appear in Article 230.

The Schengen *acquis* and opt-ins and opt-outs by the United Kingdom, Ireland and Denmark

It was further agreed at Amsterdam that the *Schengen acquis* concerning external border controls would be brought within the framework of the Union legal system. Under these arrangements, the Council, acting unanimously, is to decide which parts of the *Schengen acquis* can be properly based on Title VI of the TEU (PJCC), and which should be passed by measures promulgated within the EC system, or more particularly new Title IV.[23] This means, therefore, that some of the *Schengen* rules will be transformed into "Union" legal principles, and will take the form of common positions, framework decisions, decisions, and conventions, which will be subject in turn to the restricted forms of judicial review described above. By contrast, the *Schengen* principles that are deemed by the Council to properly fall within Title IV EC will be transformed into the Community legal system by Regulations, Directives, Decisions, and Recommendations, and be subject to review by the Court of Justice under the conditions described above.

The situation is further complicated by opt-ins and opt-outs to the Schengen arrangements that have been agreed for the benefit of Ireland, the United Kingdom, and Denmark. The details of these arrangements appear in a series of Protocols attached to the Amsterdam Treaty, and they have been discussed in detail in several learned commentaries.[24] It is sufficient to note, for present purposes, that, like the new provisions on flexibility, the failure of all Member States to agree to the incorporation of the Schengen regime will cause substantial rupturing to the uniform application of Community law. The legal effect of these norms will range from nil, for Member States which have opted out of *Schengen* principles, to the status of fully fledged EC legislation passed pursuant to Title IV, to the status of PJCC initiatives.

[23] Article 2(1) Schengen Protocol.

[24] For example, J. de Zwaan, "Opting Out and Opting In: Problems and Practical Arrangements under the Schengen Agreement" in A. Dashwood and A. Ward (eds.), (1998) 1 *Cambridge Yearbook of European Legal Studies* 107; K.Hailbronner, "European Immigration and Asylum under the Amsterdam Treaty" (1998) 35 *CMLRev* 1047.

4. CRITIQUE OF THE COURT'S AMSTERDAM JURISDICTION IN THE LIGHT OF THE EFFECTIVE REMEDIES PRINCIPLE AND UNIFORM APPLICATION OF THE LAW

The first and most obvious casualties of the above arrangements are transparency and legal certainty. Not transparency in the sense of EC law making, the absence of which is most commonly lamented, but transparency in the context of legal remedies and procedures. While the Court of Justice will, in all likelihood, retain jurisdiction to decide whether or not individual Union and Community measures have been promulgated pursuant to the correct title of the EC or EU Treaty (as the case may be),[25] this jurisdiction will be of little assistance in determining the correct channels of redress when the law has been breached. Avenues of judicial review will differ markedly, depending on the procedure with respect to which a measure has been passed, or whether allegedly unlawful conduct on the part of a Member State or Community institution is in issue.

Challenging the legality of Title IV and PJCC measures

Both Member States and Community institutions will have an automatic entitlement to bring a suit seeking the nullity of Title IV measures under the conditions laid out in Article 230 EC. Further, private parties who can prove they are directly and individually concerned by Title IV initiatives will be allowed to do the same. Further, even if not directly and individually concerned, an action for damages will be available under Article 288(2) against Community institutions for private parties suffering loss by the grace of Title IV measures. They will also be entitled to contest the validity of Title IV initiatives through the national courts.

This will not apply, however, with respect to measures or decisions relating to the maintenance of law and order and the safeguarding of internal security. Under Article 68(2) EC, the Court of Justice is precluded from reviewing these measures. This may mean that there exists no avenue of judicial review to assess the legality of these rules. This is so because the Court of Justice has been divested of jurisdiction under Article 68(2), and the *Foto-Frost* principle[26] precludes Member State courts from declaring any Community measure invalid. In the absence, therefore, of a facility in the hands of *Member State* courts to judicially review these laws, those affected by a Title IV measure promulgated with respect to the maintenance of law and order and the safeguarding of internal security (such as, for example, restrictions of immigration from an "unfriendly" State) might argue that a reference must be accepted by the Court of Justice,

[25] Case C–170/96 *Commission and the European Parliament* v. *Council* [1998] ECR I–2763 indicates that this will be so.

[26] See note 1, above.

irrespective of Article 68(2) EC. Such a contention could be based on the fundamental right to access to an effective judicial remedy, as enunciated in the *Johnston* case.[27]

However, even when the action for validity through national courts is available with respect to Title IV measures, special problems will arise which do not occur with respect to ordinary EC instruments. Under Article 68(1) EC, the only national courts who are entitled to refer questions to Luxembourg are those against whose decision there is no judicial remedy. In contrast *any* national court may refer questions on the validity of other EC measures. With respect to visa asylum and immigration policy, it will only be after the Court of Justice has issued its ruling on validity that the result of challenge to Title IV measures will be definitively decided. This will doubtlessly entail considerable delay, and one which compares unfavourably with the traditional means for challenging the validity of EC measures.

Applicants, however, who wish to contest the legality of a third pillar PJCC rule will be confronted by even more tenacious difficulties, resulting in further fragmentation of legal remedies. First, as noted above, under Article 35(6) and (7) TEU, only Member States and the Commission are entitled to bring nullity proceedings with respect to PJCC measures. This precludes the Council, the European Parliament, and private individuals from directly contesting the legality of PJCC initiatives before the Community judicature. Further, none of the alternative avenues of direct redress before the Community judicature, available in the EC Treaty, have been extended to PJCC measures. So a private party will not, for example, be entitled to sue a Community institution for damages under Article 288(2) EC with respect to loss caused by an act passed under the PJCC procedure.

However, private parties may be in a better position in the context of validity proceedings brought before national courts, depending on the scope of jurisdiction to refer to the Court of Justice which has been conferred on the national court seised of the matter. The possibility for a relatively early resolution of a dispute will exist in Member States in which inferior courts *have* been granted jurisdiction to refer. This may prove particularly expeditious in comparison with validity proceedings brought in the context of Title IV EC measures. It will be recalled that only courts of last instance will be entitled to refer.

Yet, the validity procedures prescribed under PJCC are also beset with difficulties. First, the above is a best case scenario, in which discretion to refer has been awarded by a Member State to a broad range of courts, and not just courts against whose decisions there is no judicial remedy. It is important to bear in mind that Member States are entitled, under the Amsterdam Treaty, to wholly preclude the Court of Justice from receiving PJCC references from their national courts. When this option is taken, if the *Foto-Frost* principle were to apply to PJCC rules, then no court within such Member States will have authority to review the validity of a PJCC measure. On the one hand this may seem unlikely, given that *Foto-*

[27] See note 10, above.

Frost was enunciated in the first EC pillar, and thus far has had no function in the inter- governmental second and third pillars. On the other hand, however, the Court of Justice is expressly vested, under Article 35(1) TEU to rule on the validity of PJCC initiatives. It is yet to be decided if this jurisdiction is exclusive, or if it will be shared with the national courts of the Member States.

If the *Foto-Frost* principle were extended to PJCC instruments, these instruments will be immune from review at the behest of private parties before national courts, in a similar fashion to the (possible) immunity from judicial review of Title IV EC initiatives which are concerned with the maintenance of law and order and the safeguarding of internal security. If the *Foto-Frost* principle is not to be extended to the PJCC pillar, private parties will, at the very least, be entitled to argue that national measures implementing PJCC initiatives breach *Member State* administrative and constitutional law.

Further, it is also important to recall that, even in Member States in which a comprehensive reference mechanism has been introduced, under Article 35(5) TEU the Court of Justice is precluded from reviewing the validity or proportionality of operations carried out by police or law enforcement services of a Member State, and decisions relating to the maintenance of law and order and the safeguarding of internal security. Jurisdiction over review of these measures will therefore remain with national courts.

Additional fragmentation arises with respect to the availability of an effective, non-discriminatory remedy to correct wrongdoing caused by an unlawful PJCC measure. Within the EC legal regime, these two principles operate in favour of private parties in the context of both cases concerning the compatibility of national law with EC rules, and the validity of Community measures. As has already been mentioned, these can be called on to improve the remedy ordinarily available under national law, or precipitate disapplication of an obstructive procedural rule. There would seem to be no reason for precluding the *acquis* in this field to Title IV EC litigation. However, PJCC initiatives fall within the TEU pillar, so it is by no means certain that Court of Justice case-law concerning Member State remedies and procedural rules applies *a fortiori* to PJCC review. If a private party wishes to question the legality, therefore, of a Member State sanction or procedural rule which is operative in a claim contesting the validity of a PJCC initiative, they may have to rely exclusively on principles of national law.

Contesting the compatibility of national law with Title IV EC and PJCC measures

Access to an effective judicial remedy will be easier for private parties to obtain when they question, before the national courts, the compatibility of Member State law with a Title IV EC measure, as opposed to contesting the validity of Title IV initiatives. Advantage can be found for private parties in that national courts *are* entitled to rule on the compatibility of national law with Community measures, when the meaning of the relevant Community measure is *acte clair*. Therefore, even inferior courts will be entitled to disapply national measures that are clearly incompatible with directly effective Regulations, Decisions, and Directives passed pursuant to Title IV, even in the absence of a reference mechanism. Further, as noted above, national courts will also be bound by the EC *acquis* on the availability of effective, non-discriminatory remedies and will be able to call on these rules, if necessary, to improve the sanction available at Member-State level.

The position is somewhat different with respect to PJCC initiatives. It will be recalled that, under Article 34 TEU, framework decisions and decisions are prohibited from having direct effect. Thus, even if an applicant can prove that national law breaches a framework decision or a decision, a Member State judge will not be entitled to apply it in preference to the conflicting national measure. Article 34 therefore confines the potential for Member State judges to directly enforce PJCC measures to common positions and conventions which are sufficiently clear, unconditional and precise to be directly effective.

With respect to framework decisions and decisions, at best the judge may have recourse to the doctrine of sympathetic interpretation,[28] which the Court of Justice has formulated to assist in the implementation of EC measures. However, this doctrine, like the *Foto-Frost* principle, may not extend to judicial review under PJCC, given that the sympathetic interpretation rule forms part of the "effective enforcement" *acquis* operating under the *EC* regime. Even if the doctrine were extended to PJCC rules, it will be of no assistance if national law flatly contradicts the terms of a framework decision or a decision, given that the doctrine only applies if national law is worded in a way that lends itself to a sympathetic interpretation.[29]

In addition, the Court's case-law on Member State remedies and procedural rules is unlikely to have any application in disputes concerning Framework Decisions and PJCC Treaty Articles, given that these principles are generally only applied to EC provisions satisfying the requirements for direct effect, or in actions concerning the validity of EC measures.[30] They may have a role, however, in cases in which a private party successfully argues that a provision of PJCC common position or convention has direct effect, and national law fails

[28] Case C–106/89 *Marleasing SA* v. *La Comercial Internacionale de Alimentacion SA* [1990] ECR I–4135.

[29] Case C–168/95 *Arcaro* [1996] ECR I–4705.

[30] On the action for validity and national remedies, see *FMC*, note 11, above. See however Case C–180/95 *Nils Draehmpaehl* v. *Urania* [1997] ECR I–2195 where the effective remedies rules were applied in a case concerning enforcement of a directive by one private party against another. Direct effect did not appear to be an issue. For a discussion of subsequent developments see Dougan "The Equal Treatment Directive: Retaliation, Remedies and Direct Effect" 24 *ELRev* (1999) 664; A. Ward, "New Frontiers in Private Enforcement of EC Directives" (1998) 23 *ELRev* 65; Case C–185/97 *Coote* v. *Granda Hospitality* [1998] ECR I–5199; M. Dougan, "The Equal Treatment Directive: Retaliation, Remedies and Direct Effect" (1999) 24 *ELRev* 664.

to meet its terms. But even this will only arise if the EC *acquis* on effective, non-discriminatory remedies, is applied to PJCC judicial review.

5. FUNDAMENTAL HUMAN RIGHTS AND THE AMSTERDAM TREATY

Under Article 6(2) TEU the Court of Justice has been vested with jurisdiction to test the conduct of Community institutions against human rights and fundamental freedoms as guaranteed by the European Convention on Human Rights, and as they result from constitutional provisions that are common to the Member States. While from one perspective this is a mere codification of the Court's established case-law on fundamental rights, two observations might be made. First, no mention is made in the Treaty of Amsterdam of authority in the hands of the Court of Justice to rule on Member State compliance with fundamental rights when acting within the context of Community law, even though the Court has long exercised jurisdiction in this field. While the framers of Amsterdam could surely not have intended to divest the Court of Justice of jurisdiction to adjudicate on Member State compliance with these norms, an ungainly text has resulted from the decision to refrain from making reference to the Court's role in this field, especially when Article 6(2) TEU fortifies its fundamental rights jurisdiction so unequivocally in the context of Community institutions, and indeed, along with Article 46 TEU extends the Court's jurisdiction to third pillar activities.

Of more significance, however, is the extent to which European human rights law might be called in aid by private parties seeking to cure some of the shortcomings inherent in the scheme of judicial review provided by the Amsterdam Treaty. These are principally concerned with obtaining access to a judicial remedy in areas in which none is available, and shortening the length of proceedings in judicial review of Title IV EC and PJCC initiatives. The time taken to complete proceedings has become an issue due to the fact that, in the past, national laws implementing third pillar measures were subject only to national schemes of judicial review. The introduction of a reference mechanism, and one which restricts the range of courts entitled to make a reference to the Court of Justice, is likely to precipitate a substantial lengthening of the judicial process.

As noted above, total exclusion of judicial review may be a problem with respect to challenge to the validity of both Title IV EC measures concerning the maintenance of law and order and the safeguarding of internal security, and PJCC laws in Member States which have declined to adopt a reference mechanism. The Court of Justice may, therefore, be entitled to apply the *Johnston* principle, from its fundamental rights case-law, and accept references from national courts on the validity of these measures, even in the absence of a clause in the EU Treaty mandating it to do so. Further, it is submitted that there may be scope for private parties to challenge the inavailability of a judicial remedy under the auspices of Article 6 of the European Convention on Human Rights

(ECHR). This is so because the recent *Matthews* case[31] indicates that Member States will be responsible for breaches of the Convention arising in the context of implementation of international agreements which cannot be reviewed for compliance with human rights by the European Court of Justice.[32] Given that the (possible) exclusion of judicial review here described was introduced under the Amsterdam Treaty, and that it is by no means certain that the Court of Justice can review this Treaty for compliance with its fundamental rights case-law, activation of the Strasbourg scheme of judicial review may not be completely implausible.

Undue delay in judicial proceedings is an issue which has occupied both the European Court of Justice,[33] and the European Court of Human Rights.[34] The Court of Justice has recently reduced the amount of a fine payable in competition proceedings due to unjustified delay in the deliberations of the Court of First Instance. It would seem unlikely, however, that any general principle emerging from that case would be of assistance with respect to references received from national courts, aside from placing a moral, and perhaps legal, obligation on the Court of Justice to dispose of the reference as expeditiously as is possible. Here too, therefore, the Strasbourg mechanism may come into play. Even though the Court of Human Rights has ruled that it cannot take into account the length of time taken in an Article 234 EC reference in assessing the compliance of a Member State with obligations derived from Article 6 of the Convention,[35] the *Matthews* case might indicate that any extreme delay entailed in the Title IV and PJCC reference procedures, which is not reviewable by the Court of Justice, exposes Member States' implementation of the Amsterdam Treaty to challenge from compliance with Article 6 ECHR.

6. CONCLUSION

It has been here illustrated, therefore, that fragmentation and dislocation of the EC *acquis* on uniform and effective application of Community rules has resulted from the amendments wrought at Amsterdam. Rather than simply integrating the Justice and Home Affairs Pillar into the EC Treaty, and enfolding principles formulated within its rubric into established schemes of judicial review, an independent system has been crafted, and one which, at the very least, carries the potential to undermine some of the foundation constitutional principles formulated by the European Court of Justice.

Political differences, however, militated against the "simple" solution, and more particularly concerns voiced at the Amsterdam IGC by the United

[31] See note 9, above.

[32] See Schermers (2000), note 9, above.

[33] Case C–185/95 *P Baustahlgewebe GmbH* [1998] ECR I–8417.

[34] For example, *Pammel* v. *Germany*, Application No. 17820/91 (1997) 26 EHRR 100; *Pafitis and Others* v. *Greece*, Application No. 20323/92 (1998) 27 EHRR 566.

[35] Case C–185/95, note 34, above.

Kingdom, Swedish and Danish Governments over Court of Justice involvement in a hitherto inter-governmental area of policy making.[36] It appears that, at least for the present, the imperative of national sovereignty over domestic schemes of judicial review, will remain a key motivating force behind amendment to the Union's judicial architecture, perhaps heralding a new era in "variable geometry" in judicial remedies.

[36] See De Zwaan (1998), note 25, above.

PART IV

Access to Courts and Other Forms of Remedial Control

11

Remedies for Violation of Social Rights within the Council of Europe: The Significant Absence of a Court

TONIA NOVITZ

1. INTRODUCTION

IN 1949, the founders of the Council of Europe elaborated on the essential features of their democratic project.[1] Through inter-governmental co-operation, they would seek to prevent the reoccurrence of fascism and other totalitarian forms of government which might threaten European stability.[2] The new organisation consisted of a Committee of Foreign Ministers acting as a decision-making organ, a Consultative Assembly representing the views of national Parliaments[3] and a Secretariat providing administrative support.

The aim of the Council of Europe was to achieve a "greater unity between its members for the purposes of safeguarding and realising the ideals and principles which are their common heritage and facilitating social and economic progress".[4] At this early stage the claim was made that the projects of securing civil liberties, rights of political participation and social standards would be intertwined.

Subsequently, two complementary human rights instruments were adopted by the Council of Europe. The first was the European Convention for the Protection of Human Rights and Fundamental Freedoms 1950 (the Convention), which guarantees certain civil and political rights and has come to be

[1] States involved in this project were Belgium, Denmark, France, Ireland, Italy, Luxembourg, The Netherlands, Norway, Sweden and the United Kingdom. Greece, Turkey, Iceland and Germany subsequently became members in 1949–50.

[2] Council of Europe, *Collected Edition of the "Travaux Preparatoires" of the European Convention for the Protection of Human Rights and Fundamental Freedoms* (The Hague: Nijhoff, 1975), Vol. 1, 40 and 292. *Cf.* the 1951 Treaty creating the supra-national European Coal and Steel Community, signed by the Foreign Ministers of Belgium, France, Germany, Italy, Luxembourg and The Netherlands. See A.H. Robertson, "The European Political Community" (1952) 29 *BYBIL* 383.

[3] Renamed the Parliamentary Assembly in 1975.

[4] Statute of the Council of Europe 1949, Article 1. *Cf.* The Political Resolution of the Hague Congress of 1948, Article 5 which assigned to a United Europe the task of establishing both a "democratic social system" and a "political democracy".

regarded as "the jewel in the Council of Europe crown".[5] The second instrument, long awaited and overshadowed by its predecessor, was the European Social Charter 1961 (the Charter), which elaborates on social and economic entitlements.

It is arguable that, through this "artificial dichotomy", the Council of Europe tacitly took its position in the ideological battlefield of the Cold War. As part of a Western alliance, its members sought actively to protect those civil and political rights which symbolised respect for individual liberty and capitalist enterprise. While the Council of Europe was prepared to acknowledge social and economic entitlements, these had become associated implicitly with the perils of Communism and were not to be given undue emphasis.[6]

From the perspective of an analysis of European remedies, what is interesting is the role that supervisory machinery played in determining the respective status of the Convention and the Charter and, thereby, each category of rights. Each instrument creates a particular control mechanism, designed to promote implementation of the undertakings contained therein. The Convention establishes a procedure whereby Contracting Parties and victims may bring complaints, which could fall ultimately for determination by a European Court of Human Rights. By contrast, no complaints procedure was available initially under the Charter. The presumption appears to have been that social rights were not justiciable. Over the past decade, various reforms have been made to Charter supervisory mechanisms, but no supervisory body responsible for implementation of Charter rights merits the status of a "Court", nor are litigants relying on Charter rights given access to the existing European Court of Human Rights. Enforcement of civil and political rights can be contrasted with the mere monitoring of socio-economic rights.

The official Council of Europe view is still that "civil and political rights and socio-economic rights must not constitute two distinct groups . . . All these rights are equal and indivisible . . . Democracy cannot be based on half measures".[7] Yet this does not take account of the crucial distinction between the Convention and the Charter as regards access to remedies. Indeed, it reveals the marked disparity between rhetorical claims as to the indivisibility of rights and

[5] D.J. Harris, "A Fresh Impetus for the European Social Charter" (1992) 41 *ICLQ* 659; see also A. Drzemczewski, "The European Human Rights Convention: Time for a Radical Overhaul?" (1987) 10 *Boston College International and Comparative Law Review* 9 at 11 who describes the Convention's achievements as "quite staggering".

[6] *Cf.* K. Fuchs, "The European Social Charter: Its Role in Present-Day Europe and its Reform" in K. Drzewicki, C. Krause and A. Rosas, *Social Rights as Human Rights: A European Challenge* (Abo, Finland: Abo Akademi University Institute for Human Rights, 1994), 151; Council of Europe Parliamentary Assembly, *Additional Protocol to the European Convention on Human Rights Concerning Fundamental Social Rights*, 23 March 1999, Doc. 8357, Explanatory Memorandum by Mrs Pulgar, paras. 18–19.

[7] A statement from Polys Modinos, who was formerly the Deputy Secretary General of the Council of Europe, now publicised on the Council of Europe web site. See http://www.dhdirhr.coe.fr/Intro/eng/GENERAL/SOC.HTM. For another example see the Declaration on the Occasion of the 50th Anniversary of the Universal Declaration of Human Rights (adopted by the Committee of Ministers on 10 December 1998, at the 651*bis* meeting of the Ministers' Deputies), para. 4.

the sterner realities associated with mechanisms for their implementation and review.

This paper examines developments relating to this issue, which have taken place within the Council of Europe over the past fifty years. The first part examines the dynamics surrounding the creation of a Court under the Convention, and the exclusion of social rights from its jurisdiction. The second outlines the development of supervisory mechanisms under the Charter, assessing the potential utility of recent reforms. The third evaluates the implications of the absence of a Court from the supervisory machinery of the Charter. The final section of the paper considers the most recent proposals made by the Council of Europe Assembly regarding judicial enforcement of social rights.

2. CREATION OF A EUROPEAN COURT OF HUMAN RIGHTS AND THE EXCLUSION OF SOCIO-ECONOMIC RIGHTS FROM ITS JURISDICTION

Even before the foundational Statute of the Council of Europe was signed, it was envisaged that a Declaration of Rights would be adopted under its auspices.[8] Yet the drafting of this instrument was unlikely to prove straightforward. It was necessary to determine, first, what rights would be guaranteed and, secondly, what provision would be made for the instrument's execution and enforcement. Debates over these two controversial issues were to shape the content of the European Convention on Human Rights.

The exclusion of social rights from the text of the Convention

The sociologist T.H. Marshall, writing at the time the Convention was adopted, described as "social", rights which cover "the whole range from the right to a modicum of economic welfare and security to the right to share to the full in the social heritage and to live the life of a civilised being according to the standards prevailing in society".[9] These are rights which recognise the interests of persons in their social and economic well-being, in comparison with civil and political rights which reflect established interests in liberty and political participation. The extent to which these three categories of rights are severable is debatable. Indeed, this is evident from the Universal Declaration of Human Rights 1948 (UDHR) which proclaimed that all persons were entitled to a combination of civil, political and socio-economic rights.[10]

[8] G.L. Weil, *The European Convention on Human Rights: Background, Development and Prospects* (Leyden: Sythoff, 1963), 22–4.

[9] T.H. Marshall, *Citizenship and Social Class* (Cambridge: Cambridge University Press, 1950), 11.

[10] See, for example, Universal Declaration of Human Rights 1948, Articles 22–26 which deal with what are now regarded as typical socio-economic rights. Also see Article 28 which states that: "Everyone is entitled to a social and international order in which the rights and freedoms set out in

As the text of the Council of Europe Convention was to be based on the UDHR,[11] one might have expected that social rights would receive protection alongside their civil and political counterparts. Early records of debates indicate that arguments were made for their inclusion, in particular by Irish delegates.[12] One among their number also asked that the drafters include standards set by the International Labour Organisation (ILO),[13] thereby "marrying these three concepts of human rights".[14] However, there was considerable opposition to these proposals, predominantly from the United Kingdom (UK). The reasons given were that social rights would be "too controversial and difficult of enforcement" and, perhaps more importantly, that "their inclusion would jeopardise the acceptance of the Convention".[15]

Unanimous agreement was required if the Committee of Ministers of the Council of Europe was to be able to adopt the Convention, and therefore the co-operation of the UK was vital. If the UK warned that inclusion of social rights would "jeopardise acceptance of the Convention", this could be read as an implicit threat. The matter was off the agenda. The Assembly Committee on Legal and Administrative Questions conceded subsequently that protection of social rights must be delayed to a later date.[16]

A year after this concession was made, the issue of social rights arose again, this time in relation to proposals to include in the final draft of the Convention a right to property and a right of parents to make choices relating to the education of their children. UK representatives opposed the inclusion of such rights on the grounds that they were social, as opposed to civil or political, and accordingly too broad to be susceptible to judicial interpretation.[17] Once again, it was an Irish representative who pointed to flaws in the UK position, observing that their arguments "might equally be used to justify the exclusion from the list of human rights many of those which have been incorporated in the Convention", such as those rights set out in Articles 9–12.[18] A compromise was eventually reached in the Committee of Ministers, which agreed to the inclusion of these rights in a subsequent Protocol, rather than the main text of the Convention.[19]

this Declaration can be fully realized". *Cf.* V. Viljanen, "Abstention or Involvement? The Nature of State Obligations under Different Categories of Rights", in Drzewicki *et al.*, note 6, above, 43.

[11] See the *Travaux Preparatoires*, note 2, above, Vol. I, 194, para. 8.

[12] *Ibid*, Vol. I, *per* Mr Everett (Ireland), 102–06; M. Jacquet (France), 136.

[13] An agency of the League of Nations founded in 1919, which became an agency of the United Nations (UN) after the Second World War.

[14] *Travaux Proparatoires* note 2, above, Vol. I, Mr Norton (Ireland), 128–30.

[15] *Ibid*, Vol. I, *per* Sir David Maxwell-Fife (UK), 114–18. See also the comments of Mr Nally (UK), 146.

[16] *Ibid*, Vol. I, 194, para. 5.

[17] *Ibid*, Vol. V, *per* Sir David-Maxwell (UK), 222–4; Vol. VI, *per* Mr Roberts (UK), 88 and Mr Mitchison (UK), 94.

[18] *Ibid*, Vol. V, Mr MacEntee (Ireland), 310.

[19] *Ibid*, Vol. VII, 44. Other rights have subsequently been incorporated into the Convention, by means of Protocols 4, 6 and 7, to the extent that any one of the Contracting Parties to the 1950 Convention ratifies each Protocol.

The view that fundamental social rights are difficult to interpret and enforce might seem surprising to the comparative constitutional lawyer, given that many European constitutions contain guarantees of social and economic rights which are regarded as justiciable in national courts.[20] Experience within the European Community also indicates that, when phrased in concrete terms, social rights can give rise to individual entitlements, the subject of which may be substantive or procedural, and which can constitute the subject of a justiciable claim.[21] It may simply be that the UK, having no such tradition of justiciable constitutional socio-economic rights, perceived its legal system to be threatened by such a development.[22]

Nonetheless, the notion that social rights were not justiciable was to haunt efforts to secure protection of social rights in the Council of Europe and indeed internationally. It set an important trend in the discourse of international human rights. When, in 1966, the United Nations finally adopted the International Covenant on Civil and Political Rights (ICCPR) and the International Covenant on Economic, Social and Cultural Rights (ICESCR), provision was made for a complaints mechanism only in respect of the former, not the latter. This was a trend which subsequently spawned academic commentary seeking to explain and justify the maintenance of a distinction between civil, political and social rights, in both practical and ideological terms.[23] Subsequent developments, which indicate that this stance is not sustainable, will be addressed in the third section of this paper.

Establishment of an individual petitions procedure, a Commission and a Court

While debate continued as to the nature of the rights to be guaranteed under the Convention, attention was also directed to the mechanisms by which

[20] An EC Commission *Comparative Study on Rules Governing Working Conditions in the Member States: A Synopsis*, SEC (89) 1137 found that only three Constitutions of the then twelve Member States of the European Community made no reference to social rights. B. Bercusson, "Fundamental Social and Economic Rights in the European Community" in A. Cassese, A.Clapham and J. Weiler (eds.), *Human Rights and the European Community: Methods of Protection* (Baden-Baden: Nomos, 1991), 238–9. See also K.D. Ewing, "Social Rights and Constitutional Law" [1999] *PL* 105 at 112 and 117–19.

[21] *Cf.* M. Schleinin, "Economic and Social Rights as Legal Rights" in A. Eide, C. Krause and A. Rosas (eds.), *Economic, Social and Cultural Rights: A Textbook* (Dordrecht: Martinus Nijhoff, 1995), 57–58, who cites as his key example the impact of Article 141 (ex Article 119) of the EC Treaty. Other examples arise in the context of rights of information and consultation contained in EC Directives 75/129/EEC, OJ 1975 L 48/29 and OJ 1992 L 245/3, and 77/187/EEC (as amended), OJ 1977 L 61/27 and OJ 1998 L 201/88.

[22] *Cf.* S. Greer, "A Guide to the Human Rights Act 1998" (1999) 24 *ELRev* 3 at 3–4.

[23] Examples include M. Cranston, "Human Rights Real and Supposed" in D. Raphael (ed.), *Political Theory and the Rights of Man* (London: Bodley Head, 1967); and E.G. Vierdag, "The Legal Nature of the Rights Granted by the International Covenant on Economic, Social and Cultural Rights" (1978) 9 *Netherlands Yearbook of International Law* 103.

enforcement of these rights would be secured. Once again, significant differences arose and the requirement of ultimate unanimous agreement posed a potential stumbling block.[24] French delegates insisted that if a European human rights instrument was to be effective, a supervisory mechanism had to be developed which was comparable with that available in national legal systems.[25] "In domestic law the protection of rights depended on the existence of courts. The international position could not be different".[26]

It was readily apparent that a European Court of Human Rights could not simply be a "Court" in the same sense as that which functioned in the domestic sphere. As Churchill observed, "[s]uch a Court would have no sanctions and would depend for the enforcement of their judgment on the individual decisions of the States now banded together in the Council of Europe . . ."[27] Conferring the title of a "Court" on an organ of a regional inter-governmental organisation, dependent for its efficacy on state co-operation, may seem merely a convenient fiction. Yet this title was important in that it would imbue the new supervisory organ with the "socio-linguistic insignia" of hierarchy and status.[28]

Certain forms associated with Court proceedings were to be adopted which would contribute to what Legrand refers to as the "mythology" of legitimacy.[29] There may be no single European legal system,[30] but the aim of the drafters was to identify crucial features of Court proceedings and incorporate these into a new constitutional European legal order.[31] The features identified were: (1) a right of individual petition by one or more complainants against a defendant, (2) to be heard before competent independent judges (3) who would provide a final judgment on legal principles with reasons given and, (4) where necessary, award compensation to the victim.[32] By this means, in the sphere of civil and political rights, the Council of Europe would move away from an inter-governmental

[24] See for a very detailed analysis of the debates among members of the Assembly, Committee of Ministers, the Committee of Legal Experts and the Conference of Senior Officials, A.H. Robertson, "The European Convention for the Protection of Human Rights" (1950) 27 *BYBIL* 145.

[25] See the *Travaux Preparatoires*, note 2, above, *per* M.Teitgen, Vol. 1, 194–202 and Vol. II, 172–82; *per* M. Bidault, Vol. II, 162; *per* M. Chaumont, Vol. IV, 114 and 138.

[26] *Ibid*, *per* M. Chaumont, Vol. IV, 114.

[27] *Ibid*, Vol. I, 34.

[28] *Cf*. P. Goodrich, *Legal Discourse: Studies in Linguistics, Rhetoric and Legal Analysis* (London: Macmillan, 1987), 171; and M. Shapiro, "The European Court of Justice" in P. Craig and G. de Búrca (eds.), *The Evolution of EU Law* (Oxford: Oxford University Press, 1999), 327–8.

[29] *Cf*. P. Legrand, "European Legal Systems are Not Converging" (1995) 45 *ICLQ* 52 at 61.

[30] *Ibid*. See also P. Legrand, "Against a European Civil Code" (1997) 60 *MLR* 44.

[31] *Travaux Preparatoires*, note 2, above, *per* M. Jacquet (France), Vol. I, 136: "This Court would receive petitions, it would investigate complaints and would, thereafter, pronounce its judgment. If the State concerned failed to comply with the judgment, the Council of Europe would have to take such action as it considered appropriate".

[32] This is very much the "prototype" which Shapiro identified as generally employed by "students of Courts" involving "(1) an independent judge applying (2) pre-existing legal norms after (3) adversarial proceedings in order to achieve (4) a dichotomous decision in which one of the parties was assigned the legal right and the other found wrong". Shapiro is critical of this model, investigating the role of triad structures in conflict resolution, but recognises the cultural prominence of this more familiar standard prototype in the very first page of his text. See M. Shapiro, *Courts: A Comparative and Political Analysis* (Chicago: University of Chicago Press, 1981), chapter 1.

model towards a new type of pan-European legal system which constrained state discretion and could be seen to provide meaningful protection to the individual.

Under Article 1 of the 1950 Convention, those rights guaranteed under the Convention could be claimed by all those lawfully resident in a Contracting State. In addition to complaints by one Contracting State against another,[33] there was provision for "individual petition". Any person, non-governmental organisation or group of individuals claiming to be a victim of a violation by a Contracting State could lodge complaints, if the State concerned had made a declaration under the Convention to this effect.[34] The requirement of a declaration reflected the fact that this was a novel development, for traditionally only States constituted legitimate subjects of international law and therefore held the monopoly on an ability to make complaints before supra-national tribunals.[35] One contemporary commentator observed that this was the "the first time in history", the individual was recognised by international law as having "direct access to an international instance before which he can bring his case against a government . . .".[36]

Inter-State cases before the Court are relatively rare. It has been "the *individual* who, in protecting his own interests, plays the role of a useful stimulus and contributes indirectly to build up a body of law . . .".[37] In recognition of this, there is no longer any optional declaration. Under Protocol 11 to the Convention, which came into force on 1 November 1998, all State parties are now obliged to accept the right of individual petition.[38]

The scrutiny of complaints by a European Commission on Human Rights was perceived to be imperative so as to avoid "shoals of applications" which were pursued solely for the purpose of political propaganda.[39] The requirement of exhaustion of domestic remedies placed the focus of remedies on the national courts, who along with other state organs, must bear the principal responsibility for the protection of human rights.[40] This appeared necessary in the context of European-level supervisory jurisdiction and is similar to admissibility

[33] European Convention on Human Rights 1950 (prior to amendment by Protocol 11), Article 24.

[34] European Convention on Human Rights 1950 (prior to amendment by Protocol 11), Article 25.

[35] *Cf.* M. Janis, "Individuals as Subjects of International Law" (1984) 17 *Cornell International Law Journal* 61.

[36] A.H. Robertson, *The Council of Europe: Its Structure, Functions and Achievements* (London: Stevens & Sons, 1956), 168.

[37] J.A.C. Salcedo, "The European System of Protection of Human Rights" in F. Carpi and C.G. Orlandi (eds.), *Judicial Protection of Human Rights at the National and International Level: International Congress on Procedural Law for the Ninth Centenary of the University of Bologna September 22–24 1998*, Vol. 1, 364.

[38] European Convention on Human Rights 1950 (post amendment by Protocol 11), Article 34.

[39] See, for example, the concerns of Mr Ungoed-Thomas (UK), *Travaux Preparatoires*, note 2, above, Vol. I, 100.

[40] This is evident from European Convention on Human Rights 1950 (prior to amendment by Protocol 11), Articles 13, 26 and 60. *Cf.* A. Drzemczewski, "The European Human Rights Convention: A New Court of Human Rights in Strasbourg as of November 1, 1998" (1998) 55 *Wash & Lee L. Rev* 697, 715.

requirements under other international human rights instruments, such as the ICCPR.[41] Scrutiny of admissibility is maintained under Protocol 11, but now will be carried out by Committees and Chambers of the Court.[42] "Friendly settlement" was to minimise potential for conflict and avoid exposure of state conduct in European legal proceedings. This process of negotiation and conciliation was first undertaken by the Commission,[43] but has now passed to the Court,[44] although the extent to which the latter is able to perform the same role is questionable.[45]

Until 1998, there was not only potential for "friendly settlement" but also "political settlement" of complaints. The Commission's report could be referred either to the Court for a final and binding judgment or to the Committee of Ministers for a decision.[46] This potential for intervention by the Committee of Ministers, a political body, illustrates the initial attraction of Council of Europe members to a model that maximised opportunities for governmental control. Just how far the Convention apparatus has come from these shaky beginnings is evident from Protocol 11, which abolishes this anomalous procedure, ensuring that "a fully judicial system" prevails.[47]

In 1950, the establishment of a European judicial system was novel and therefore alarming. There was no comforting precedent, for no such Court had been created previously at a regional level.[48] The only potentially useful comparator was the International Court of Justice (ICJ).[49] Various delegates, including those from the UK, expressed their opposition to the creation of a judicial supervisory organ under the Convention.[50] Eventually, a compromise was sought and obtained, whereby Contracting Parties were not obliged to accede to the jurisdiction of the Court, but could do so by a declaration under Article 46.[51] The result was that the European Court of Human Rights only began sitting in

[41] *Cf.* First Optional Protocol to the ICCPR 1966, Article 2.

[42] European Convention on Human Rights (post amendment by Protocol 11), Articles 28, 29 and 35.

[43] European Convention on Human Rights 1950 (prior to amendment by Protocol 11), Article 28.

[44] European Convention on Human Rights (post amendment by Protocol 11), Article 38.

[45] P. Mahoney, "Speculating on the Future of the Reformed European Court of Human Rights" (1999) 20 *Human Rights Law Journal* 2; A. Drzemczewski, "A Major Overhaul of the European Human Rights Convention Control Mechanism: Protocol No. 11" (1995) VI(2) *Collected Courses of the Academy of European Law: The Protection of Human Rights in Europe* 206–07.

[46] European Convention on Human Rights 1950 (prior to amendment by Protocol 11), Article 32. *Cf.* A. Tomkins, "The Committee of Ministers: Its Roles under the European Convention on Human Rights" [1995] 1 *EHRLR* 49.

[47] Salcedo (1998), note 37, above, 383–5; Drzemczewski (1995), note 45, above, at 13.

[48] Although the creation of a European Community Court of Justice was to follow shortly thereafter. Robertson (1956), note 36, above, at 389.

[49] This is evident from the Draft Statute of the European Court which contained many provisions based on the Statute of the International Court of Justice. See Weil (1963), note 8, above, 26.

[50] *Travaux Preparatoires*, note 2, above, Vol. III, 268.

[51] The parallels with the compromise position agreed *via-à-vis* the individual petition procedure are readily observable. Indeed, many governments regarded the two issues as closely connected. Also Contracting Parties, like the UK, eventually submitted the two declarations simultaneously. For the UK, this was done in 1966. See also *Travaux Preparatoires*, note 2, above, Vol. IV, 138.

1959.[52] Yet what was once strange and threatening has since become a matter of course. As the composition of the Court has developed, its credibility has been enhanced.[53] All State parties now accept the jurisdiction of the single, permanent Court.[54]

This Court will give reasons for its judgment which is final. Such a judgment cannot "annul, repeal or modify any legislation or individual decision of a competent State" but the Court is empowered to determine whether a domestic administrative act, court decision or law is in breach of the Convention and, in giving reasons for its judgment, may specify the obligations incumbent on the State concerned.[55] The Court may also make provision for compensation to an injured party. The judgment is then transmitted to the Committee of Ministers which will supervise its execution.[56] The Committee of Ministers has no actual sanctions at its disposal to ensure the obedience of recalcitrant states, but relies on the weapon of international embarrassment and the ultimate penalty of expulsion from the Council of Europe.[57]

This court-based system is not the only means by which the Convention provides for supervision of its implementation. In addition, Article 57 confers on the Secretary-General the ability to request reports from States on the manner in which national laws implement Convention rights. This power has been exercised a number of times and provides an alternative source of documentation.[58] Yet it would seem that it is the judicial mechanism created by the Convention which has undoubtedly attracted the greater attention.

It has been claimed that the Convention created a "constitutional" or "quasi-constitutional Court".[59] Gomien, Harris and Zwaak go so far as to assert that, at the present date, in its theory and practice, the Court parallels that of the United States Supreme Court.[60] This is perhaps overly ambitious, when one

[52] V. Berger, *Case Law of the European Court of Human Rights* (Dublin: The Round Hall Press, 1989), Vols. 1, 3.

[53] This is largely due to Protocols 5, 8 and 11 to the Convention. On qualifications of the judges, see European Convention on Human Rights 1950 (prior to amendment by Protocol 11), Article 39; and European Convention on Human Rights (subsequent to amendment by Protocol 11), Articles 21 and 22. See also H.G. Schermers, "Election of Judges to the European Court of Human Rights" (1998) 23 *ELRev* 568.

[54] *Cf.* Drzemczewski (1995), note 45, above; and H.G. Schermers, "The Eleventh Protocol to the European Convention on Human Rights" (1994) 19 *ELRev* 367.

[55] Salcedo (1998), note 37, above, 374–6.

[56] European Convention on Human Rights 1950 (prior to amendment by Protocol 11), Articles 49–54 and (post amendment by Protocol 11), Articles 41–6. Note also the capacity of the Court to provide advisory opinions, previously under Protocol No. 2 and now, post amendment by Protocol 11, Articles 47–9.

[57] D. Gomien, D. Harris and L. Zwaak, *Law and Practice of the European Convention on Human Rights and the European Social Charter* (Strasbourg: Council of Europe Publishing, 1996), 90–1.

[58] F.G. Jacobs and R.C.A. White, *The European Convention on Human Rights*, 2nd edn. (Oxford: Clarendon Press, 1996), 11–13.

[59] Drzemczewski (1987), note 5, above at 14; Drzemczewski (1995), note 45, above at 715; and Mahoney (1999), note 45, above at 4.

[60] Gomien *et al.* (1996), note 57, above, 19.

compares the operation of the Strasbourg Court with two classic features of a "Constitutional Court", identified by Jacobs when examining the function of the European Court of Justice. These are, first, "judicial review of legislation to ensure its conformity with the constitution or other fundamental law; and in particular to ensure the observance of fundamental rights" and secondly, adjudication "in disputes over the respective powers of the organs of the State".[61] It is only to the extent that the Court of Human Rights provides an authoritative assessment of the extent to which national laws and practice comply with the fundamental rights set out in the Convention, that it may claim a partial resemblance to domestic constitutional courts.[62] Yet, the significance of the Convention's control machinery lies not so much in its constitutional aspect, but in that it utilises one of the key icons of legal mythology, the "Court".

The nationals of Contracting Parties became aware of the significance of the rights contained in the instrument, because of a supervisory mechanism which had a peculiar cultural resonance. They could go to a European "Court", employing many of the same procedures with which they were familiar in their national legal system and which they associated with authoritative statements of law. A European-level "judgment", binding on a State, was therefore a newsworthy event. The media delighted in the constraints which this mechanism claimed to place on national laws and authorities. Their actions, in publicising the Court's findings, secured its public profile.[63] While there has been criticism of certain aspects of its procedure and jurisprudence, the prominence of the Court in the national systems and legal culture of Council of Europe Member States cannot be denied.[64]

3. THE SUPERVISORY FRAMEWORK DEVELOPED IN RESPECT OF THE EUROPEAN SOCIAL CHARTER

In records of debates relating to the creation of a European Social Charter, it is possible to detect a tussle between certain State delegates who did not wish to cede any control over national determination of social standards, and others who clung to the idealism of earlier days, fearing that neglect of social rights

[61] F.G. Jacobs, "Is the Court of Justice of the European Communities a Constitutional Court?" in D. Curtin and D. O'Keeffe (eds.), *Constitutional Adjudication in European Community and National Law* (Dublin: Butterworths Ireland Ltd, 1992), 25. In the same collection, O. Due, "A Constitutional Court for the European Communities", at 3–10, finds it more difficult to arrive at a straightforward definition. However, he reaches the same conclusion as Jacobs, namely that the European Court of Justice within the European Union is a constitutional court, in so far as it ascertains compliance of Community law with fundamental rights and determines the balance of power between Community organs.

[62] See *Xth Conference of the European Constitutional Courts*, Budapest, 6–10 May 1996, Address by R. Ryssdal, President of the European Court of Human Rights, Cour (96) 364.

[63] M. Janis, R. Kay and A. Bradley, *European Human Rights Law* (Oxford: Oxford University Press, 1995), 70.

[64] *Ibid*, 8; Gomien *et al.* (1996), note 57, above, 19.

could defeat their common democratic project.[65] This conflict was resolved by a compromise, according to which social rights were set out in the Charter, and even elaborated upon in subsequent Protocols, but whereby no effective system of remedies was established.

Initial decisions on supervisory machinery appropriate to a European Social Charter

The substantive rights guaranteed under the 1961 Charter have their limitations. First, while Convention rights are extended to all those resident within a Contracting Party, Charter rights only apply to nationals of the State in question.[66] Also, Article 20 gave State parties substantial choice as to the Charter provisions they might choose to adopt.[67] There is no core of rights to which every party to the instrument has to adhere.[68] In addition, certain Charter provisions are phrased in very general terms, so that they seem like aspirational statements rather than concrete rights.[69] Yet, from the beginning, these restrictive elements inherent in the text of the Charter proved less controversial than one overriding question: how could Contracting States be prevailed upon to confer these rights on their citizens?

Gomien, Harris and Zwaak claim that "[a]t the outset, the rights covered by the European Social Charter were not intended to be legal rights in the sense that an individual resident of a European country could invoke them in a court of

[65] See, for example, *Report of the Ad Hoc Committee of Social Experts to the 13th Session of the Committee of Ministers*, Strasbourg, 12 September 1953, CM (53) 99; European Social Charter, *Collected Travaux Preparatoires (provisional edition)*, Vol. 1, 1953–4, Section III. *Cf.* A.G. Mower, *International Co- operation for Social Justice: Global and Regional Protection of Economic/Social Rights* (Westport: Greenwood Press, 1985), 187–93.

[66] See Appendix to the 1961 Charter. *Cf.* protection for stateless persons discussed in the Appendix to the Revised Social Charter 1996.

[67] Article 20(2) of the 1961 Charter requires that each Contracting Party consider itself bound by at least five of the "core" articles contained in the Part II of the Charter. These are Articles 1, 5, 6, 12, 13, 16 and 19. In addition, a contracting party is required to consider itself bound by such a number of articles or numbered paragraphs contained in Part II of the Charter as it may select, provided that the total number of articles or numbered paragraphs is not less than ten articles or forty-five numbered paragraphs. These must be notified to the Secretary General of the Council of Europe. *Cf.* the extension of the number of core articles under Part III, Section A of the Revised Social Charter 1996.

[68] D.J. Harris, "The European Social Charter", (1964) 13 *ICLQ* 1076, 1080–2. *Cf.* D.J. Harris, *The European Social Charter* (Charlottesville: University Press of Virginia, 1984), 293.

[69] Examples include Articles 1(1), 2(1), 12(3), 14 and 15. The jurisprudence developed by the Committee of Independent Experts relating to these Charter provisions is summarised in L. Samuel, *Fundamental Social Rights: Case Law of the European Social Charter* (Strasbourg: Council of Europe Publishing, 1997).These have been considered "progressive" or "dynamic" provisions, so that state compliance is to be assessed according to whether the State appears to be seeking actively to improve the relevant social circumstances. See Gomien *et al* (1996), note 57, above, 381. *Cf.* the characterisation of social rights as aspirational, in K.Lenaerts, "Fundamental Rights to be Included in a Community Catalogue" (1991) *ELRev* 389.

law, either domestically or internationally".[70] This is not strictly accurate, as the rights contained in the Charter were stated to be "binding" on Contracting Parties, to the extent that they had consented to particular provisions under Article 20. It is for this reason that courts in the Netherlands accepted that Article 6(4) of the Charter could be considered a "self-executing provision of international law which was binding on every one in the Netherlands", and therefore capable of enforcement in domestic courts.[71]

It is true that none of the early proposals for a Social Charter suggested that individuals should be able to invoke social rights before the Court of Human Rights or a similarly constituted organ. Instead, there were initial suggestions that enforcement of the Charter be linked to that of the Convention, by finding a role for the Commission on Human Rights in the Charter's supervisory machinery.[72] This would have been more consistent with the notion that civil, political and social rights are indivisible, but the proposal was rejected.[73]

Subsequent debate focused on an alternative suggestion, namely the potential for control by a tripartite body, containing government, employer and trade union representatives, according to a model already well-established within the ILO.[74] Despite vocal support for the involvement of a tripartite body in the supervisory process, in particular at a Tripartite Conference which immediately preceded the final adoption of the Charter,[75] the Committee of Ministers main-

[70] Gomien *et al.* (1996), note 57, above, 14.

[71] *NV Dutch Railways* v. *Transport Unions FNV, FSV and CNV* (1986) 6 *International Labour Law Reports* 3. This determination was made under Article 66 of the Netherlands Constitution of 1956 which gives provisions of international treaties "which, according to their nature, are capable of binding the citizens" precedence over national law. This is the same constitutional provision which was the subject of a reference to the European Court of Justice in Case 26/62 *Van Gend en Loos* [1963] ECR 1, but no reference was possible or considered necessary in respect of the European Social Charter. *Cf.* T. Koopmans, "Judicial Review of Legislation in the Netherlands" in D. Curtin and D. O'Keeffe (eds.), note 61, above, 275; and E. Stein, "Lawyers, Judges and the Making of a Transnational Constitution" (1981) 75 *American Journal of International Law* 1, at 3–10. See on domestic applicability of Charter provisions in Dutch and German courts, L. Betten and T. Jaspers, "Implementation of the European Social Charter: The Netherlands", and E.-M. Hohnerlein "Implementation of the European Social Charter: Federal Republic of Germany", in A.Ph.C.M. Jaspers and L. Betten (eds.), *25 Years: European Social Charter* (Deventer: Kluwer, 1988). As regards Belgium, see Committee of Independent Experts on the European Social Charter, *Conclusions XIII–4* (1996), 360.

[72] Consultative Assembly, *European Social Charter and European Economic and Social Council Draft Recommendation* (1955) Doc. 403. European Social Charter, *Collected Travaux Preparatoires (provisional edition)*, Vol. II, 1955, Section II.

[73] *Cf.* Consultative Assembly, *Economic Social Charter and European Economic and Social Conference, Draft Recommendations and Reports, presented on behalf of the Committee on Social Questions* (1956) Doc. 488, Report by M. Heyman, 22. European Social Charter, *Collected Travaux Preparatoires (provisional edition)*, Vol. III, 1956, Section IV.

[74] See ILO, *Comparison of the Provisions of the Draft European Social Charter with Corresponding ILO Standards* (Geneva, International Labour Office, 1958), vi–vii.

[75] ILO, *Record of Proceedings: Tripartite Conference Convened by the ILO at the request of the Council of Europe, Strasbourg 1–12 December 1958* (Geneva, International Labour Office, 1959), at 76 *per* Mr Eggerman (representative of the International Federation of Christian Trade Unions), at 82 *per* Mr Ventejol (workers' delegate, France), and at 84 *per* Mr Alders (workers' delegate, Netherlands).

tained its opposition. The procedure devised by the latter allowed for a legal interpretation of the text of the Charter by qualified experts, but was ultimately designed to ensure the maximum political control over the supervisory process.[76]

There was no complaints mechanism in the 1961 Charter. Instead, Contracting Parties were obliged to provide reports on the extent of their compliance with Charter obligations.[77] National trade unions and employers' organisations were to be given the opportunity to make observations on such reports. Afterwards a Committee of Independent Experts (CIE) would conduct a legal assessment of compliance with Charter provisions.[78] The CIE was appointed by the Committee of Ministers, but would be assisted by a representative from the ILO. The governmental reports, the supplementary reports and the "Conclusions" of the CIE would then be examined by a Governmental Committee, consisting of ministerial representatives. The Governmental Committee would also be attended by representatives of international organisations of employers and workers (at present the ETUC and UNICE) who could not vote but would act in a consultative capacity. The reports of the CIE and Governmental Committee would be examined by the Assembly, which would give its own opinion. The reports of all these bodies would be considered by the Committee of Ministers which had the discretion to issue recommendations to States which have violated a guarantee of the Charter, by a two-third majority vote.[79]

On average it took four years for a supervisory cycle to be completed. Trade unions and employers' organisations appeared distinctly underwhelmed by its efficacy, as was reflected in their apathy when it came to supplying observations.[80] It was also a procedure whereby government ministers possessed both control over appointment of the Experts and the ability to undermine their findings when this was politically convenient. CIE conclusions were often disregarded by the Governmental Committee, whose findings, largely based on pragmatic political considerations, were given precedence by the Committee of Ministers.[81] Moreover, Council of Europe Member States which had not ratified any part of the Charter could participate in the determination whether the Committee of Ministers would issue a recommendation. The result was that, for thirty years, no recommendation was directed to a State by the Committee of

[76] *Cf.* Fuchs (1994), note 6, above, 157.

[77] These are directed to the Secretary General. See European Social Charter 1961, Articles 21–3.

[78] *Ibid*, Articles 24 and 25.

[79] *Ibid*, Articles 26–9.

[80] *Cf.* Harris (1984), note 68, above, 264. This can be contrasted with the conduct of such organisations within the ILO, where they have showed themselves willing and able to submit observations. See ILO, *Report of the Committee of Experts on the Application of Conventions and Recommendations*, International Labour Conference, 87th Session (Geneva, International Labour Office, 1999), 43–4.

[81] See Parliamentary Assembly, *Opinion No. 137 on the application of the European Social Charter* (1988), para. 3.

Ministers.[82] In comparison with the Convention, the Charter was "little known, rarely referred to and often ignored in practice".[83] It led a "twilight existence".[84]

Recent reforms to Charter supervisory machinery

By 1989, radical political and social changes were taking place in Central and Eastern Europe, and the membership of the Council of Europe was expanding.[85] Reunification of Europe encouraged the Committee of Ministers to address the disjuncture between their stated commitment to equal protection of civil, political and social entitlements and the inferior treatment of Charter rights. A spate of additional Protocols were adopted in an attempt to "revitalise" the Charter.[86] Some were designed to supplement the existing Charter rights.[87] Others were concerned with modification of the supervisory machinery. There was to be both improvement of the existing reporting mechanism and creation of a new collective complaints procedure. However, there was to be no co-ordination with the system already developed for enforcement of the Convention.

The Turin Amending Protocol, adopted in 1991, revised various facets of the reporting procedure. This Protocol has received a significant number of ratifications, but has yet to enter into force as it requires the unanimous acceptance of all Contracting Parties to the 1961 Charter.[88] In the meantime, certain aspects of the Protocol have been introduced, following a decision to this effect by the Committee of Ministers.[89]

The length of the supervisory procedure has been addressed by removing reference to the Parliamentary Assembly as a step in the supervisory process; instead the Assembly will hold periodic debates on what it considers to be vital issues concerning enforcement of the Charter.[90] The Governmental Committee

[82] See V. Shrubsall, "The European Social Charter: Employment, Unions and Strikes", in R. Beddard and D.M. Hill (eds.), *Economic, Social and Cultural Rights: Progress and Achievements* (London: Macmillan, 1992), 154; and L. Betten, "Committee of Ministers of the Council of Europe Call for Contracting States to Account for Violations of the European Social Charter" (1994) 10 *IJCLLIR* 147.

[83] B. Hepple, "25 Years of the European Social Charter" (1989) 10 *Comparative Labor Law Journal* 460.

[84] Harris (1992) note 5, above, 659.

[85] Membership of the Council of Europe currently stands at forty-one, including Croatia (1996), Russia (1996) and the Ukraine (1995).

[86] In the informal Rome Conference of 1990, the Committee for the European Social Charter (known as "Charte-Rel") was created to investigate and suggest appropriate reforms. Many of these were adopted by the Ministerial Conference in Turin 1991. See Council of Europe, *The Social Charter of the 21st Century: Colloquy Organised by the Secretariat of the Council of Europe 14–16 May 1997* (Strasbourg: Council of Europe Publishing, 1998), *per* P.P. di Benisichi at 43–49 and *per* B. Lidal at 71; and Fuchs (1994), note 6, above, 151–2.

[87] Additional Protocol to the European Social Charter 1988 and the Revised Social Charter 1996.

[88] Protocol Amending the European Social Charter 1991, Article 8.

[89] Gomien *et al.* (1996), note 57, above, 415.

[90] Protocol Amending the European Social Charter 1991, Article 6. The first such debate in the Assembly was held on 7 October 1992.

has also revised its working methods, giving the CIE exclusive competence to make the necessary assessments of compliance with the Charter.[91] However, the Governmental Committee may still advise the Committee of Ministers on the subject of recommendations, with reference to "social, economic and other policy considerations". Finally, the Committee of Ministers has adopted new voting procedures. A two-thirds majority is still required for the making of recommendations, but States which have not ratified the Charter are not allowed to vote.[92] Since this procedure was put in place, the Committee of Ministers has issued a number of recommendations to States who have contravened Charter provisions.[93] These modifications represent an improvement in the reporting procedure; but, taken as a whole, this remains a largely political as opposed to a legal process, deferential to government interests.

This is not to say that a system of supervision involving expert interpretation and governmental consideration of State reports has no merit. A routine reporting mechanism may deliver more information than the occasional complaint and is less confrontational.[94] It removes the onus on the victim of a violation to defend their rights and is less reliant on their possession of the resources to do so. Yet a reporting procedure is most likely to be effective where it is supplemented by an alternative complaints procedure. The co-existence of supplementary mechanisms is notable in the Convention,[95] the ICCPR,[96] the ILO[97] and the European Community.

Therefore, a more significant and promising development was the Collective Complaints Protocol 1995 (CCP), which came into force in 1998.[98] This was based on a pre-existing complaints procedure which had long been in operation within the ILO, relating to freedom of association.[99] The aim of the CCP was to complement the existing reporting mechanism, increasing participation by worker, employer and non-governmental organisations. It would also be much shorter, ensuring a swift response to legitimate concerns about enforcement of the Charter.[100] However, there are numerous differences between the Charter and Convention complaints machinery.

First, only "unsatisfactory application" of the Charter is at issue under the CCP; whereas applications under the Convention are made in respect of "a

[91] *Cf.* Turin Amending Protocol 1991, Article 4.

[92] *Cf.* Turin Amending Protocol 1991, Article 5.

[93] A summary of Recommendations made is listed on the Council of Europe's web site at http://www.coe.fr/cm/indexes/rc.O.html.

[94] E. Landy, *The Effectiveness of International Supervision: Thirty Years of ILO Experience* (London: Stevens & Sons, 1966), 210.

[95] European Convention on Human Rights 1950, Article 57.

[96] ICCPR, Article 40 and First Optional Protocol.

[97] See L.Swepston, "Supervision of ILO Standards" (1997) 13 *IJCLLIR* 327.

[98] Admissibility of the first complaint under this procedure has recently been decided. See *International Commission of Jurists* v. *Portugal*, Complaint No. 1/1998, 10 March 1999.

[99] *Explanatory Report to the 1995 Additional Protocol Providing for a System of Collective Complaints*, para. 1.

[100] *Ibid*, para. 2.

violation . . . of rights".[101] The latter is implicitly a much more serious matter. The CIE decision to rename itself the "European Committee of Social Rights" does stress that Charter provisions entail "rights". While this invokes the powerful rhetoric of entitlement, the reality is that these provisions are not to be regarded as justiciable, in the same sense as Convention rights.

This becomes apparent when one investigates who is entitled to make a complaint, for there is no right of "individual petition". Articles 1 and 2 of the CCP provide only for complaints by certain trade unions, employers' organisations and non-governmental organisations (NGOs).[102] Individual complainants have no access to the process. To defend their social rights, they are required to form organisations. The instrument fails to acknowledge that adequate representation will not always be achieved. Moreover, the Explanatory Report to the CCP goes further, stating that "individual situations" will not be regarded as the legitimate subject of a complaint.[103]

The CIE will decide on admissibility, collect information on the complaint, and draw up a "report" of its conclusions.[104] This "report" does not appear to have the same force as a "judgment" delivered by the European Court of Human Rights. No financial compensation of complainants is contemplated. More importantly, the report is not binding on the contracting party who is the respondent to a complaint. It is possible that no recommendation will be issued to the State concerned.[105] Much depends on the reaction of the Committee of Ministers.

This is difficult to predict as the first collective complaint has just been decided by the European Committee of Social Rights and the report was forwarded to the Committee of Ministers on 10 September 1999. The Committee of Ministers responded to the Report only by adopting a brief Resolution in December 1999, noting its contents and stating its expectation that Portugal would report in due course. There is considerable controversy over the wording of Article 9 of the CCP and whether it requires the Committee of Ministers to make a recommendation to a Contracting Party found in the report not to be in conformity with the Charter. The use of mandatory language suggests that this is compulsory.[106] However, the requirement that the recommendation be made by a two-thirds majority suggests some room for discretion. Moreover, if the Committee of Ministers considers that the report of the European Committee

[101] European Convention on Human Rights 1950 (post amendment by Protocol 11), Article 34.

[102] *Explanatory Report to the 1995 Additional Protocol Providing for a System of Collective Complaints*, para. 18.

[103] *Ibid*, para. 31. Although this is not binding it is likely to be influential. See Council of Europe, *Social Charter of the 21st Century*, note 86, above, *per* D. Harris, 101–05. Also Parliamentary Assembly, *Opinion No. 167 (1993) on the Draft Second Additional Protocol of the Social Charter of the Council of Europe Providing for a System of Collective Complaints*, para. 4.

[104] CCP, Articles 6–8.

[105] *Cf*. Council of Europe, *Social Charter of the 21st Century*, note 86, above, *per* D. Harris, 108.

[106] CCP, Article 9 states "the Committee of Ministers shall adopt . . . a recommendation . . .". See *Explanatory Report to the 1995 Additional Protocol Providing for a System of Collective Complaints*, para. 46.

on Social Rights raises new issues, it can decide, again by a two-thirds majority, to consult the Governmental Committee.[107]

It is doubtful that the operation of a collective complaints mechanism, as envisaged in the CCP, will bestow the kiss which transforms the Charter from a frog into a prince. There is still potential for the findings of the European Committee on Social Rights to be thwarted by an unco-operative Committee of Ministers or Governmental Committee, whose agenda may be dominated by their own immediate political concerns. Its report will be made public in due course[108] but without support from the Committee of Ministers the status of its findings is likely to be diminished and is unlikely to approach that of a judgment delivered by the European Court of Human Rights. Indeed, despite its change of name, it is clear that the Committee on Social Rights is unable to claim the status of a "Court" with all the cultural connotations of legitimacy and authority which that would entail.

4. COMPLICATIONS ARISING FROM THE DIVISION OF SUPERVISORY MACHINERY AND THE INDIVISIBILITY OF RIGHTS

If there were any truth to the Council of Europe's claim that civil, political and social rights are "universal, indivisible, interdependent and interrelated",[109] complications would be bound to arise from the creation of two separate instruments, each with its own distinctive supervisory mechanisms. There would be an inevitable overlap between enforcement of Convention rights (over which the European Court of Human Rights has jurisdiction) and Charter rights (over which it does not).

An applicant cannot directly rely on Charter rights in an application to the Court, but the European Court of Human Rights has ventured into the arena of social rights in the course of interpretation of provisions contained in the Convention.[110] In *Airey*, the Court found that:

> the mere fact that an interpretation of the Convention may extend into the sphere of social and economic rights should not be a decisive factor against such an interpretation; there is no watertight division separating that sphere from the field covered by the Convention.[111]

[107] CCP, Articles 8–9.

[108] At least four months after receipt by the Committee of Ministers, *Explanatory Report to the 1995 Additional Protocol Providing for a System of Collective Complaints*, paras. 43–44.

[109] Declaration on the Occasion of the 50th Anniversary of the Universal Declaration of Human Rights, adopted by the Committee of Ministers on 10 December 1998 at the 651bis meeting of the Ministers' Deputies, para. 4.

[110] Parliamentary Assembly, *Additional Protocol to the European Convention on Human Rights concerning Fundamental Social Rights*, 23 March 1999, Doc. 8357, Explanatory Memorandum by Mrs Pulgar, paras. 48–9.

[111] *Airey* v. *Ireland* (1980) 2 EHRR 305. Cited in C. Flinterman, "Economic, Social and Cultural Rights and the European Convention on Human rights" in R. Lawson and M. de Blois (eds.), *The Dynamics of the Protection of Human Rights in Europe: Essays in Honour of Henry G. Schermers* (Dordrecht: Nijhoff, 1994), 173.

In that case, access to a "fair and public hearing" under Article 6 of the Convention was found to be dependent on the provision of free legal assistance. Protection of Article 6(1) has since been applied in the context of claims for social security benefits.[112] In this manner, despite the reality of separate guarantee of civil and political rights under the Convention and socio-economic rights under the Charter, the Court appears to have accepted the rhetoric of unity, that is, the view that these rights are in fact intricately interconnected.

In addition, the Court has become involved in determining the scope of social entitlements, when assessing the extent of legitimate exceptions to Convention rights. For example, Article 11(1) of the Convention which guarantees freedom of association is not absolute, but is subject to Article 11(2) which permits restrictions "such as are prescribed by law and are necessary in a democratic society . . . for the protection of the rights and freedoms of others". The Court has determined that Article 11 does not encompass the rights of a trade union to be consulted, to engage in collective bargaining and to take strike action (contained in core Articles 5 and 6 of the Charter). The reason given in the *Belgian Police* and *Swedish Engine Drivers* cases was that Article 20 of the Charter permitted a ratifying State not to accept as binding all the undertakings contained in the Charter, including a choice between core Articles, and that it would therefore be unreasonable to impose a Charter obligation on a State under Article 11 of the Convention.[113] Such is the artificial apportionment of rights between the Charter and the Convention. Nevertheless, the Court will still adjudicate on the scope of rights to collective bargaining and industrial action if an argument is made by a State that these constitute grounds for an exception under Article 11(2). This is illustrated by *Gustafsson* v. *Sweden*, where the Court balanced an employer's negative right not to associate under Article 11(1) against a trade union's legitimate interest in pursuing collective bargaining and taking industrial action under Article 11(2).[114]

It is ironic that in such circumstances, by acknowledging the overlap between civil, political and social entitlements, the Court has the potential to undermine the substance of Charter rights. While members of the Court might congratulate themselves on developing case-law which recognises the indivisibility of rights, this is being done in an *ad hoc* and arbitrary fashion, skewed by the emphasis the Court places on Convention as opposed to Charter rights. In this fashion, a Court steeped in a tradition devoted to primary protection of civil and political rights has given negative liberty (or freedom to disassociate) implicit priority over collective activities (bargaining through a trade union or industrial action).[115]

[112] See, for example, *Feldbrugge* v. *The Netherlands*, Judgment of 29 May 1986, A/99 and *Salesi* v. *Italy*, Judgment of 26 February 1993 A/257–E. Discussed extensively in Schleinin (1995), note 21, above.

[113] *National Union of Belgian Police* v. *Belgium* (1979) 1 EHRR 578. See also *Swedish Engine-Drivers' Union Case* (1979) 1 EHRR 617 at 628.

[114] *Gustafsson* v. *Sweden* (1996) 22 EHRR 409. See T. Novitz, "Negative Freedom of Association" (1997) 26 *ILJ* 79.

[115] *Young, James and Webster* v. *UK* (1982) 4 EHRR 38.

At present, decisions reached by the Court have greater authority than those of the European Committee of Social Rights. They are "judgments", binding on States. So should the Court decide tangentially on an issue relating to the scope of a Charter right, it is this finding that is likely to prevail, rather than the pre-existing jurisprudence developed under the Charter supervisory procedure. The Committee's sea-change on the issue of negative freedom of association, following the Court's decision in *Young, James and Webster*, is an example of this phenomenon.[116] This has the potential to make a mockery of the Charter's supervisory machinery, whatever superficial improvements are made to its operation. The question is how this structural problem is to be corrected.

5. PROPOSALS FOR COURT PROCEEDINGS IN RESPECT OF CHARTER RIGHTS

Since 1989 the Council of Europe has spent considerable time and effort considering and reconsidering the appropriate form of remedies for civil, political and social rights. Not only has the supervisory machinery under the Convention and Charter been subject to reform, but there is now to be a Commissioner for Human Rights. The Commissioner, who took office in January 2000,[117] has the potential to provide "advice and information" on protection of a broad spectrum of "human rights" embodied in all the human rights instruments of the Council of Europe. Much is dependent upon how the new appointee interprets this task, but it is possible that his work will promote recognition of the connections between these previously distinct categories of rights.[118]

There are indications that this period of change is not over and that further developments can be anticipated. The most recent proposals stem from the Assembly Committee on Social Health and Family Affairs, whose findings have led to the adoption of Assembly Recommendations on the subject of Social Charter enforcement over two consecutive years.

Recommendation No. 1354 (1998) regarding the "Future of the European Social Charter" revived a much earlier proposal made in 1978.[119] Recognising that the European Court of Human Rights "is a central authority for the

[116] Despite initial indications in the *Travaux Preparatoires*, note 2, above, Vol. IV, 262, that the drafters had decided to exclude the negative aspect of freedom of association from the ambit of Article 11, the Court reached a different conclusion in *Young, James and Webster*. Prior to this judgment, the CIE had ruled that governments could not impose compulsory trade unionism, but that it was permissible for workers themselves to negotiate a "closed shop" with their employers. See *Conclusions of the Committee of Independent Experts IV*, 47. However, the CIE changed their position after the matter had been decided by the Court. See Samuel (1997), note 69, above, 116–23.

[117] See Council of Europe Press Release 21.09.99 announcing appointment of Alvaro Gil-Robles as Human Rights Commissioner.

[118] *Committee of Ministers Resolution (99) 50 on the Council of Europe Commissioner for Human Rights*, Human Rights Information Bulletin No. 46, March–June 1999, 56. However, he will not be able to take up individual complaints under Article 1 of the resolution. *Parliamentary Assembly Request for an Opinion by the Committee of Ministers*, Doc. 8196 (1998).

[119] Parliamentary Assembly, *Recommendation No. 839* (1978). *Cf.* Harris (1984), above, note 70, 266.

protection of human rights and human dignity", the Assembly advised that either one of two options be pursued. Either a "parallel European Court of Social Rights" should be established, or individual rights should be transferred from the Charter to the Convention "in order to create the basis for stricter legal observance".[120] The CIE has given its support to this Recommendation.[121]

In Recommendation No. 1415 (1999) "Additional Protocol to the European Convention on Human Rights Concerning Fundamental Social Rights", the Assembly elaborated on its earlier proposal. It stated that, while certain Charter provisions are not an appropriate subject of Court proceedings, others are potentially justiciable and merit more effective enforcement. In doing so, it adopted a stance similar to that of the EC Commission's Committee of Experts considering the inclusion of social rights in an EU Charter of Fundamental Rights.[122] The Assembly recommended that, as a preliminary step, the Committee of Ministers should carry out a survey to examine which social rights are guaranteed by constitutions of Member States and are considered enforceable in national courts. Recognising that certain social rights are already guaranteed under the Convention, the European Court of Human Rights was to be asked for its view on what further social rights could be considered enforceable and added to present Convention provisions. The end result should be an optional Protocol to the Convention setting out certain social rights which would be justiciable before the Court.[123] The 1999 Recommendation conceded that this will not be easy to accomplish; only asserting that the attempt should be made. The mechanics of change will have to be considered carefully.

The comparative study recommended by the Assembly should establish that judicial mechanisms are appropriate for the enforcement of social rights, but other problems are likely to arise when implementation of their proposals are seriously considered. For example, the new permanent Strasbourg Court already suffers under the weight of a backlog of cases and it may be prudent to ensure that this is overcome before new litigation on social rights is allowed to add to its burden.

Also, the Court has not fared well in its interpretation of social rights to date, especially in the field of labour standards. It is doubtful whether, merely by including a specific social mandate in the Convention, a significant shift will take place in the cultural bias of the Court, given the legacy of its case-law to

[120] Parliamentary Assembly, *Recommendation No. 1354 on the Future of the European Social Charter* (1998), para. 18. See also the Report Doc. 7980, 12 January 1998.

[121] European Social Charter Committee of Independent Experts, *Conclusions XIV–1, Vol. 1* (1998), 26–7; *Conclusions XIV–2, Vol. 1* (1998), 28–9.

[122] Report of the Expert Group on Fundamental Rights, *Affirming Fundamental Rights in the European Union:Time to Act* (Brussels: European Commission on Employment, Industrial Relations and Social Affairs, 1999). *Cf.* Report by the Comite des Sages, *For a Europe of Civic and Social Rights* (1996), published in L. Betten and D. MacDevitt (eds.), *The Protection of Fundamental Social Rights in the European Union* (The Hague: Kluwer, 1996), Annex VI.

[123] See also the Report by the Assembly Social, Health and Family Affairs Committee Doc. 8357, 23 March 1999 and the Opinion presented by the Committee on Legal Affairs and Human Rights, Doc. 8433, 2 June 1999.

date. More thought may need to be given to the experience, expertise and training of appointees to the Court and possibly even their advisers in the Court's Secretariat.[124]

In addition, it will be important to ensure that the Charter is not undermined by the transfer of its core social provisions to the Convention. For this reason, development of the collective complaints procedure into a judicial mechanism could present a more profitable and immediate route to justiciable social rights, even if this delays achievement of integrated enforcement of Convention and Charter rights. If this is the option chosen, there must be the funding to support a larger judicial body and greater numbers of Secretariat staff. The rhetoric which apportions civil, political and social rights equal importance must be reflected in the distribution of budgetary resources.

Given these complications, why does the Assembly continue to push for this kind of reform? The answer takes us full circle, back to the debates surrounding the initial Convention on Human Rights. In 1950, a French delegate at the Council of Europe commented that:

> If we really wish to have collective protection in Europe of rights and fundamental freedoms, it is necessary to go beyond a simple Recommendation or the mere publication of a Report. We must refer the matter to the only force which, in these countries, has a final authority, that is justice; there must be a Court and judges.[125]

It seems that, despite the exploration of alternative sources of remedies for social rights, this sentiment survives.

The creation of the European *Court* of Human Rights under the Convention was not a coincidence. The drafters deliberately borrowed a rhetorical device which would lend status to that supervisory body. In addition, this Court was given a procedural form which had powerful connotations. Individuals and groups were given standing to bring claims to enforce their rights. A Court was required to give a final and binding judgment, containing reasons for its decisions which were legal rather than political. Compensation was envisaged for those whose rights had been violated. These procedures may be imperfect, but the familiar authority which they have the capacity to confer on the decisions reached by a supervisory organ is significant. It is by recognising this cultural context that it is possible to make sense of the Assembly's proposals for enforcement of social rights by a Court.

The Council of Europe has declared that parity of protection for civil, political and social rights is essential to their democratic project. It may be time for this rhetoric to mesh with reality. As long as supervision of the Charter turns on recommendations and reports, it will be difficult for the jurisprudence developed under this instrument to achieve the same prestige and stature as that created by the European Court of Human Rights.

124 Schermers (1994), note 54, above.
125 *Travaux Preparatoires*, note 2, above, Vol. VII, *per* M. Teitgen (France), 174.

12

Social Democracy and Judicial Review in the Community Order

PHIL SYRPIS

1. INTRODUCTION

UNDER THE social dialogue mechanism, the content of Community-level legislation is determined by the social partners, the representatives of management and labour at the European level. They have the power to make agreements which may be implemented either "in accordance with the procedures and practices specific to management and labour and the Member States" or "by a Council decision on a proposal from the Commission".[1] This chapter considers the extent to which agreements made by the social partners and implemented in either of the above ways are subject to normative controls. It considers the role of the social partners, the Commission, the Council and particularly the Courts in ensuring the legitimacy of the social dialogue, in the light of the decision of the Court of First Instance (CFI) in *UEAPME*.[2]

UEAPME involved a challenge to the legality of the Parental Leave Directive, a piece of Community legislation based on an agreement between UNICE, CEEP and the ETUC.[3] The challenge was ruled inadmissible on the ground that *UEAPME* (an employers' organisation representing the interests of small and medium-sized undertakings) was not "individually concerned" by the Directive.[4]

I consider that the decision is, in two important respects, flawed. First, the CFI adopted a typically narrow test regarding access to judicial review. Under the social dialogue, as in many other areas of Community law, the standing test should be reconsidered. Second, as will be seen below, the Court did not review the agreement between the social partners. Instead, it only reviewed the fulfilment of the obligations of the Commission and Council at the implementation stage of the social dialogue. This approach is misconceived. Under the social

[1] Article 139(2) EC.

[2] Case T–135/96 *UEAPME* v. *Council* [1998] ECR II–2335.

[3] UNICE, CEEP and the ETUC are three, general, cross-industry, European-level social partner organisations with a long history of involvement in the social dialogue. UNICE represents private sector employers, CEEP public sector employers, and the ETUC represents trade unions.

[4] Article 230(4) EC.

dialogue mechanism, social partner organisations are given the power to create European Community law. Their agreements, however implemented, must be subject to normative control.

This chapter examines the reasons for the Court's rather conservative approach. There are two competing models according to which the social dialogue mechanism can be analysed; a democratic (or constitutional law) model, and an industrial relations (or labour law) model.[5] In *UEAPME*, the Court acknowledged both traditions. However, the Court overlooked some important lessons from labour law and failed to afford sufficient weight to the constitutional role of the social partners. If it is to contribute to the development of social democracy within the Community order, the Court must rethink its approach.

2. THE SOCIAL DIALOGUE MECHANISM

The Agreement on Social Policy introduced "new institutional arrangements for the production of EU labour law",[6] with a greatly enhanced role for the representatives of the two sides of industry. These arrangements, termed the social dialogue mechanism, have now been incorporated into the main body of the Treaty.[7]

The origins of the social dialogue date back to the 1980s. The Single European Act made the promotion of dialogue between management and labour one of the official tasks of the Commission. Under the Agreement on Social Policy, whose wording reflects an agreement between UNICE, CEEP and the ETUC,[8] the obligations of the Commission were extended. After the Treaty of Amsterdam, Article 138(1) EC (formerly Article 3(1) of the Agreement on Social Policy) states that the Commission "shall have the task of promoting the consultation of management and labour at Community level and shall take any relevant measure to facilitate their dialogue by ensuring balanced support for the parties".

The legislative process under the social dialogue mechanism has three separate stages; a consultation stage, a negotiation stage and an implementation stage. At the consultation stage, there is an obligation on the Commission to consult management and labour before submitting proposals in the social

[5] See also S. Fredman, "Social Law in the European Union" in P. Craig and C. Harlow (eds.), *Lawmaking in the European Union* (The Hague/London: Kluwer, 1998) at 408–11; and B. Bercusson, "Democratic Legitimacy and European Labour Law" (1999) 28 *ILJ* 153.

[6] B. Bercusson, "The Collective Labour Law of the European Union" (1995) 1 *ELJ* at 176–8. The Agreement on Social Policy was attached to Protocol 14, annexed to the Treaty on European Union.

[7] When the EC Treaty was amended at Amsterdam in 1997, the Agreement on Social Policy was incorporated within the main body of the Treaty. In this chapter I make reference to the EC Treaty as amended and consolidated by the Treaty of Amsterdam.

[8] See B. Hepple, *European Social Dialogue – Alibi or Opportunity?* (London: Institute of Employment Rights, 1993) at 12–19.

policy field, and again on the content of any envisaged proposal.[9] At this stage, the Commission chooses which social partner organisations are to be involved. It has insisted that the organisations consulted must fulfil three criteria. They must be "cross-industry or relate to specific sectors or categories and be organized at European level", they must "consist of organizations which are themselves an integral and recognised part of Member States' social partner structures", and they must "have adequate structures to ensure their effective participation in the consultation process".[10] This set of criteria has been condemned as insufficient.[11] The focus of the criticism relates to the representativity and mandate of the European-level social partner organisations. According to the European Parliament:

> the participation of the social partner organizations at the various levels of the social dialogue must take due account of the principle of representativeness and of the independence of the associations.[12]

In similar vein, Lord Wedderburn has stated that "the social dialogue can be a 'democratization' only if the organizations concerned are 'representative' and 'speak for their members' ".[13]

The negotiation stage is distinct. After the consultation stage, management and labour may inform the Commission of their wish to initiate the process provided for in Article 139 EC. Article 139(1) EC states that the dialogue between the social partners may lead to contractual relations, including agreements. The groups involved "will be those who agree to negotiate with each other".[14] Thus, while it is the Commission which decides which organisations are to be involved at the consultation stage, it is the social partners themselves who decide who will be involved in the negotiation stage. Every time legislation has been adopted under the social dialogue, it has been only UNICE, CEEP and the ETUC which have been involved at the negotiation stage. They have exercised their autonomy in a way which has excluded the remaining organisations consulted by the Commission and has created a *de facto* monopoly in relation to the negotiation stage of the social dialogue.[15]

At the third stage, the agreements between the social partners are implemented in one of two ways. They are implemented either "in accordance with

[9] Article 138(2) and (3) EC.

[10] See COM (93) 600, para. 24, repeated in COM (98) 322 at 4–5. The most recent list of the organisations which, according to the Commission, comply with these criteria appears in COM (98) 322, Annex I.

[11] E. Franssen and A. Jacobs, "The Question of Representativity in the European Social Dialogue" (1998) 35 *CMLRev* 1295 at 1300–01.

[12] OJ 1997 C286 at 338.

[13] Lord Wedderburn, "Labour Standards, global markets and labour laws in Europe", in W. Sengenberger and D. Campbell (eds.), *International Labour Standards and Economic Interdependence* (Geneva: International Institute for Labour Studies, 1994) at 250–3.

[14] COM (93) 600, para. 31.

[15] Directive 96/34 on Parental Leave (OJ 1996 L145/4), Directive 97/81 on Part-Time Work (OJ 1998 L14/9) and Directive 99/70 on Fixed-Term Contracts (OJ 1999 L175/43) are all based on agreements between UNICE, CEEP and the ETUC.

the procedures and practices specific to management and labour and the Member States or, in matters covered by Article 137, at the joint request of the signatory parties, by a Council decision on a proposal from the Commission".[16]

The three-stage social dialogue mechanism described above operates in tandem with more traditional forms of European Community law making. If management and labour decide not to negotiate with each other, or if their negotiations fail to yield any agreement, it is open to the Commission to advance legislation under Article 137 EC, using a procedure which involves the participation of the Council, the European Parliament, the Economic and Social Committee and the Committee of the Regions.[17] The existence of an alternative legislative route which bypasses management and labour has led Bercusson to describe the social dialogue as "bargaining in the shadow of the law".[18] Indeed, there is some evidence that employer groups in particular are only willing to come to the negotiating table where the "threat" of legislation adopted under the traditional route is perceived to exist.[19]

The social dialogue mechanism described above defies easy characterisation.[20] Building on the work of Fredman and Bercusson,[21] I identify two models with reference to which the social dialogue can be analysed. Neither model fully captures the social dialogue. However, the relationship between the two models creates an analytical framework within which the social dialogue mechanism may be located. Such a framework may provide courts with the means to develop social democracy within the Community order and to assess the legitimacy of the social dialogue mechanism.

The first is a *participatory democracy* (or *constitutional law*) model. This model views the social dialogue mechanism simply as a means by which legislation is adopted. The model is plausible. It is possible to evaluate the social dialogue mechanism without stepping outside the confines of the constitutional law approach. Under this democratic model, the social dialogue mechanism is said to derive legitimacy as a result of the fact that the incorporation of the social partners into the legislative process goes "some way towards remedying the democratic deficit at EC level".[22] However, although it is no doubt uncontroversial that "the democratic principle favours the maximum involvement of

[16] Article 139(2) EC. Where I refer to agreements between the social partners, I refer to agreements implemented via one of these routes. I do not argue that the same principles should apply to agreements between the social partners which do not have their origins in Commission proposals for Community legislation.

[17] Directive 94/45 (OJ 1994 L245/64), the European Works Councils Directive, was adopted under this route after the social partners decided not to open negotiations.

[18] B. Bercusson, *European Labour Law* (London: Butterworths, 1996) at 538–52.

[19] See (1998) 299 *EIRR* at 19–21, reporting the views of Jean Lapeyre, deputy general secretary of the ETUC, and Olivier Richard, a UNICE social affairs advisor.

[20] It has been described as a "quasi neo-corporatist form of social policy law making". L. Betten, "The Democratic Deficit of Participatory Democracy in Community Social Policy" (1998) 23 *ELRev* 20 at 28.

[21] See note 5, above.

[22] Fredman (1998), note 5, above, at 409.

employers and workers in the formulation of the rules governing their relationship",[23] the social dialogue mechanism has met with criticism premised on democracy.[24] The concerns are three-fold. Concerns are raised first as a result of the exclusion of the European Parliament. The European Parliament "regards its rights as being curtailed by the procedure used".[25] It is not easy to demonstrate that the democracy forfeit as a result of the exclusion of the European Parliament can be regained through the inclusion of the social partners in the legislative process. There are also concerns, alluded to above, in relation to the criteria adopted by the Commission at the consultation stage, and to the way in which UNICE, CEEP and the ETUC have exercised the right to choose their negotiating partners.

The second model is rather more problematic. Nevertheless, if one posits an analogy with collective bargaining, it is possible to create an *industrial relations* (or *labour law*) model. Collective bargaining is essentially a voluntary, autonomous and organic process. The social dialogue mechanism as a whole does not share these characteristics. However, the negotiation stage of the social dialogue does parallel collective bargaining. This may have implications both for whether, and if so, how, access to the negotiation stage is controlled, and for the fate of agreements adopted at the negotiation stage. It is indicative of the difficulties in this area that the autonomy of the social partners – prized under an industrial relations approach – may be condemned when the social dialogue mechanism is analysed from a democratic perspective.

3. ACCESS TO JUDICIAL REVIEW

It is fundamental to the maintenance of the rule of law in society and to the legitimacy of a legal order that the arbitrary and excessive use of state power and authority is controlled. Judicial review provides a means through which those who are granted access to the relevant court are permitted to challenge the legality of the exercise of executive power. In all legal orders there are a number of rules which govern judicial review actions. In the European legal order, access to judicial review is limited. It is only interested parties who have standing to bring actions for judicial review in order to challenge the legality of the exercise of executive power. The existence of a standing test has the effect of excluding

[23] B. Bercusson, "The European Community's Charter of Fundamental Social Rights of Workers" (1990) 53 *MLR* 624 at 641.

[24] Betten (1998), note 20, above, at 30–6.

[25] OJ 1997 C371/63, para.16. The Commission's pledge to inform the European Parliament of developments under Articles 3 and 4 of the Agreement on Social Policy (COM (98) 322 at 16) is unlikely to allay these concerns. Betten argues that the growth of the social dialogue process is a factor which "confirms, once again the consistent marginalisation of the European Parliament which fails to obtain the tools it needs to achieve its *raison d'etre*: to represent the peoples of Europe"; L. Betten, "The Amsterdam Treaty: Some General Comments on the New Social Dimension" (1997) 13 *IJCLLIR* 188 at 192.

many applicants from the judicial review process and of limiting their ability to keep the executive in check.

Under the EC Treaty, Member States, the Council and the Commission, so-called privileged applicants, are granted access to the Court of Justice without needing to demonstrate any particular interest.[26] The European Parliament, the Court of Auditors and the European Central Bank have semi-privileged status. They have standing, but only for the purpose of protecting their prerogatives.[27] Beyond these groups, putative applicants including, it seems, social partner organisations, must demonstrate an interest in the act which they wish to challenge. Article 230(4) EC (ex Article 173(4)) states that natural or legal persons only have standing to challenge decisions which are of "direct and individual concern" to them. The individual concern limb of the test has proved to be the most difficult for applicants. In *UEAPME*, the Court of First Instance, repeating the well-worn *Plaumann* formula, stated that natural or legal persons can claim to be individually concerned by a measure "only if it affects them by reason of certain attributes peculiar to them or by reason of circumstances which differentiate them from all other persons".[28]

Two rather different types of interest may lead to a finding of individual concern. The first is an interest in the *outcome* of the legislative process; the second, an interest in *participation* in the legislative process. It is well known that neither the Court of Justice nor the Court of First Instance have tended to be responsive to claims based on the outcome of the legislative process, that is to claims based on being affected by the contested act.[29] Subject to certain limited exceptions,[30] it is only where the applicant can demonstrate membership of a closed class of affected persons, whose number and identity is fixed and ascertainable,[31] that it will be possible to demonstrate individual concern within the meaning of the *Plaumann* formula on the basis of an interest in the outcome of the legislative process. This line of case-law is much criticised, in particular in the environmental field.[32]

Claims based on participation in the legislative process are more likely to be successful. Where individuals have the *right* to participate in the European

[26] Article 230(2) EC.

[27] Article 230(3) EC. The TEU brought the Treaty position into line with the position of the Court in Case C–70/88 *European Parliament* v. *Council* (Chernobyl) [1990] ECR I–2041.

[28] *UEAPME* [1998] note 2, above, para. 69. See Case 25/62 *Plaumann* v. *Commission* [1963] ECR 95.

[29] See Cases T–585/93 and C–321/95P *Stichting Greenpeace* v. *Commission* [1995] ECR II–2205 and [1998] ECR I–1651.

[30] The approach in Case C–309/89 *Codorniu* v. *Council* [1994] ECR I–1853, in which the challenge was ruled admissible on the ground that the contested regulation infringed the applicant's trade mark rights, has not been adopted in later cases. The reasoning in Case C–358/89 *Extramet Industrie* v. *Council* [1991] ECR I–2501 is also broad, but may be confined to anti-dumping.

[31] Cases 106 and 107/63 *Alfred Toepfer* v. *Commission* [1965] ECR 405, Case 11/82 *Piraiki-Patraiki* v. *Commission* [1985] ECR 207.

[32] See L. Kramer, "Public Interest Litigation in Environmental Matters before the ECJ" (1996) 8 *Journal of Environmental Law* 1; S. Schikhof, "Direct and Individual Concern in Environmental Cases: The Barriers to Prospective Litigants" (1998) 7 *EELR* 276.

legislative process, they may be granted standing, even though they are not regarded as directly and individually concerned by the outcome of the measure. The Court of Justice held in *COFAZ* that:

> where a regulation accords undertakings procedural guarantees entitling them to request the Commission to find an infringement of Community rules, those undertakings should be able to institute proceedings in order to protect their legitimate interests.[33]

This again is a strict test. Standing is conditional on the existence of participation *rights*. In the Community order, judicial review operates so as to cement existing rights to participate, but does not make the connection between the *fact* of participation and standing.

In *UEAPME*, the Commission and Council contested the applicant organisation's right to invoke the jurisdiction of the Court. The arguments of the applicant in relation to individual concern were based on the premiss that it possessed "special rights in the context of the procedural mechanisms established by the Agreement (on Social Policy) for the adoption of measures falling within its purview, and that these rights have been set at naught".[34] Thus, in order to establish whether or not *UEAPME*'s action would be admissible, the Court examined the extent of *UEAPME*'s rights under the Agreement on Social Policy (now Articles 138 and 139 EC).

4. THE DECISION IN *UEAPME*

UEAPME brought an action against the Council to annul Directive 96/34/EC of 3 June 1996 on the framework agreement on parental leave concluded by UNICE, CEEP and the ETUC.[35] *UEAPME* was consulted by the Commission but was not involved in the negotiation stage. It was only UNICE, CEEP and the ETUC who together informed the Commission that they wished to negotiate a framework agreement at the Community level. They reached an agreement which was implemented by Directive 96/34, adopted by the Council on a proposal from the Commission. *UEAPME* challenged the legality of the Directive.

Putting the autonomy of the social partners to the fore, the CFI held that no social partner organisation had the right to be involved in the *negotiation* stage.[36] However, contrary to what one might have expected, the absence of such a right to participate was not fatal to *UEAPME*'s claim.[37] The CFI held that the participation of Commission and Council at the *implementation* stage had the effect of "endowing an agreement concluded between management and

[33] Case 169/84 *COFAZ* v. *Commission* [1986] ECR 391, para. 23.
[34] *UEAPME* [1998] note 2, above, para. 70.
[35] Directive 96/34 is at OJ 1996 L145/4.
[36] *UEAPME* [1998] note 2, above, para. 78.
[37] *Ibid*, para. 83.

labour with a Community foundation of a legislative character".[38] Accordingly, it held that the Commission and Council were under certain obligations, and that these were subject to judicial review by the Court. Among these obligations, was the obligation to verify that the signatories to an agreement were truly representative. This obligation, "derived from a fundamental democratic principle",[39] was regarded as particularly significant. The Court held that:

> the principle of democracy on which the Union is founded requires – in the absence of the participation of the European Parliament in the legislative process – that the participation of the people be otherwise assured.[40]

Therefore, the Court of First Instance held that where an agreement between the social partners lacks "sufficient collective representativity", those representatives of management and labour consulted by the Commission, whose particular representation, in relation to the content of an agreement, is necessary to raise the collective representativity of the signatories to the required level, are to be regarded as individually concerned.[41] The Court concluded that the signatories, UNICE, CEEP and the ETUC, possessed sufficient collective representativity in relation to the content of the Parental Leave Directive, and that therefore *UEAPME*'s challenge was inadmissible.[42] The Court's analysis of collective representativity in effect confirmed the legality of the monopoly which UNICE, CEEP and the ETUC have carved out for themselves at the negotiation stage of the social dialogue; at least in relation to cross-industry agreements.[43]

5. REFLECTIONS ON THE INDIVIDUAL CONCERN TEST IN THE LIGHT OF *UEAPME*

The "sufficient collective representativity" criterion developed by the Court in *UEAPME* represents an attempt by the Court draw on both the constitutional and the labour traditions of the social dialogue. As such, it is welcome. However, I would argue that while the representativity of signatories should play a role in any assessment of the legality of an agreement, it should not be the decisive factor in relation to access to judicial review.

The Court must be given some credit for avoiding some of the pitfalls into which it may have been drawn. First, *UEAPME* could have been held to be individually concerned on the basis of the fact that it *had the right to be consulted* under Article 3 of the Agreement on Social Policy (now Article 138 EC). If the Court had adopted this approach, a closed class of applicants whose number and identity was fixed and ascertainable,[44] could have been afforded access to

[38] *UEAPME* [1998] note 2, above, para. 88.
[39] *Ibid*, para. 110.
[40] *Ibid*, para. 89.
[41] *Ibid*, para. 90.
[42] *Ibid*, para. 111.
[43] In relation to more limited agreements, see Bercusson (1999) note 5, above at 165–8.
[44] See note 31, above.

judicial review. This approach is superficially attractive. Nevertheless, the Court was right to reject it. First, the Court was correct to emphasise the distinction between the consultation and the negotiation stage of the social dialogue and to recognise that the representatives of management and labour should be given some autonomy at the negotiation stage. Second, if standing were to be conditional on having the right to be consulted by the Commission, the importance of the criteria employed by the Commission in relation to the consultation stage,[45] would be exaggerated. Only if the Commission succeeds in developing a more sophisticated set of criteria should the Court be prepared to endow them with any greater significance. Third, it should be noted that organisations such as the Economic and Social Committee and the Committee of the Regions have the right to be consulted in a number of areas, and yet do not have standing before the Court.[46] A mere right to be consulted in the decision-making process tends not to be a sufficient basis for the creation of a right of access to judicial review.

Second, the Court might plausibly have held that *UEAPME had the right to participate in the negotiation stage* of the social dialogue mechanism. Such an approach would run counter to the industrial relations tradition of the social dialogue. Neither the Commission nor the Council should be in a position to insist that particular social partner organisations participate in the negotiation stage of the social dialogue. It is perhaps worth adding that it is only if a right to participate in the negotiation stage of the social dialogue mechanism were held to exist, that it would be worth pursuing a parallel with the "semi-privileged" status which has been afforded to the European Parliament. This status allows the European Parliament to bring judicial review actions in order to protect its prerogatives.[47] Unless an organisation such as *UEAPME* were afforded a right to participate at the negotiation stage, its prerogatives would not be infringed by a decision of other social partner organisations to proceed to the negotiation stage without it.

The test adopted by the Court represents a compromise between the constitutional and the labour law traditions. While the Court did not go so far as to hold that *UEAPME* had the right to participate in the social dialogue, it did insist that the Commission and the Council were under an obligation to ensure that the signatories to any agreement possessed "sufficient collective representativity". There are two difficulties with this approach. First, as discussed below, the Court should have reviewed the representativity of the agreement itself, not merely the Commission and Council's obligations in relation to collective representativity of the agreement.

[45] COM (93) 600, para. 24. See note 10, above.

[46] G. de Búrca, "The Institutional Development of the EU: A Constitutional Analysis" in P. Craig and G. de Búrca (eds), *The Evolution of EU Law* (Oxford: Oxford University Press, 1999) at 60.

[47] This point appears to have been overlooked by A. Jacobs and A. Ojeda-Aviles, "The European Social Dialogue – Some Legal Issues" in ETUI, *A Legal Framework for European Industrial Relations* (Brussels: ETUI, 1999) at 72.

Second, the Court's analysis of collective representativity is far too simplistic. All assessments of the representativity of parties to collective bargaining are fraught with difficulty, and "national experience should have taught the Court that this is a minefield".[48] The grounds on which the Court held that UNICE, CEEP and the ETUC possessed "sufficient collective representativity" can be criticised. The CFI, somewhat unrealistically, held that UNICE could sufficiently represent the interests of small and medium-sized undertakings, as it counted among its members associations of small and medium-sized undertakings, many of which were also affiliated to *UEAPME*.[49] The CFI stated that:

> by contrast to the applicant's situation, it is clear that if CEEP had not been one of the signatories to the framework agreement, this alone would have fundamentally affected the sufficiency of the collectively representational character of those signatories in view of the contents of that agreement, because then one particular category of undertakings, that of the public sector, would have been wholly without representation.[50]

Many factors which would seem to go to the collective representativity of the agreement were not considered by the Court. The fact that UNICE, CEEP and the ETUC "do not represent a majority of employers and workers",[51] was ignored, as were the internal structures of the social partner organisations. Peter Cane has noted that:

> an association cannot properly represent the views and interests of others unless there is an effective mechanism for ascertaining what those views and interests are and for ensuring that the views put forward by the association are a fair reflection of the views represented.[52]

As has been demonstrated elsewhere, such mechanisms are, at best, uneven as regards UNICE and the ETUC.[53]

Nevertheless, I contend that the "sufficient collective representativity" criterion, amended to take account of these difficulties, should play a part in the assessment of the legality of agreements reached via the social dialogue mechanism. However, it should not be used at the standing stage. As regards access to judicial review, an altogether more radical approach would be preferable.

UEAPME should have been granted the right to challenge the Parental Leave Directive on the ground that it was *excluded from participation in the negotiation stage*. *Les Verts* provides an albeit isolated precedent for such an approach.[54] In *Les Verts*, the Green Party was allowed to challenge the reim-

[48] Jacobs and Ojeda-Aviles (1999) note 47, above, at 73. See also Bercusson (1999) note 5, above, at 158–9.

[49] *UEAPME* [1998] note 2, above, paras. 98, 99.

[50] *Ibid*, para. 100. Thus, *UEAPME*'s position would have been stronger if its membership, and that of UNICE, had been separate.

[51] Betten (1998), note 20, above, at 32.

[52] P. Cane, "Standing, Representation, and the Environment" in I. Loveland (ed.), *A Special Relationship? American Influences on Public Law in the UK* (Oxford: Clarendon Press, 1999) at 136.

[53] See the discussion in Bercusson (1999) note 5, above, at 161.

[54] Case 294/83 *Parti ecologiste "Les Verts"* v. *Parliament* [1986] ECR 1339.

bursement rules for the 1984 European elections on the grounds that they discriminated in favour of political groupings already represented in the European Parliament. The ECJ stated that "it cannot be considered that only groupings which were represented and which were therefore identifiable at the date of the adoption of the contested measure are individually concerned by it".[55] It was imperative that *non-participants* should be entitled to challenge the rules established by the European Parliament.

In *Les Verts*, as in *UEAPME*, the democratic credentials of the Community were at stake. However, while, exceptionally, in *Les Verts*, the Court was prepared to grant access to judicial review to those excluded from the decision-making process, the Court was not prepared to make the same leap in *UEAPME*. It is only if those excluded from the legislative process are granted access to judicial review, that the Court can provide "a surrogate political process to ensure the fair representation of a wide range of affected interests in the process of administrative decision",[56] and that it can contribute to the development of social democracy within the Community order.

6. SHOULD THE ACTS OF THE SOCIAL PARTNERS BE SUBJECT TO JUDICIAL SCRUTINY?

In *UEAPME*, the CFI placed great emphasis on the obligations of the Commission and Council at the implementation stage. Paragraph 90 merits careful consideration. The Court stated that the representatives of management and labour whose particular representation is necessary in order to raise the collective representativity of the signatories to an agreement to the required level, have the right "to prevent the Commission and the Council from implementing the agreement at Community level by means of a legislative instrument".[57] Thus, such applicants have the right to prevent an agreement being implemented by the Council, but they do not have the more fundamental right to contest the legality of the agreement itself.

In a Communication of 1993, the Commission stated that its task at the implementation stage is to consider:

> the representative status of the contracting parties, their mandate, the "legality" of each clause in the collective agreement in relation to Community law, and the provisions regarding small and medium-sized undertakings.[58]

[55] *Ibid*, para. 35. Compare the Opinion of AG Mancini who stated (at para.9) that the application should have been held to be inadmissible as the applicants were not in a position to demonstrate that they were individually concerned.

[56] R. Stewart, "The Reformation of American Administrative Law" (1975) 88 *Harvard Law Review* (1975) 1667 at 1670.

[57] *UEAPME* [1998] note 2, above, at para. 90.

[58] COM (93) 600, para. 39. The Commission Communication, "of course, does not constitute any legal authority for the Commission to assume the powers it asserts"; Bercusson (1999) note 2, above, at 162.

The Court quoted this passage with approval in *UEAPME*. It added that the Council was required to verify whether the Commission had fulfilled the above obligation. If the Council did not do so, it would run the risk of "ratifying a procedural irregularity capable of vitiating the measure ultimately adopted by it" [59]

Thus, in *UEAPME*, the Court avoided the difficult issue of judicial review of the acts of the social partners by focusing its attention on the acts of the Commission and the Council. In failing to review the acts of the social partners, who are responsible for the content of their agreements, the Court overlooked the constitutional role of the social partners within the social dialogue mechanism. While the Commission and Council have extensive obligations at the implementation stage, they accept that they do not have the power to alter the substance of the social partner agreement.[60] Thus, the ultimate responsibility for the content of the agreement, if not for its subsequent implementation, always rests with the social partners. The seeming reluctance of the Court to subject the agreements of the social partners to judicial scrutiny may reflect its unease with the social partners' relatively new legislative role. Any such unease must now be overcome.

Grainne de Búrca has stated that:

> the Constitutional legitimacy of the Union remains substantially contested, and its fragility is inevitably exacerbated if the growth and diversification of the EU's institutional manifestations are not accompanied by adequate normative controls.[61]

Although Article 230(1) EC seems to preclude the judicial review of acts of the social partners,[62] there is a precedent for the extension of the scope of judicial review. Again, the precedent is *Les Verts*. In *Les Verts*, the Court established, contrary to the wording of Article 173 as it then was, that the acts of the European Parliament were judicially reviewable. The Court stated that the Community was "based on the rule of law",[63] and argued that the review of measures adopted by the European Parliament was necessary on the grounds that the European Parliament "could encroach on the powers . . . of the other institutions".[64] It is possible to draw an analogy with the social dialogue mechanism. At the negotiation stage, the social partners encroach on the powers of the Community institutions. When the social partners decide to initiate the process provided for in Article 139 EC, the Commission must suspend its activities, and must give the social partners up to nine months in which to negotiate an agreement.[65]

[59] *UEAPME* [1998] at paras. 86, 87.

[60] COM (96) 448 at 13; and COM (93) 600 at para. 38.

[61] De Búrca (1999) note 46, above, at 56.

[62] Article 230(1) EC states that the "Court of Justice shall review the legality of acts adopted jointly by the European Parliament and the Council, of acts of the Council, of the Commission and of the ECB [European Central Bank], other than recommendations and opinions, and of acts of the European Parliament intended to produce legal effects vis-à-vis third parties".

[63] *Les Verts* [1986] note 54, above, at para. 23.

[64] *Ibid*, para. 25.

[65] Article 138(4) EC. See also COM (96) 448, Annex I at v.

These concerns are magnified in relation to agreements implemented not by Council decision, but "in accordance with the procedures and practices specific to management and labour and the Member States". Where, as in *UEAPME*, agreements are implemented by Council decision, there will be an act of the Community institutions to which a judicial review action can attach. In relation to agreements implemented via the alternative labour law route, the Commission and Council have no obligations, and so, presumably, if the resulting agreement is to be subject to any form of normative control, it must be the acts of the social partners which will be subject to review.

However, in *UEAPME*, the Court appeared to hint that agreements implemented under the labour law route could not be subject to judicial review at the Community level. The CFI held that the participation of the Commission and Council at the implementation stage had the effect of endowing the agreement between the social partners "with a Community foundation of a legislative character".[66] The necessary inference must be that if a social partner agreement were implemented by the alternative route, the agreement would lack legislative character.

If the Court were to rule that judicial review actions could not attach to agreements implemented via the labour law route, it would create an important, and to my mind, insupportable distinction between the more traditional constitutional law, and more innovative labour law, implementation routes. Every time the Commission proposes legislation in the social policy field, it must consult management and labour. Management and labour can then decide to embark on the negotiation stage. The dialogue between them can lead to agreements. Such agreements will then be implemented via the labour law route unless the signatory parties request that their agreement is implemented by Council decision. Thus, Commission proposals can be transformed into social partner agreements implemented in accordance with the procedures and practices specific to management and labour and the Member States, without the Commission or Council having any further say. Social partner agreements implemented in this way encroach on the powers of the Community institutions, and should be subject to judicial control.

7. CONCLUSION

In this chapter I have argued for a bold approach to judicial review. I have argued that the Court should hear applications from parties who have been excluded from the legislative process, and that it should review not only the acts of the Commission and the Council, but also the agreements of the social partners.[67] Carol Harlow has highlighted the dangers associated with the growth of judicial review. She cautions that over-extensive judicial review, such as that

[66] *UEAPME* [1998] note 2, above, at para.88.
[67] See note 16, above.

encountered in the US, may lead to sterile proceduralism and to the unwelcome politicisation of the Court. She is convinced that "law cannot fill the void created by the absence of democratic politics".[68]

Nevertheless, there is a need for action. The social dialogue mechanism has failed to create "a real political Community with a rich and plural political discourse".[69] If the legitimacy of this particular manifestation of the Community order is to be enhanced, improvements need to be achieved. All the actors have a role to play. The Commission must formulate more satisfactory criteria at the consultation stage.[70] The social partners themselves also have a responsibility. They must be more inclusive at the negotiation stage.[71]

The focus of this chapter has, however, been on the role of the Court. The European Court of Justice has an activist tradition. The challenge before it is to provide a public law underpinning to the social dialogue mechanism. In order to do so, it must review the agreements of the social partners. As regards their content, the Court should apply the same standards as it does to other forms of Community legislation.[72] However, the Court must also be prepared to scrutinise the identity of the signatories to social partner agreements.

This will involve forging a new relationship with the representatives of management and labour. The Court should treat them seriously as institutional actors, recognising the extent of their powers and the extent of their responsibilities. Social partner agreements, however implemented, should be subject to judicial review. The review should be based on broad notions of democracy, which can apply to both the constitutional and the labour law contexts. *UEAPME* may come to be seen as the Court's first faltering steps towards a review of the social dialogue which contributes to the growth of social democracy in the Community order.

[68] C. Harlow, "European Administrative Law and the Global Challenge" in P. Craig and G. de Búrca (eds.), *The Evolution of EU Law* (Oxford: Oxford University Press, 1999) 261 at 281; C. Harlow, "A Special Relationship? American Influences on Judicial Review in England" in I. Loveland (ed.), *A Special Relationship? American Influences on Public Law in the UK* (Oxford: Clarendon Press, 1995) at 79; and C. Harlow and R. Rawlings, *Pressure through Law* (London: Routledge, 1992).

[69] Harlow (1999), note 67, above, at 281.

[70] The signs are encouraging. The Commission has stated that it is to launch a major study on the representativeness of the cross-industry and sectoral social partner organisations. See COM (98) 322 at 4.

[71] Again, the signs are encouraging. A co-operation agreement was concluded between UNICE and *UEAPME* in December 1998 (see (1999) 300 *EIRR* at 3), which has had the result that *UEAPME* has abandoned both its appeal to the ECJ in the Parental Leave Directive case (Case C–316/98 was removed from the register on 2 February 1999), and a further challenge which it had made to the Part-Time Work Directive (Case T–55/98was removed from the register on 14 January 1999).

[72] Under Article 230 EC (ex Article 173) the grounds for judicial review are "lack of competence, infringement of an essential procedural requirement, infringement of this Treaty or of any rule of law relating to its application, or misuse of powers".

13

Engaged Elites. Citizen Action and Institutional Attitudes in Commission Enforcement

RICHARD RAWLINGS[1]

1. INTRODUCTION: THREE FACES OF INFRINGEMENT PROCEEDINGS

> for never before would he have issued so cordial an invitation:
> and from that moment, invisibly, began the decline of his prestige.
> From *The Leopard* by Lampedusa

Article 226 of the EC Treaty, formerly the famous Article 169, is a great survivor. The scale and complexity of the process of regional integration notwithstanding, the wording is the original set down in the Treaty of Rome. The clue lies in the skeletal quality of the formal legal language and in particular the strong element of discretionary powers afforded the Commission. The provision presents to this effect a dual character. It remains a central legal tool in the pivotal role assigned to the Commission as "the Guardian of the Treaties".[2] And it has served to mask the interplay of different modalities of law enforcement, which bear in turn on the issue of the proper role for official action or public advocacy in the Community legal system.

A central theme of this article is the involvement in the public law machinery of private actors. Most obviously because of limited investigative powers and resources, the Commission has relied on the efforts of complainants in effect to sustain its position in law enforcement.[3] Which in turn has engendered a further dynamic, in the form of pressure from complainants to discipline Commission

[1] This chapter is a revised version of a paper presented at the EU/International Law Forum in Bristol, May 1999 and was published recently in the *European Law Journal* (Vol. 6, No. 1, March 2000). It was written prior to the discussions on institutional reform at the European Council in Helsinki (December 1999).

[2] Article 226 being the general legal procedure by which the Commission can take action to "ensure that the provisions of this Treaty and the measures taken by the institutions pursuant thereto are applied" (Article 211).

[3] Most cases stem from complaints made by "individuals" (957 of 1218 cases in 1997). Other sources are questions in, and petitions to the Parliament, as well as suspected infringements detected by the Commission. See for details, Commission, *Fifteenth Annual Monitoring Report*, COM (1998) 317 final, 8–11.

decision-making. Biting the hand that feeds it is a facet of this form of private policing.

And a good thing too! Much has rightly been made in recent years of the need for greater transparency in the Union, involving more rational forms of decision-making, and in the expanded sense of greater accessibility and permeability of decision-making networks. The general powers of Commission enforcement have typically been something of a "no-go" area in this respect. Yet the more that complainants have engaged with it, the less convincing Commission claims to an "objective" procedure[4] operating in the public interest have become. A re-balancing is in order, one that preserves regulatory choice by the Commission, but also provides for greater procedural recognition of complainants, and, further, for the structuring and confining of otherwise strong discretion, better to secure the public legitimacy of the process. Expressed slightly differently, a form of regulatory proceeding that more accurately reflects the demands for more responsive and participatory forms of decision-making, which are associated with ideas of a Community "public sphere" and active citizenship.

European integration is familiarly characterised as "an affair of the elites". A development that increasingly has an air of vulnerability, as people come to perceive themselves as being directly affected by European decisions.[5] Commission enforcement is seen in this chapter as a paradigm case. To explicate, the infraction process has been the classic example in Community law of so-called "non-contradictory procedure"; the Commission not being required to exchange views and arguments with the party that has actually drawn its attention to the possible infringement. The fact that this itself has increasingly become a target of complaint fits with the broad trajectory of constitutional and legal development in the Union. Reference need only be made to the elaboration of more advanced codes of procedural protection in certain sectors,[6] and, at a more fundamental level, to the rise of citizenship as a political and social as well as market construct. A more populist age in which the "People" are demanding "Voice" appears to be upon us.[7]

Of course care must be taken to retain effective control of decisions, so reflecting a proper sense of administrative and professional responsibility. Complainants are naturally self-selecting, and the concern to vindicate the rule of (Community) law will typically be a product of private interest or prejudice. It is irksome for an elite to have to listen, conceptualise and explain. But such is

[4] Commission, *Thirteenth Annual Monitoring Report*, COM (96) 600 final, 8.

[5] D. Obradovic, "Policy Legitimacy and the European Union" (1996) *JCMS* 191.

[6] As for example in public procurement and state aids policy (below, text accompanying note 133). See further B. Vesterdorf, "Complaints Concerning Infringements of Competition Law within the Context of European Community Law" (1994) 31 *CMLRev* 77; and C. Kerse, "The Complainant in Competition Cases: A Progress Report" (1997) 34 *CMLRev* 213.

[7] Y. Meny, "The People, the Elites and the Populist Challenge" (Jean Monnet Chair Paper No. 47) (Florence: EUI, 1998). And see C. Harlow, "Citizen Access to Political Power in the European Union" (RSC Paper No. 99/2) (Florence: EUI, 1999).

the common currency of administrative law enforcement in conditions of democracy and pluralism, strong or otherwise. Unimpressive are the generalised and unsubstantiated pleas of cost and efficiency that Commission officials have customarily made in this context.[8] Part of the argument is that the Commission has not been sufficiently exposed to the disciplines of New Public Management;[9] and, in particular, to the downward pull of a more service-oriented administrative culture. Commission representatives have also engaged in an "Aunt Sally" form of argumentation: the setting up of a model of full party rights for the individual, only to shoot it down together with other forms of procedural protection.[10] *Per contra*, the matter is appropriately analysed in terms of a series or ladder of obligations that might be imposed on the Commission.[11] So for example confirmation that the Commission has discretion not to pursue court proceedings does not deny the obligation properly to examine the matters of fact and law set out in a complaint.

The role and interplay of different institutional attitudes is another major theme of the chapter. In this respect the Office of the European Ombudsman calls for special attention. It has been the chief conduit for the expression of citizens' grievances concerning the operation of Article 226 procedure; in turn, the investigation reports supply cogent evidence of stress points in the modalities of Commission enforcement. A classic role for ombudsmen is to function as a "window on the administration", by which is meant the role of opening up to public scrutiny and debate internal administrative policies and practices. This is all the more significant in the case of the infringement procedure, precisely because of the old dictates of a closed bipolar process.[12] The European Ombudsman is also a means of side-stepping a failure by the Court of Justice effectively to police the Article 226 process; an aspect that points up the broader potential of the development in European administrative law of machinery for alternative dispute resolution. The Ombudsman has however started slowly, with the task of stimulating improvement in Commission working practices being treated less as a sprint than a marathon. A legalistic approach has been adopted, so limiting the creativity of the Office. Investigations of Commission enforcement, it is argued, demonstrate that the potential of the Office has not been properly realised.

A third theme concerns a proper place for the principle of complementarity in the Community legal system. Let us remember that Article 169 was originally

[8] See, for example, C. Timmermans, "Judicial Protection Against the Member States: Articles 169 and 177 Revisited" in D. Curtin and T. Heukels (eds.), *Institutional Dynamics of European Integration* (Dordrecht: Martinus Nijhoff, 1994), 399.

[9] This is not to overlook the heavy reliance on outsourcing, which as recent events demonstrate has been all too undisciplined. See Committee of Independent Experts, *First Report on Allegations of Fraud, Mismanagement, and Nepotism* (15 March 1999); Second Report on Reform of the Commission (September 1999).

[10] As in the *Newbury Bypass* case, see note 69, below.

[11] See in this fashion I. Maselis, I. and H. Gilliams, "Rights of Complainants in Community Law" (1997) 22 *ELRev* 103.

[12] As associated with the elite model of regulatory bargaining, discussed below.

envisaged as the standard means of law enforcement. Introduced by the Court of Justice, individual legal action via national courts and reference procedure has ascended in a way simply unimagined when the Treaty of Rome was drafted. Attention is rightly drawn in this context to the problems of Commission law enforcement that this kind of private policing solves or ameliorates: central overload and lack of regulatory knowledge or information, remedies and the conflicting institutional and policy interests of the multi-functional agency that is the Commission.[13] But the analysis so easily becomes one-sided, thus glossing over the limitations of the private model of enforcement. These are many and various. Blockages of law, where there are no private rights correlative with the duties of national authorities, are demonstrated in cases of failure to transpose directives. Technical constraints are imposed by doctrines such as standing to sue. Meanwhile the standard international law characterisation of all private litigants as "individuals" serves only to obscure the many disparities in terms of legal understanding, resources and empowerment. In this article it will be shown that infringement proceedings, far from withering away in the face of private legal action, are in the course of reinvigoration. The better targeting of Commission resources on the gaps in the coverage left by the private model is however a part of the challenge.[14] Public advocacy should to this effect remain of vital importance in underwriting the implementation of Community law.

The final theme concerns the dynamic character of this regulatory process. It is a regime viewed in this article as an increasingly fluid mix of competing administrative models and procedural constructs. As indicated, the old sense of proceedings as a secretive affair between Commission and Member State is today rightly challenged. Pressures for change further reflect a greater concern in the Union with problems of implementation, involving calls for a firmer and more effective means of centralised enforcement.[15] In fact the current position, far from representing either a "steady state" or deliberative process of reform, demonstrates a diverse pattern of incremental change. An example of the smooth path of legal and administrative "evolution" in the Community, it is not.

Triangular relations

Let us develop the argument. While much has been written on the subject of Commission enforcement, insufficient attention has been paid to basic conflict

[13] See, for example, P. Craig, "Once upon a Time in the West: Direct Effect and the Federalization of EEC Law" (1992) 12 *OJLS* 453.

[14] Insistence on the principle of complementarity as between public and private forms of legal action is obviously one element in a larger project. Commission enforcement also requires adaptations in light of common trends towards de-centralised and network models of European regulation.

[15] "Implementation" and "enforcement" are notoriously slippery terms. In this article implementation represents the process whereby Community legal obligations are fulfilled, and enforcement the techniques available to ensure that implementation takes place.

over the institutional purposes and design and to the different properties of the process as expressed at various stages of European integration.[16] This chapter introduces a trilateral framework of analysis, which is expressive both of competing administrative aims and functions and of different forms of evaluation.

Behind the formal legal mask the enforcement process is thus seen in ideal-typical fashion to present three faces. The first face represents the classic or older idea of an "international procedure"; or, drawing on the literature of administrative law, an elite model of regulatory bargaining. Which means an informal, discretionary, co-operative and closed process. The model reflects the origins of the Community as a reworked form of intergovernmental relations, and as such the convoluted wording of the Treaty Article underwrites it.

Complaint procedure constitutes the second aspect, that is Article 226 as machinery for redress of grievance against Member States by a range of actors, in particular in situations where the private model of legal protection is seen to be defective. Typically there is a major problem of "fit" associated with the wording of the Treaty provision, and the Commission has in the past vigorously opposed this view of enforcement proceedings. Yet, as indicated, the model has come to be vigorously asserted, and with some success, on the back of demands for more advanced rights of citizenship in the Union. A different set of evaluative criteria is thus imported; elements like accessibility and due process, timeliness and remedy, at the expense of official concerns of flexibility and co-operation.

The third face is technocratic in character. It encompasses a sharper, more streamlined approach to centralised enforcement, with particular reference to accelerated investigation procedures and the design of a tariff system. The idea of formalisation and routinisation, first to foster the uniform application of Community law, and, second, to ensure equality of treatment between Member States, is not a new theme in Commission law enforcement. Yet it has gained greater impetus in recent years, being explicitly linked to further demands for market liberalisation associated with the introduction of a single currency, as also the immediate prospect of enlargement. Again, the process now incorporates an element of quasi-criminal jurisdiction, by way of judicial competence to impose penalties for continued non-compliance by Member States.[17] The pressure for formalisation, and, further, the attraction of Commission enforcement for private actors, is in this way magnified.

Reconciliation of some of the competing demands of the different models is clearly possible. But other tensions are more intractable, such that accentuating the features or moulding proceedings in the image of one face serves to disfigure another. A clear example is the conflict between a closed bargaining model of dispute resolution and an open and participatory form of complaint procedure.

[16] But see F.Snyder, "The Effectiveness of European Community Law: Institutions, Processes, Tools and Techniques" (1993) 56 *MLR* 19.

[17] Article 228 (formerly Article 171 as amended by the Treaty on European Union).

There is, to coin a phrase, a "regulatory trilemma" at the heart of Commission law enforcement.

The discussion could not be more topical. Reform is in the air, even perhaps a Treaty amendment. The trilateral framework used in this chapter is also metaphor for much of the contemporary constitutional and legal contest in the Union. How the balance is struck between the competing demands of political (international) co-operation, citizen participation and effective law enforcement is clearly fundamental to the development of European administrative law in particular and the Community legal system in general.

2. FIRST FACE: INTERNATIONAL PROCEDURE AND ELITE REGULATORY BARGAINING

Discretion and the decision-making chain

According to the case-law, the enforcement procedure involves a power on the part of the Commission to consider the most appropriate means and time limits for the purposes of putting an end to an infringement.[18] To this end the classic model of international procedure envisages a dialogue and mutual accommodation with the Member State.[19] The aim is not protection of the individual but to obtain compliance. Complaints are merely a "source of information for detecting problems".[20] This aspect of enforcement proceedings is appropriately analysed in terms of a series of familiar concepts in administrative justice.

Thus the "decision-making chain" is elongated, and so generates many opportunities and incentives for negotiation and settlement.[21] Take the pre-pre-litigation procedure that the Commission has created: an administrative graft onto the formal legal framework.[22] Nothing better illustrates the twin themes of informality and confidentiality, the aim being in the case of a valid complaint to achieve some form of quiet accommodation with the Member State. Then there is the formal "administrative phase", inaugurated by the "Article 226 letter" or formal request to the Member State to submit observa-

[18] Case 7/71 *Commission* v. *France* [1971] ECR 1003.

[19] Early confirmation of the scope for different emphases was provided by a move under the Commission Presidency of Roy Jenkins to instituting more infringement actions. See C.-D. Ehlermann, "Die Verfolgung von Vertragsverletzungen der Mitgliedstaaten durch die Kommission" in *Festschrift für Hans Kutscher* (Baden-Baden: Nomos, 1981); and on the ensuing cases, U. Everling, "The Member States of the European Community before their Court of Justice" (1984) 9 *ELRev* 215.

[20] Timmermans (1994), note 8, above.

[21] The different stages are well known and so are briefly summarised here. The classic account is H. Audretsch, *Supervision in European Community Law*, 2nd edn. (Amsterdam: Elsevier, 1986). See also now, A. Mattera, "La procedure en manquement et la protection des droits des citoyens et des operateurs leses (1995/3) *Revue du Marche Unique* 123; A. Ibanez, *The Administrative Supervision and Enforcement of EC Law* (Oxford: Hart Publishing, 1999).

[22] That is investigation of a possible breach, involving discussions with the Member State in an attempt to ascertain the facts.

tions. The scope for protracted negotiation is demonstrated, the Commission having adopted the norm of a year in which to decide whether or not to close a file.[23] The next stage, the concretising of the dispute via the obligation on the Commission to give a reasoned opinion, is also identified as hybrid in character. Recording the infringement and defining the issues serves not only to prepare the way for court action but also to establish the parameters of a possible final settlement. It is long-established practice for the Commission to bargain proactively at this stage by means of suggestions of what action would be appropriate to end an infringement.[24] Last but not least, the classic design of maximising the opportunities for voluntary compliance is demonstrated at the "judicial phase" of referral to the Court. The "enormous discretionary power to do nothing"[25] is to this effect famously underwritten by the Treaty.

A related concept is that of the "complaint pyramid", representing in empirical terms the diminution in the caseload over the different stages of the process. Typically this pyramid has been seen to be broad at the base, with substantial portions of settlement and compromise in the conditions of informality and confidentiality, such that only a tiny proportion of cases has gone before the Court.[26] There is also support for the twin elements of filtering out the trivial and passing serious matters upwards, which in terms of institutional design constitute the rationale of the pyramid. Whereas many internal market cases have settled early, disputes in such sensitive sectors as customs union and taxation and fisheries have typically proved more intractable.[27]

Infringement proceedings on the classic model are a brilliant illustration of regulation operating "in the shadow of the law".[28] Court proceedings are thus seen as a sanction of last resort against which compliance is sought through negotiation, bargaining and threats. Attention correctly focuses on the "hidden jurisprudence" of the Commission and not merely on the (judicial) "tip of the iceberg". So too the Commission has consistently emphasised the need to preserve the co-operative model of decision-making that is typified by regulatory bargaining; and with it the close and fluid workings of its closed relationships with the Member States as "the Guardian of the Treaties." Mutual trust or confidence is a notion that has been repeatedly invoked.

[23] See for details Secretariat General, *Improvement of the Commission's Working Methods in relation to Infringement Proceedings*, SEC (1998) 1733.

[24] See, for example, Case C–247/89 *Commission* v. *Portugal* [1991] ECR I–3659.

[25] K.C. Davis, *Discretionary Justice. A Preliminary Inquiry* (Baton Rouge: Louisiana State University Press, 1969).

[26] As demonstrated by the following "snapshot" figures for 1993: 1040 complaints, 1209 letters of formal notice, 352 reasoned opinions, 44 court referrals: Commission, *Eleventh Annual Monitoring Report 1993* COM (94) 500 final. See further, Snyder (1993), note 16, above.

[27] Similarly "tough nuts" in the form of misapplication cases are disproportionately represented at the later stages of the enforcement process. See for discussion, M. Mendrinou, "Non-compliance and the European Commission's Role in Integration" (1996) 3 *JEPP* 1.

[28] C. Veljanovski, "The Regulation Game" in C. Veljanovski (ed.), *Regulators and the Market* (London: Institute of Economic Affairs, 1991).

It is not surprising to learn that the Commission has clung tenaciously to the elite model of regulatory bargaining. Considerations of institutional self-interest inevitably play a significant role in the operation of the procedure;[29] for which the closed, informal model is such a useful vehicle. Viewed in a positive light, the Commission can seek via "test-casing" to establish basic principles and "play for rules",[30] that is itself to structure the framework for bargaining. The potential for integrating enforcement action with the Commission's other activities, most obviously its agenda-setting role, is highlighted. Then there is the space left for political considerations, the hallmark of "international procedure" and so a recurrent theme especially in the older accounts of the process.[31] At best the Commission has been able to steer clear of certain highly sensitive areas, as shown by its policy of non-enforcement in respect of the activities of the national court systems.[32] At worst it is seen in individual cases effectively to have surrendered in the face of the political intransigence of, or organised defiance in, a Member State.[33]

Selective enforcement is a basic element of a good enforcement policy and the Commission is no exception. Reference need only be made to the "black hole" that is non-compliance in the Union,[34] that is the systemic but elusive quality of the phenomenon, as also the limited resources available, even supposing that the Commission was run properly. The criticism is the familiar one of a failure to specify clear and appropriate criteria structuring and confining the selective exercise of enforcement powers. To anticipate an argument, only recently has the Commission begun to articulate a policy in this field.[35] A typical consequence in individual cases is the complaint that the Commission has somehow been "got at" by the Member State,[36] a popular manifestation of the theory of

[29] See Mendrinou (1996), note 27, above. This is not to suggest that the Commission is a monolith; see further below.

[30] Snyder (1993), note 16, above; and see generally, T. Christiansen, "A Maturing Bureaucracy? The role of the Commission in the policy process" in J. Richardson (ed.), *European Union: Power and Policymaking* (London: Routledge, 1996).

[31] A. Evans, "The Enforcement Procedure of Article 169 EEC: Commission Discretion" (1979) 6 *European Law Review* 442; Everling (1984) note 19 above; A. Dashwood and R. White, "Enforcement Actions Under Articles 169 and 170 EEC" (1989) 14 *ELRev* 388.

[32] This policy, justified by reference to the constitutional traditions of judicial independence in the Member States, has recently been the subject of an unsuccessful complaint to the European Ombudsman. See Decision on complaint 176/97/JMA; *Annual Report 1998*, 97.

[33] The episodic violence by French farmers protesting at imports springs readily to mind. See now Case C–265/95 *Commission* v. *France* [1997] ECR I–6959; and for discussion, T. Hartley, *Constitutional Problems of the European Union* (London: Hart Publishing,1999), chapter 6.

[34] See generally P. Haas, "Compliance with EU directives: insights from international relations and comparative politics" (1998) 5 *JEPP* 17. And see for useful legal accounts, P. Van den Bossche, "In Search of Remedies for Non-Compliance: The Experience of the European Community" (1996) 3 *Maastricht Journal of Comparative Law*, 371; C. Harding, "Member State Enforcement of European Community Measures: The Chimera of 'Effective' Enforcement" (1997) 4 *Maastricht Journal of Comparative Law* 5.

[35] See text accompanying note 106, below. See further on the internal priorities of the Commission in different periods, Ibanez (1999), note 21, above.

[36] A recurrent theme in the complaints to the European Ombudsman: see below. See also R. Mastroianni, "The Enforcement Procedure Under Article 169 of the EC Treaty and the Powers of the European Commission: Quis Custodiet Custodes?" (1995) 1 *EPL* 535.

"agency capture". Again, attention naturally focuses on some prime output of the strong discretionary model: the differential rates of compliance among Member States, or that which is tendentiously described in terms of "the usual suspects" or "north-south gradient".[37] Whither the uniform application that is stated *ad nauseam* as a basic principle of Community law?

The problem however is more fundamental. The classic model of international procedure lacks credibility in light of the trajectory of European integration. It is increasingly challenged in terms of the other faces of the enforcement process, that is, both by complainants or third parties and via technocratic concerns of efficiency and effectiveness. In fact one reason why the model has dominated for so long is the support given by the Court of Justice. On the one hand, enough has been said to identify the familiar concern of administrative law with procedural safeguards and accountability. On the other hand, the judges have operated to bolster, even legitimise the model of elite regulatory bargaining. The point has a general significance in European administrative law where the slant of the argument has typically been on control by the courts.[38] Let us look more closely.

Judicial sustenance

Reference to the dual model of international procedure and regulatory bargaining casts fresh light on the approach of the ECJ in this sphere. On the one hand, procedural protection for the Member States has been developed, to the extent that it "over-protects [them] under the administrative phase".[39] In fact the Court, in imposing strict legal requirements for enforcement action as a means of discipline, has also increased the incentives for the Commission to engage in regulatory bargaining as a way of achieving compliance. Complainants on the other hand, that is third parties potentially disruptive of the closed, bipolar relationship, have been poorly treated. The judges have in this respect proceeded by means of self-denying ordinance.

Important is collateral review, in its broad sense in administrative law of defensive legal action. Member States have thus been able to plead procedural impropriety under the rubric of inadmissibility.[40] To give the flavour, the Court has imposed on the Commission substantial information requirements; duties

[37] Hartley (1999), note 33, above.

[38] Epitomised in the Germanic tradition by J. Schwarze, *European Administrative Law* (London: Sweet & Maxwell, 1992).

[39] A. Ibanez, *A Deeper Insight into Article 169* (Harvard: Jean Monnet Working Paper 11/98) (1998), 43.

[40] Good illustrations are Case 211/81 *Commission* v. *Denmark* [1982] ECR 4547; Case 325/82 *Commission* v. *Germany* [1984] ECR 777; and Case C–296/92 *Commission* v. *Italy* [1994] ECR I–1. The jurisprudence is well known and so is only briefly summarised here. See for details T. Hartley, *The Foundations of European Community Law* (Oxford: Clarendon Press, 1998) 4th edn., chapter 10.

to give reasons; a bar on introducing new elements; and waiting periods before Member States have to achieve compliance. Typically, this is a product not only of the language of the Treaty but also of judicial creativity via the "general principles" of Community law.[41]

Complainants seeking to contest the closure of a file have run up against two key procedural obstacles. The individual is not a party to the proceedings, either in the administrative stage or before the Court, and so the first "roadblock" is standing to sue.[42] Second but related, the reasoned opinion is not a reviewable act since it is not legally binding.[43] Speaking more generally, the Court has consistently emphasised the breadth of the discretionary power afforded the Commission: it " alone is . . . competent to decide whether it is appropriate to bring proceedings".[44] The basic separation between a pluralist system of private legal action via national courts and Article 234 (formerly 177) reference procedure, and the monopoly of public advocacy through Article 226 proceedings,[45] is underscored in the case-law.

For the complainant the net effect is to render Article 226 process a judicial "no-go" area. Many practical illustrations could be given but one will suffice. *World Wildlife Fund*[46] is one of the best-known cases in European administrative law. Typically however it is analysed in terms of the line of cases dealing with the emergent general obligations on Community institutions of transparency and access to documents.[47] Fresh light is shed if the case is approached in terms of the administrative process that prompted the dispute: Article 226 infringement proceedings. The case is in fact a litmus test of judicial attitudes in the area. It represents an apologia for the model of regulatory bargaining.

The case is part of the saga of Mullaghmore, one of a series of legal challenges by conservation groups associated with the decision of the Irish authorities to build a tourist facility in the Burren National Park using European structural funds for the purpose. Following the failure of an annulment action in respect of the Commission's refusal to take legal proceedings,[48] the groups sought to

[41] See especially H. Nehl, *Principles of Administrative Procedure in European Community Law* (Oxford: Hart Publishing, 1999); also K. Lenaerts and J. van Hamme, "Procedural Rights of Private Parties in the Community Administrative Process" (1997) 34 *CMLRev* 531.

[42] See, for example, Case 247/87 *Star Fruit Co.* v. *Commission* [1989] ECR 291, para 13.

[43] Case 48/65 *Lütticke* v. *Commission* [1966] ECR 19.

[44] Case C–431/92 *Commission* v. *Germany* [1995] ECR I–2189 at para. 22. Also Case C–87/89 *Sonito* v. *Commission* [1990] ECR I–1981, para. 6: "It is clear from the scheme of Article [226] . . . that the Commission has no obligation to commence proceedings; it has a discretionary power precluding the right of individuals to require it to adopt a particular position and to bring an action for annulment against its refusal to take action".

[45] Typically the Commission has sought to blur the distinction to its own advantage by intervening as a "repeat-player" in Article 234 proceedings.

[46] Case T–105/95 *WWF (UK)* v. *Commission* [1997] ECR II–313.

[47] M. De Leeuw (1997) 3 *EPL* 339; P. Neill, "The Duty to Give Reasons: The Openness of Decision-Making" in C. Forsyth and I. Hare, *The Golden Metwand and the Crooked Cord* (Oxford: Clarendon Press, 1998); M. O'Neill, "The Right of Access to Community-Held Documentation as a General Principle of EC Law" (1998) 4 *EPL* 403.

[48] Case T–461/93 and Case C–325/94 P *An Taisce and WWF (UK)* v. *Commission* [1994] ECR II–733 (CFI) [1996] ECR I–3727.

penetrate the infringement decision-making process. Requests were made for access to all documents relating to the investigation of the project including, in particular, the use of structural funds. Naturally the Commission refused, falling back on two exceptions in the Code on public access to documents.[49] The first was the discretionary bar of general or "horizontal" application, which protects the institution's interest in the confidentiality of its proceedings. The second was the mandatory bar directly targeted on the infraction process, applying, under the rubric of protection of public interest, to cases where disclosure could undermine court proceedings and investigations. In fact, the regulatory bargaining model was specifically invoked by the Commission to justify secrecy. Not only did co-operation with Member States permit "negotiation between the parties with a view to reaching a settlement", it was also the possibility of "precisely such frank and open dialogue" that had "enabled a compromise" in the present case. Again, both France and the United Kingdom made much of "the vital need to foster a climate of mutual confidence", it being "clearly in the interest of the Community" that pre-litigation discussions could be conducted "in conditions of absolute confidentiality".[50] These arguments proved successful, on the basis that "the confidentiality which the Member States are entitled to expect of the Commission" warranted protection, even where a period of time has elapsed since the closure of the investigation.

All this has tended to be overshadowed by the annulment of the decision for failure to give adequate reasons. In fact, while the Court would not accept a whole "class" (of documents) claim to public interest immunity, its approach to the testing of "contents" claims was muted. Explanation could suffice of why categories of documents related to the possible opening of an infringement procedure, their subject-matter, and whether they involved investigations. It would be "impossible" to give reasons justifying confidentiality for individual documents without "depriving the exception of its very purpose". It suffices to observe that so minimal are these requirements that they would not tax any official worth her salt.

Speaking more generally, the case crystallises the legal position of a closed, bipolar process. Notably the Commission in its argument claimed to distinguish the investigation of infringements, a "particular type of quasi-judicial procedure", from "internal procedures or deliberations of an executive nature". We note the irony. "Quasi-judicial" procedure commonly involves the kind of transparency requirements that was in this case strictly denied.

[49] Code of Conduct Concerning Public Access to Council and Commission Documents, Council Decision 93/731 OJ 1993 L34; Commission Decision 94/90, OJ 1994 L46.

[50] Sweden intervened on the other side, neatly illustrating the divergent national traditions in law and administration in this area.

3. SECOND FACE: CITIZENS' EUROPE AND REDRESS OF GRIEVANCE

The unknown citizen

Complainants of course have no right to require the Commission to adopt a specific position. There is nonetheless a good instrumental reason for improving their position in the infraction process. Precisely because the Commission is largely dependent on private individuals and firms to detect infringements, the legitimacy of the process in the eyes of citizens is vital. The problem of delay, since it is an inevitable by-product of the model of regulatory bargaining, is a pertinent example. There is pressure to streamline procedures both for reasons of efficiency and effectiveness and to help ensure that potential complainants do not lose interest.[51] But further the idea of complainants as some kind of information fodder, to be deployed as and when the Commission chooses, runs counter to the emergent concept of a European citizenship. As indicated, conflict has resulted as the Commission has faced demands for enhanced procedural recognition of complainants. A Commission lament further suggests a basic confusion:

> the Commission is perceived as capable of solving every individual situation – a kind of Community Supercourt, as it were, whereas in fact the object of the Article 169 procedure is to induce a Member State to come back into line with Community law . . . There is thus a gap between what the Commission can do and what the citizen expects of it.[52]

In fact the Commission's monitoring reports on the application of Community law betray a lack of proper complaint analysis. Take the view that "the success of the . . . procedure . . . demonstrates the public's growing awareness of the Community's importance". "Success" is nowhere explained for this purpose, let alone the linkage between a thousand or so complaints and broad perceptions.[53] Again, it may be true that "the Community's citizens are ever keener to see their rights properly respected", but how is this demonstrated by an increase in complaints back towards previous levels?[54] Guff of this kind should not be lightly dismissed as amusing propaganda. It represents a failure by the Commission to take the role and status of the citizen seriously.

Not of course that the Commission is a monolith. Take the fact that many of the Article 226 complaints concern environmental issues. Clearly one explanation is adverse conditions for private enforcement: the familiar problem of organising and winning legal recognition for diffuse interests. But we cannot overlook the role of personal factors, as demonstrated by the proactive work of

[51] See Commission, *Fourteenth Annual Monitoring Report* (1997) COM (97) 299 final, 11.

[52] *Ibid*, 12.

[53] Commission, *Eleventh Annual Monitoring Report*, note 26, above, 6. In fact the number of complaints fell in the relevant year!

[54] Commission, *Fifteenth Annual Monitoring Report 1997*, note 3, above, 11.

some Commission lawyers in encouraging and facilitating environmental complaints.[55] Attention is further drawn to the potential of lobbying for legal action by interest groups, an important dimension of "pressure through law"[56] that works to soften the distinction between public and private legal initiative. A point that is highlighted in this context by the large scale funding for Brussels-based environmental NGOs provided by the Commission.[57]

Closer inspection also reveals a measure of internal dispute concerning recognition of the citizen in the machinery of public advocacy. Notably the Legal Service has been at the heart of the opposition. Formal legal considerations have clearly had a role to play in this respect: at one level, the skeletal Treaty procedure to which the individual concerned is not a party; and, at another, the potential liability of the Commission in Article 288 proceedings if formal procedural protections were established.[58] Enough has been said however to indicate a wider issue: an internal legal culture that has insufficient regard, at least from an Anglo-American perspective, for the due process norms of contemporary administrative law systems.

Encouraging noises have come from the Secretariat General, to the effect of aiding a learning process in the Commission. Important in this respect is a staff paper produced in late 1998 on working methods in infringement cases.[59] The complainant's role, it conceded, had been "underestimated"; it was "vital that they be kept informed and have the situation explained to them at each stage of the procedure". Whereas two years earlier reform had taken place that had virtually nothing to say on the status of complainants, their expectations were now accepted as a justification for extending procedural recognition. Perhaps this is a pointer to the future. All the more striking then that the practical development will be seen to have remained partial and fragmented.

Some pressure for change has come from the Parliament, the obvious body to press the claims of the individual in this regard being the Committee on Petitions. Yet this Committee, here as elsewhere in European administrative law, has made only a muted contribution.[60] A product in part it appears of a lack of professional resources and expertise in complaint handling to underpin the work.[61] As indicated, the medium through which the competing vision of infraction process as complaint machinery has been most clearly asserted is the European Ombudsman.

[55] Most notably Ludwig Kramer, as Head of Legal Affairs in the Environment Directorate.

[56] C. Harlow and R. Rawlings, *Pressure through Law* (London: Routledge, 1992).

[57] See for discussion, J. Greenwood, *Representing Interests in the European Union* (London: Macmillan, 1997), chapter 8.

[58] Case 9/69 *Sayag* v. *Leduc* [1969]ECR 329.

[59] Secretariat General, *Improvement of the Commission's Working Methods*, note 23, above.

[60] See generally E. Marias, "The Right to Petition the European Parliament after Maastricht" (1994) 19 *ELRev* 169. This is not to overlook the work of the Committee on Legal Affairs and Citizen's Rights, which has focused in particular on the issue of selective enforcement. See text accompanying note 106 below.

[61] See for discussion of the difficulties, Committee on Petitions Annual Report 1997–98, EP Doc. A4–0250/98, 10–15.

The Ombudsman's challenge

A distinctive jurisdiction is one consideration. The Ombudsman, Mr Soderman, in investigating complaints concerning the conduct of Article 226 investigations does not face the same "roadblocks" as exist under the jurisprudence of the Court of Justice. By virtue of his more flexible jurisdiction "non-decisions" and concerned citizens or "non-addressees" of decisions find a place in the sun. Only one side of the bipolar "bargaining" process can be tested however, given the absence of jurisdiction over the activities of Member States. The Ombudsman's contribution further involves a reworking in his own image of the infraction process as complaint machinery. It is however a partial reworking, which is not only respectful of the "international" character of the legal framework but also demonstrates a conservative view of the Ombudsman function. All the more so, in the case of a young agency that is still feeling its way. Expressed slightly differently, both institutional and personal factors are seen to be important.

Maladministration, which the Office is set up to investigate, is a famously elastic concept. But it is one that Mr Soderman has approached in legalistic fashion, operating to this effect like a surrogate court. While it is correct to say that to act unlawfully constitutes maladministration, it is wrong to treat the concepts as if they were synonymous.[62] Mr Soderman has to this effect deferred to the Court of Justice, first in terms of what constitutes an acceptable ground of complaint, and second as regards constraint on the review of the exercise of discretionary power. In his words: "The Ombudsman does not seek to question discretionary administrative decisions provided that the institution or body concerned has acted within the limits of its legal authority. General limits on such authority are established by the jurisprudence of the Court".[63] To push home the point, the Ombudsman has opportunities to expand on the competence of the Court both by invading judicial "no-go" areas and by developing in creative fashion his own principles of review. In Article 226 cases his legalism shows Mr Soderman choosing the one but not the other.

Co-operation and ongoing dialogue with the Commission also characterise the elite regulatory model that is the Ombudsman. To explicate, operating as a guardian of "the Guardian of the Treaties", the European Ombudsman is in administrative law terms an instrument of bureaucratic regulation.[64] He is the archetypal "repeat player", with the ability easily to return to a problem on the basis of further complaints or on his own initiative. Thus, despite a lack of mandatory remedies, the Ombudsman has the capacity, over time and in incremental fashion, to prod the Commission towards a more citizen-oriented

[62] See for the basic meaning ascribed to maladministration, *European Ombudsman Annual Report 1995*, 17.

[63] *Annual Report 1997*, 26.

[64] That is, the regulation of government bodies by other government bodies. See for discussion in the United Kingdom context, C. Hood, C. Scott, O. James, G. Jones and T. Travers, *Regulating Inside Government* (Oxford: Clarendon Press, 1999).

approach.[65] The style however is once again conservative. A reactive approach has been prioritised: the targeting of the independent power of investigation on administrative problems that have generated multiple complaints.[66] The consequences are made very apparent in Article 226 matters. There is at one level, a high degree of repetition of certain kinds of grievance, tedious alike for Ombudsman and complainants; and, at another, failure fully to exploit the potential to attack what is seen as a poor quality and, on occasion, Kafkaesque style of Commission administration.

The investigations by the Ombudsman can be divided into three main elements. He is first seen in classic complaint-handling mode, as the scale of complainant dissatisfaction with enforcement procedures is quickly made evident.[67] Predictably many of these early complaints concerned the immediate procedural difficulties that individuals faced when requesting Commission action. That is delay in the processing of complaints, lack of information about progress, and non-receipt of reasoning for a decision to close a file.[68] The two leading cases, both of which derive from allegations of non-compliance with the Environmental Impact Assessment Directive, further illustrate the potential of the Ombudsman as a magnet for pressure group activity.

The protesters in the *Newbury Bypass* case[69] complained that the Commission, by accepting the Government's view that the project was exempt because planning procedures were already under way before the Directive came into force, had prevented an authoritative ruling on the issue at the heart of the dispute. The case highlights the Commission's initial attitude to the Ombudsman: very defensive. His capacity to find maladministration was challenged on the basis of the absence under Article 226 of specific procedural rights for complainants, and of the Commission exercising discretion "as fully recognised by the Court". Mr Soderman's insistence on playing a role brilliantly illustrates the function of the Ombudsman in reaching those parts that the judges cannot reach. It is precisely in such circumstances of strong discretion coupled with an absence of legal constraint that the case for scrutiny by an institution like the Ombudsman is so compelling. In the event, a lack of clarity was found in the official reasoning. Discretion, it was said, was exercised to close the file on the basis of no infringement even though Article 226 renders a belief in the fact of an infringement a condition precedent to the exercise of agency discretion.

[65] The Office being established on the Danish model of wide investigative powers coupled not with mandatory remedies but with powers to criticise, conciliate and recommend. See for discussion, K. Heede, "Enhancing the Accountability of the Community Institutions and Bodies: The Role of the European Ombudsman" (1997) 3 *EPL* 587.

[66] See *Annual Report 1995*, 21–2. Limited resources constitute a partial explanation.

[67] Article 226 cases accounted for one-third of all the admissible complaints made to the Ombudsman in his first full year of operations. See *Annual Report 1996*, 105.

[68] See J. Soderman, *The Citizen, The Administration and Community Law* (Stockholm: FIDE, 1998), 17–18.

[69] Decision on Complaint 206/27.10.95/HS/UK; *Annual Report 1996*, 59. See further, P. Kunzlik, "The Enforcement of EU Environmental Law: Article 169, the Ombudsman and the Parliament" (1997) 6 *EELR* 46.

The legalistic approach of the Ombudsman is also highlighted. The conclusion that the project was exempt was examined under the rubric of "maladministration in interpretation of the law" before being accepted as "probably correct".

The affair illustrates both the limited role and positive contribution of the Ombudsman. Take the complaint that the Commission in closing the file was motivated by political considerations. A typical allegation of abuse of power, it represents a direct attack on the model of international procedure. The Ombudsman was notably unenthusiastic, giving as the reason that the doubts raised were insufficient to merit a close examination.[70] "Catch-22": how from outside the closed bipolar process is convincing evidence of bad faith to be obtained? In contrast, take the complaint that the complainants first heard of closure of the file from a press release. The Ombudsman took the opportunity to signal a more inclusive approach to the giving of reasons. Extending the requirement beyond the legal rights of the formal parties to the process could be justified on the basis of good administrative practice.

The theme was pursued in the *M40* case.[71] Denied an explanation why the scheme did not require certain assessments, the objectors turned first to the national ombudsman and then to Mr Soderman. Operating as a "window on administration", the Ombudsman shed light on the Commission's policy in cases of complex appraisal of limiting review to grounds like manifest error and misuse of powers.[72] Mr Soderman correctly considered that this was reasonable, given the evidential burden that the Commission must discharge if it brings a Member State before the Court of Justice. It followed that in this case detailed investigation of the claims was unnecessary and that the Commission was entitled to close the file on the basis of the replies received from the UK Government. But why was none of this ever explained to the complainants? Instead they were left to pursue redress of grievance – "reasonably and understandably"– for years afterwards. The attitude of officials in this case, and by implication the prevailing administrative culture, could only be regarded as arrogant and high-handed.

The second element is the "own initiative inquiry" that was prompted by such cases.[73] The manner of proceeding "without prejudice" to the issue of whether principles of Community law might require more developed procedural rights shows once again the European Ombudsman occupying the administrative hin-

[70] Strictly this was not the end of the matter, since the protesters were able to pursue the matter via the parallel political process of the Committee on Petitions. It suffices to say that in that forum the affair quickly fell by the wayside.

[71] Decision on Complaint 132/21.9.95/AH/EN; *Annual Report 1996*, 67.

[72] By analogy with the principles used by the Court in Case 42/84 *Remia* v. *Commission* [1985] ECR 2545 to review Commission decisions based on complex economic matters.

[73] *Annual Report* 1997, 270. It is one of a series launched by Mr Soderman in his quest for greater transparency in the Union. See in particular, *Special Report and Decision by the European Ombudsman following the Own-Initiative Inquiry into Public Access to Documents held by Community Institutions and Bodies*, December 1997. See also J. Soderman, "The Role and Impact of the European Ombudsman in Access to Documentation and the Transparency of Decision-Making" (1997) (available on the Ombudsman's website: http://www.euro-ombudsman.eu.int/home/en/default.htm).

terland of the formal law. The argument of the Legal Service that discretion was being exercised "as fully recognised by the Court" could effectively be turned on its head. Precisely because it was a matter of internal management, procedural rights could be developed under the rubric of good administrative behaviour in a way that was consistent with the jurisprudence of the Court denying individuals a legal challenge. In the event, and responding to issues raised in the early cases, some basic procedural minima were established, in the form of Commission assurances regarding complainant information and registration, as also, save in "special cases", the use of the one-year time limit for closing a file. The proactive role of the Ombudsman is further illustrated, there now being a chance to contest the view of the Commission before a final decision is taken. The suggestion was made and adopted that complainants be made aware of the intention to close a file together with the reasons why there is considered to be no infringement.[74]

The own initiative inquiry has been much trumpeted by the Ombudsman. Yet it was largely a wasted opportunity. One feature is the way in which Mr Soderman, impressed by the "constructive and service minded" approach of the Commission to the inquiry, took its assurances at face value. There was for example no statistical analysis of the treatment of complaints, nor any apparent probing of "special cases". Remarkable as it may seem, it has not always been the case that complaints to the Commission are registered.[75] Again, a promise of citizen participation once a provisional conclusion is reached is of limited value. Experience teaches that for such input to be effective, it would have to happen much earlier in the decision-making process, as indeed is the case in the Ombudsman's own investigation of admissible complaints.[76] Nor should the narrow focus of the inquiry on the preliminary stages of the "complaint pyramid" be overlooked. Take the internal time limit for closing a file. As anyone with experience of waiting lists knows, such a requirement hardly guarantees speedy action elsewhere in a decision-making chain. In sum, the quality of the procedural change produced was tepid.

This aspect is brilliantly illustrated by the third element: individual investigations in recent cases. The Office has continued to receive many complaints about infringement proceedings;[77] further, there is evidence of a qualitative change, with complainants pressing beyond straightforward procedural matters to test the character and style of Commission decision-making. The limited role

[74] Except where a complaint is manifestly unfounded or where the complainant appears to have lost interest in the complaint. See Commission, *Fifteenth Annual Monitoring Report*, note 3, above, 10.

[75] As the Ombudsman later found in Decision on Complaint 250/97/OV; *Annual Report 1998*, 236.

[76] Where the complainant, in light of the opinion of the institution concerned, has the opportunity to submit observations to the Ombudsman. See Article 4 of the Ombudsman's Implementing Provisions.

[77] Approximately 8 per cent of admissible complaints in 1997, and 5 per cent in 1998. There is however some overlap in the form of decisions on complaints of poor procedure arising before the Commission's response to the own initiative investigation.

played by the Ombudsman in policing infringement proceedings has in this way been increasingly exposed. Mr Soderman has adhered to the line that in the review of discretionary power his marching orders are taken from the Court of Justice. The formula that "the institution acted within the limits of its legal authority and therefore no instance of maladministration has been established" is to this effect a standard one. The theme that because the Treaty and jurisprudence give limited guidance, the Commission has broad discretion to determine the procedures as well as decisional criteria, is another refrain.[78]

Examples demonstrate the interplay of the legal, institutional and personal factors. In an important case for civil liberties and freedom of movement, the organisation *Liberty* complained that UK nationals had wrongfully been included on Member State "blacklists" of football hooligans.[79] On the basis that the Court has confirmed the aim as being to afford an opportunity to remedy non-compliance, the Ombudsman declined to censure the Commission, which could find no existing infringement, for refusal to examine past conduct. So the case highlights the tension between the first two faces of enforcement proceedings: machinery for compliance or redress. Again, complaints have been made to the Ombudsman concerning the refusal to release documents relating to the Commission's contacts with Member States. In light of the *World Wildlife Fund* case, Mr Soderman has accepted that "in the present state of Community law" the practice "does not appear" to constitute maladministration.[80] On occasion the Ombudsman has failed to practise what he preaches. The novel element in a case concerning animal experiments[81] was that the Commission, in determining that on the basis of the evidence submitted Community legislation had not been breached, had failed to respond to requests to assist in identifying the elements necessary for a successful complaint. The Ombudsman refused to act as citizen's advocate and establish under the rubric of good administration a positive duty on the Commission of aid and advice. As an issue of effective access for citizens, this contradicts the theme of a consumerist orientation for the public service that elsewhere Mr Soderman has espoused.[82] In fact the Ombudsman failed to explain the matter in rejecting the complaint. Applying the standard that he has applied against the Commission,[83] the Ombudsman's decision "was accordingly insufficient in its reasoning".

A case related to the free movement of goods further illustrates the contrast in Article 226 proceedings with the position of the complainant in competition cases.[84] The Commission, having decided to issue a reasoned opinion, struck a deal with the UK authorities that the original complainant, a company, consid-

[78] See, for example, Decision on Complaint 176/97/JMA; *Annual Report 1998*, 97.

[79] Decision on Complaint 259/27.11.95/PL/UK/PD; *Annual Report 1997*, 59.

[80] Decision on Complaint 783/01.08.96/LBR/ES/KH/(JMA); *Annual Report 1998*, 212.

[81] Decision on Complaint 1003/97/PD (available on the Ombudsman's website, note 73, above).

[82] See, for example, J. oderman, "The role of the European Ombudsman" (available on the Ombudsman's website, note 73, above).

[83] See Decision on Complaint 472/6.3.96/XP/ES/PD; *Annual Report 1998*, 191.

[84] Decision on Complaint 651/97/IJH; *Annual Report 1998*, 111.

ered was unsatisfactory. Investigation by the Ombudsman revealed informal steps to allow the company an opportunity of notice and comment: a fine example of unstructured procedural discretion. But Mr Soderman, on the basis of the closed model of regulatory bargaining, rejected a complaint that the company was refused participation in a meeting with the UK authorities to discuss a solution. Whereas this "would be *prima facie* unreasonable in a normal administrative procedure in which the complainant is a party", the lack of a formal legal base was considered by the Ombudsman a conclusive answer to the claim of maladministration.

In only one important case[85] has the Ombudsman penetrated deep into the jungle that is Commission decision-making. Notably it involves a concept, "due diligence", that the Court has recognised as a principle of good administration.[86] To explicate, Mr Soderman has recently been flirting with this principle, to the effect that the Commission "should actively seek" to ensure that a Member State puts an end to an infringement, while generally being satisfied by evidence of regular contact with the national authorities.[87] His patience is not inexhaustible. The saga began in 1990 when the Commission, in receipt of complaints concerning the recognition by Spain of South American diplomas that did not meet the requirements of the Directives, sent a formal notice. Six years later, one of the complainants, understandably frustrated by the apparent lack of progress, complained to the Ombudsman. It emerged from his enquiries that in 1992 the Commission had issued a reasoned opinion, but that the next four years had been taken up with "further requests" to Spain for "additional information". Eventually, in 1996, the Commission had adopted a decision to take Spain before the Court; this decision was however suspended in 1998 because the Commission had now had positive results in negotiations. The case shows once again the practical relevance of the competing models of infraction process. Boldly, and on the basis of regulatory bargaining, the Commission claimed that "its attitude has been very active". The time-span could thus be explained in terms of legal and political complexity: national courts had frustrated initiatives by the Spanish Government to comply with the Directives; recognition was based on pre-accession Treaty obligations and raised delicate issues of international relations. From the complainant's perspective, however, the Commission was "a technical body" primarily charged with upholding the law: it "could not possibly justify" the long delay on the basis of political reasons. Belatedly in light of his own initiative inquiry, the Ombudsman extended the testing of timeliness to encompass the substantive dealings with Member States. The Commission had "failed to provide clear, precise and transparent information" to support its claim of great activity and this constituted maladministration.

[85] Decision on Complaint 783/01.08.96/LBR/ES/KH(JMA); *Annual Report 1998*, 212.

[86] See, for example, Case 179/82 *Lucchini* v. *Commission* [1983] ECR 3083. The potential for taking oral evidence from officials is demonstrated by Decision on Complaint 1140/97/IJH.

[87] See, for example, Decision on Complaint 260/97/JMA; *Annual Report 1998*, 99.

To summarise, the disputation between Commission and Ombudsman reflects a difference in outlook. In contrast to the Legal Service, which has prayed in aid the idea all too familiar in administrative law that individual procedural protection cannot be given unless formally mandated, the Ombudsman has articulated the need for a more permissive or citizen-oriented administrative culture. But to repeat, Mr Soderman in engaging with the Commission has made a slow start, and only now is there beginning to be signs of a significant contribution.[88] This aspect is further illustrated by his call in the latest annual report for the citizen's right to complain under Article 226 to be enshrined in the Treaty, in effect to guarantee the status of the citizen as a party in the enforcement process. This, it was said, is "the only way . . . to ensure proper and transparent dealing with their complaints in the future".[89] Given the potential of the Ombudsman's Office, enough has been said to show that this is not the whole story. Mr Soderman should have done more to meet the challenge.

4. THIRD FACE: FORMALISATION, EFFICACY AND TARIFF

At Amsterdam the European Council endorsed a Single Market Action Plan presented by the Commission.[90] Although obscured by the widespread disappointment felt at the general conclusions of the Inter-Governmental Conference (IGC), the Plan has in fact been central to the contemporary development of European administrative law. Thus, together with renewed political efforts to tackle key market distortions and remove obstacles to market integration, it has signalled greater emphasis on rendering the regulatory rules more effective, as also on enhancing citizen awareness and non-judicial tools of redress of grievance. A reworking of enforcement strategy is involved, indicative of the third, technocratic face of infringement proceedings. To push home the point, this is a development that must be seen in broad perspective. The importance of ensuring that Community law is properly implemented within Member States has been a central theme in EU discourse throughout the 1990s.[91] But the Action Plan may be seen as providing a sharper edge to the enterprise, and, further, a context in which the potential of Commission enforcement has been reasserted. Reference has already been made to the trend towards greater formalisation and routinisation in infringement proceedings, linking on to the practical reality of a jurisdiction to specify penalties for non-compliance.

[88] For the work by the Ombudsman on a code of good administrative behaviour for officials, see *infra* for official explanation, accompanying note 126, below.

[89] *Annual Report 1998*, 11. Very recently, the Ombudsman has called for a "fundamental right" to an open, accountable and service-minded European administration to be included in the proposed EU Charter of Fundamental Rights.

[90] See Commission, *Assessment of the Single Market Action Plan, June 1997–December 1998*, COM (99) 74 final.

[91] See especially Commission, *Reinforcing the Effectiveness of the Internal Market*, COM (93) 256 final (1993).

Then there is the single currency. The Commission has stressed the need for extra vigilance in its role as "the Guardian of the Treaties" given the incentives to raise other barriers to the free flow of goods, services, people and capital that are associated with the removal of exchange rates as an instrument of economic policy.[92] Expressed slightly differently, infringement proceedings are seen taking on a new lease of life as one of a number of techniques for shoring up confidence in a reinvented Single Market; all the more so, in light of the parallel policy context of EU enlargement. Notable in this regard is the invocation of league tables, a technique associated in the United Kingdom with the Citizen's Charter, and one of the disciplinary tools of the New Public Management. Thus the Single Market Scoreboard, published regularly by the Commission, has provided detailed indicators of the state of the Single Market and of the level of commitment of Member States to implementation.[93] In the words of the Commission, a "cycle of measurement, evaluation, adaptation, and implementation will be at the heart of the future strategy of the Single Market".[94]

Reshaping the administrative process

Changes to internal working practices reflect and reinforce the new priority assigned to centralised enforcement. The effort to accelerate the investigation of complaints typically involves shortening the early part of the decision-making chain. Recourse to informal letters to Member States prior to opening formal infringement procedures has since 1996 been strictly limited, with the formal Article 226 letter being reinvented in Commission jargon as a "de-dramatised" request for observations.[95] So too the internal one-year time limit for adopting a position on a suspected infringement has come to be more vigorously asserted.[96] The complaint statistics serve to highlight the way in which the "complaint pyramid" is thus reshaped by administrative action. As a consequence of streamlining, the number of reasoned opinions and referrals to the Court is increased.[97]

Timeliness is a continuing struggle, not least because of Member State delay and the cumbersome nature of the Treaty provisions. The staff paper in 1998 was in part prompted by the limited success of previous attempts to speed up the handling of cases. The length of time between the Commission opening a case and a court judgment typically stands at two to three years in cases of non-communication of transposition, and averages over five years in cases of

92 See, for example, Commission, *Single Market Scoreboard* (No. 3) (October 1998), 1.

93 See, in particular, Commission, *Single Market Scoreboard* (No. 4) (June 1999).

94 *Ibid*, 1. The Scoreboard, expanded and given permanency, is central to this exercise. The knock-on effects of the selective targets will be interesting to observe!

95 See for details, Commission, *Fourteenth Annual Monitoring Report*, note 51, above, 9–10.

96 Secretariat General, *Improvement of the Commission's Working Methods*, note 23, above, 4.

97 Commission, *Single Market Scoreboard* (No. 4) (June 1999), 9.

incorrect transposition or application.[98] In an attempt to preserve the credibility of the process, Commission departments are now instructed to move straight to proposing a reasoned opinion or court referral whenever Member States fail to adhere strictly to the prescribed time limits.[99]

A more vigorous approach is also signalled by the increased use of publicity as a lever for enforcement. To explicate, the model of regulatory bargaining still dominates as far as the Article 226 letter is concerned, the principle of confidentiality being seen as appropriate in a situation where the formal notice has been "de-dramatised". Otherwise, and following on an earlier experiment that "had a generally positive effect on the settlement of infringement cases", the Commission now intends to have recourse to the media via prompt and detailed briefings.[100] So far have we travelled from the simple model of an international procedure.

The move to diversify the administrative ways of dealing with infringements of Community law other than by the Article 226 procedure is a continuing one.[101] At one level this involves classic techniques of complaint filtering, a way of freeing up resources for tackling the more complex cases. So-called "one-off cases" involving individual citizens where a speedy, less formal approach to dispute resolution is appropriate are a prime example.[102] This is in fact very much the realm of the Action Plan, which has provided for the setting-up of national co-ordination centres as an informal means of solving problems in the operation of the Single Market, and of administrative "contact points" for businesses and members of the public.[103] At another level are the "package meetings" that the Commission holds with national authorities in major sectors with a view to early dispute resolution. The contacts between the national chairpersons that are now being developed represent a further shift from the bilateral model of regulatory enforcement.[104]

A reform that has been under consideration could prove the most significant. It appears that belatedly the Commission may be entering the information technology age in terms of complaint procedure. An opportunity to use e-mail[105] should help complainants with the daunting task of approaching an institution the internal organisation of which is notoriously labyrinthine. The

[98] Commission, *Making Single Market Rules More Effective*, SEC (1998) 903, 10.

[99] Commission, *Improvement of the Commission's Working Methods*, note 23, above, 5.

[100] *Ibid*, 6.

[101] The way in which the changes to working methods consolidate and advance previous initiatives can be traced by reference to F. Snyder (1993), note 16, above. For a general legal discussion, see A. Ibanez, *Commission Tools for the Supervision and Enforcement of EC Law Other Than Article 169 EC Treaty: An Attempt at Systematisation* (Harvard: Jean Monnet Working Paper 12/98 (1998)).

[102] See Commission Press Release, *Citizens: Commission Tackles Single Market Problems* (15 October 1998).

[103] Reference may also be made to the Dialogue with Citizens Signpost Service and the Eurojus network of advisers on EC law (accessible through the Commission's Representations in each Member State).

[104] See Commission, *Making Single Market Rules More Effective*, note 98, above, 7–8.

[105] As suggested by the Secretariat General, note 23, above, 7.

numbers of complaints could be expected to increase rapidly. But further the procedure would help to underpin proper complaint analysis and use as a tool of effective supervision. Once again the different dynamics, on the one hand for citizen access and redress of grievance, and on the other for more efficient and streamlined enforcement, would be demonstrated.

In sum, the changes outlined are necessary but insufficient. Greater stress is appropriately laid on infringement proceedings as one piece in the mosaic that is the effectiveness of Community law; and, further, on innovative techniques and collective methods of dispute resolution inside the infraction process. The hole in the heart is the lack of a convincing policy of selective enforcement. In the light of criticism in the Parliament the Commission has begun to articulate some priorities in the processing of complaints: notably failures of transposition, horizontal cases of incorrect application and infringements in relation to Community co-financing.[106] But such a list is too rudimentary to provide a proper basis for the structuring and confining of enforcement discretion. We will return to this point.

Penal competence: new dynamics

What then of the new apex of the enforcement system? By which is meant the penal competence introduced at Maastricht and now contained in Article 228, whereby Member States can be fined if they fail to obey a judgment of the Court of Justice; powers that will typically be invoked in the context of Article 226 proceedings. As is well known, legal sanction for tackling the problem of post-litigation non-compliance was previously lacking, with action being limited to further declaratory proceedings.[107] Criticised correctly as a basic weakness in the machinery of law enforcement, this was in fact a typical manifestation of the international model of co-operative and closed decision-making.

Doubts are properly raised concerning the efficacy of the new machinery.[108] A procedure whereby the Commission, prior to exercising its new power to propose a fine when referring a matter back to the Court, has once again to go through the different stages of formal notice, submission of observations and reasoned opinion, is self-evidently convoluted. Again, the absence on the one hand of the typical common law remedy of injunction, and on the other of a clear collection mechanism, mark the strict limits of this quasi-criminal jurisdiction.

[106] See Commission, *Fourteenth Annual Monitoring Report*, note 51 above, 8–9; and for input from the Committee on Legal Affairs and Citizens' Rights, EP Doc. A4–0008/98.

[107] As highlighted by the notorious "Sheepmeat" affair: Case 232/78 *Commission* v. *France* [1979] ECR 2729; Joined Cases 24 and 97/80 R *Commission* v. *France* [1980] ECR 1319. Not forgetting the power of the Court to prescribe interim measures (Article 243).

[108] D. Curtin, "The Constitutional Structure of the Union: A Europe of Bits and Pieces" (1993) 30 *CMLRev* 17; J. Diez-Hochleitner, "Le traité de Maastricht et l'inexecution des arrêts de la Cour de justice par les États membres" (1994) 2 *Revue du Marché Unique Européen* 111.

Yet formal legal analysis, so typical of European administrative law, should not be allowed to obscure the broader significance of penal competence in terms of the dynamics of the enforcement process. Effectiveness, formalisation and deterrent: these themes are both highlighted at the new apex and cast a long shadow. Especially noteworthy for present purposes is the interplay, on the one hand, with Commission and Member State strategies in elite regulatory bargaining; and on the other, with the expression of citizen grievance.

The form of the complaint pyramid is once again reconstituted. Whereas the initial, informal phase of infringement proceedings is now streamlined, the penal competence has been integrated as one stage in the decision-making chain that constitutes the infraction process. Commission policy serves to emphasise this aspect. The French model of *astreinte*[109] is preferred to lump sum payments, precisely because the Commission "intends to use [the new power] to persuade the Member State concerned to regularize its position". So too, "both the criteria selected and the way they are applied will be dictated by the need to ensure that Community law is effectively enforced".[110]

Operating in a new area where (in Euro-speak) Member States have powerful "rights of the defence," the Commission has determined on "a spirit of openness." By this is meant the legitimacy gains of "a clear and consistent method," as also the need for defensible practice in a field where the Court of Justice, notably applying the proportionality principle, has final decision-making power.[111] The design involves an application of the "soft-law" techniques that are so familiar in the Community.[112] Discretion to make rules has been publicly exercised by means of Communications from the Commission, so enabling the standard formula of structuring and confining discretion in individual cases. It is precisely what has not happened in respect of the other links in the decision-making chain. In fact the tariff scheme is so detailed that the style of decision-making is taken to the other extreme. A complex mathematical formula is involved,[113] which presents its own problems of transparency, and is itself subject to modification as rulings from the Court come on stream.[114]

[109] Whereby the Commission calculates penalty payments in respect of each day of delay.

[110] Commission, *Method of Calculating the Penalty Payments Provided for Pursuant to Article 171 of the EC Treaty*, OJ C 063 of 28 February 1997, para. 1; *Memorandum on Applying Article 171 of the EC Treaty*, OJ C 242 of 21 August 1996, para. 2. See further, A. Bonnie, "Commission discretion under 171(2) EC" (1998) 23 *ELRev* 537.

[111] *Memorandum*, *ibid*, para. 2; *Method of calculating*, *ibid*, para. 1.

[112] In the broad sense of rules of conduct that have limited or no legally binding force. See F. Snyder, "Soft Law and Institutional Practice in the European Community" in S. Martin (ed.), *The Construction of Europe* (Dordrecht: Kluwer, 1994).

[113] $Pd = (Fr \times Cs \times Cd) \times n$. Where Pd = daily penalty payment; Fr = flat-rate amount; Cs = seriousness coefficient; Cd = duration coefficient; n = factor taking into account the Member State's ability to pay. At the time of writing the Court of Justice has not determined a penalty case. The Commission however has issued a series of reasoned opinions. See for illustrations, Commission, *Single Market Scoreboard* (No. 4) (June 1999).

[114] See further on the difficulties of the development in competition law, W.Wils, "The Commission's New Method for Calculating Fines in Antitrust Cases" (1998) 23 *ELRev* 252.

The Commission has stressed that the new power will not lead it to neglect the co-operative element of negotiations with Member States.[115] But this is not the whole story. For example, in proposing a fine, the Commission will have regard to "any financial advantage the Member State might gain" from post-litigation non-compliance.[116] In other words the "purchase of illegality", as the French call it, should not come cheap. Such a criterion considerably alters the terms and conditions of bargaining "in the shadow of the law". The tariff scheme is predicated on the strengthening of incentives for early settlement by reason of deterrent.

It is fine irony that the first place in the infringement procedures where the importance and effect of non-compliance for the citizen is publicly recognised is in the assessment of penalty. The "economic or other damage suffered by individuals" will thus be counted, under the rubric of the seriousness of the infringement.[117] Typically in the view of the Commission the original complainant is otherwise rendered invisible at this stage of the infraction process. Enough has been said however to show that this will not wash. Increased visibility of the enforcement process, coupled with the prospect of paying back national authorities for continued intransigence, can only work to encourage more complaints into the system. Repeat players such as the major environmental groups will have the most incentive. Again the European Ombudsman will surely become engaged sooner rather than later, as citizen-complainants, unable to attack Commission decision-making and procedures via the Court, claim maladministration. Expressed slightly differently, the demand for more participation, whereby citizens play a greater role in the machinery of public advocacy, far from being satiated, is liable to grow in light of the exercise of penal competence. The dynamic properties of this regulatory process are once again highlighted.

5. RE-INVENTING INFRINGEMENT PROCEEDINGS. OR CAN THE COMMISSION CHANGE ITS SPOTS?

The aloof and unresponsive character of Commission administration revealed in the Ombudsman's reports should offend even the most committed Europhile. It can be seen as one aspect of a broader malaise, which has now struck home in the report from the Committee of Independent Experts into allegations of fraud and mismanagement.[118] There is indeed the sense of a lack of "responsibility" in the conduct of infringement proceedings, which is underwritten by the

[115] Commission, *Eleventh Annual Monitoring Report*, note 53, above, 8.

[116] *Method of Calculating*, note 110, above, para. 3.1.2.

[117] As a victim-oriented factor it will require careful handling, since the prospect opens up of double counting in the light of state liability under the *Francovich* principle. Case C–6/90 (*Francovich and Bonifaci* v. *Italy*[1991] ECR I–5357).

[118] Committee of Independent Experts, note 9, above. And for discussion, see A. Tomkins, "Responsibility and Resignation in the European Commission" (1999) 62 *MLR* 744.

negativity to citizens displayed by the Legal Service. Various improvements notwithstanding, the reality is far removed from Commission rhetoric of "fostering a real People's Europe".[119] General administrative reform, targeted on a bureaucratic culture that is only too redolent of the France of the 1950s, is a precondition of an effective and transparent enforcement process.

In fact the work programme of the Commission for 1999 claimed to attach key importance to its own modernisation,[120] the stated aims being to decentralise, assign responsibility, monitor more closely, and simplify internal management. Fortunately however the idea of a "gradual" reform has been overtaken by events, with the recent confirmation of Romano Prodi as President of the Commission representing an unrivalled window of opportunity for change.[121] Let us hope that the infraction process features in the list for proper audit and management discipline. The fact that the Commission has clearly been over-stretched[122] only underscores the case for concentrating resources on core functions like the guardianship of the treaties. And the Legal Service far from being immune is a prime candidate for reform, better to inculcate the principles of citizenship and justice in administration.

A double standard has persisted for far too long. By this is meant restrictive application in the Commission of the kind of New Public Management techniques increasingly familiar in and targeted on the Member States. One example is the lack of publicly available performance indicators on the conduct of enforcement proceedings. Why not an independently audited Commission "Scoreboard", incorporating such elements as speed of processing, rates of settlement and measures of complainant satisfaction? It could do much to sharpen up case management by the Commission, with the benefit to public confidence in the regulatory system.

Developments in information technology widen the options. Take the project, previously mentioned, of an e-mail facility for Article 226 complainants. This can only be an improvement on the outdated and skeletal complaint form that the Commission has insisted on using.[123] In fact one would expect to see a professionally designed website, incorporating a detailed explanation of procedures, press releases and lists of contacts, and indexed records of past and pending cases.[124] That is if the Commission intends to take its role as "the Guardian of the Treaties" seriously. Indeed, why not an interactive facility designed for interested third parties: a model for the new millennium of the class action?

[119] Which has been stated as one aim of attempts to encourage the use of Article 226 procedure: Commission, *Tenth Annual Monitoring Report*, COM (93) 329 final, 7.

[120] See OJ 1998 C 366.

[121] See, most recently, *Reforming the Commission. A Consultative Document* (G3/2000) 1/17 (January 2000).

[122] A central theme in the report from the Committee of Independent Experts.

[123] See OJ 1989 C26/6.

[124] Items that are all found on the website of the European Ombudsman. Is it not maladministration for the Commission now to do otherwise?

Then there is what should now be called the citizen's charter movement in public administration. The Commission has been slow to respond to the idea, now widely accepted both at national and supranational levels, of providing statements of the standards of service that citizens can expect to have delivered by an agency. In the event a statement that appeared in March 1999[125] demonstrates not so much a shift towards, as the distance from, a service-oriented administrative culture. Commitments to give correct advice and act with courtesy, and to state reasons particularly for negative decisions, may be useful, but they are no substitute for detailed commitments to quality of service. Again, the Commission has recently rejected a proposal for a Code of Good Administrative Behaviour for EU officials in their relations with the public that the European Ombudsman had finally got round to preparing.[126] Elite dialogues, fine words: the case of Commission enforcement demonstrates that this does not suffice.

The European Ombudsman should play an important role. Notably, rather than extend his jurisdiction to implementation by the Member States, Mr Soderman favours the development of network and liaison arrangements with national ombudsmen and similar bodies.[127] Let us hope that liaison matures into arrangements for joint investigation: especially in Article 226 cases given the delays that are associated with the model of regulatory bargaining. We cannot overlook the consequences of Mr Soderman's conservative and legalistic approach; in particular the fact that in a prototypical area of strong discretion like infringement proceedings the Ombudsman is unable to penetrate very far into the jungle. Substance not shadow in terms of bureaucratic regulation is what is wanted.

Both the style and substance of infringement proceedings need to be revamped.[128] One idea that has surfaced in this context is that of a European Administrative Enforcement Act.[129] Like the general argument of which it is a variant that procedures at Community level should be enshrined in a formal codification, this has a certain superficial attraction: formal coherence and rationalisation in place of a patchwork of general and specialised infringement procedures.[130]

[125] The timing was hardly coincidental, the Commission rushing out a series of codes in an unsuccessful pre-emptive strike against the Committee of Independent Experts. See Commission, *For a European political and administrative culture: Three codes of conduct*. The statement was contained in the final section of the code of conduct for staff.

[126] *Code of Good Administrative Behaviour*; Draft Recommendation of the European Ombudsman in the own initiative inquiry OI/1/98/OU. The Commission prefers a weaker code of conduct annexed as "supplementary measures" to its internal code of conduct.

[127] See *Annual Report 1998*, 11.

[128] Other important issues that fall outside the scope of this chapter include the adequacy of interim remedies and the suitability of state-focused infringement proceedings in light of the rise of meso or regional government in Europe.

[129] Ibanez (1999), note 21, above.

[130] A typical product of the incremental and fragmented process of EU regulatory development: see for discussion, S. Wilks, "Regulatory Compliance and Capitalist Diversity in Europe" (1996) 3 *Journal of European Public Policy* 536. The full list of arguments for and against such codification bears no repetition here. See especially, C. Harlow, "Codification of EC Administrative Procedures? Fitting the Foot to the Shoe or the Shoe to the Foot" (1996) 2 *ELJ* 3; and M. Shapiro, "Codification of Administrative Law: the US and the Union" (1996) 2 *ELJ* 26.

However, bearing in mind that legal rules are not in themselves sufficient to ensure a high standard of administration, one of the dangers of such a scheme is that it would deflect attention from the more important need to promote a more responsible and service oriented administrative culture. It is also important to limit the negative aspect of "juridification", the contemporary tendency all too familiar in the Union to formalise and encase social relations in terms of law. In tackling Article 226 infringement proceedings, care must be taken not to throw out the baby with the bath water, in the guise of the competing administrative values of flexibility and responsiveness. All the more so, when one considers the heterogeneous activities covered by this general procedure. The use of secondary legislation would to this effect be more appropriate.

Fons et origo of Commission enforcement, the general procedure is today an exception. In other areas where the Commission is directly responsible for administration the procedures are commonly well-established and have been formulated in regulations. In fact the recent reform of the supervision of state aids provides a possible role model.[131] By this is meant an insistence via Council Regulation on time limits for Commission decisions; on additional information gathering better to verify compliance; and on notice and comment rights for third parties, which does not burden the Commission with full "contradictory procedure" at each stage of the process.[132] Of course it would mean amending Article 226 to provide a legal base for secondary rule making powers: a project, given the advantages to Member States of the basic framework of international procedure, that is perhaps only for the longer term.

Urgent consideration should thus be given to applying to the general procedure the kind of "soft law" techniques that previously have characterised state aids policy and practice.[133] Open and flexible guidelines furnish the means to an appropriate balance of regulatory choice for the Commission, proper procedural protections, and more rational forms of decision-making. Looking forward, there are pointers here to a soft form of European administrative law able to escape the worst excesses of juridification. It would involve coupling such guidelines with a proper charter of service standards, so as to secure for citizens both an information and expectation base. Techniques of alternative dispute resolution, for example the European Ombudsman, would be facilitated.

Practical steps to improve the procedural position of complainants could usefully begin with acceptance of a general administrative obligation of advice and assistance. Complainant interviews and visits, in difficult cases professional aid to formulate grievance: such measures ought not to pose problems if resources are properly targeted, and are vital if the role of "the Guardian of the Treaties" is to be taken seriously. Attention should further be given to enabling com-

[131] Council Regulation 659/99 OJ 1999 L 83.

[132] See in this context Case C–367/95 P *Commission* v. *Sytraval* [1998] ECR I–1719.

[133] See G. della Cananea, "Administration by Guidelines: The Policy Guidelines of the Commission in the Field of State Aids" in I. Harden (ed.), *State Aid: Community Law and Policy* (Cologne: Bundesanzeiger, 1993).

plainants to make timely representations as the procedure unfolds, including detailed representations in cases of complex and disputed facts. The role of active citizenship would be amply demonstrated, without having to afford complainants full legal party status.

Commission discretion allows, and scarce resources dictate, an ordered policy of selective enforcement. There is a strong case for the reordering of Commission priorities. The efforts of the Commission need to be more closely targeted on areas where the potential for action by "private attorneys general" at national level is illusory or limited. Moving on from the problem of non-transposition, this would involve those areas of EU law where relevant interests are diffuse or fragmented, and in particular where the practical barriers to access to justice – cost, delay, lack of legal awareness, etc. – are formidable. To this effect the potential contribution of centralised enforcement would be clearly assessable in inverse proportion to the capacity of market actors to mount effective legal challenge. It is precisely this kind of prioritisation that is required if fostering a "People's Europe" is to be more than rhetoric.

In conclusion, a mature system of European administrative law demands a positive approach to both public and private forms of law enforcement. The principle of complementarity should thus be a guiding light of the system. Different institutional attitudes help to explain the progress of Commission enforcement, with the elite regulatory model increasingly under challenge in a less deferential or "trusting" world. Central to the development is the coupling of public advocacy with private initiative, which points in turn to a greater recognition of the role of the citizen in the shaping of the process. There is after all no going back. The Commission set out to use complainants: complainants came to see the Commission as part of the problem. Lampedusa would have understood.

Index